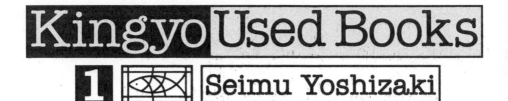

Kingyo Used Books

1 Seimu Yoshizaki

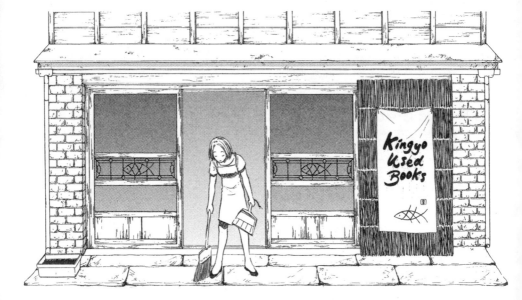

Kingyo Used Books

Contents

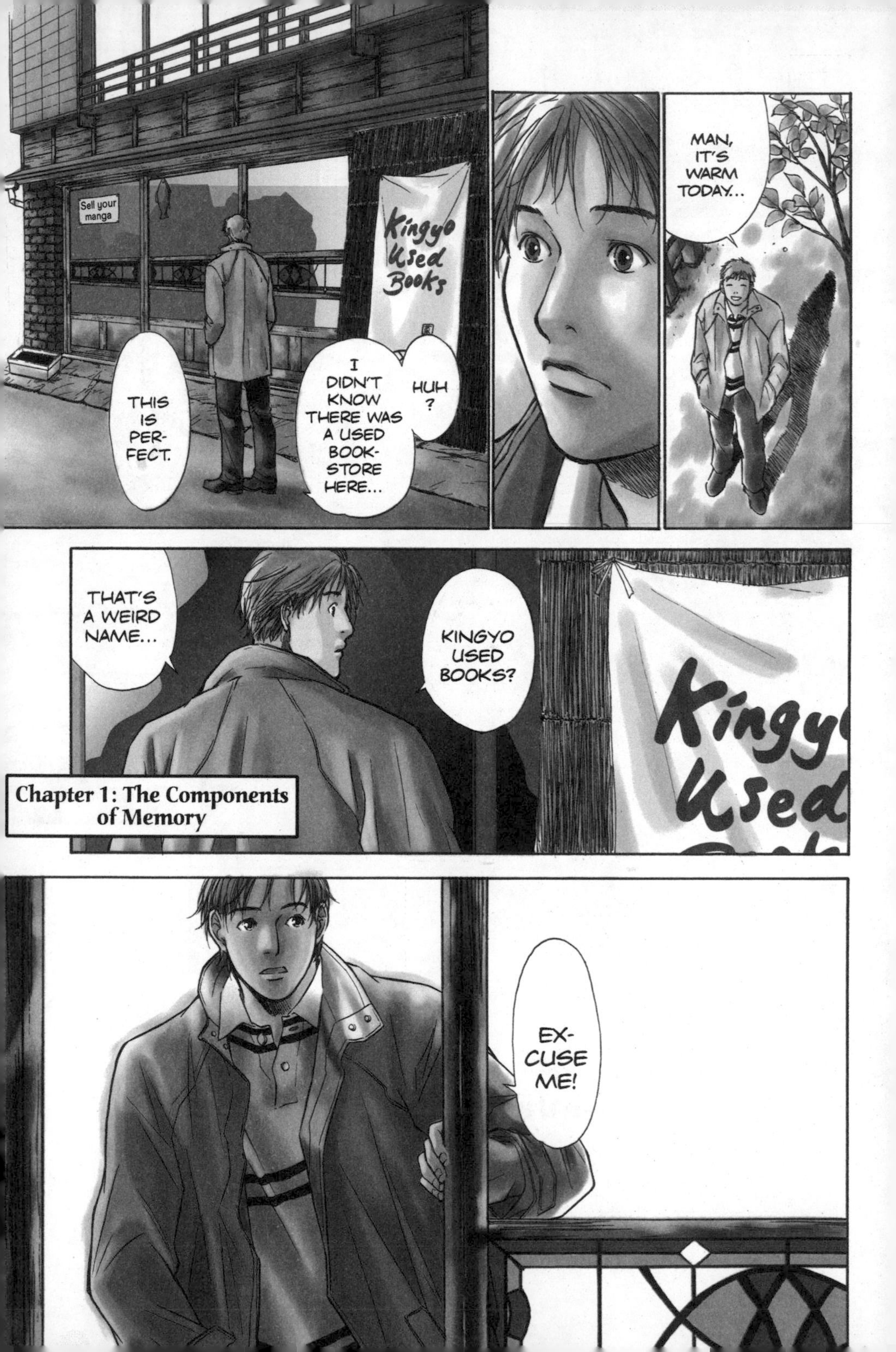
MAN, IT'S WARM TODAY...
HUH?
Kingyo Used Books
I DIDN'T KNOW THERE WAS A USED BOOK-STORE HERE...
Sell your manga
THIS IS PER-FECT.
Kingyo Used
KINGYO USED BOOKS?
THAT'S A WEIRD NAME...
Chapter 1: The Components of Memory
EX-CUSE ME!

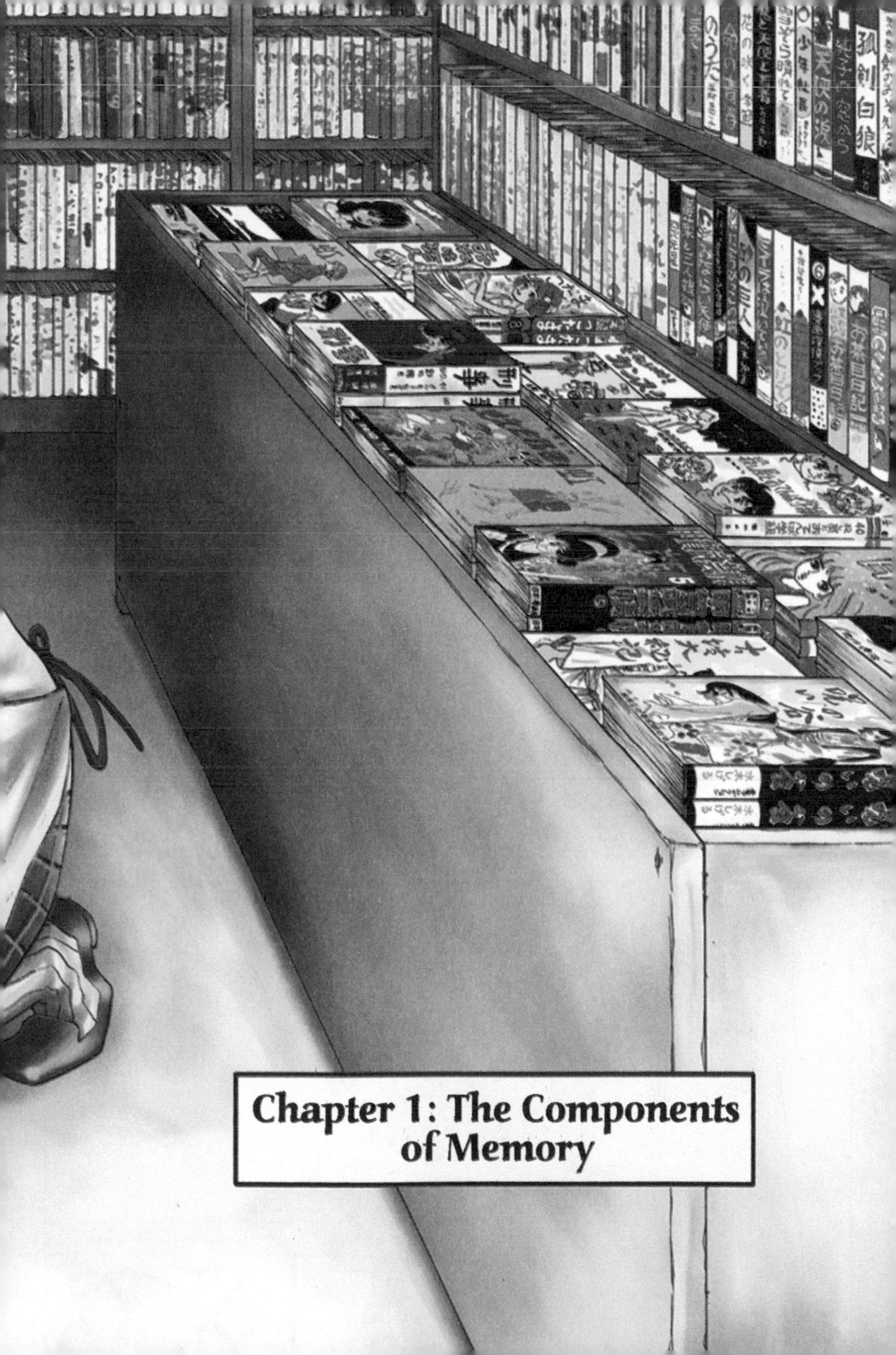
Chapter 1: The Components of Memory

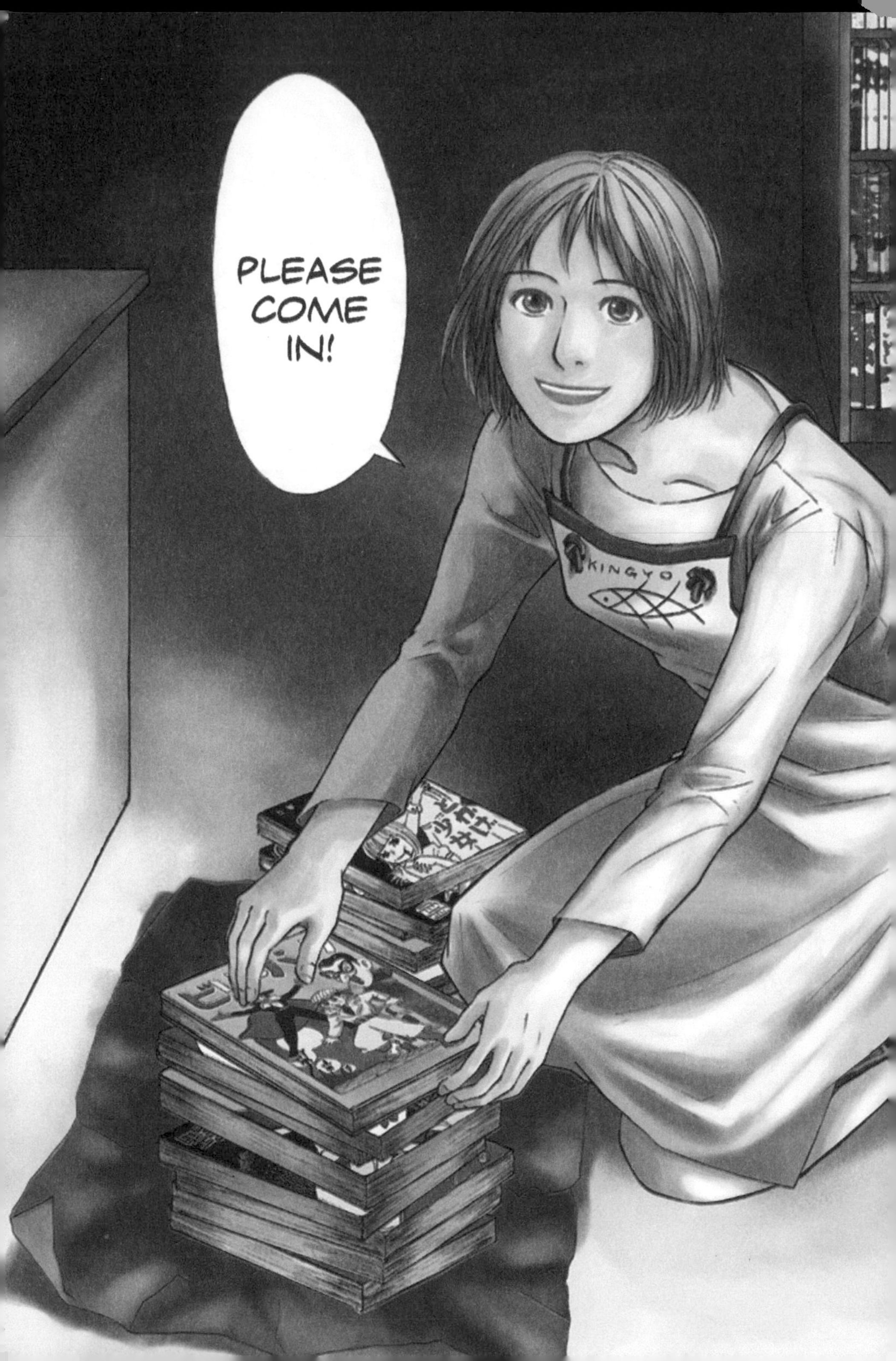
PLEASE COME IN!
KINGYO

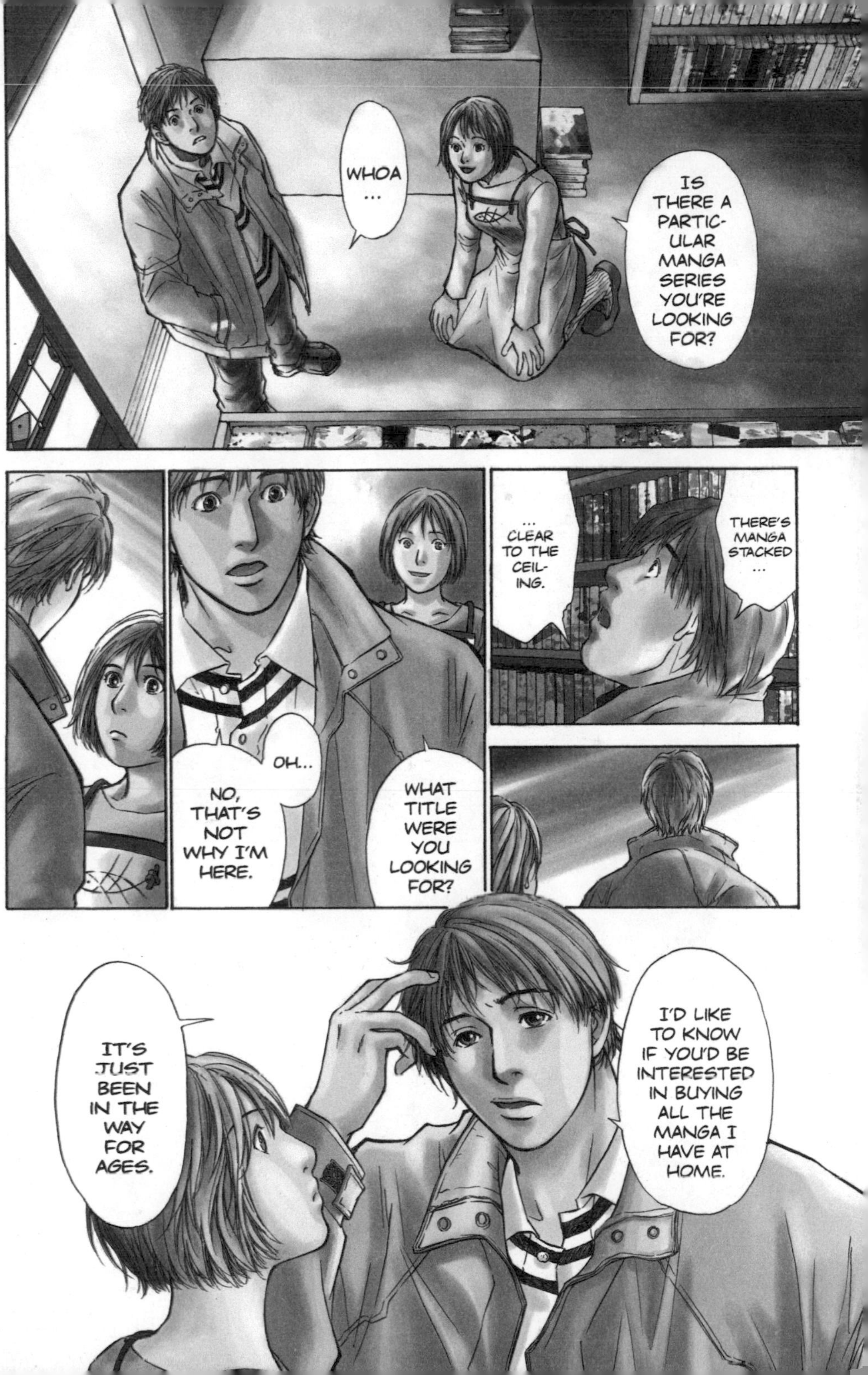
IS THERE A PARTICULAR MANGA SERIES YOU'RE LOOKING FOR?
WHOA ...
THERE'S MANGA STACKED ...
... CLEAR TO THE CEILING.
WHAT TITLE WERE YOU LOOKING FOR?
OH...
NO, THAT'S NOT WHY I'M HERE.
I'D LIKE TO KNOW IF YOU'D BE INTERESTED IN BUYING ALL THE MANGA I HAVE AT HOME.
IT'S JUST BEEN IN THE WAY FOR AGES.

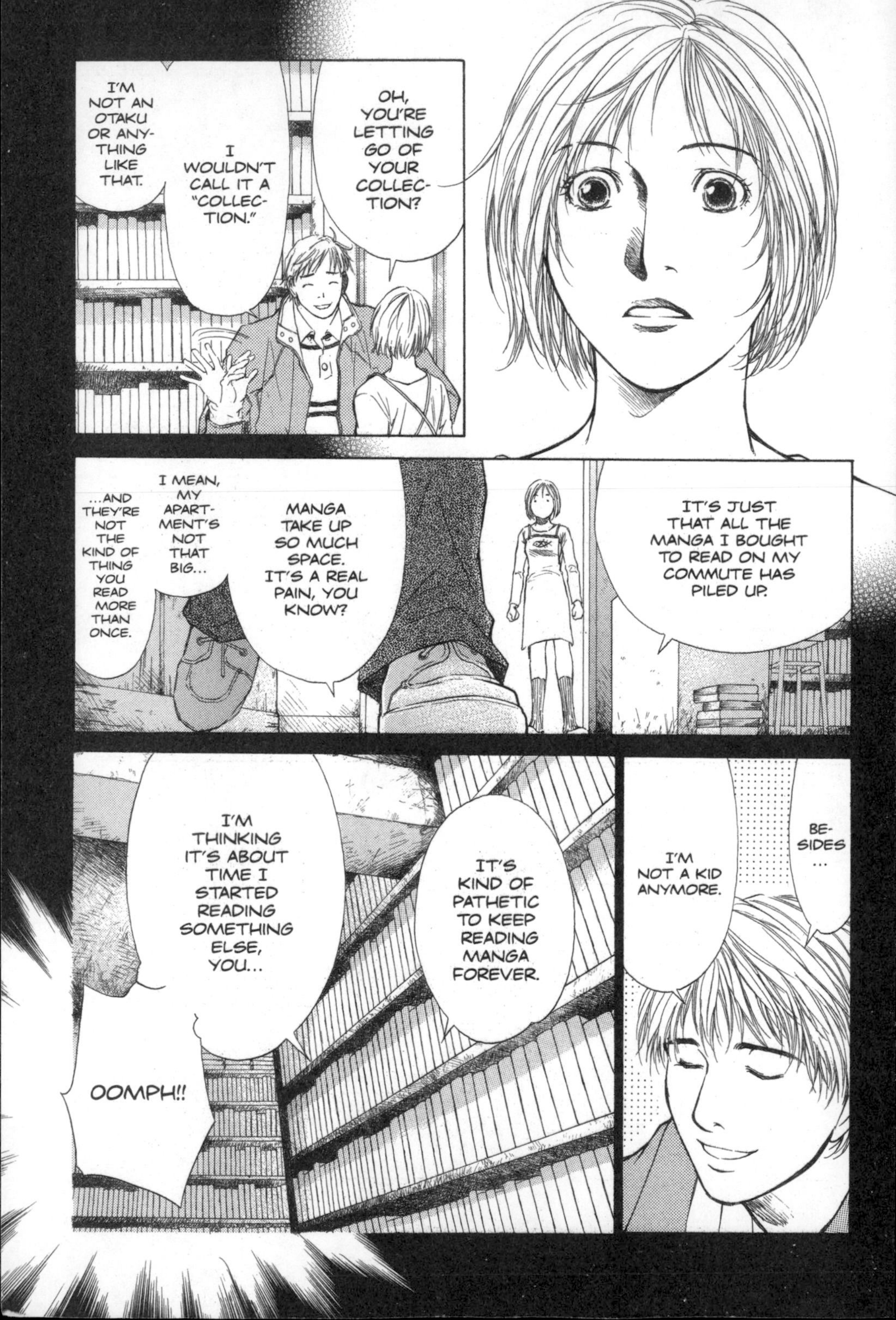
OH, YOU'RE LETTING GO OF YOUR COLLECTION?
I WOULDN'T CALL IT A "COLLECTION."
I'M NOT AN OTAKU OR ANYTHING LIKE THAT.
IT'S JUST THAT ALL THE MANGA I BOUGHT TO READ ON MY COMMUTE HAS PILED UP.
MANGA TAKE UP SO MUCH SPACE. IT'S A REAL PAIN, YOU KNOW?
I MEAN, MY APARTMENT'S NOT THAT BIG...
...AND THEY'RE NOT THE KIND OF THING YOU READ MORE THAN ONCE.
BESIDES...
I'M NOT A KID ANYMORE.
IT'S KIND OF PATHETIC TO KEEP READING MANGA FOREVER.
I'M THINKING IT'S ABOUT TIME I STARTED READING SOMETHING ELSE, YOU...
OOMPH!!

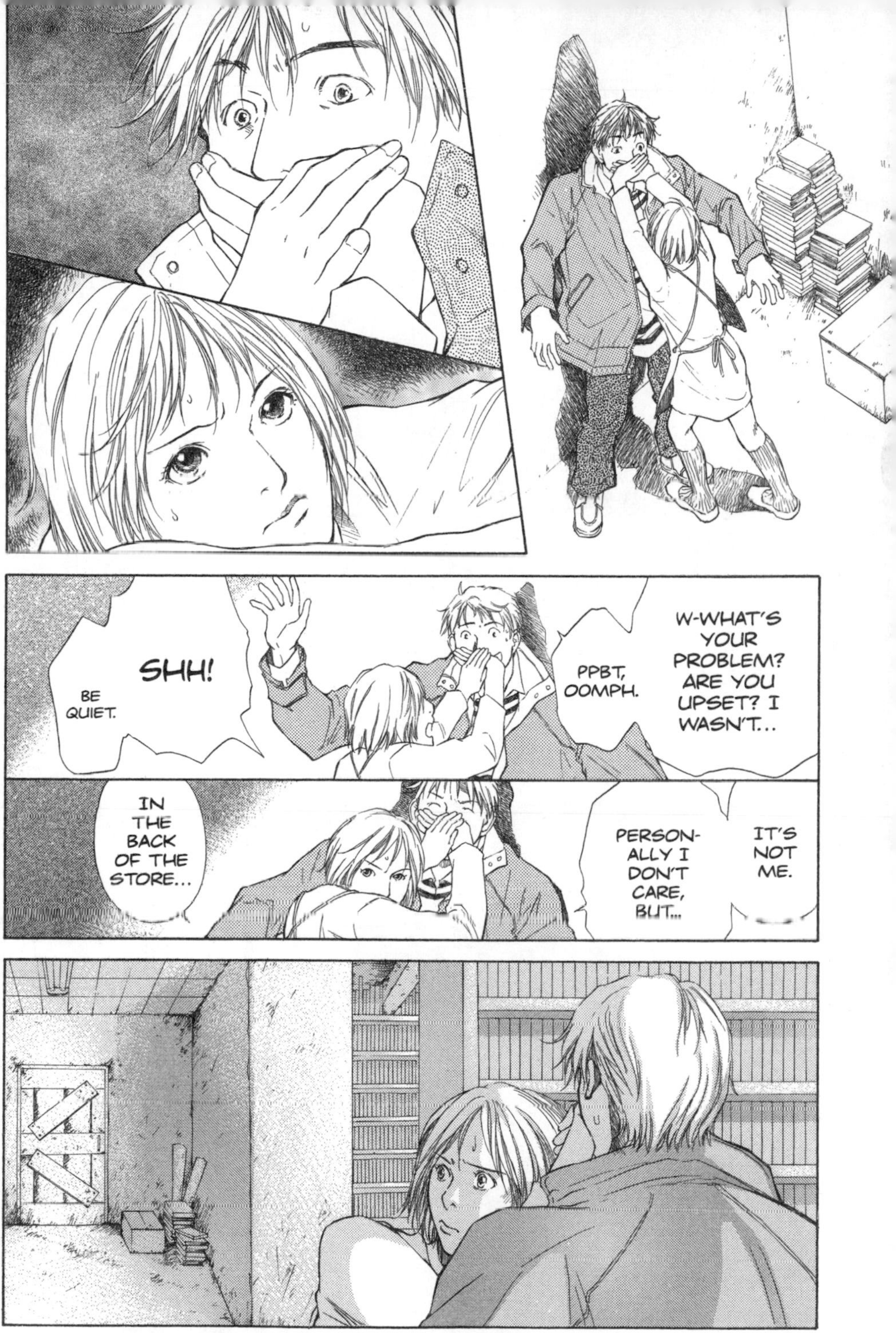
W-WHAT'S YOUR PROBLEM? ARE YOU UPSET? I WASN'T...
PPBT, OOMPH.
SHH!
BE QUIET.
IT'S NOT ME.
PERSON-ALLY I DON'T CARE, BUT...
IN THE BACK OF THE STORE...

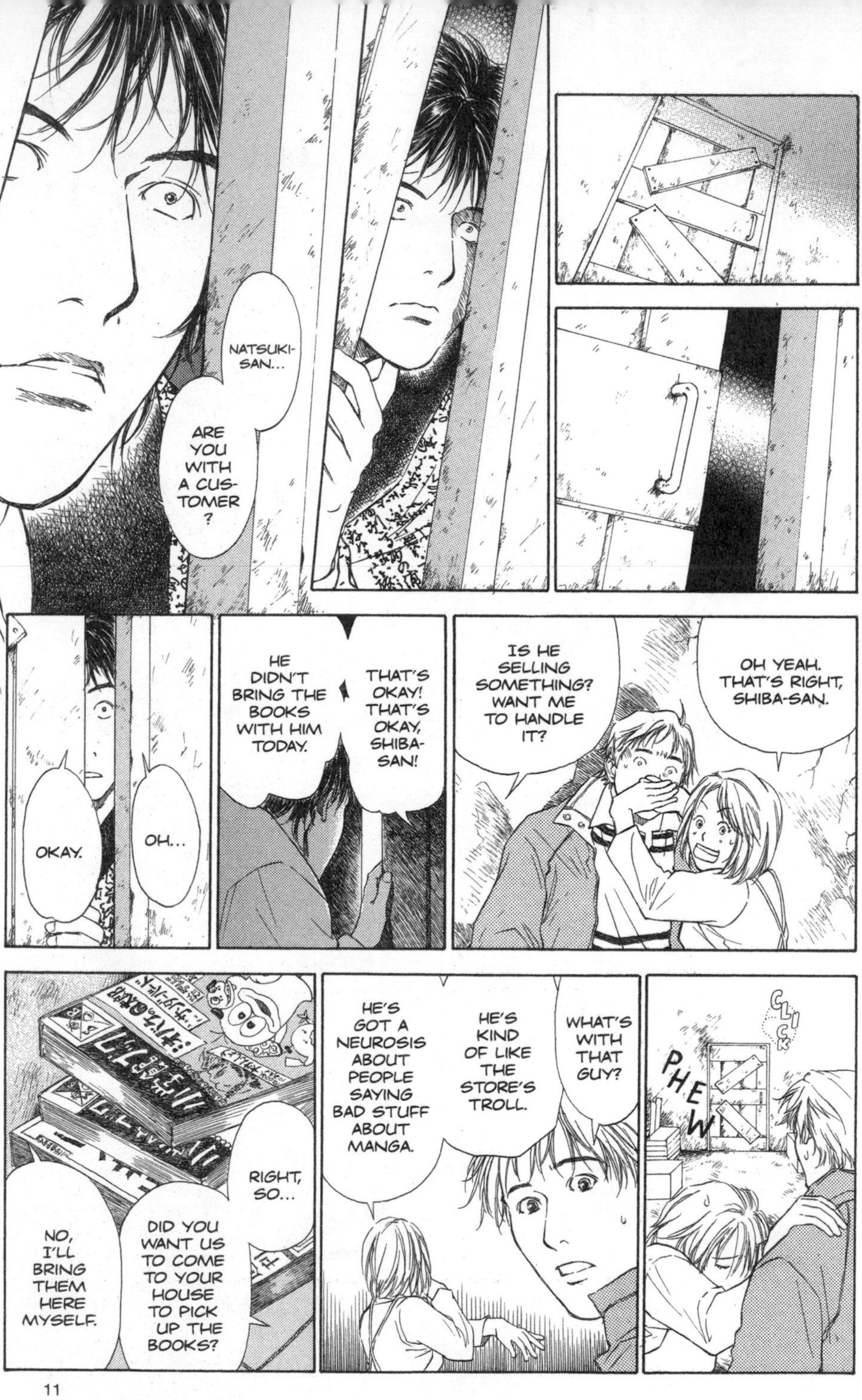
NATSUKI-SAN...
ARE YOU WITH A CUSTOMER?
OH YEAH. THAT'S RIGHT, SHIBA-SAN.
IS HE SELLING SOMETHING? WANT ME TO HANDLE IT?
THAT'S OKAY! THAT'S OKAY, SHIBA-SAN!
HE DIDN'T BRING THE BOOKS WITH HIM TODAY.
OH...
OKAY.
CLICK
PHEW
WHAT'S WITH THAT GUY?
HE'S KIND OF LIKE THE STORE'S TROLL.
HE'S GOT A NEUROSIS ABOUT PEOPLE SAYING BAD STUFF ABOUT MANGA.
RIGHT, SO...
DID YOU WANT US TO COME TO YOUR HOUSE TO PICK UP THE BOOKS?
NO, I'LL BRING THEM HERE MYSELF.

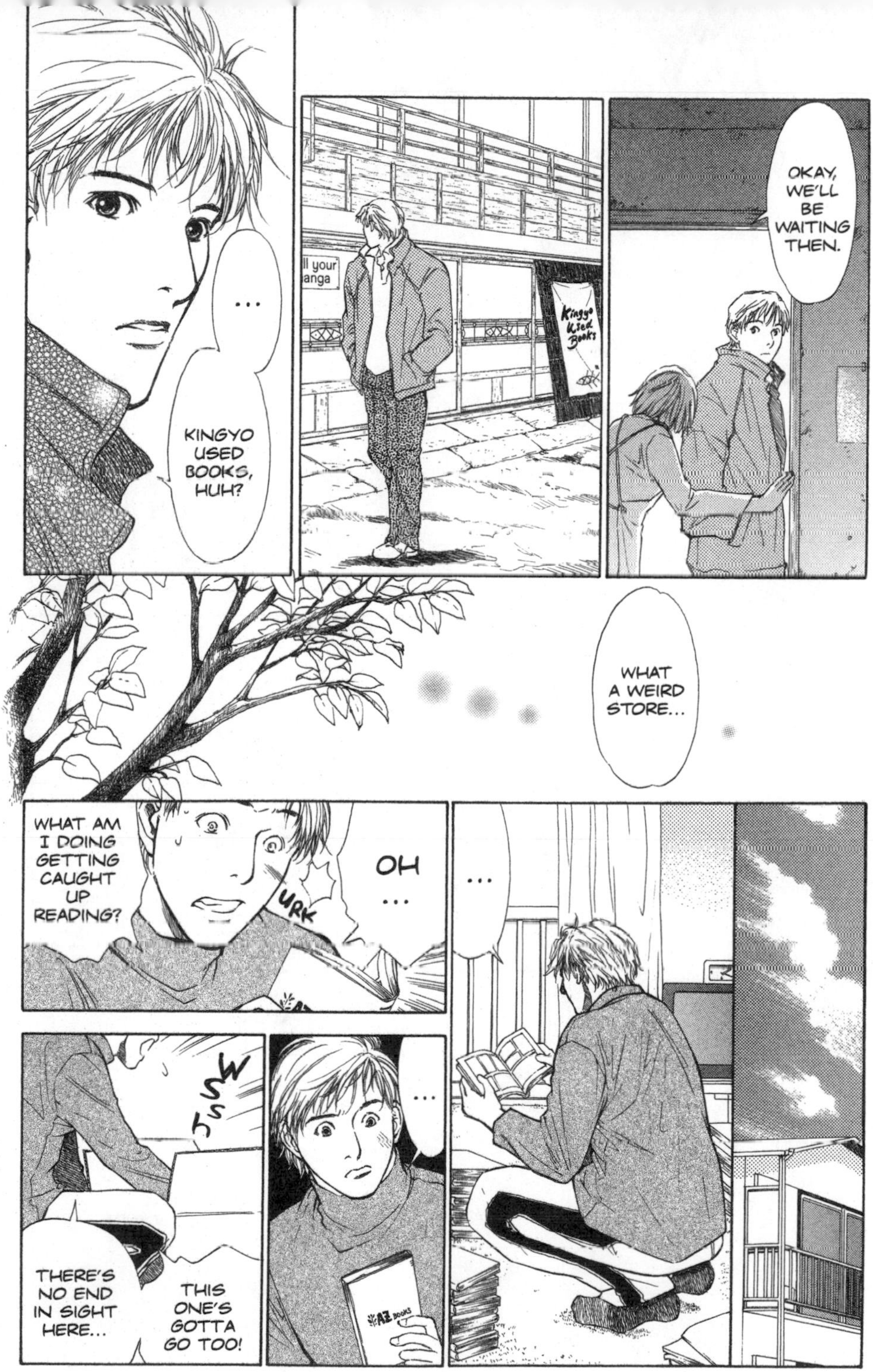
OKAY, WE'LL BE WAITING THEN.
ll your
anga
Kingyo Used Books
...
KINGYO USED BOOKS, HUH?
WHAT A WEIRD STORE...
...
OH ...
URK
WHAT AM I DOING GETTING CAUGHT UP READING?
...
AZ BOOKS
THIS ONE'S GOTTA GO TOO!
THERE'S NO END IN SIGHT HERE...

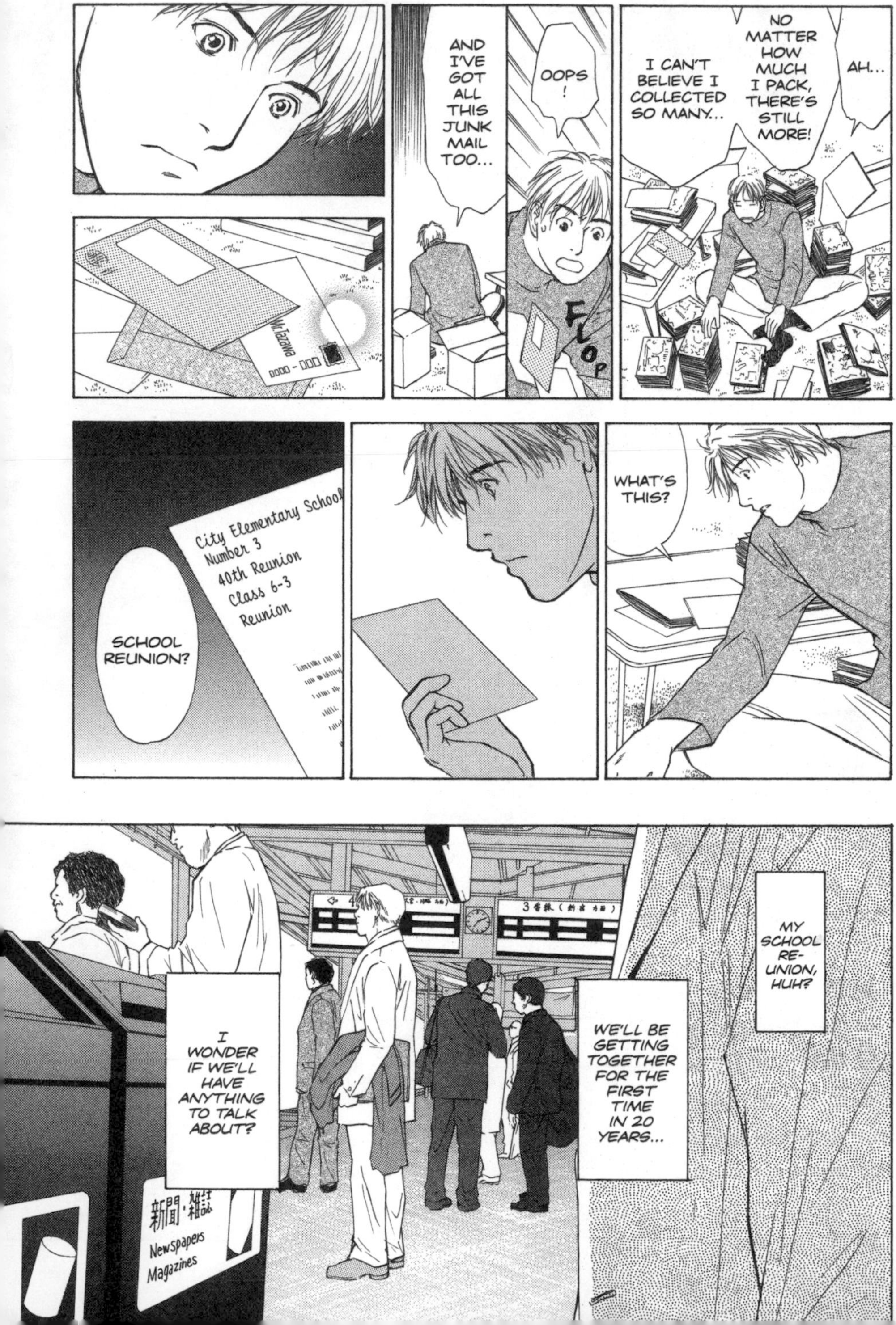
AH...
NO MATTER HOW MUCH I PACK, THERE'S STILL MORE!
I CAN'T BELIEVE I COLLECTED SO MANY...
OOPS!
FLOP
AND I'VE GOT ALL THIS JUNK MAIL TOO...
Mr. Tazawa
WHAT'S THIS?
City Elementary School
Number 3
40th Reunion
Class 6-3
Reunion
SCHOOL REUNION?
MY SCHOOL RE-UNION, HUH?
WE'LL BE GETTING TOGETHER FOR THE FIRST TIME IN 20 YEARS...
I WONDER IF WE'LL HAVE ANYTHING TO TALK ABOUT?
新聞・雑誌
Newspapers
Magazines

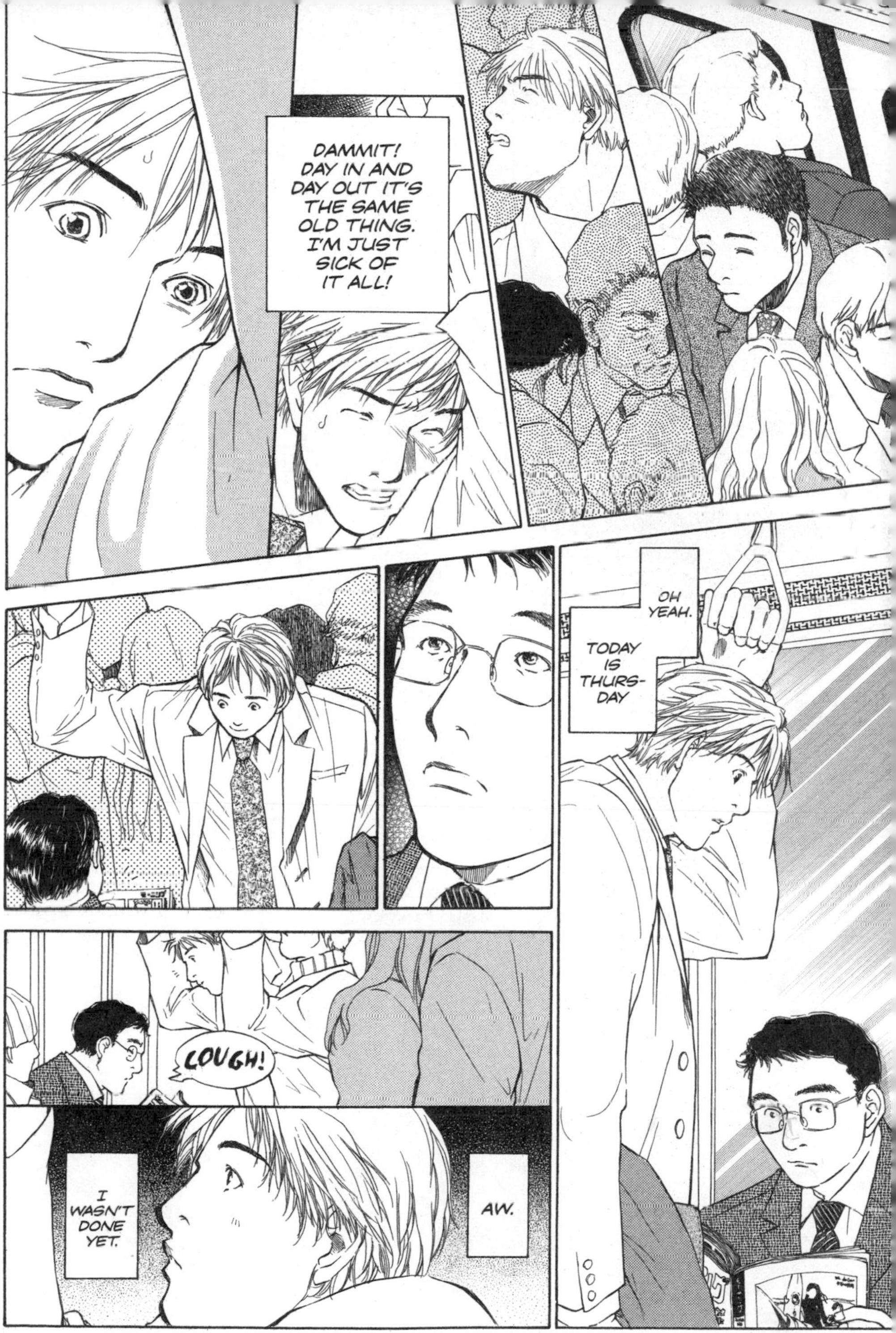
DAMMIT! DAY IN AND DAY OUT IT'S THE SAME OLD THING. I'M JUST SICK OF IT ALL!
OH YEAH.
TODAY IS THURS-DAY
COUGH!
AW.
I WASN'T DONE YET.

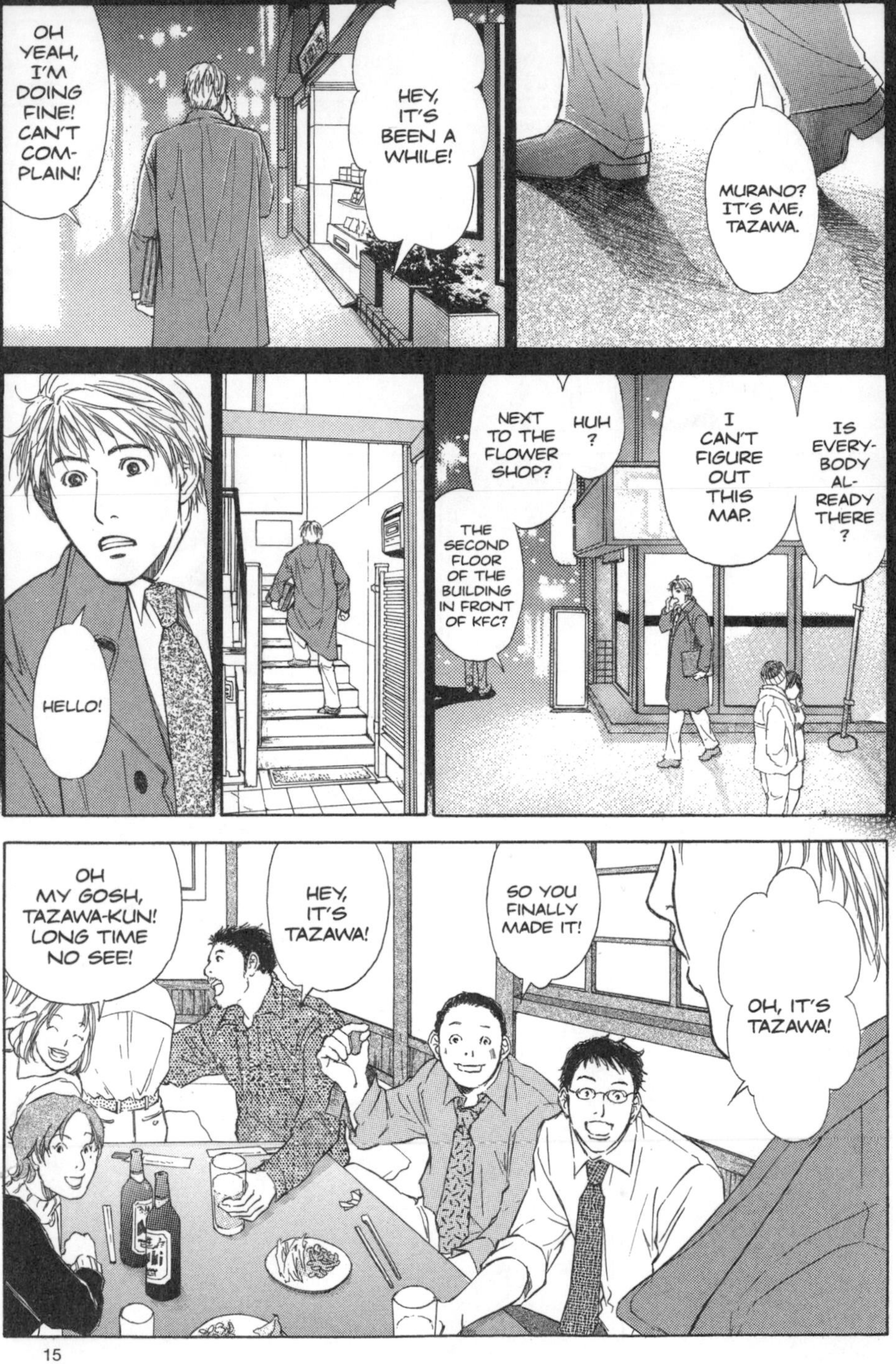
MURANO? IT'S ME, TAZAWA.
HEY, IT'S BEEN A WHILE!
OH YEAH, I'M DOING FINE! CAN'T COMPLAIN!
IS EVERYBODY ALREADY THERE?
I CAN'T FIGURE OUT THIS MAP.
HUH?
NEXT TO THE FLOWER SHOP?
THE SECOND FLOOR OF THE BUILDING IN FRONT OF KFC?
HELLO!
OH, IT'S TAZAWA!
SO YOU FINALLY MADE IT!
HEY, IT'S TAZAWA!
OH MY GOSH, TAZAWA-KUN! LONG TIME NO SEE!

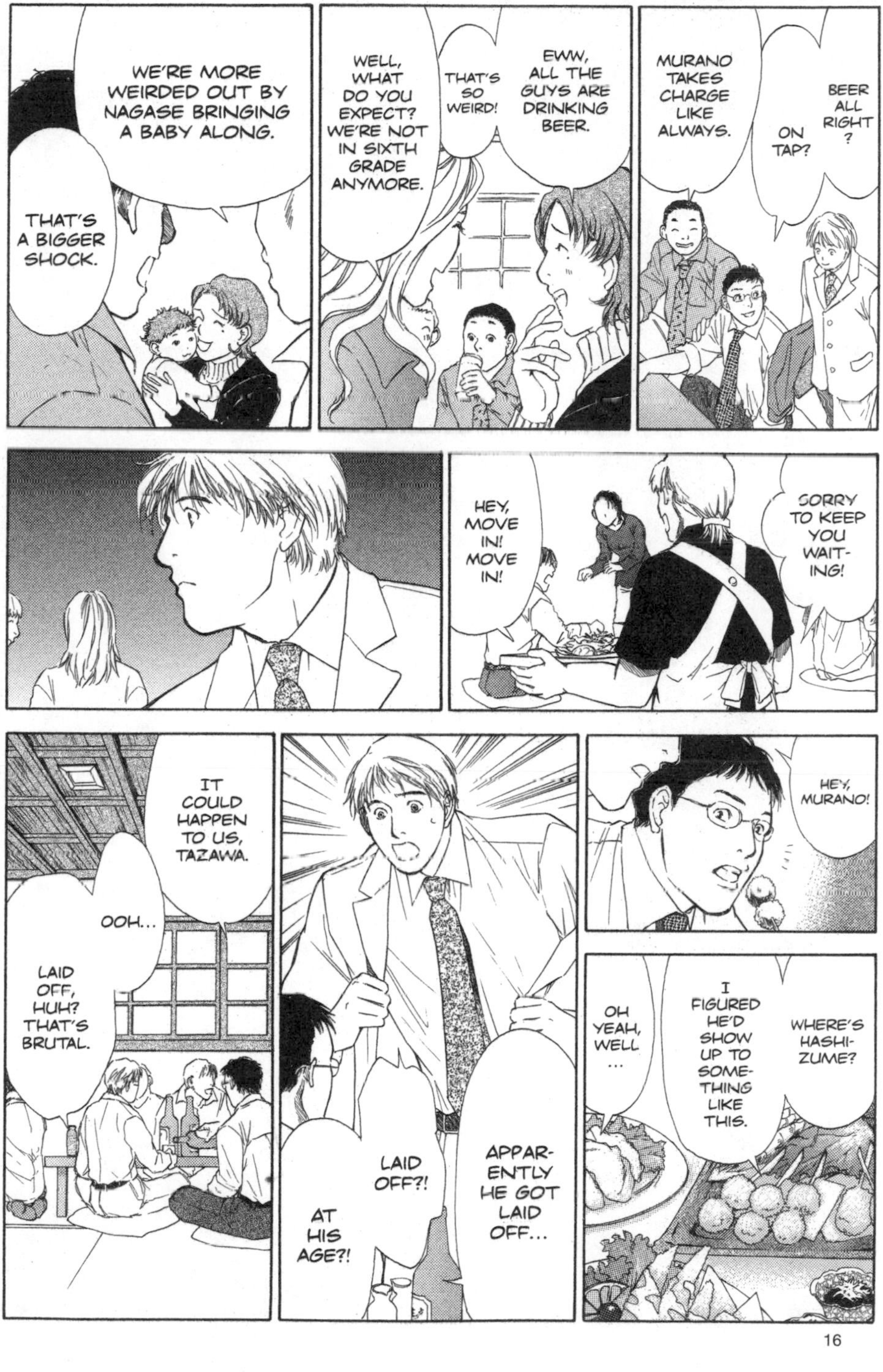
BEER ALL RIGHT?
ON TAP?
MURANO TAKES CHARGE LIKE ALWAYS.
EWW, ALL THE GUYS ARE DRINKING BEER.
THAT'S SO WEIRD!
WELL, WHAT DO YOU EXPECT? WE'RE NOT IN SIXTH GRADE ANYMORE.
WE'RE MORE WEIRDED OUT BY NAGASE BRINGING A BABY ALONG.
THAT'S A BIGGER SHOCK.
SORRY TO KEEP YOU WAIT-ING!
HEY, MOVE IN! MOVE IN!
HEY, MURANO!
WHERE'S HASHI-ZUME?
I FIGURED HE'D SHOW UP TO SOME-THING LIKE THIS.
OH YEAH, WELL ...
APPAR-ENTLY HE GOT LAID OFF...
LAID OFF?!
AT HIS AGE?!
IT COULD HAPPEN TO US, TAZAWA.
OOH...
LAID OFF, HUH? THAT'S BRUTAL.

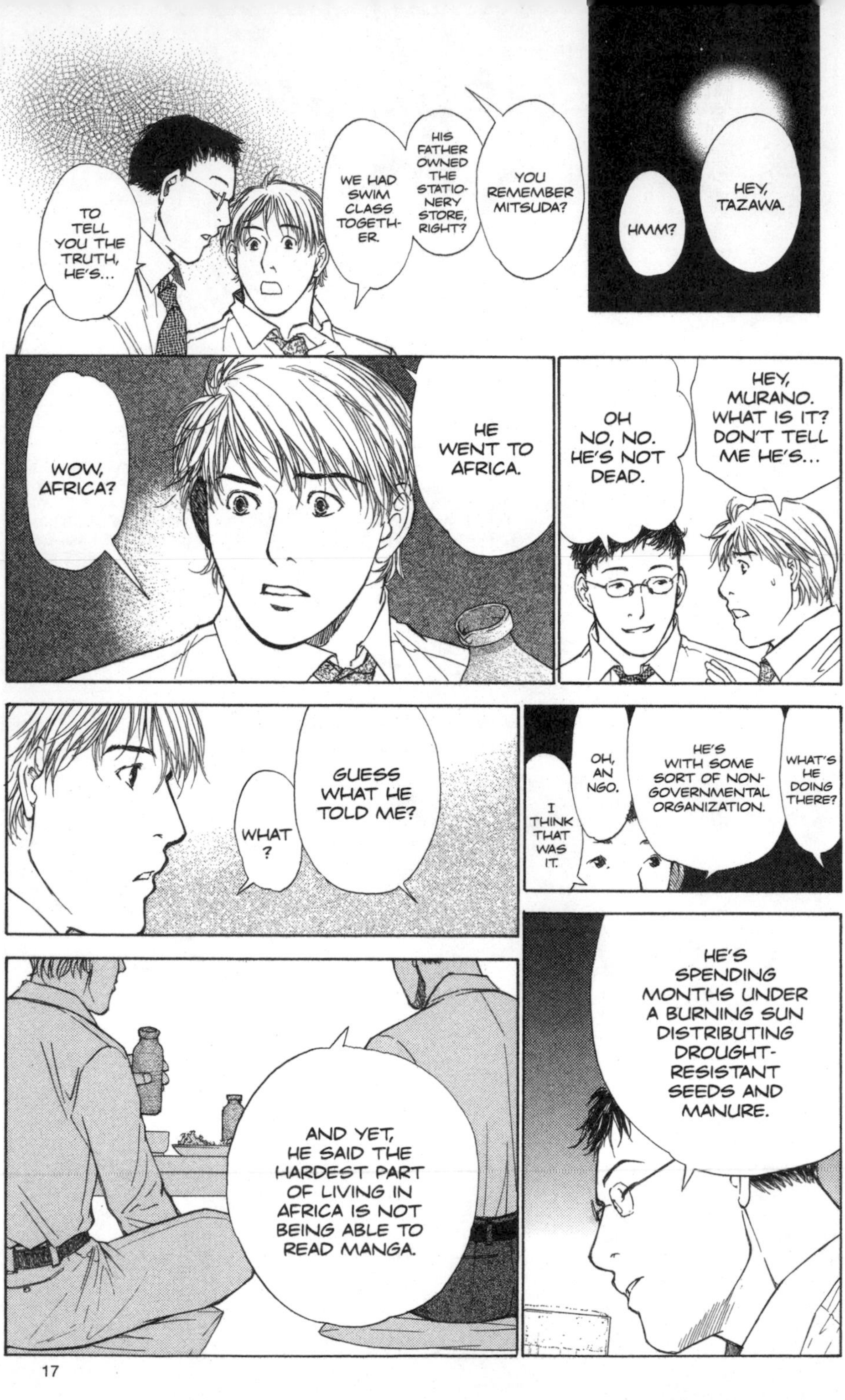
HEY, TAZAWA.
HMM?
YOU REMEMBER MITSUDA?
HIS FATHER OWNED THE STATIONERY STORE, RIGHT?
WE HAD SWIM CLASS TOGETHER.
TO TELL YOU THE TRUTH, HE'S...
HEY, MURANO. WHAT IS IT? DON'T TELL ME HE'S...
OH NO, NO. HE'S NOT DEAD.
HE WENT TO AFRICA.
WOW, AFRICA?
WHAT'S HE DOING THERE?
HE'S WITH SOME SORT OF NON-GOVERNMENTAL ORGANIZATION.
OH, AN NGO.
I THINK THAT WAS IT.
GUESS WHAT HE TOLD ME?
WHAT?
HE'S SPENDING MONTHS UNDER A BURNING SUN DISTRIBUTING DROUGHT-RESISTANT SEEDS AND MANURE.
AND YET, HE SAID THE HARDEST PART OF LIVING IN AFRICA IS NOT BEING ABLE TO READ MANGA.

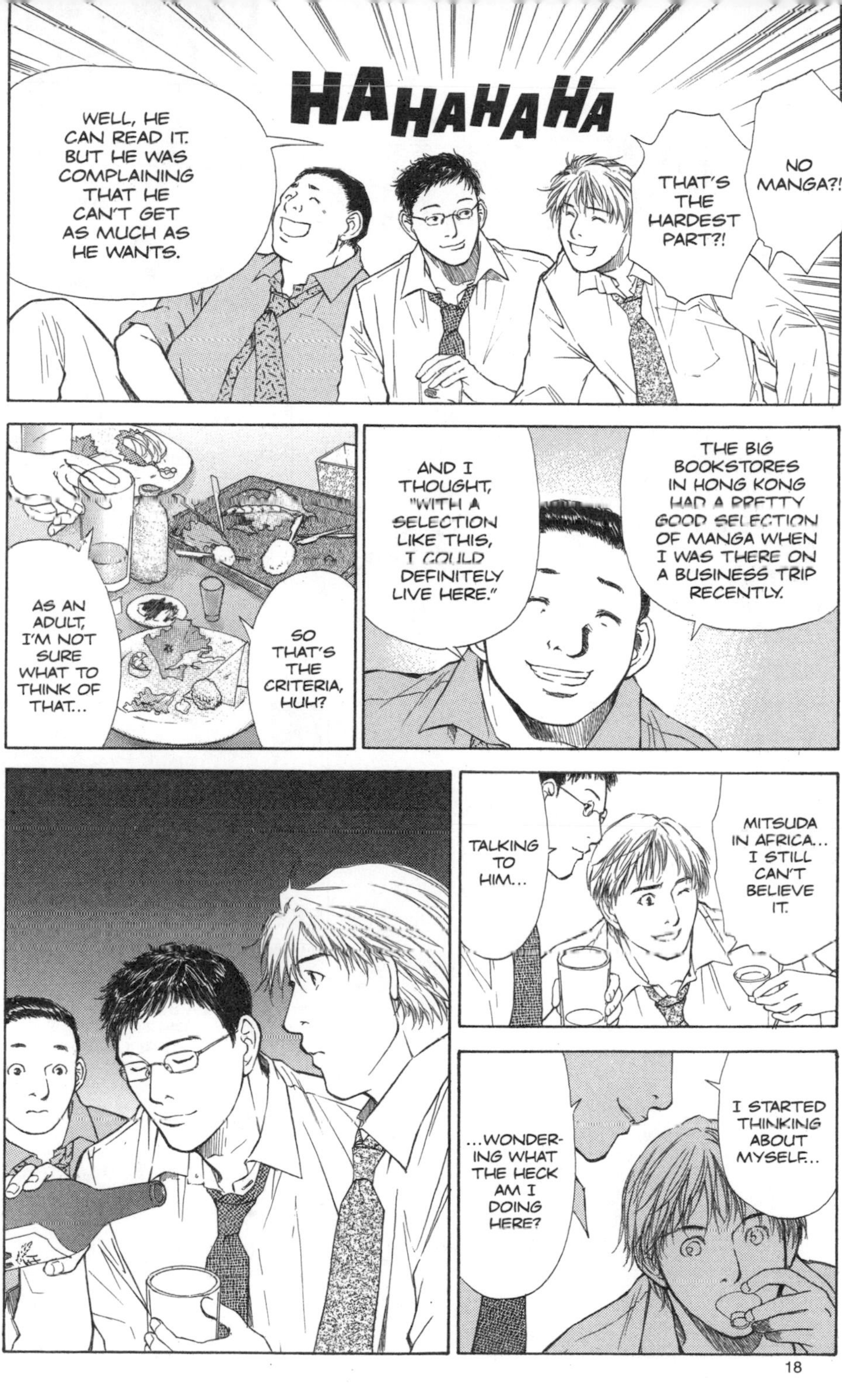
NO MANGA?!
THAT'S THE HARDEST PART?!
HAHAHAHA
WELL, HE CAN READ IT. BUT HE WAS COMPLAINING THAT HE CAN'T GET AS MUCH AS HE WANTS.
THE BIG BOOKSTORES IN HONG KONG HAD A PRETTY GOOD SELECTION OF MANGA WHEN I WAS THERE ON A BUSINESS TRIP RECENTLY.
AND I THOUGHT, "WITH A SELECTION LIKE THIS, I COULD DEFINITELY LIVE HERE."
SO THAT'S THE CRITERIA, HUH?
AS AN ADULT, I'M NOT SURE WHAT TO THINK OF THAT...
MITSUDA IN AFRICA... I STILL CAN'T BELIEVE IT.
TALKING TO HIM...
I STARTED THINKING ABOUT MYSELF...
...WONDERING WHAT THE HECK AM I DOING HERE?

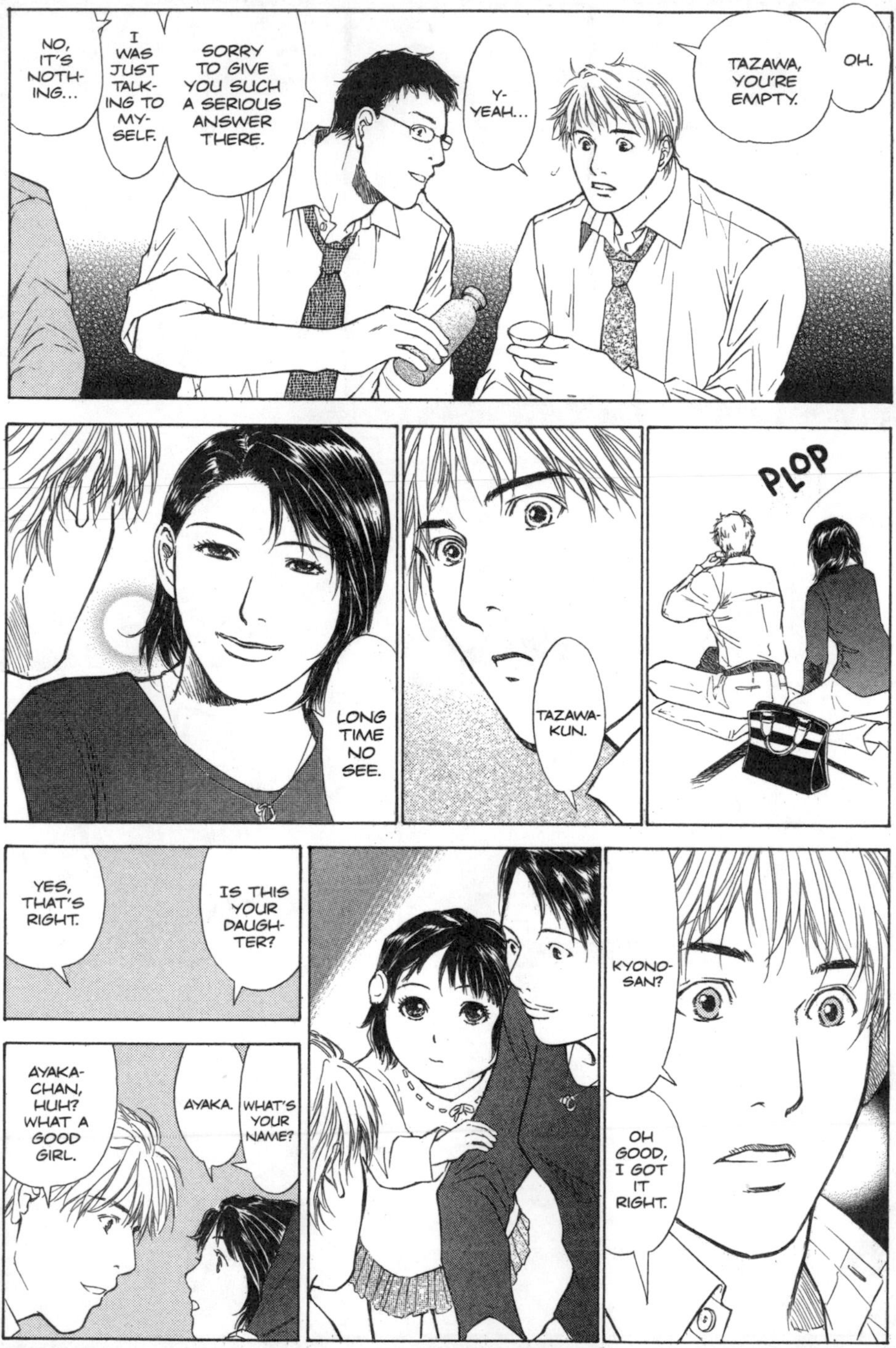
OH.
TAZAWA, YOU'RE EMPTY.
Y-YEAH...
SORRY TO GIVE YOU SUCH A SERIOUS ANSWER THERE.
I WAS JUST TALKING TO MYSELF.
NO, IT'S NOTHING...
PLOP
TAZAWA-KUN.
LONG TIME NO SEE.
KYONO-SAN?
OH GOOD, I GOT IT RIGHT.
IS THIS YOUR DAUGHTER?
YES, THAT'S RIGHT.
WHAT'S YOUR NAME?
AYAKA.
AYAKA-CHAN, HUH? WHAT A GOOD GIRL.

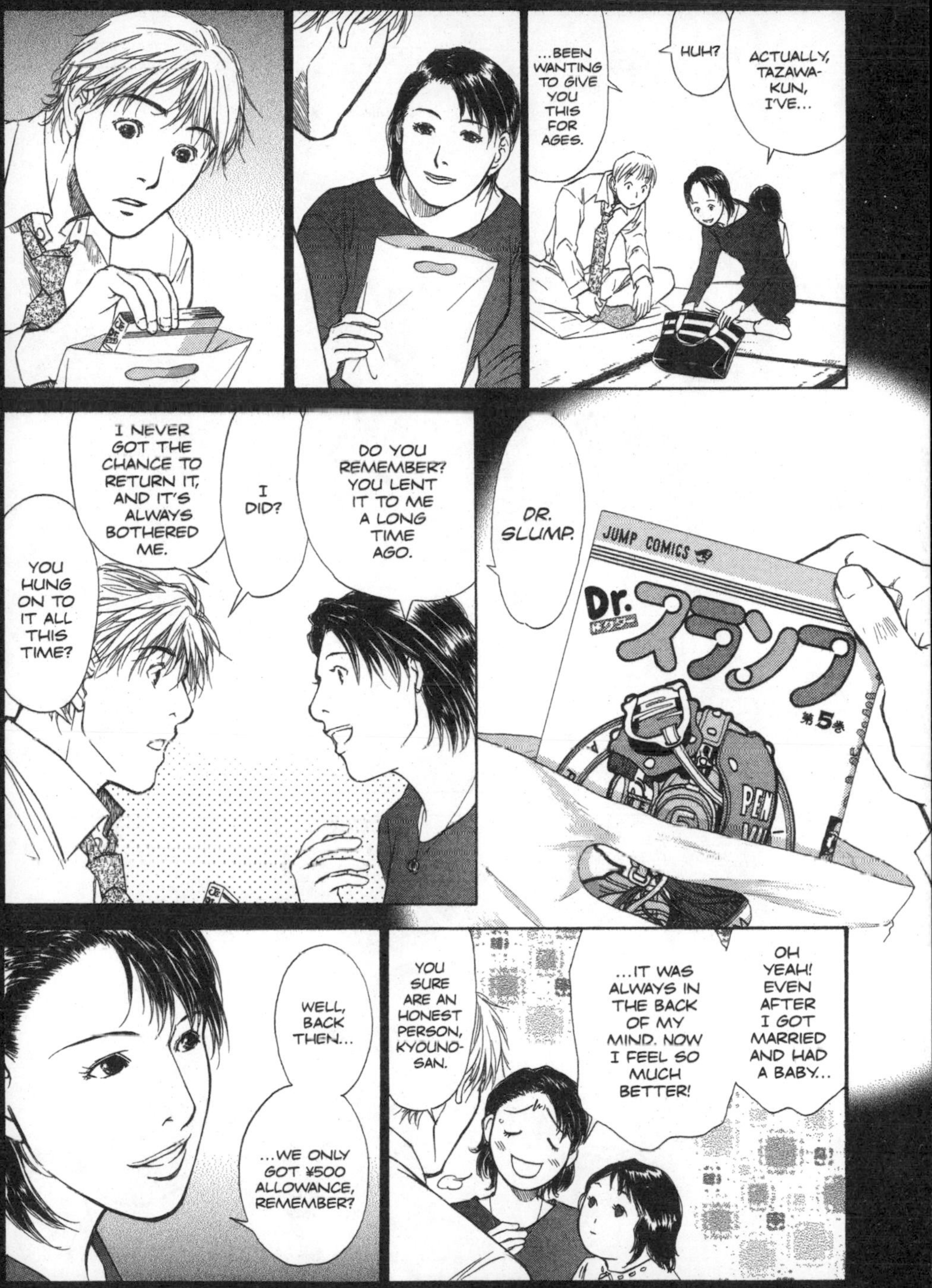
ACTUALLY, TAZAWA-KUN, I'VE...
HUH?
...BEEN WANTING TO GIVE YOU THIS FOR AGES.
DR. SLUMP.
JUMP COMICS
Dr. スランプ
第5巻
DO YOU REMEMBER? YOU LENT IT TO ME A LONG TIME AGO.
I DID?
I NEVER GOT THE CHANCE TO RETURN IT, AND IT'S ALWAYS BOTHERED ME.
YOU HUNG ON TO IT ALL THIS TIME?
OH YEAH! EVEN AFTER I GOT MARRIED AND HAD A BABY...
...IT WAS ALWAYS IN THE BACK OF MY MIND. NOW I FEEL SO MUCH BETTER!
YOU SURE ARE AN HONEST PERSON, KYOUNO-SAN.
WELL, BACK THEN...
...WE ONLY GOT ¥500 ALLOWANCE, REMEMBER?

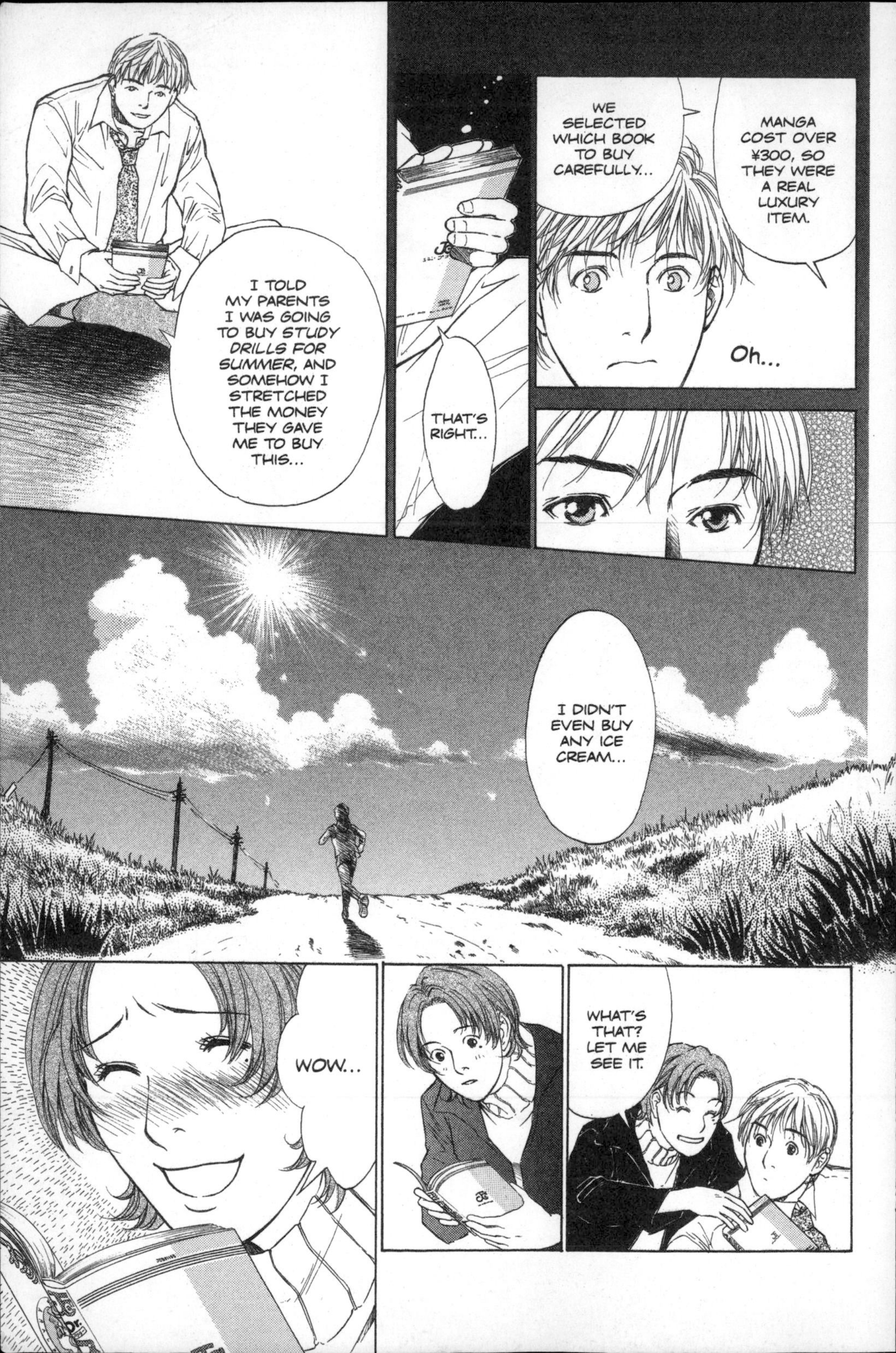

MANGA COST OVER ¥300, SO THEY WERE A REAL LUXURY ITEM.
WE SELECTED WHICH BOOK TO BUY CAREFULLY...
Oh...
THAT'S RIGHT...
I TOLD MY PARENTS I WAS GOING TO BUY STUDY DRILLS FOR SUMMER, AND SOMEHOW I STRETCHED THE MONEY THEY GAVE ME TO BUY THIS...
I DIDN'T EVEN BUY ANY ICE CREAM...
WHAT'S THAT? LET ME SEE IT.
WOW...

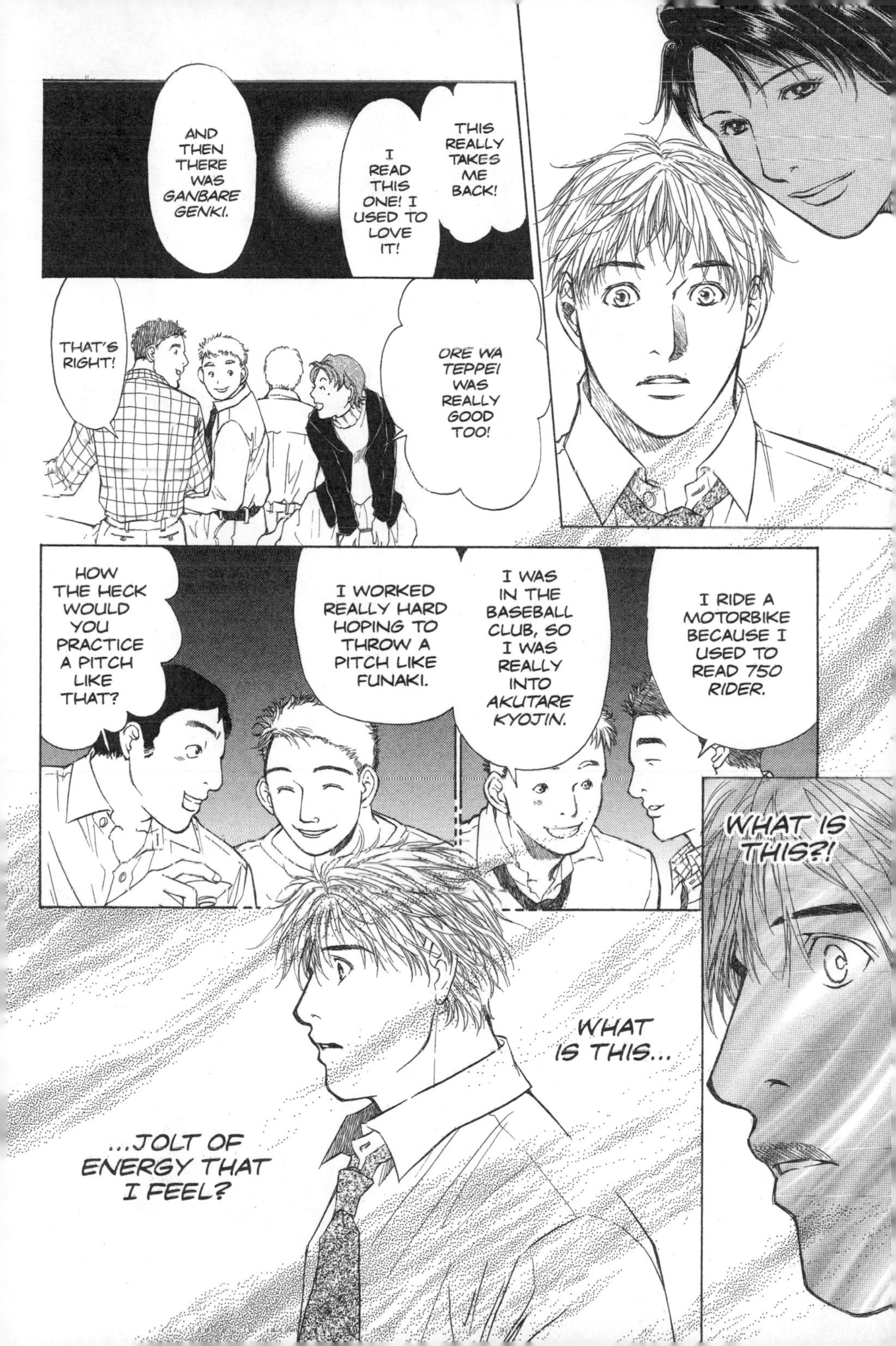
THIS REALLY TAKES ME BACK!
I READ THIS ONE! I USED TO LOVE IT!
AND THEN THERE WAS GANBARE GENKI.
ORE WA TEPPEI WAS REALLY GOOD TOO!
THAT'S RIGHT!
I RIDE A MOTORBIKE BECAUSE I USED TO READ 750 RIDER.
I WAS IN THE BASEBALL CLUB, SO I WAS REALLY INTO AKUTARE KYOJIN.
I WORKED REALLY HARD HOPING TO THROW A PITCH LIKE FUNAKI.
HOW THE HECK WOULD YOU PRACTICE A PITCH LIKE THAT?
WHAT IS THIS?!
WHAT IS THIS...
...JOLT OF ENERGY THAT I FEEL?

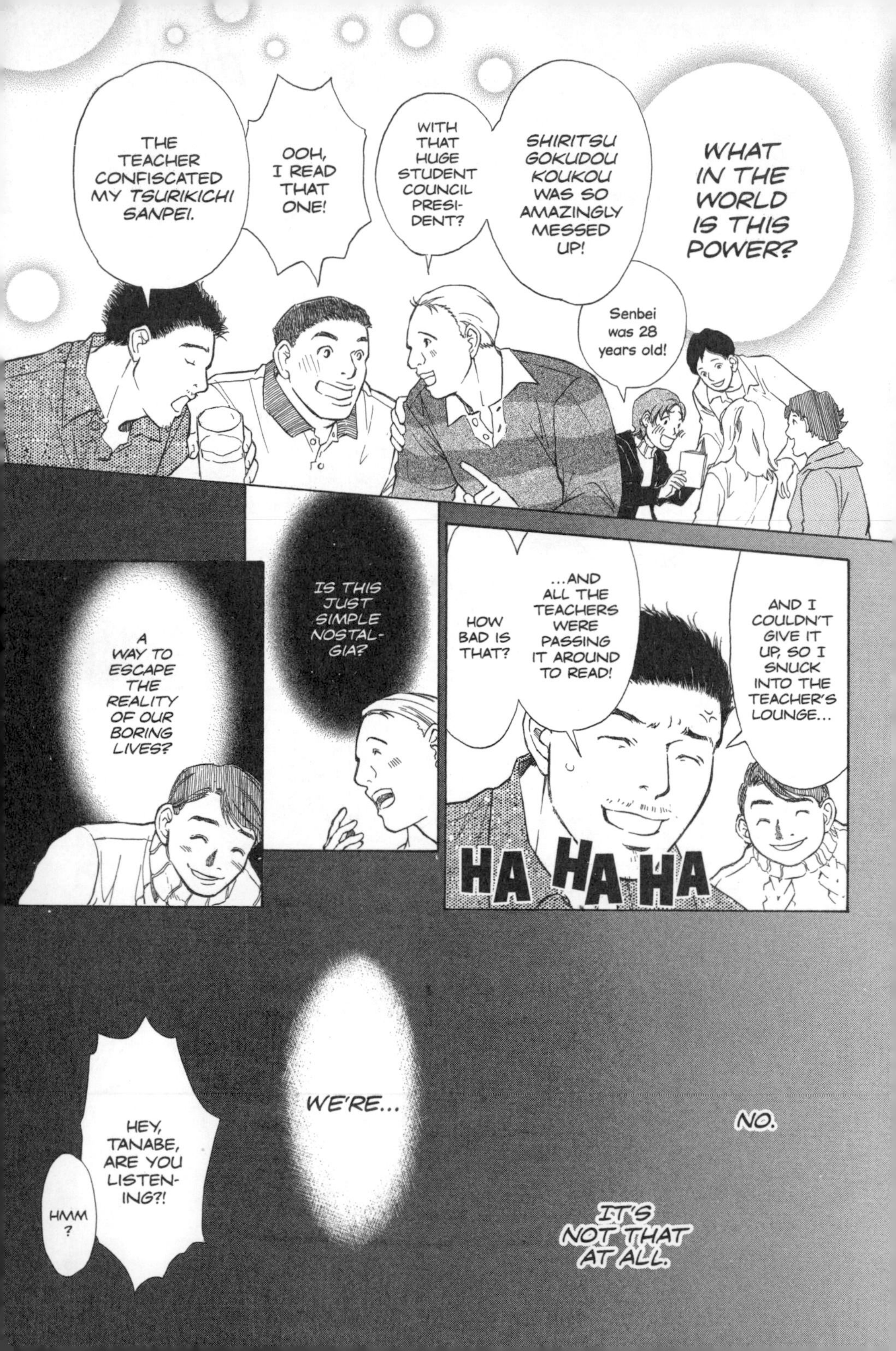
WHAT IN THE WORLD IS THIS POWER?
SHIRITSU GOKUDOU KOUKOU WAS SO AMAZINGLY MESSED UP!
Senbei was 28 years old!
WITH THAT HUGE STUDENT COUNCIL PRESIDENT?
OOH, I READ THAT ONE!
THE TEACHER CONFISCATED MY *TSURIKICHI SANPEI*.
AND I COULDN'T GIVE IT UP, SO I SNUCK INTO THE TEACHER'S LOUNGE...
...AND ALL THE TEACHERS WERE PASSING IT AROUND TO READ!
HOW BAD IS THAT?
HA HA HA
IS THIS JUST SIMPLE NOSTAL-GIA?
A WAY TO ESCAPE THE REALITY OF OUR BORING LIVES?
NO.
IT'S NOT THAT AT ALL.
WE'RE...
HEY, TANABE, ARE YOU LISTEN-ING?!
HMM?

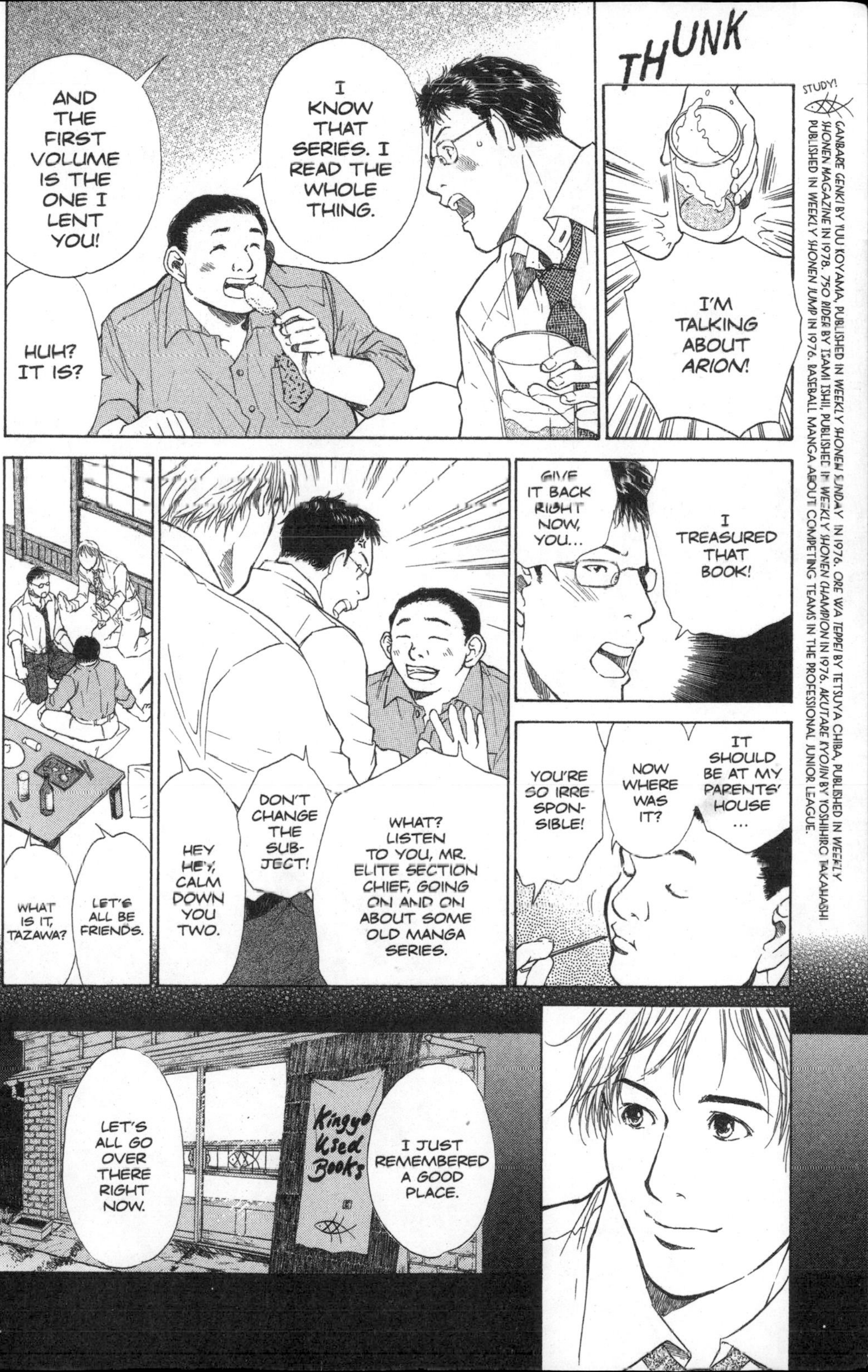
THUNK
STUDY!
I'M TALKING ABOUT ARION!
I KNOW THAT SERIES. I READ THE WHOLE THING.
AND THE FIRST VOLUME IS THE ONE I LENT YOU!
HUH? IT IS?
I TREASURED THAT BOOK!
GIVE IT BACK RIGHT NOW, YOU...
IT SHOULD BE AT MY PARENTS' HOUSE...
NOW WHERE WAS IT?
YOU'RE SO IRRE-SPON-SIBLE!
WHAT? LISTEN TO YOU, MR. ELITE SECTION CHIEF, GOING ON AND ON ABOUT SOME OLD MANGA SERIES.
DON'T CHANGE THE SUB-JECT!
HEY HEY, CALM DOWN YOU TWO.
LET'S ALL BE FRIENDS.
WHAT IS IT, TAZAWA?
I JUST REMEMBERED A GOOD PLACE.
Kingyo Used Books
LET'S ALL GO OVER THERE RIGHT NOW.

GANBARE GENKI BY YUU KOYAMA, PUBLISHED IN WEEKLY SHONEN SUNDAY IN 1976. *ORE WA TEPPEI* BY TETSUYA CHIBA, PUBLISHED IN WEEKLY SHONEN MAGAZINE IN 1978. *750 RIDER* BY ISAMI ISHII, PUBLISHED IN WEEKLY SHONEN CHAMPION IN 1976. *AKUTARE KYOJIN* BY YOSHIHIRO TAKAHASHI PUBLISHED IN WEEKLY SHONEN JUMP IN 1976. BASEBALL MANGA ABOUT COMPETING TEAMS IN THE PROFESSIONAL JUNIOR LEAGUE.

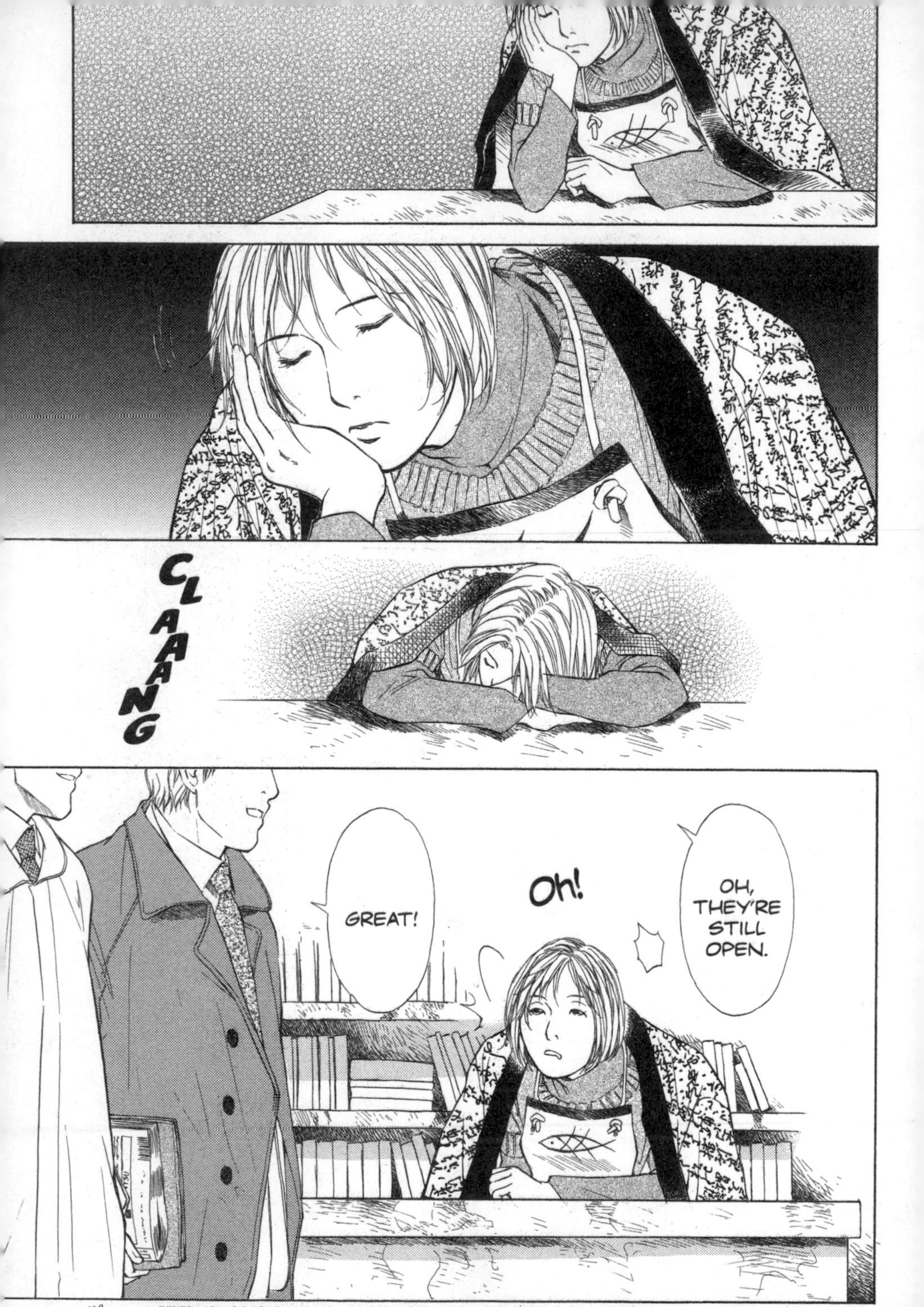
CLAAANG
OH, THEY'RE STILL OPEN.
Oh!
GREAT!

STUDY! *SHIRITSU GOKUDO KOKO* WAS AKIRA MIYASHITA'S DEBUT WORK, PUBLISHED IN *WEEKLY SHONEN JUMP* IN 1979. *TSURIKICHI SANPEI* BY TAKAO YAGUCHI, PUBLISHED IN *WEEKLY SHONEN MAGAZINE* IN 1973. *ARION*, YOSHIKAZU YASUHIKO'S DEBUT WORK, PUBLISHED IN *GEKKAN RYU* [MONTHLY RYU] IN 1979. A MANGA WHICH FOLLOWS THE GROWTH OF ITS HERO, ARION, BASED ON THE GREEK MYTHS.

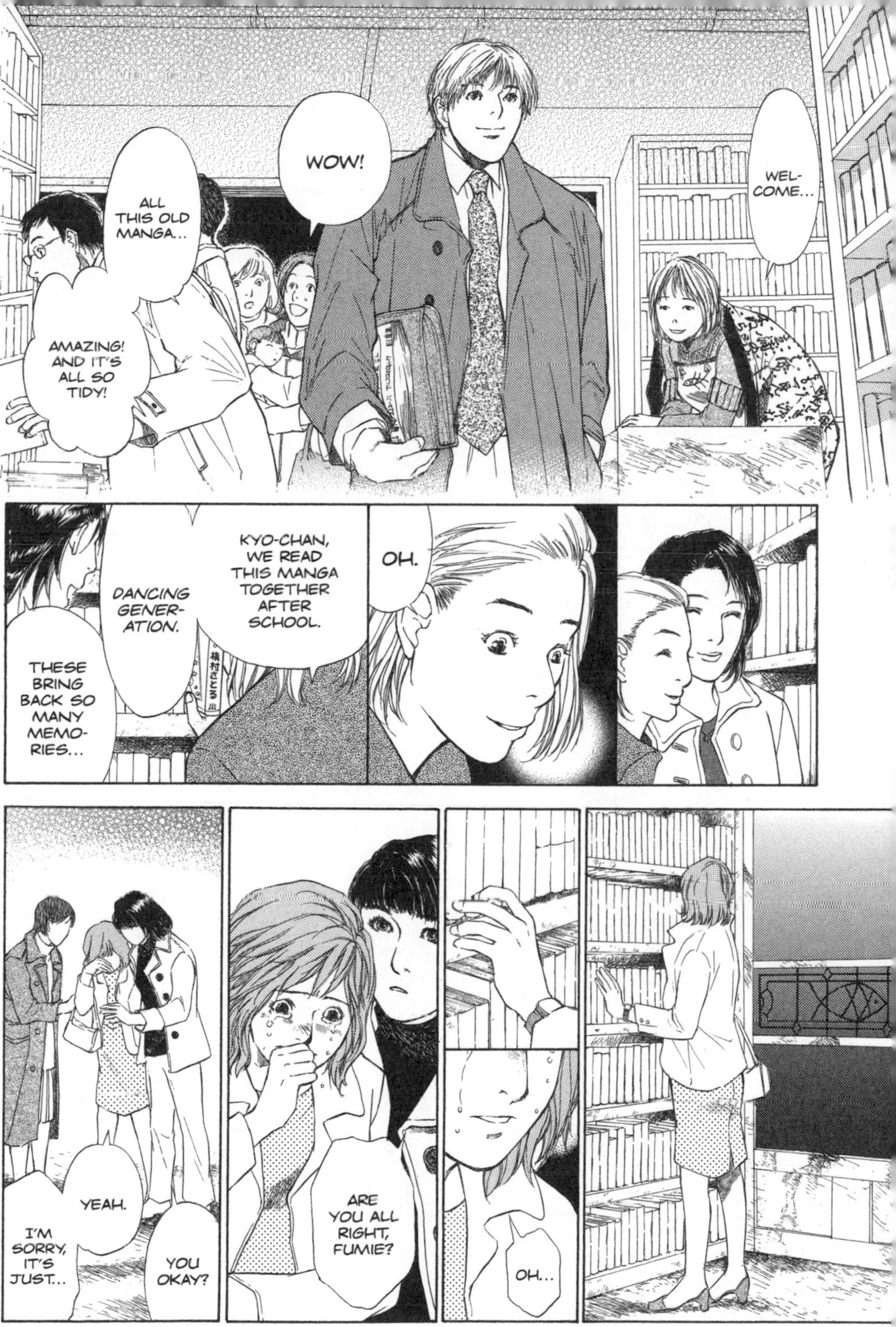
WEL-COME...
WOW!
ALL THIS OLD MANGA...
AMAZING! AND IT'S ALL SO TIDY!
OH.
KYO-CHAN, WE READ THIS MANGA TOGETHER AFTER SCHOOL.
DANCING GENER-ATION.
THESE BRING BACK SO MANY MEMO-RIES...
OH...
ARE YOU ALL RIGHT, FUMIE?
YOU OKAY?
YEAH.
I'M SORRY, IT'S JUST...

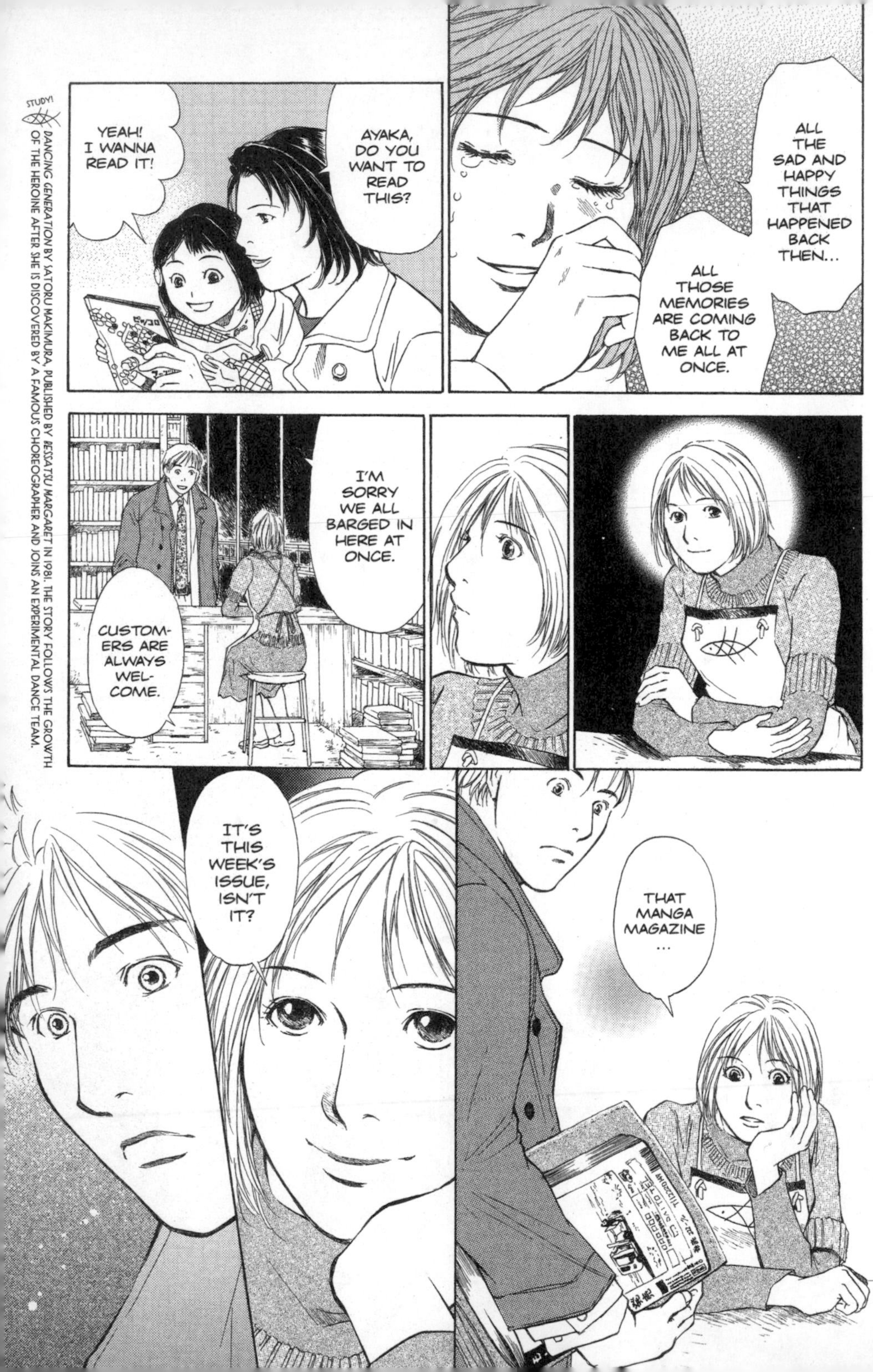
ALL THE SAD AND HAPPY THINGS THAT HAPPENED BACK THEN...
ALL THOSE MEMORIES ARE COMING BACK TO ME ALL AT ONCE.
AYAKA, DO YOU WANT TO READ THIS?
YEAH! I WANNA READ IT!
I'M SORRY WE ALL BARGED IN HERE AT ONCE.
CUSTOMERS ARE ALWAYS WEL-COME.
THAT MANGA MAGAZINE ...
IT'S THIS WEEK'S ISSUE, ISN'T IT?

STUDY!

DANCING GENERATION BY SATORU MAKIMURA, PUBLISHED BY BESSATSU MARGARET IN 1981. THE STORY FOLLOWS THE GROWTH OF THE HEROINE AFTER SHE IS DISCOVERED BY A FAMOUS CHOREOGRAPHER AND JOINS AN EXPERIMENTAL DANCE TEAM.

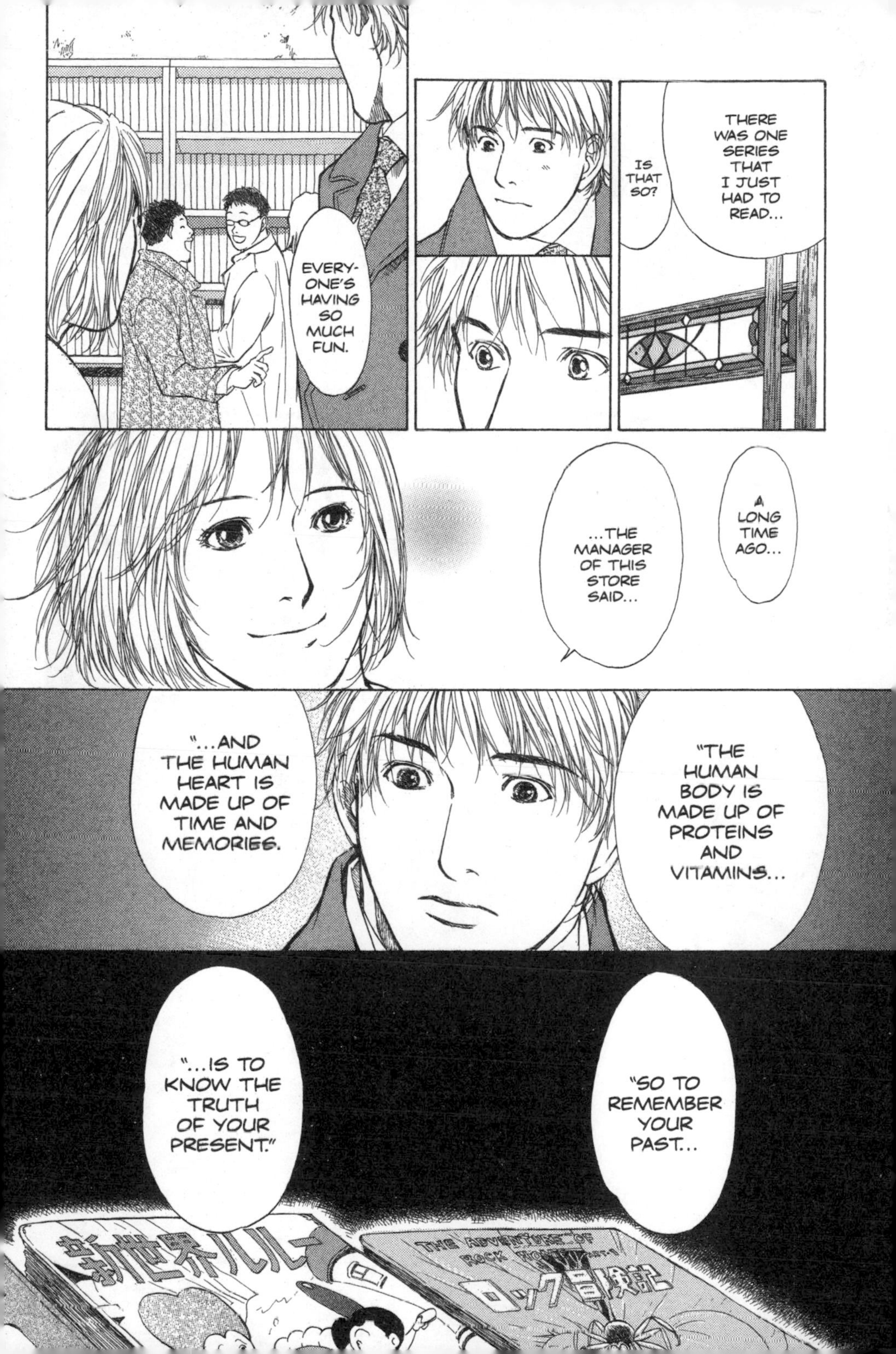
THERE WAS ONE SERIES THAT I JUST HAD TO READ...
IS THAT SO?
EVERY-ONE'S HAVING SO MUCH FUN.
A LONG TIME AGO...
...THE MANAGER OF THIS STORE SAID...
"THE HUMAN BODY IS MADE UP OF PROTEINS AND VITAMINS...
"...AND THE HUMAN HEART IS MADE UP OF TIME AND MEMORIES.
"SO TO REMEMBER YOUR PAST...
"...IS TO KNOW THE TRUTH OF YOUR PRESENT."
新世界ルルー
ロック冒険記

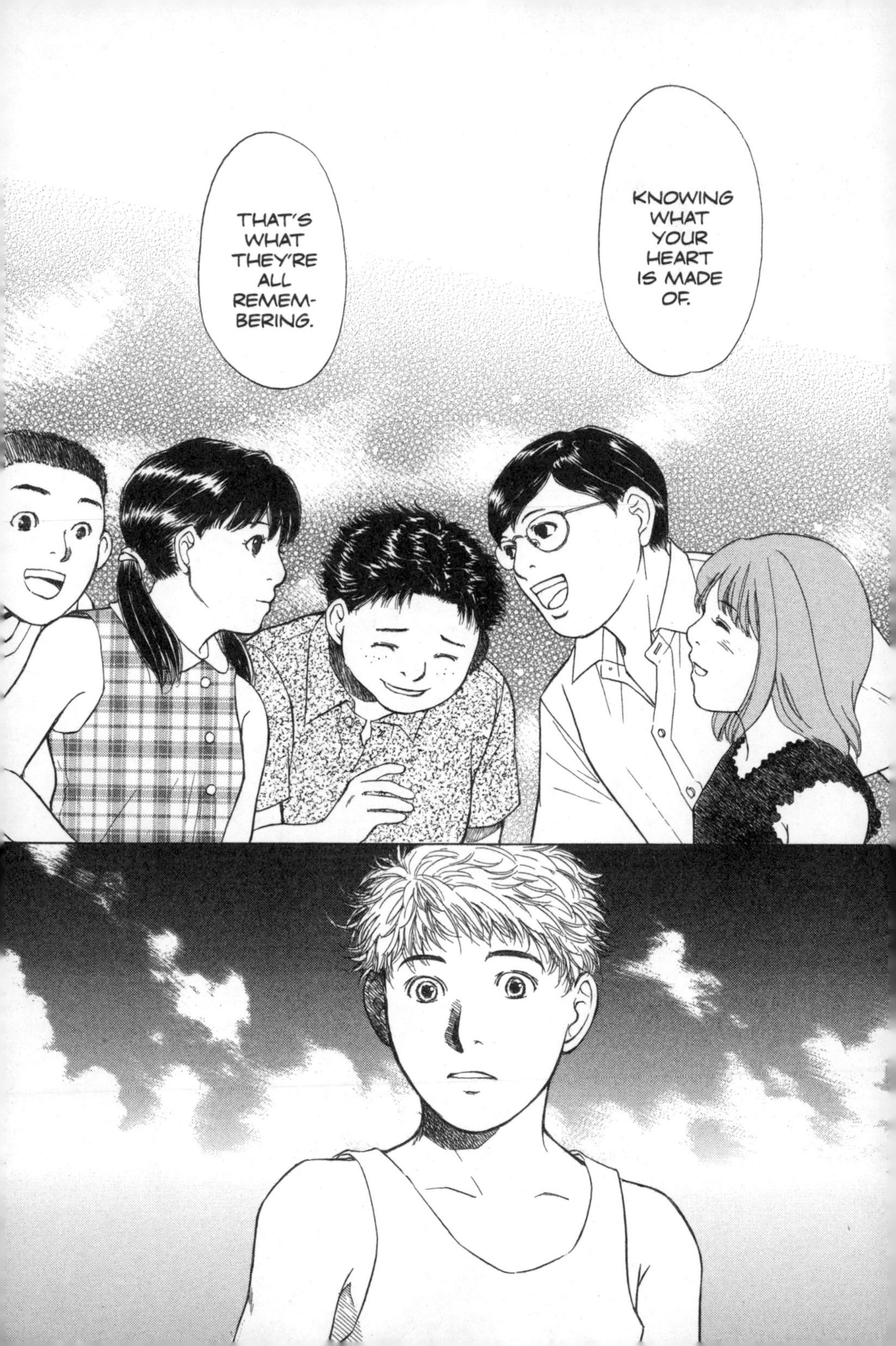
KNOWING WHAT YOUR HEART IS MADE OF.
THAT'S WHAT THEY'RE ALL REMEMBERING.

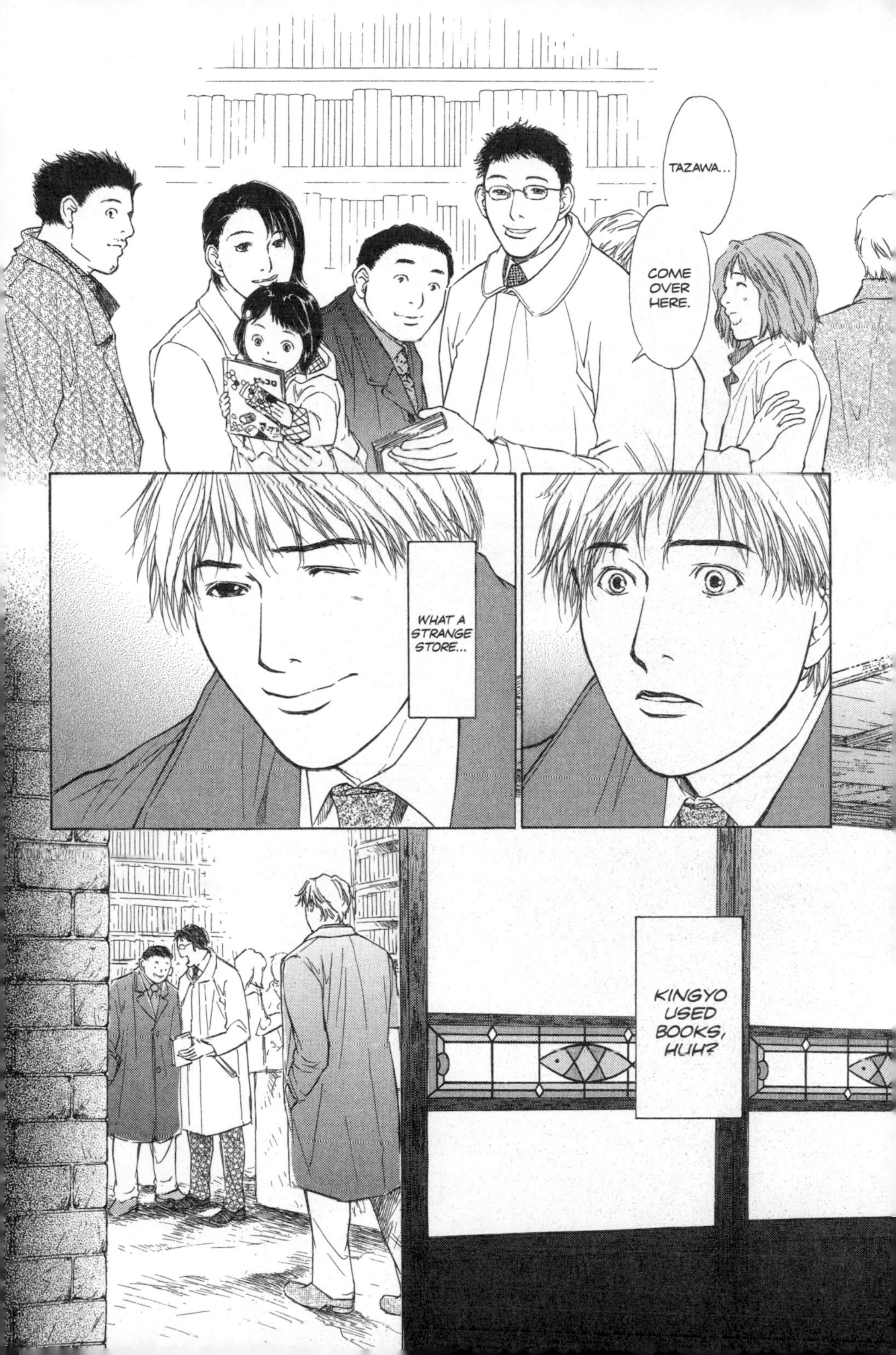
TAZAWA...
COME OVER HERE.
WHAT A STRANGE STORE...
KINGYO USED BOOKS, HUH?

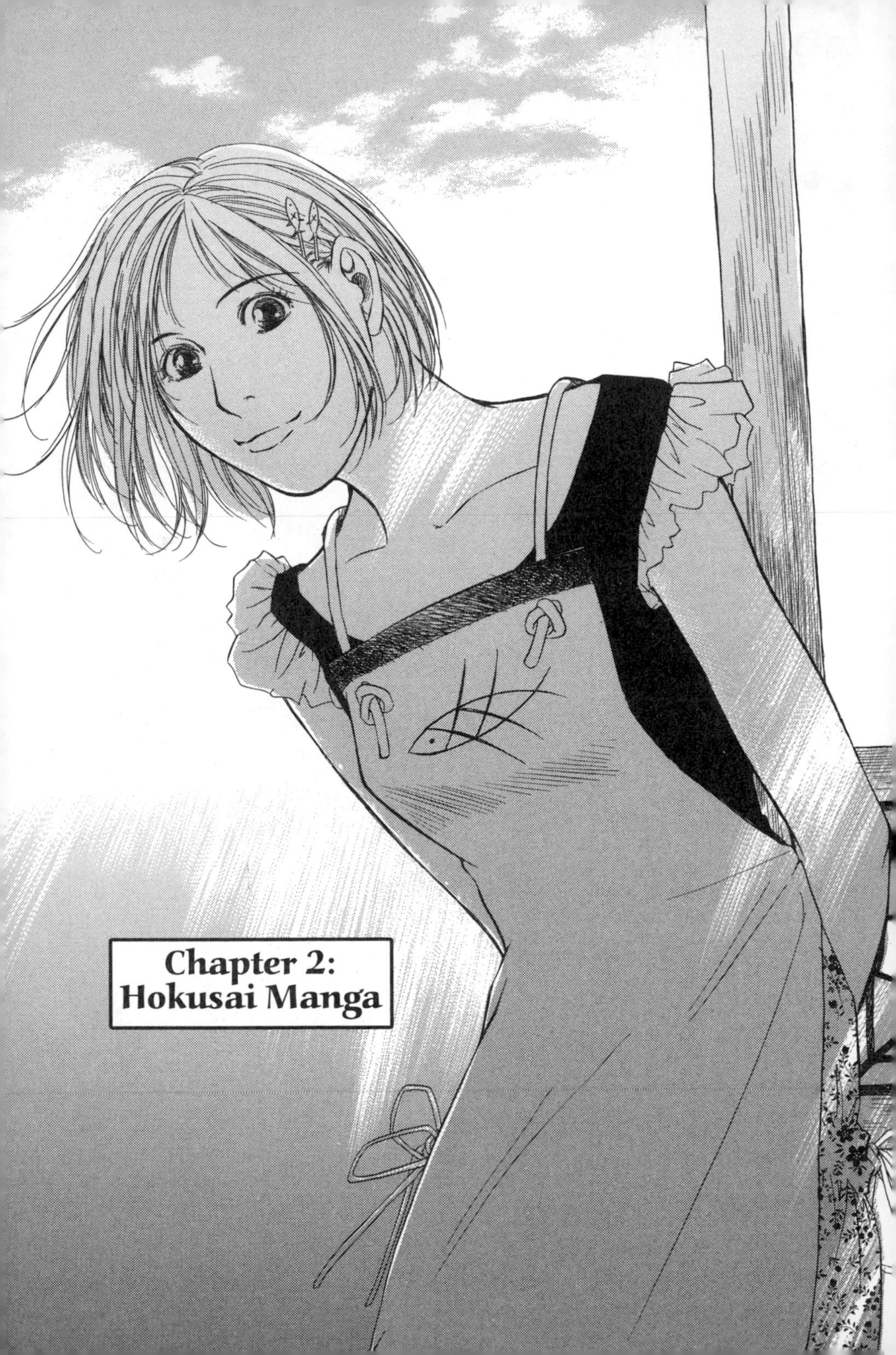
Chapter 2:
Hokusai Manga

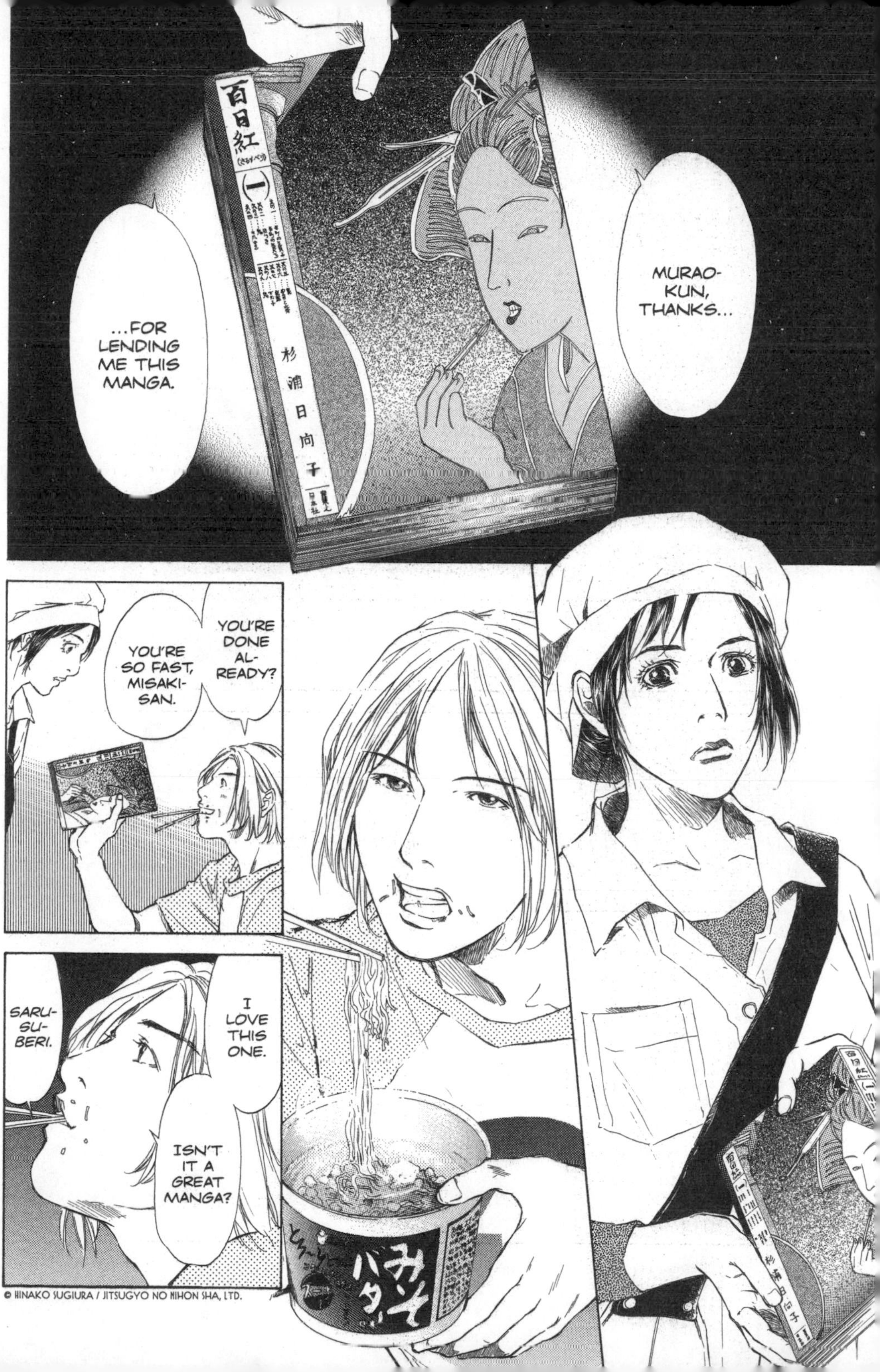
MURAO-KUN, THANKS...
...FOR LENDING ME THIS MANGA.
百日紅
杉浦日向子
YOU'RE DONE AL-READY?
YOU'RE SO FAST, MISAKI-SAN.
I LOVE THIS ONE.
SARU-SUBERI.
ISN'T IT A GREAT MANGA?

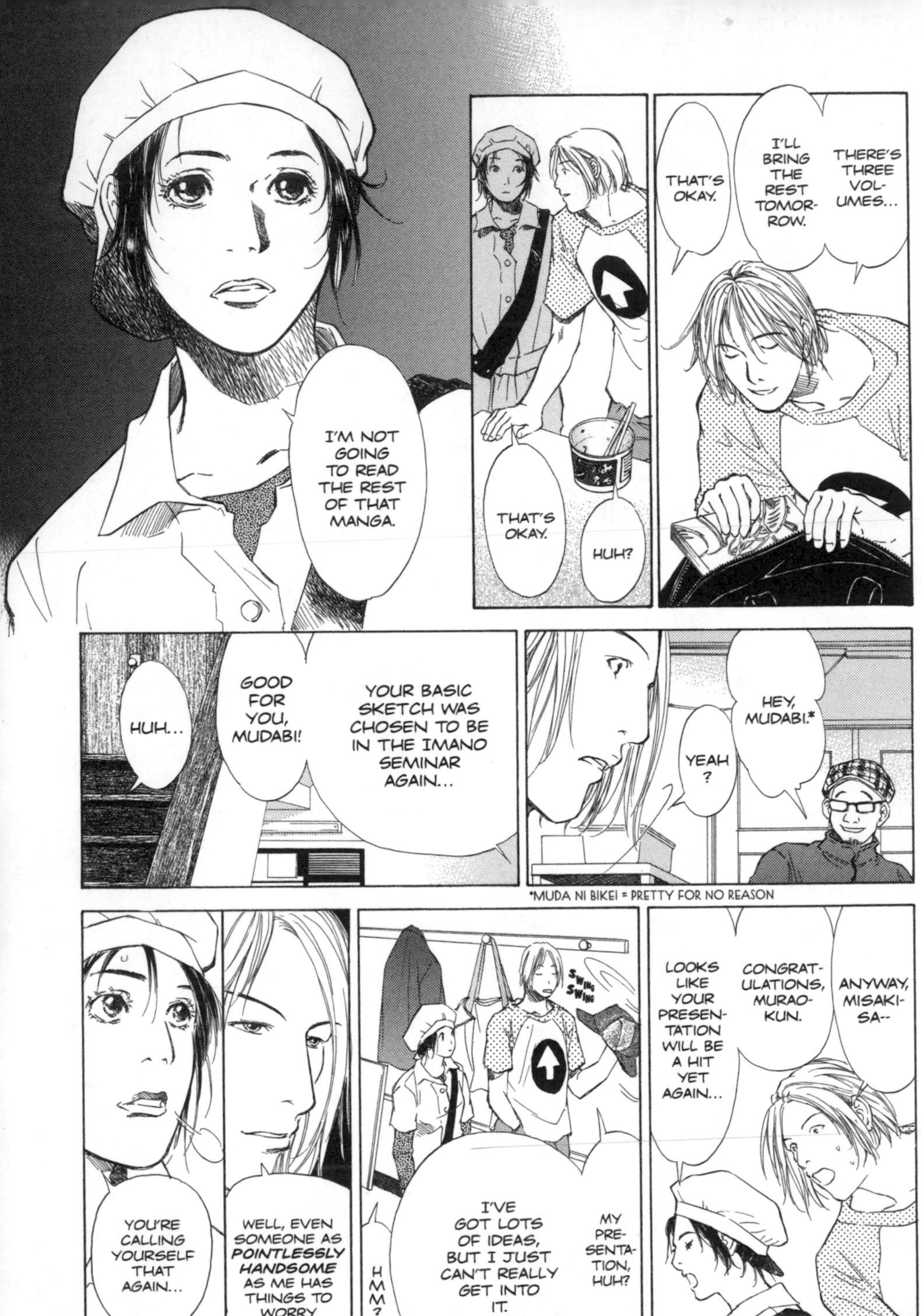
THERE'S THREE VOLUMES...
I'LL BRING THE REST TOMORROW.
THAT'S OKAY.
THAT'S OKAY.
HUH?
I'M NOT GOING TO READ THE REST OF THAT MANGA.
HEY, MUDABI.*
YEAH?
YOUR BASIC SKETCH WAS CHOSEN TO BE IN THE IMANO SEMINAR AGAIN...
GOOD FOR YOU, MUDABI!
HUH...
*MUDA NI BIKEI = PRETTY FOR NO REASON
ANYWAY, MISAKI-SA--
CONGRATULATIONS, MURAO-KUN.
LOOKS LIKE YOUR PRESENTATION WILL BE A HIT YET AGAIN...
SWING SWING
MY PRESENTATION, HUH?
I'VE GOT LOTS OF IDEAS, BUT I JUST CAN'T REALLY GET INTO IT.
HMM?
WELL, EVEN SOMEONE AS ***POINTLESSLY HANDSOME*** AS ME HAS THINGS TO WORRY ABOUT.
YOU'RE CALLING YOURSELF THAT AGAIN...

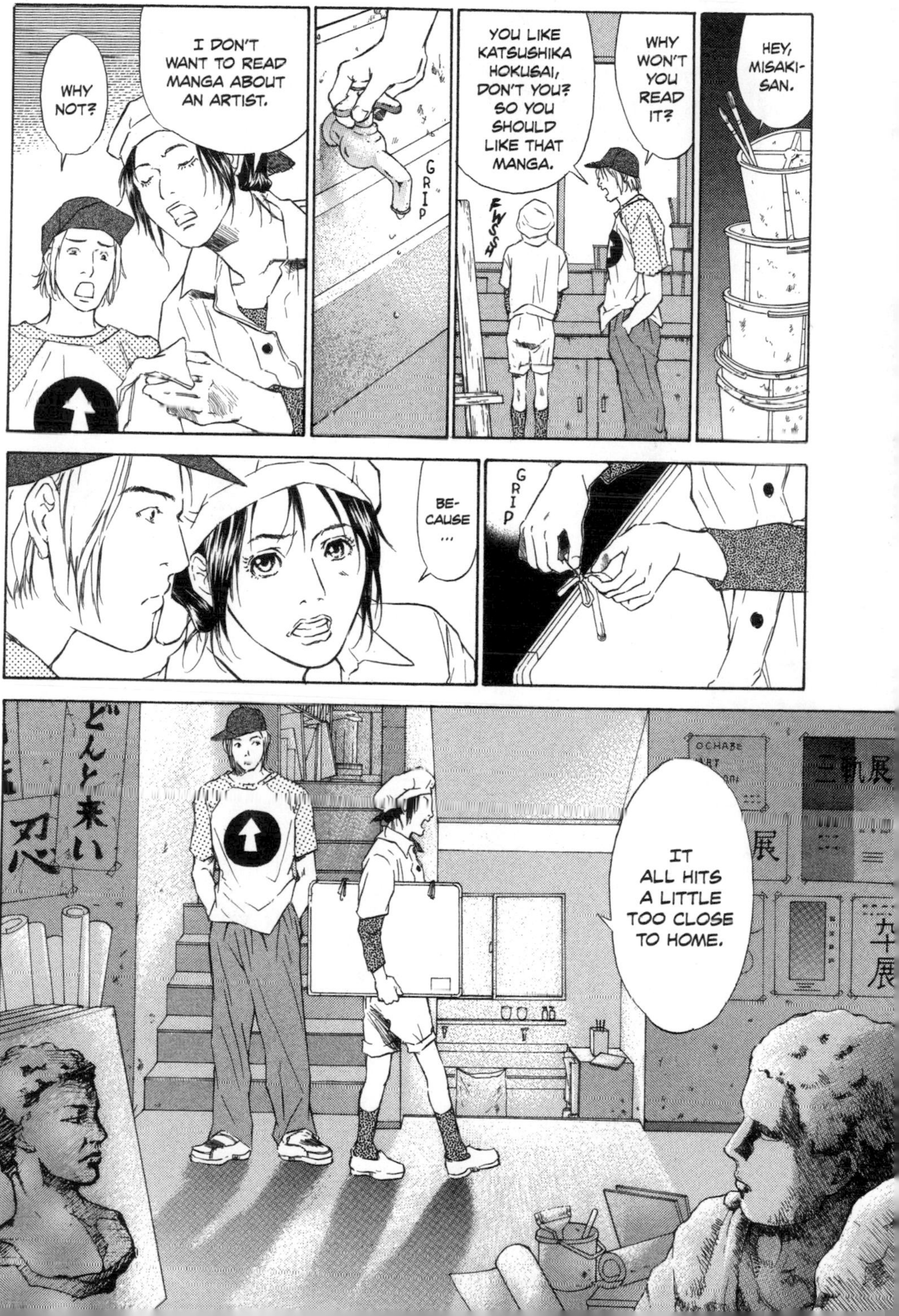
HEY, MISAKI-SAN.
WHY WON'T YOU READ IT?
YOU LIKE KATSUSHIKA HOKUSAI, DON'T YOU? SO YOU SHOULD LIKE THAT MANGA.
FWSSH
GRIP
I DON'T WANT TO READ MANGA ABOUT AN ARTIST.
WHY NOT?
GRIP
BE-CAUSE ...
三軌展
展
九十展
IT ALL HITS A LITTLE TOO CLOSE TO HOME.
どんと来い
忍

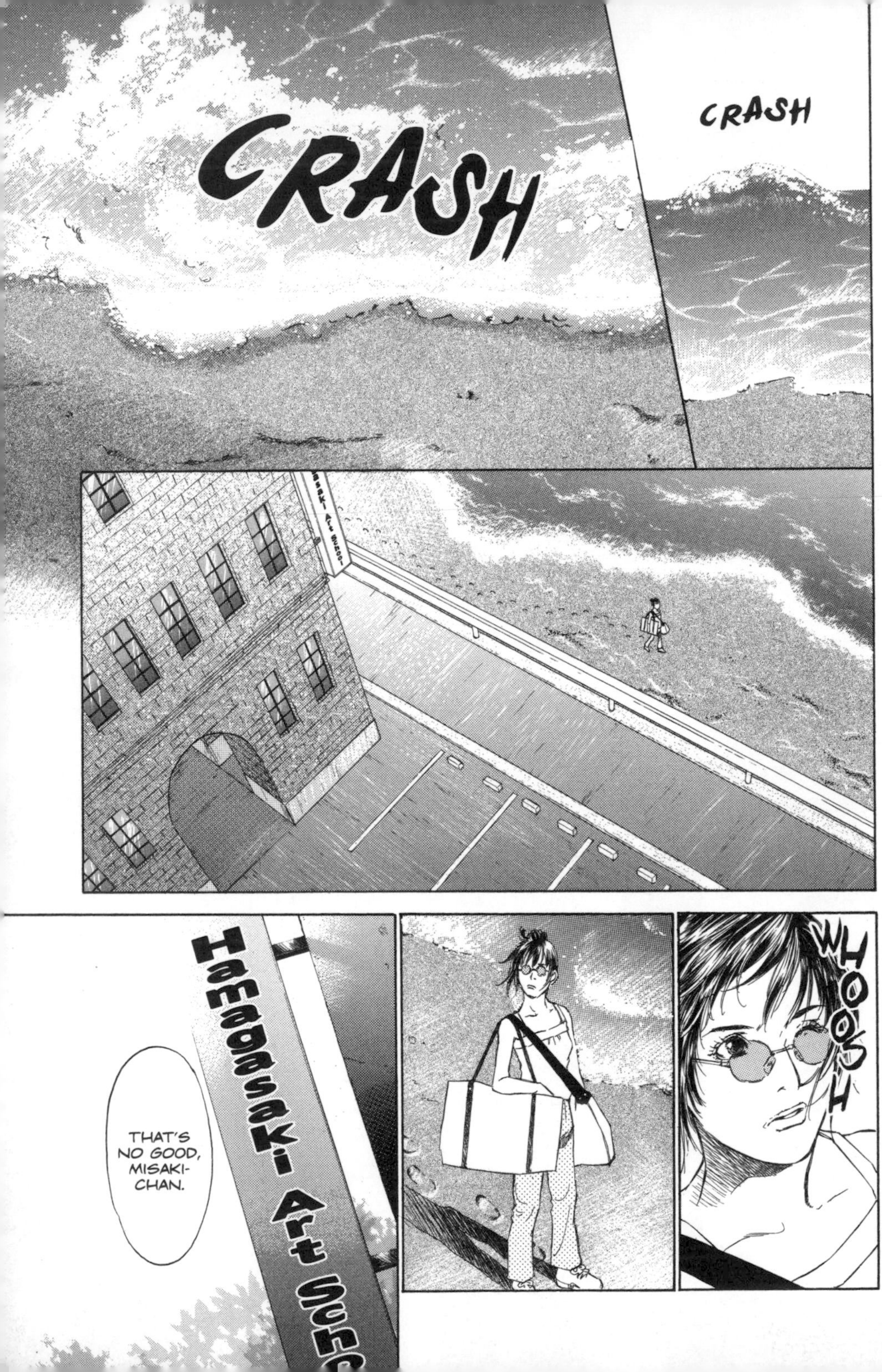
CRASH
CRASH
WHOOSH
Hamagasaki Art Sch
THAT'S NO GOOD, MISAKI-CHAN.

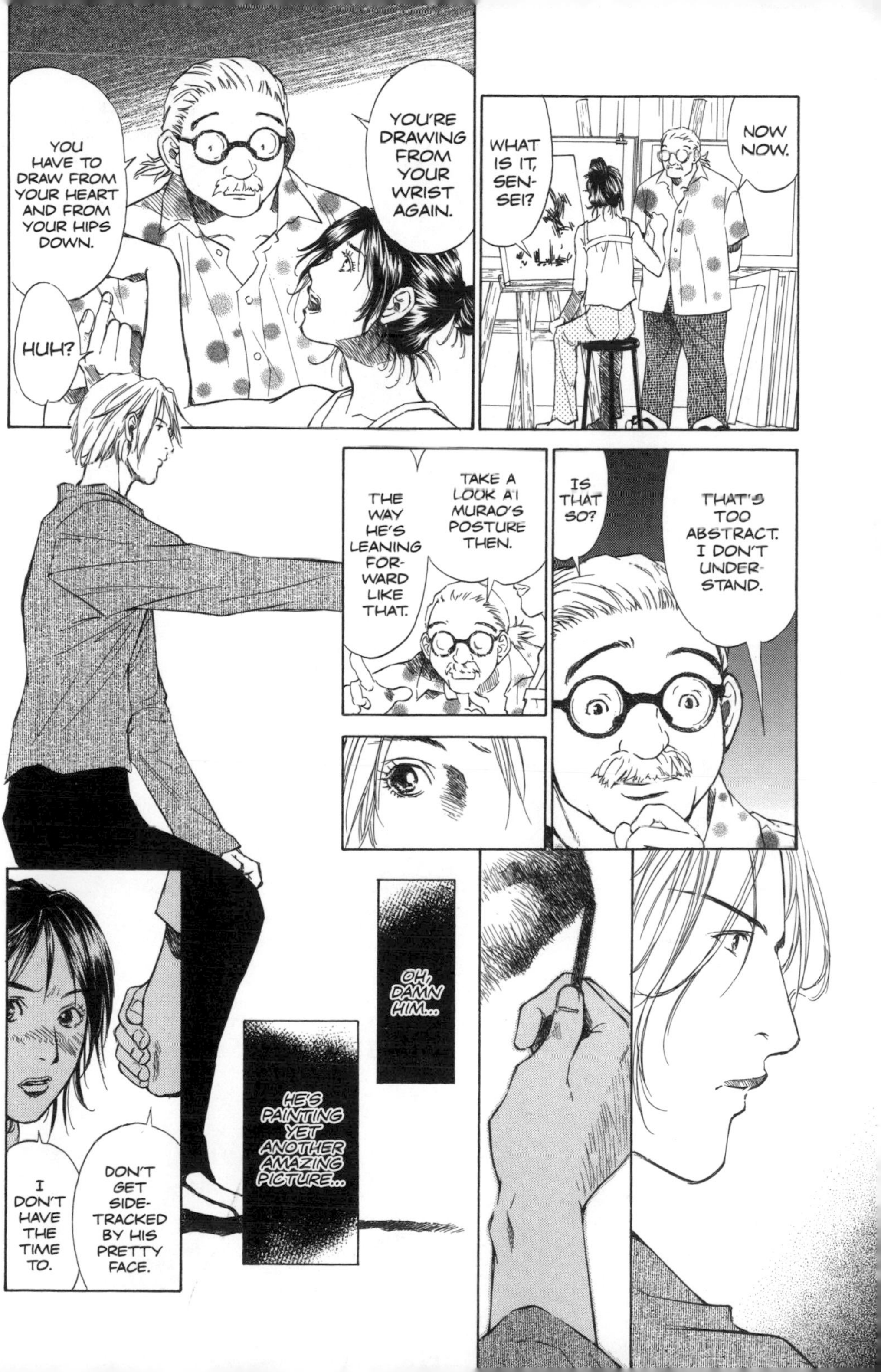
NOW NOW.
WHAT IS IT, SEN-SEI?
YOU'RE DRAWING FROM YOUR WRIST AGAIN.
YOU HAVE TO DRAW FROM YOUR HEART AND FROM YOUR HIPS DOWN.
HUH?
THAT'S TOO ABSTRACT. I DON'T UNDER-STAND.
IS THAT SO?
TAKE A LOOK AT MURAO'S POSTURE THEN.
THE WAY HE'S LEANING FOR-WARD LIKE THAT.
OH, DAMN HIM...
HE'S PAINTING YET ANOTHER AMAZING PICTURE...
DON'T GET SIDE-TRACKED BY HIS PRETTY FACE.
I DON'T HAVE THE TIME TO.

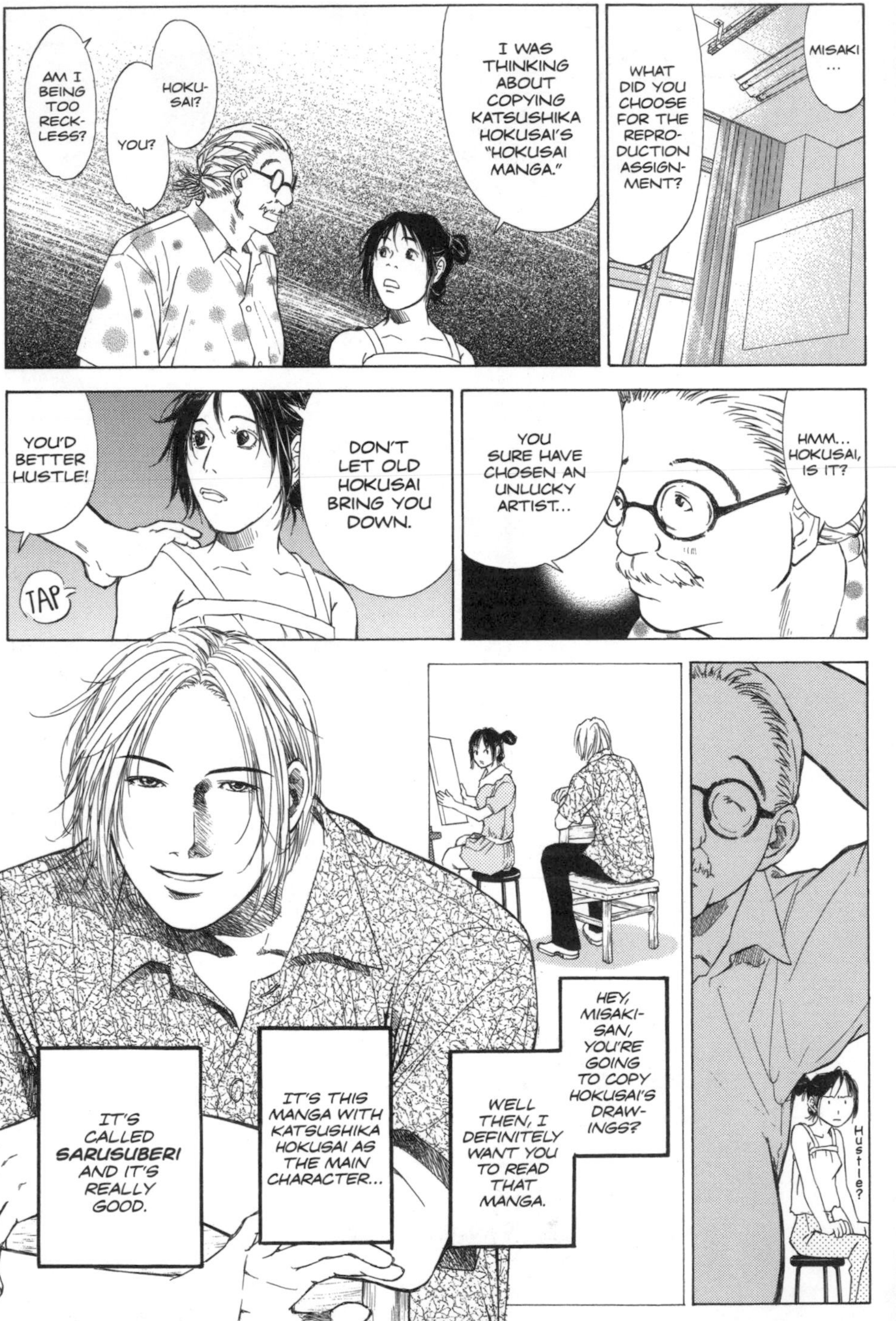
MISAKI ...
WHAT DID YOU CHOOSE FOR THE REPRODUCTION ASSIGNMENT?
I WAS THINKING ABOUT COPYING KATSUSHIKA HOKUSAI'S "HOKUSAI MANGA."
HOKUSAI?
YOU?
AM I BEING TOO RECKLESS?
HMM... HOKUSAI, IS IT?
YOU SURE HAVE CHOSEN AN UNLUCKY ARTIST...
DON'T LET OLD HOKUSAI BRING YOU DOWN.
YOU'D BETTER HUSTLE!
TAP
Hustle?
HEY, MISAKI-SAN, YOU'RE GOING TO COPY HOKUSAI'S DRAWINGS?
WELL THEN, I DEFINITELY WANT YOU TO READ THAT MANGA.
IT'S THIS MANGA WITH KATSUSHIKA HOKUSAI AS THE MAIN CHARACTER...
IT'S CALLED SARUSUBERI AND IT'S REALLY GOOD.

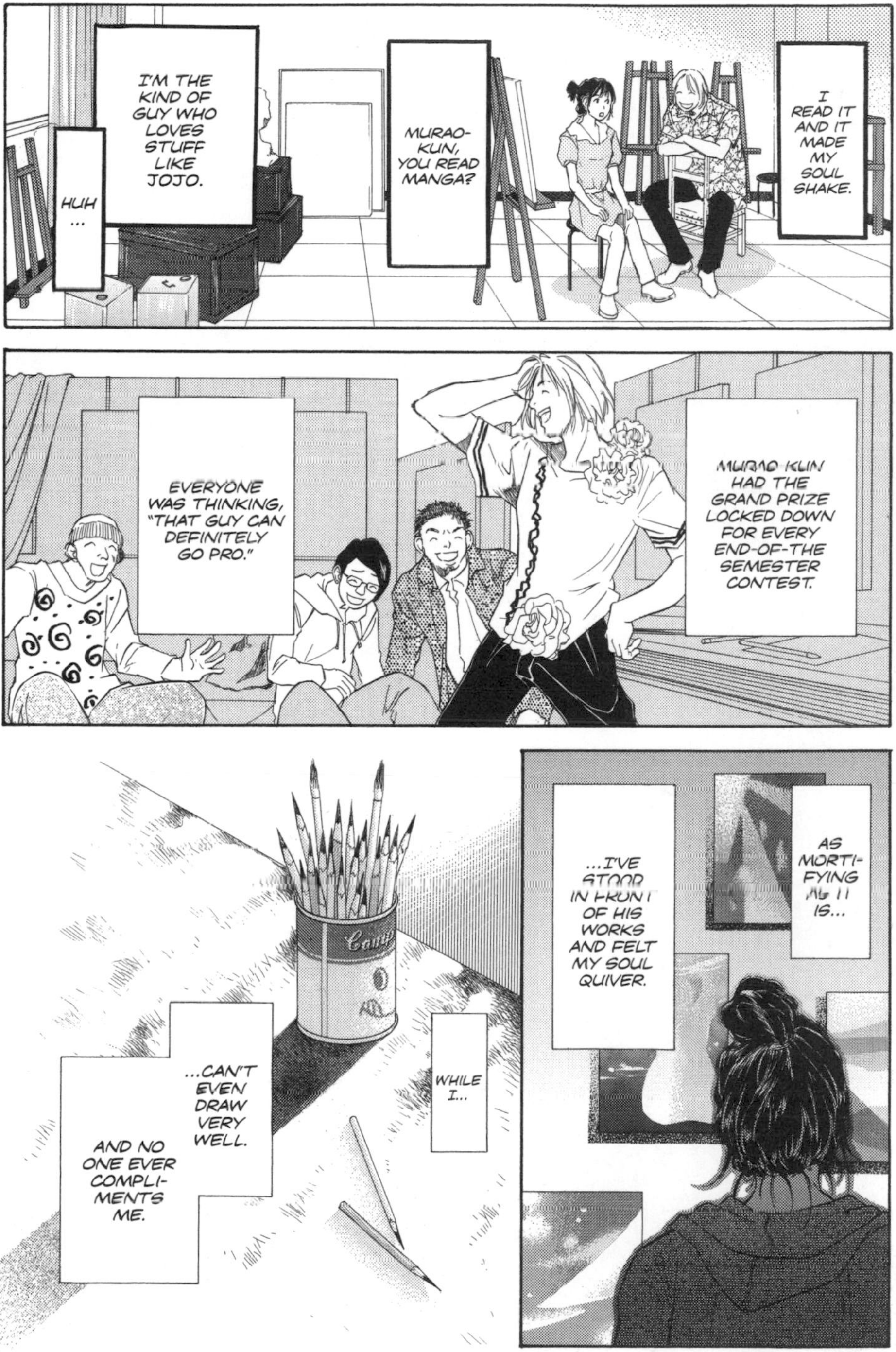
I READ IT AND IT MADE MY SOUL SHAKE.
MURAO-KUN, YOU READ MANGA?
I'M THE KIND OF GUY WHO LOVES STUFF LIKE JOJO.
HUH...
MURAO-KUN HAD THE GRAND PRIZE LOCKED DOWN FOR EVERY END-OF-THE SEMESTER CONTEST.
EVERYONE WAS THINKING, "THAT GUY CAN DEFINITELY GO PRO."
AS MORTIFYING AS IT IS...
...I'VE STOOD IN FRONT OF HIS WORKS AND FELT MY SOUL QUIVER.
WHILE I...
...CAN'T EVEN DRAW VERY WELL.
AND NO ONE EVER COMPLIMENTS ME.

STUDY!

JOJO: JOJO NO KIMYONA BOUKEN (ENG: JOJO'S BIZARRE ADVENTURE) BY HIROHIKO ARAKI. 1986 – SHONEN JUMP. EACH STORY ARC RECOUNTS BATTLES OF VARIOUS MAIN CHARACTERS ALL NAMED JOJO. CURRENTLY THE SIX ARC HAVE BEEN COMPLETED. THE AUTHOR'S UNIQUE TOUCH HAS GARNERED MUCH POPULARITY. JOJO NO KIMYONA BOUKEN (63 VOLUMES) AND JOJO NO KIMYONA BOUKEN PART 6: STONE OCEAN (17 VOLUMES) CURRENTLY AVAILABLE.

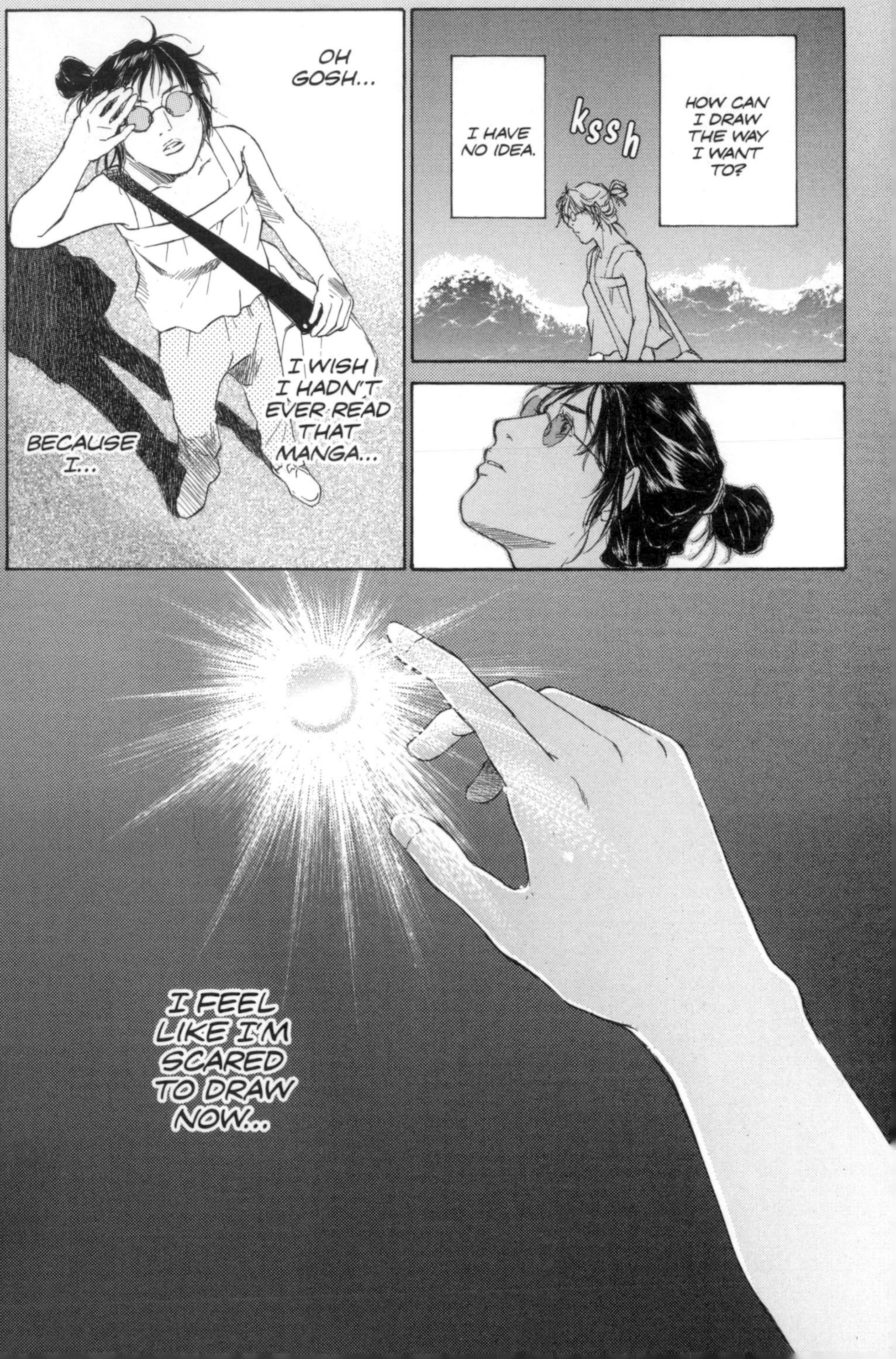
HOW CAN I DRAW THE WAY I WANT TO?
kssh
I HAVE NO IDEA.
OH GOSH...
I WISH I HADN'T EVER READ THAT MANGA...
BECAUSE I...
I FEEL LIKE I'M SCARED TO DRAW NOW...

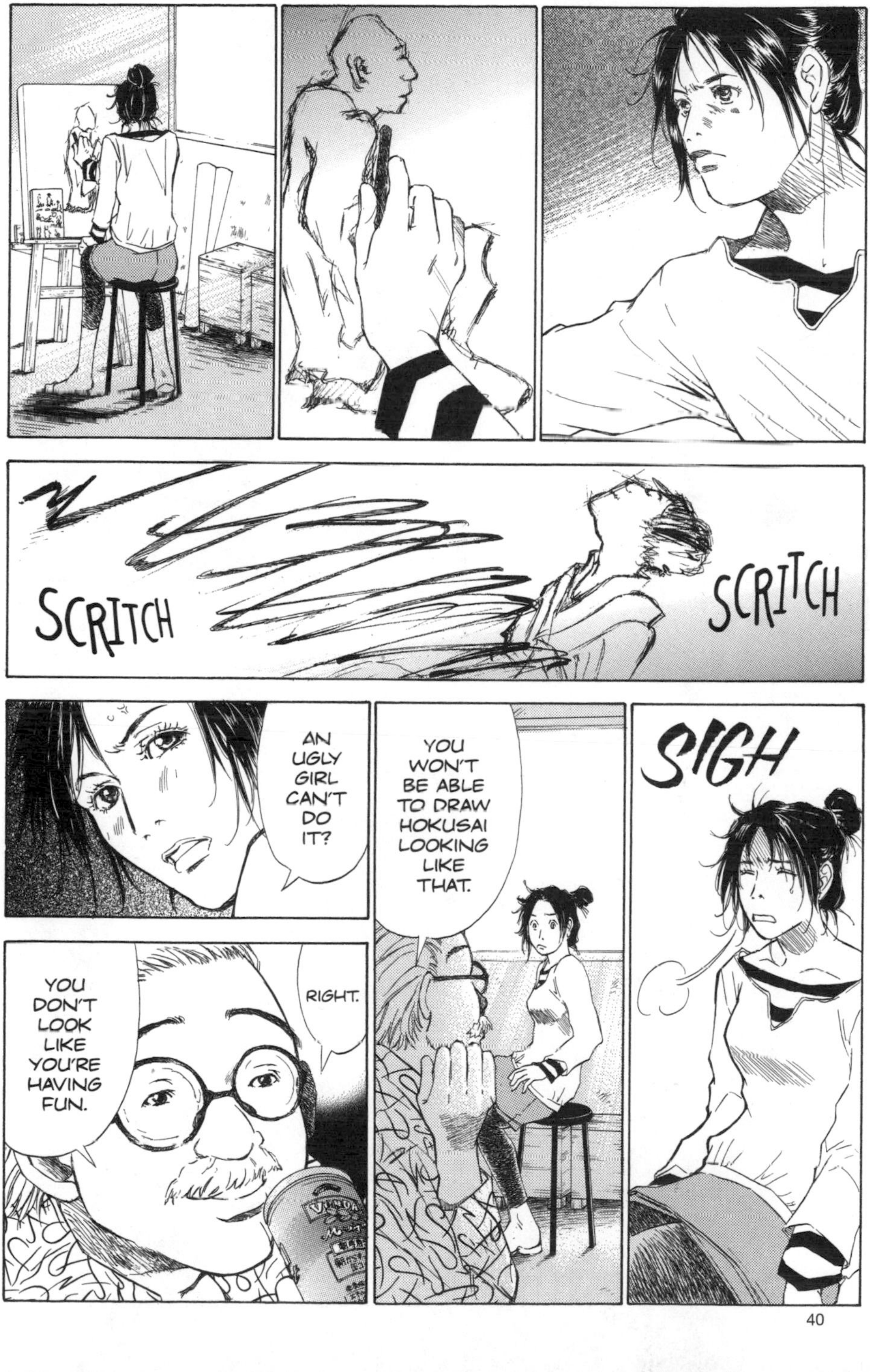
SCRITCH
SCRITCH
SIGH
YOU WON'T BE ABLE TO DRAW HOKUSAI LOOKING LIKE THAT.
AN UGLY GIRL CAN'T DO IT?
RIGHT.
YOU DON'T LOOK LIKE YOU'RE HAVING FUN.

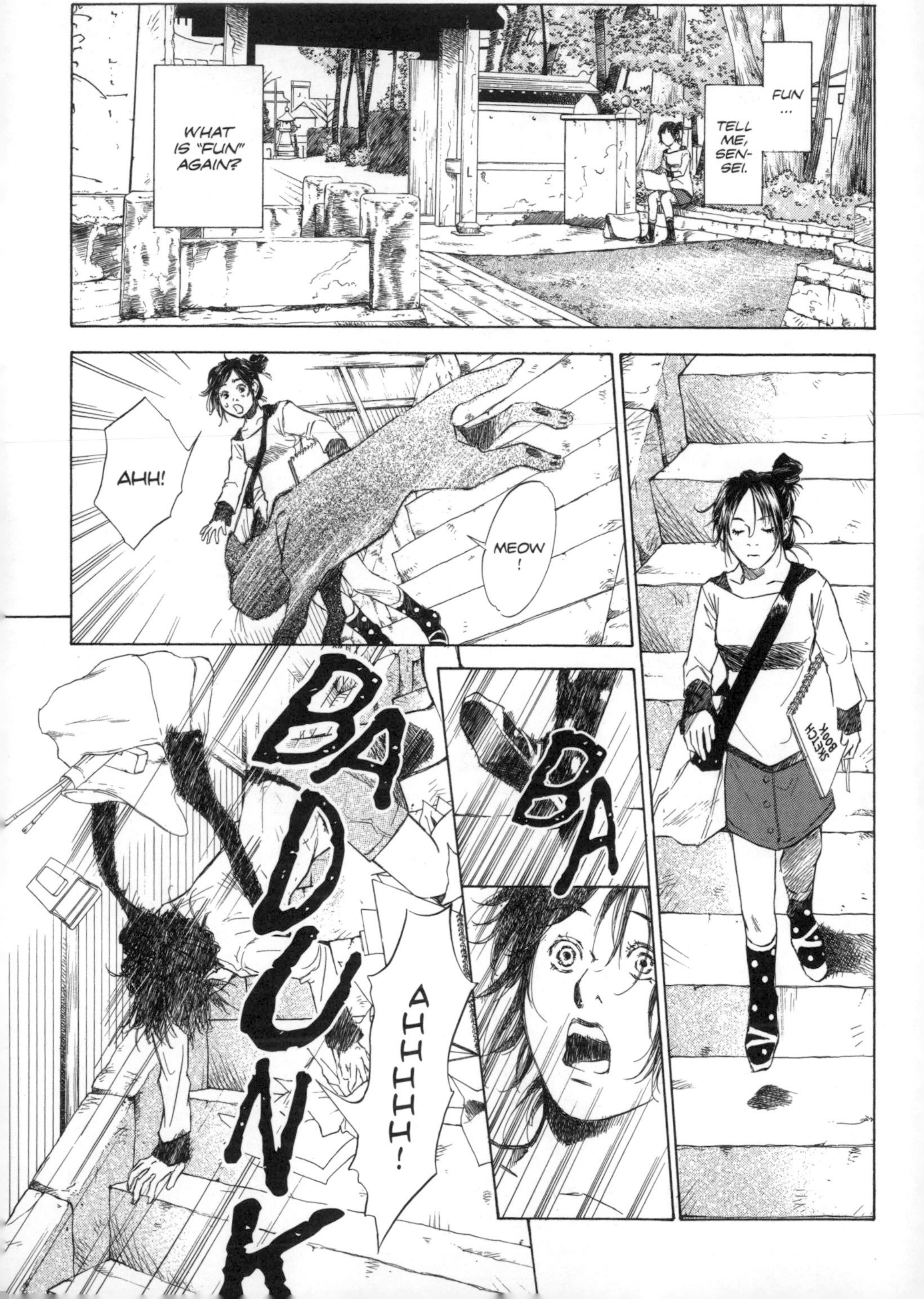
FUN ... TELL ME, SENSEI.
WHAT IS "FUN" AGAIN?
SKETCH BOOK
MEOW!
AHH!
BA BA
AHHHHH!
BADUNK

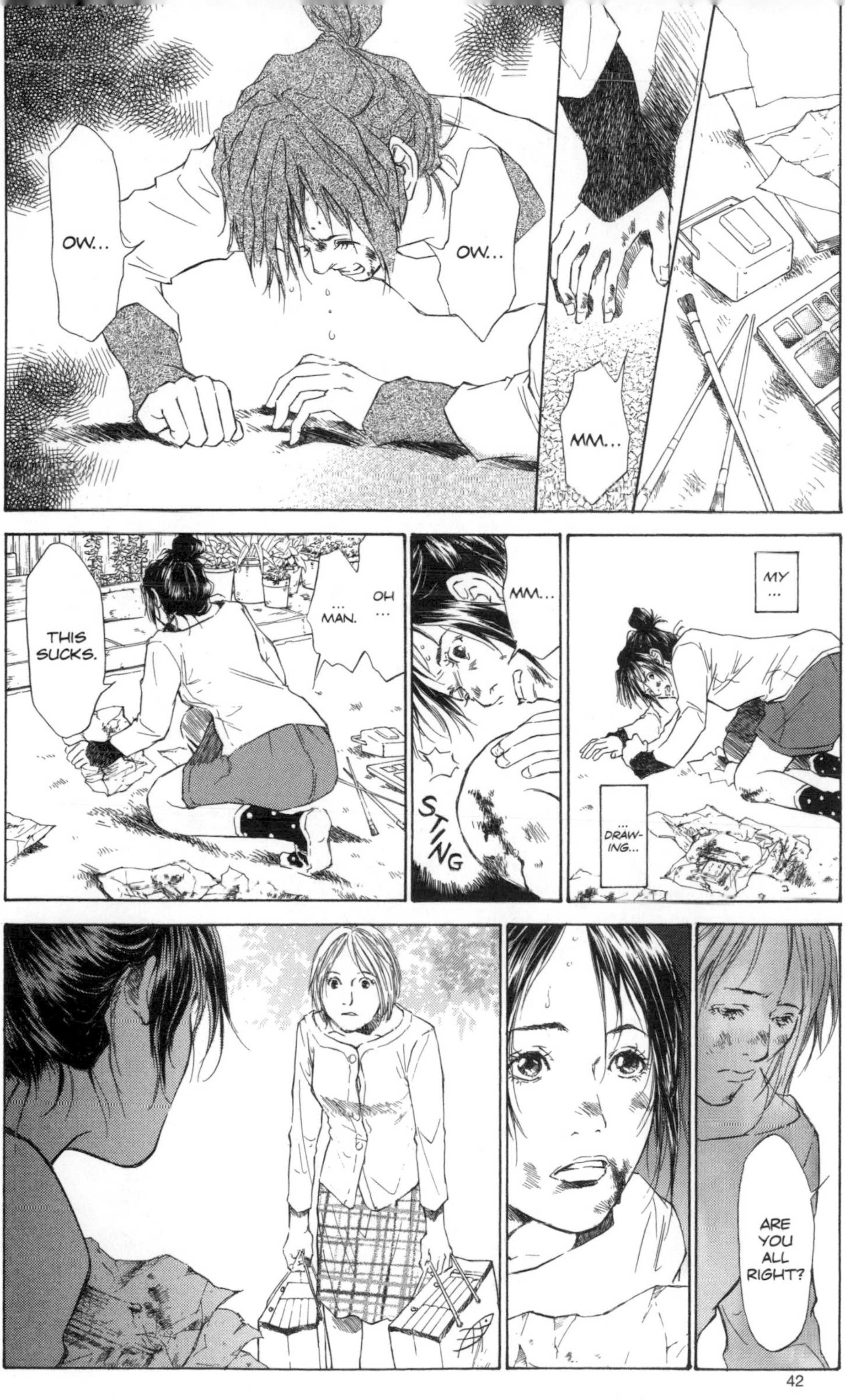
MM...
OW...
OW...
MY ...
... DRAWING...
MM...
STING
OH ... ... MAN.
THIS SUCKS.
ARE YOU ALL RIGHT?

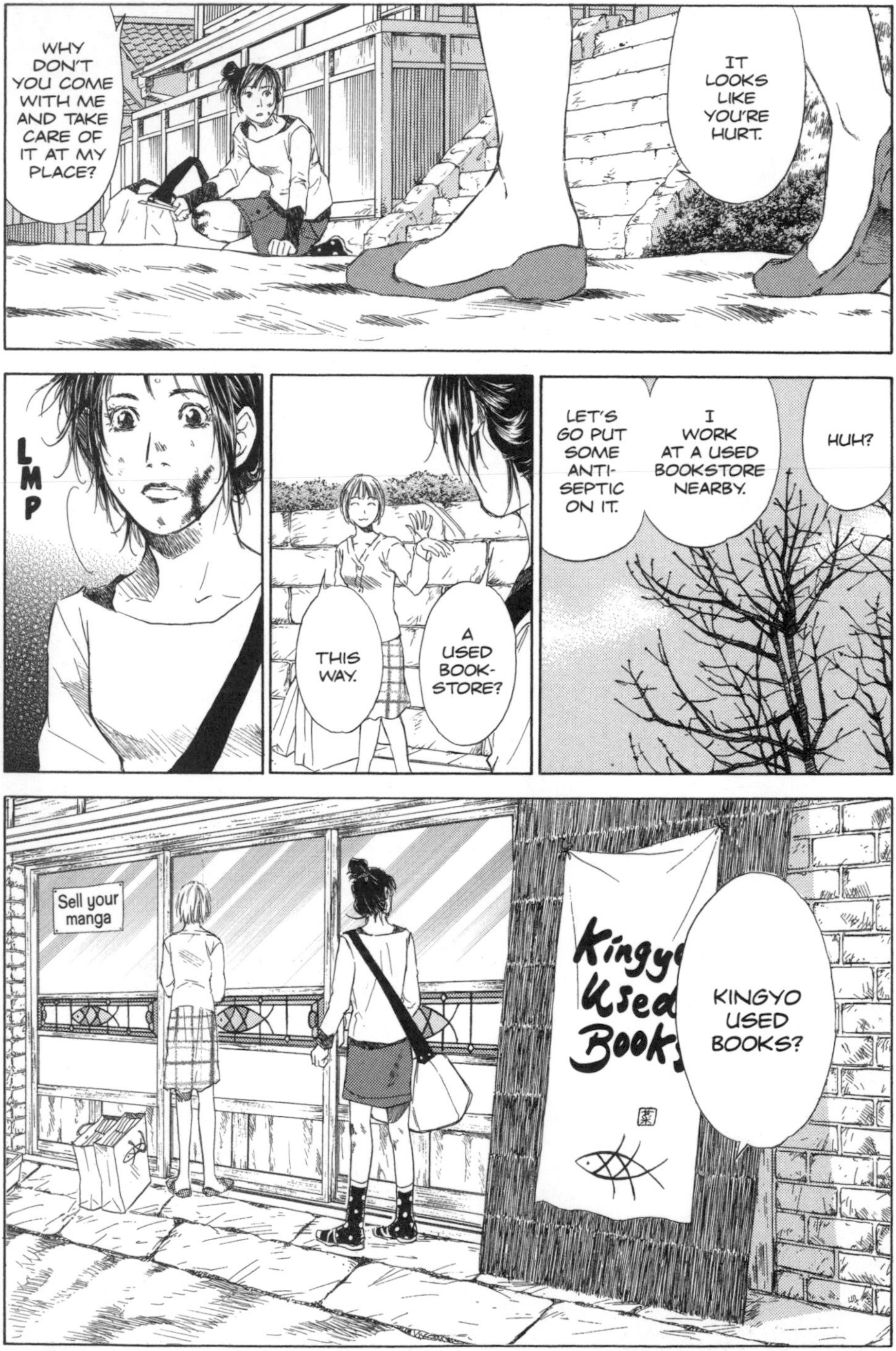
IT LOOKS LIKE YOU'RE HURT.
WHY DON'T YOU COME WITH ME AND TAKE CARE OF IT AT MY PLACE?
HUH?
I WORK AT A USED BOOKSTORE NEARBY.
LET'S GO PUT SOME ANTI-SEPTIC ON IT.
A USED BOOK-STORE?
THIS WAY.
LMP
KINGYO USED BOOKS?
Kingyo Used Books
Sell your manga

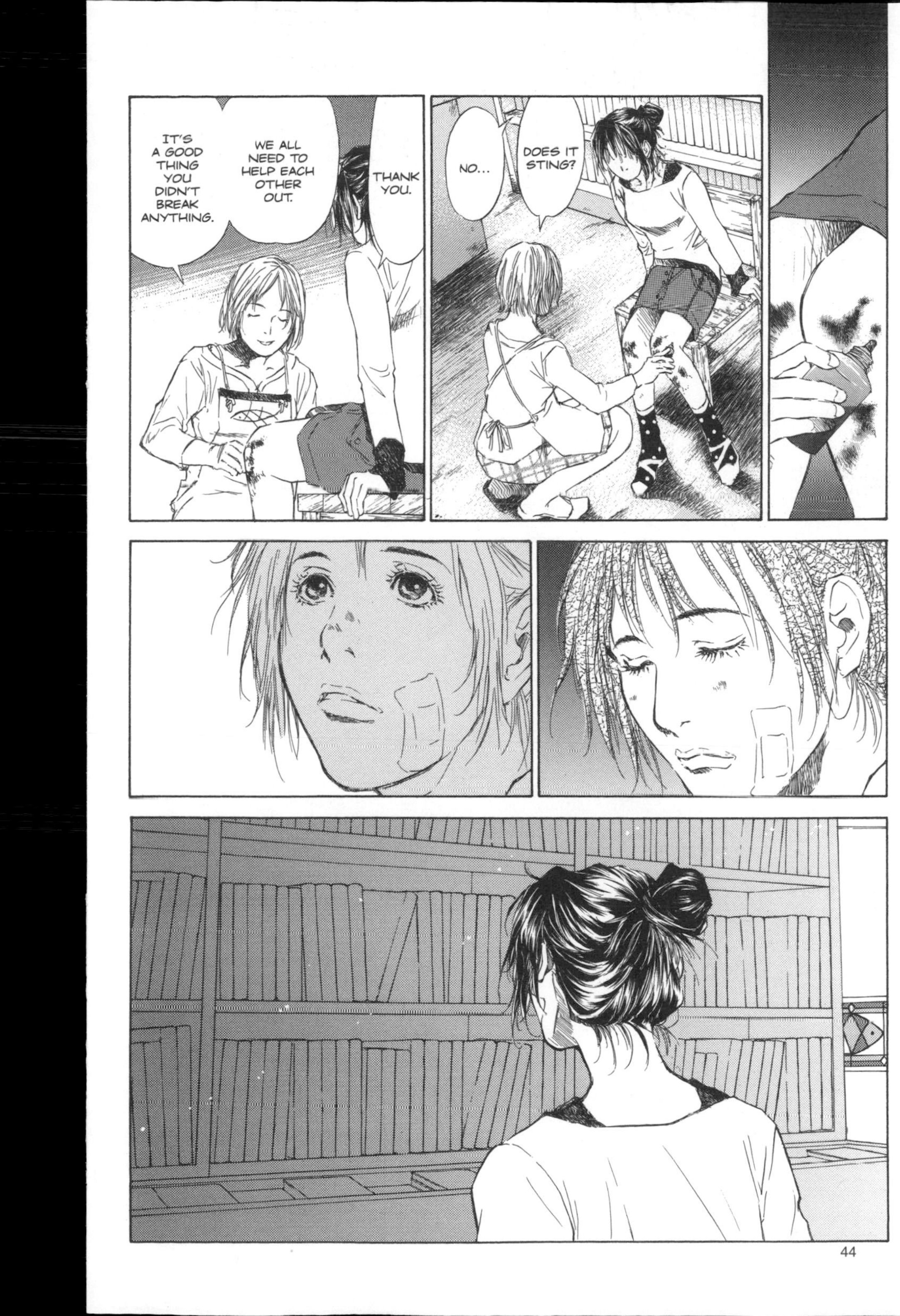
DOES IT STING?
NO...
THANK YOU.
WE ALL NEED TO HELP EACH OTHER OUT.
IT'S A GOOD THING YOU DIDN'T BREAK ANYTHING.

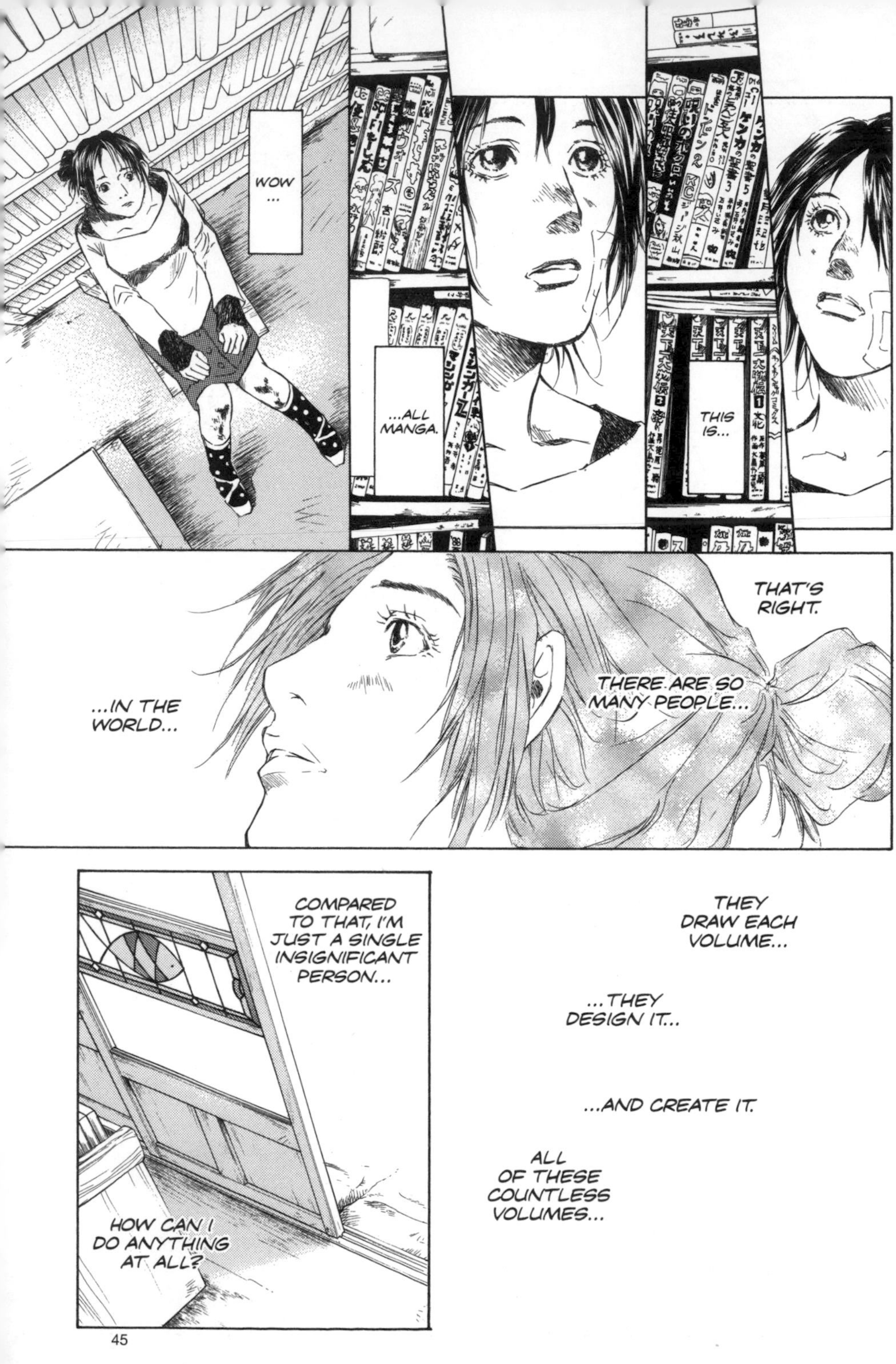
THIS IS...
...ALL MANGA.
WOW ...
THAT'S RIGHT.
THERE ARE SO MANY PEOPLE...
...IN THE WORLD...
THEY DRAW EACH VOLUME...
...THEY DESIGN IT...
...AND CREATE IT.
ALL OF THESE COUNTLESS VOLUMES...
COMPARED TO THAT, I'M JUST A SINGLE INSIGNIFICANT PERSON...
HOW CAN I DO ANYTHING AT ALL?

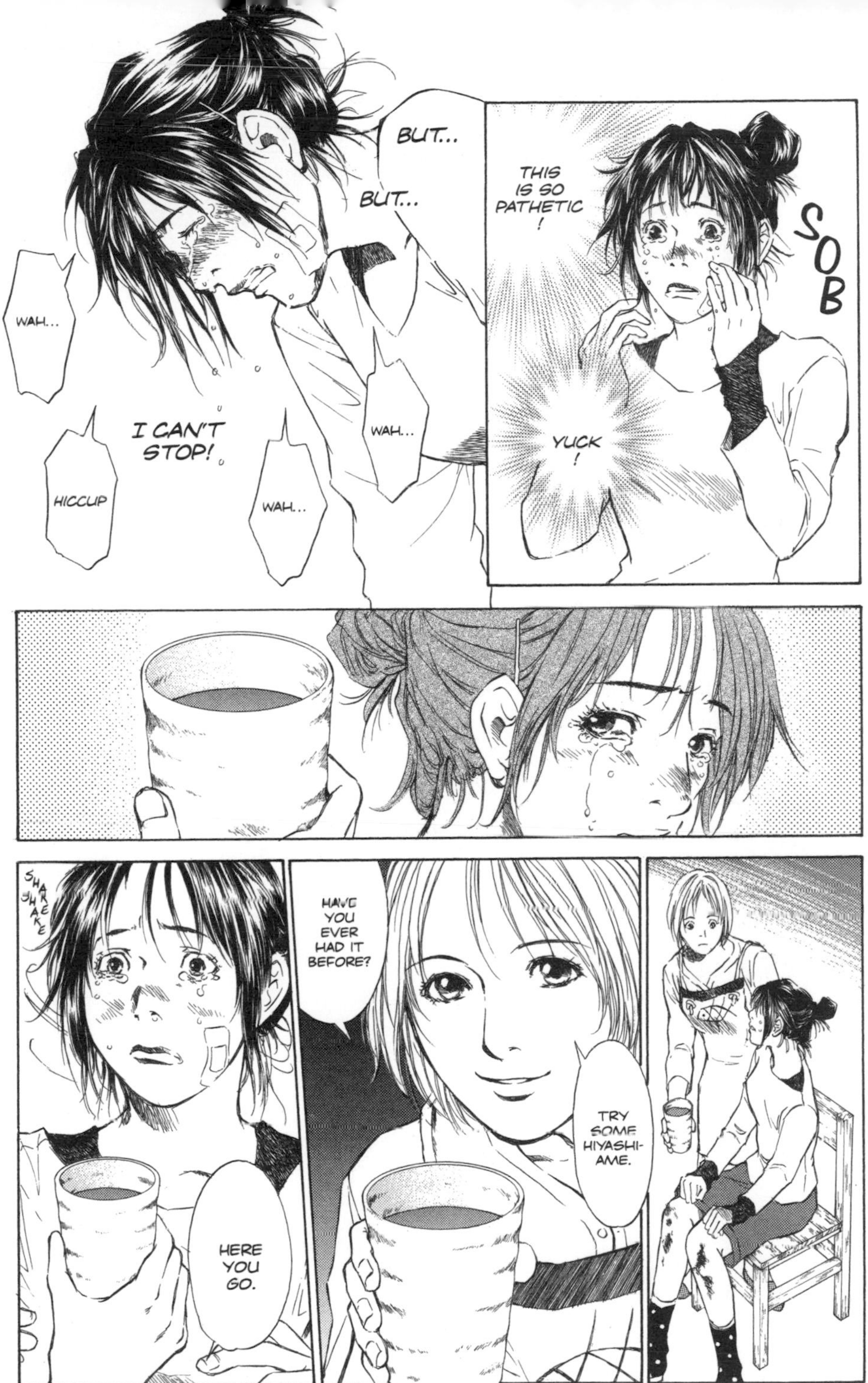
THIS IS SO PATHETIC!
SOB
YUCK!
BUT...
BUT...
WAH...
WAH...
I CAN'T STOP!
WAH...
HICCUP
TRY SOME HIYASHI-AME.
HAVE YOU EVER HAD IT BEFORE?
SHAKE SHAKE
HERE YOU GO.

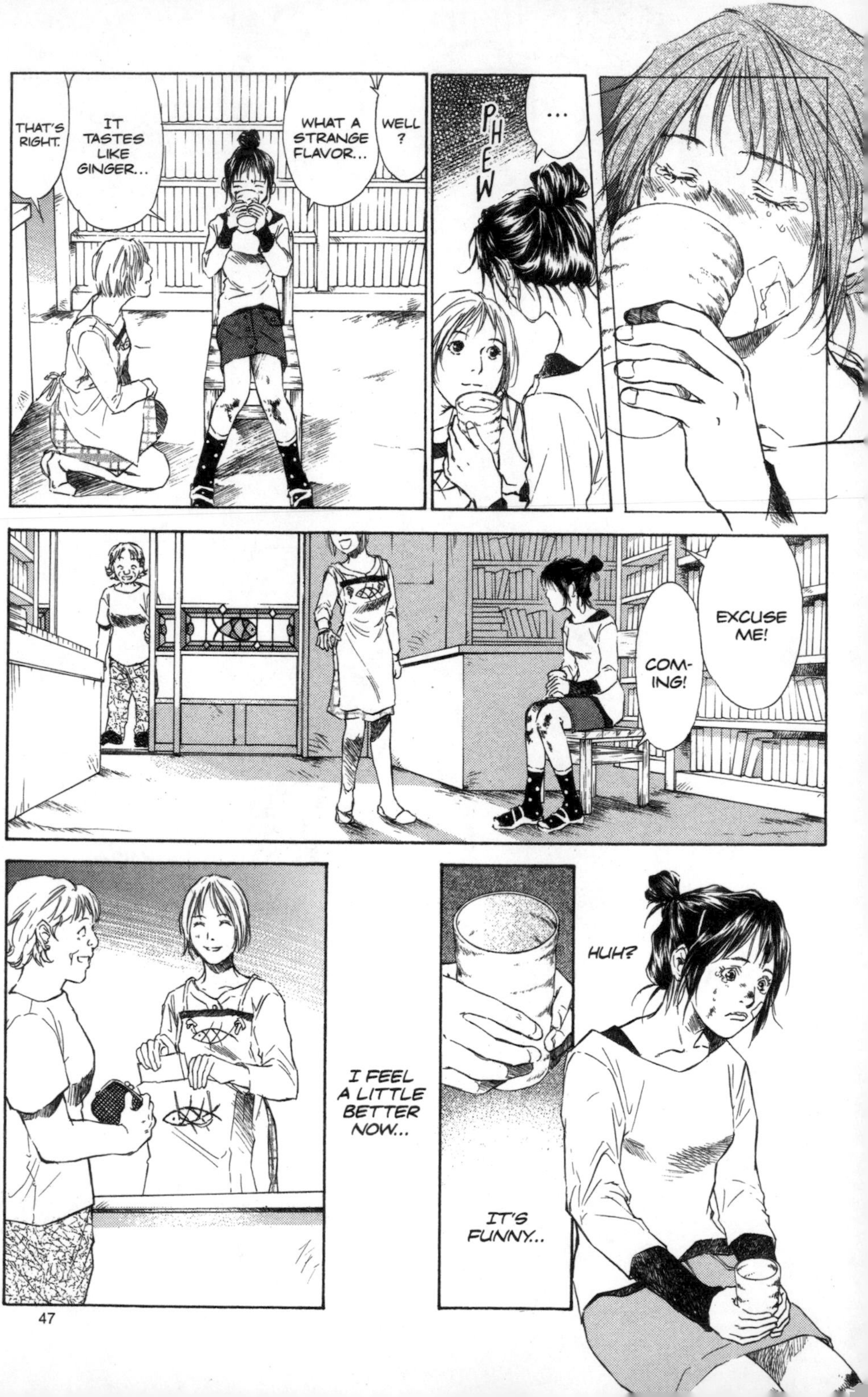
...
PHEW
WELL?
WHAT A STRANGE FLAVOR...
IT TASTES LIKE GINGER...
THAT'S RIGHT.
EXCUSE ME!
COMING!
HUH?
IT'S FUNNY...
I FEEL A LITTLE BETTER NOW...

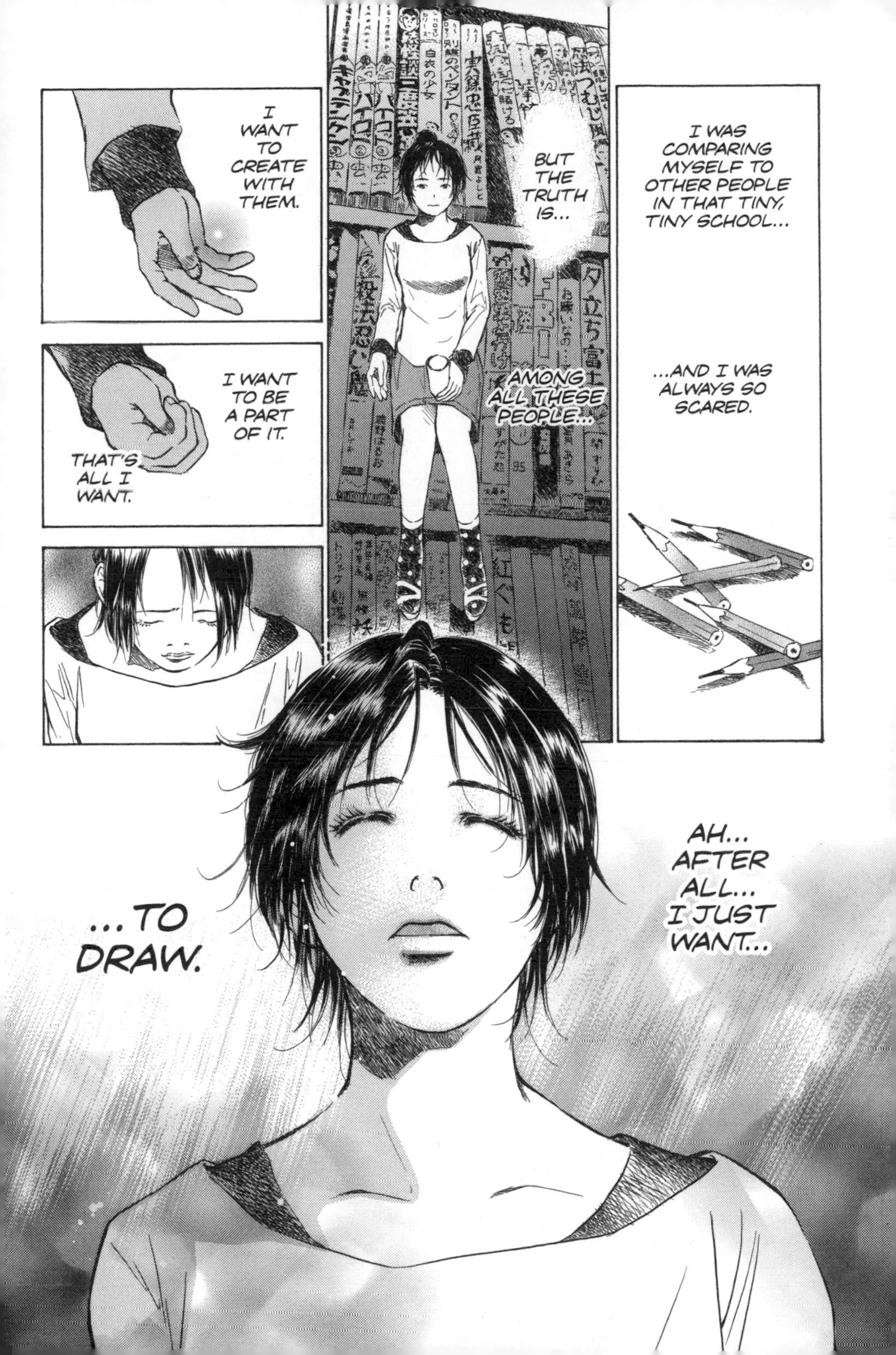
I WAS COMPARING MYSELF TO OTHER PEOPLE IN THAT TINY, TINY SCHOOL...
...AND I WAS ALWAYS SO SCARED.
BUT THE TRUTH IS...
AMONG ALL THESE PEOPLE...
I WANT TO CREATE WITH THEM.
I WANT TO BE A PART OF IT.
THAT'S ALL I WANT.
AH... AFTER ALL... I JUST WANT...
...TO DRAW.

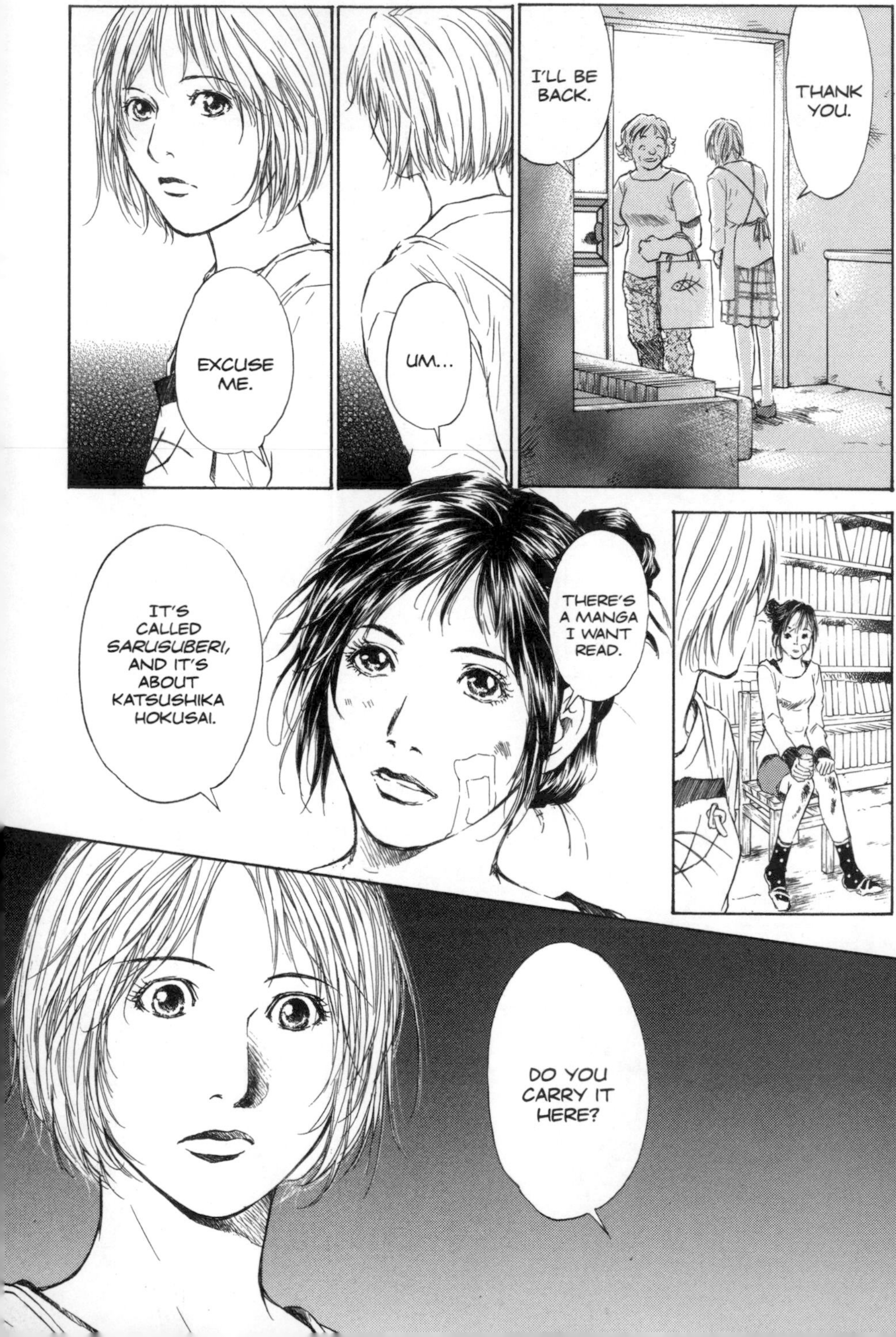
THANK YOU.
I'LL BE BACK.
UM...
EXCUSE ME.
THERE'S A MANGA I WANT READ.
IT'S CALLED SARUSUBERI, AND IT'S ABOUT KATSUSHIKA HOKUSAI.
DO YOU CARRY IT HERE?

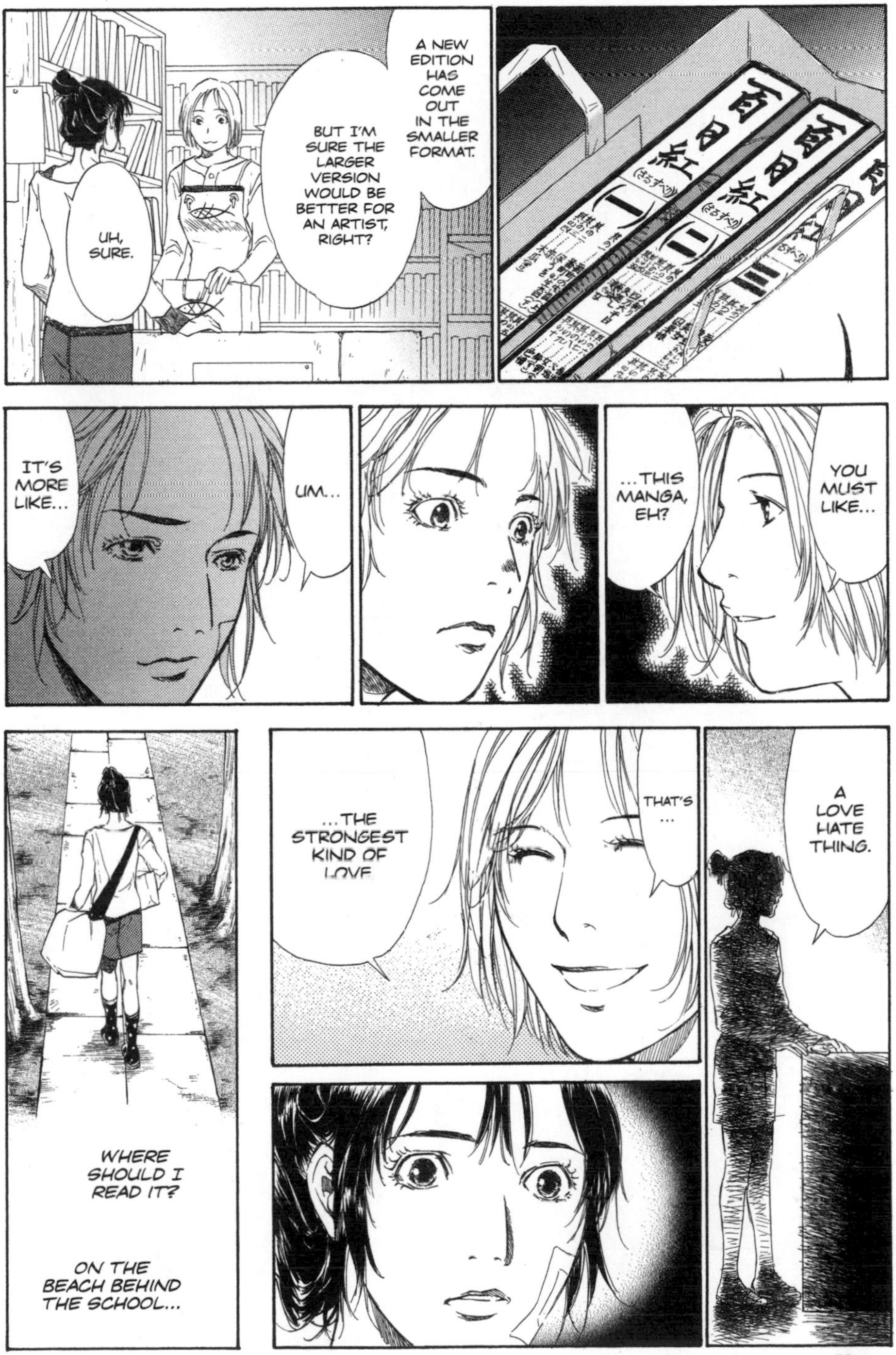

百日紅
A NEW EDITION HAS COME OUT IN THE SMALLER FORMAT.
BUT I'M SURE THE LARGER VERSION WOULD BE BETTER FOR AN ARTIST, RIGHT?
UH, SURE.
YOU MUST LIKE...
...THIS MANGA, EH?
UM...
IT'S MORE LIKE...
A LOVE HATE THING.
THAT'S ...
...THE STRONGEST KIND OF LOVE
WHERE SHOULD I READ IT?
ON THE BEACH BEHIND THE SCHOOL...

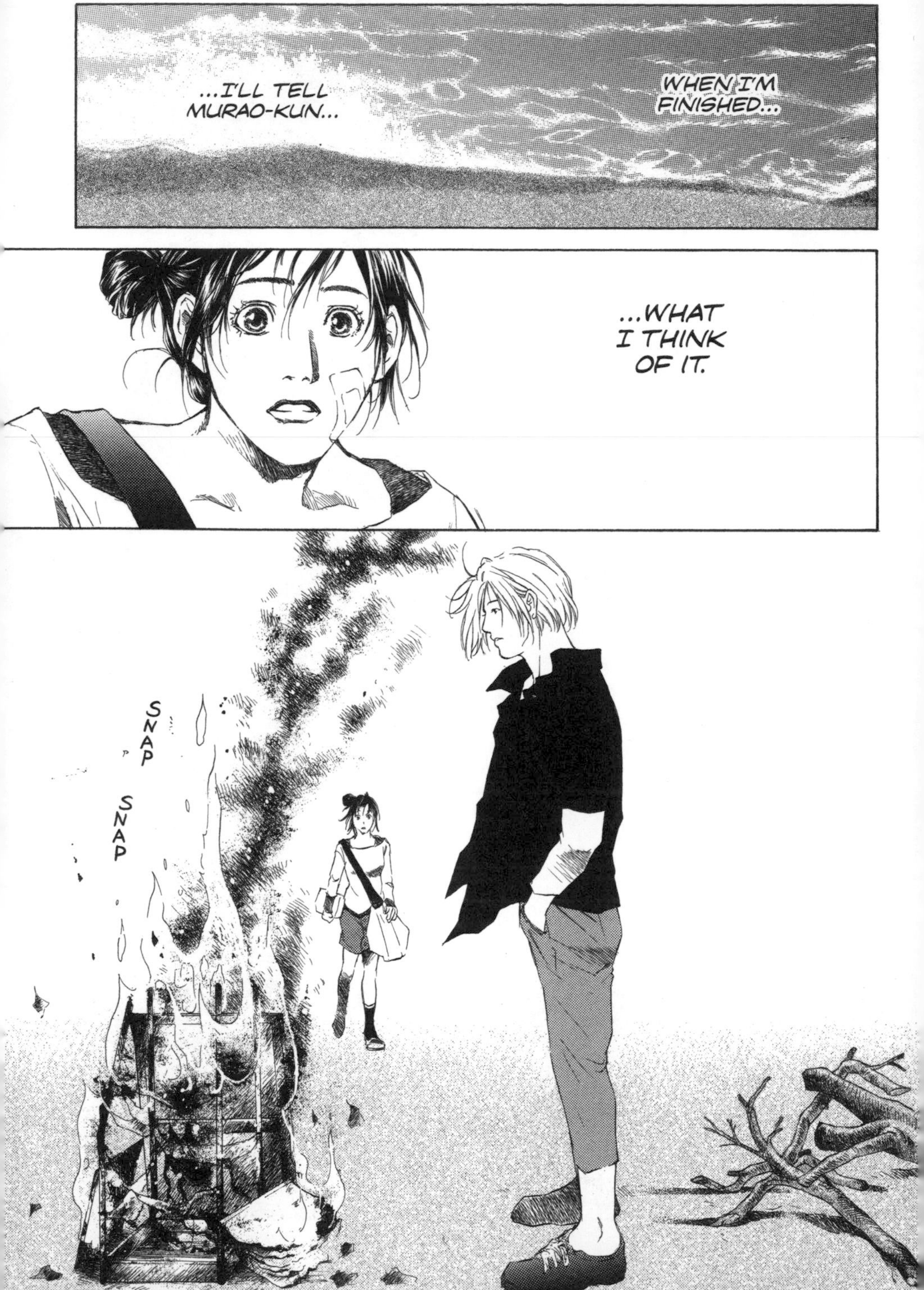
WHEN I'M FINISHED...
...I'LL TELL MURAO-KUN...
...WHAT I THINK OF IT.
SNAP
SNAP

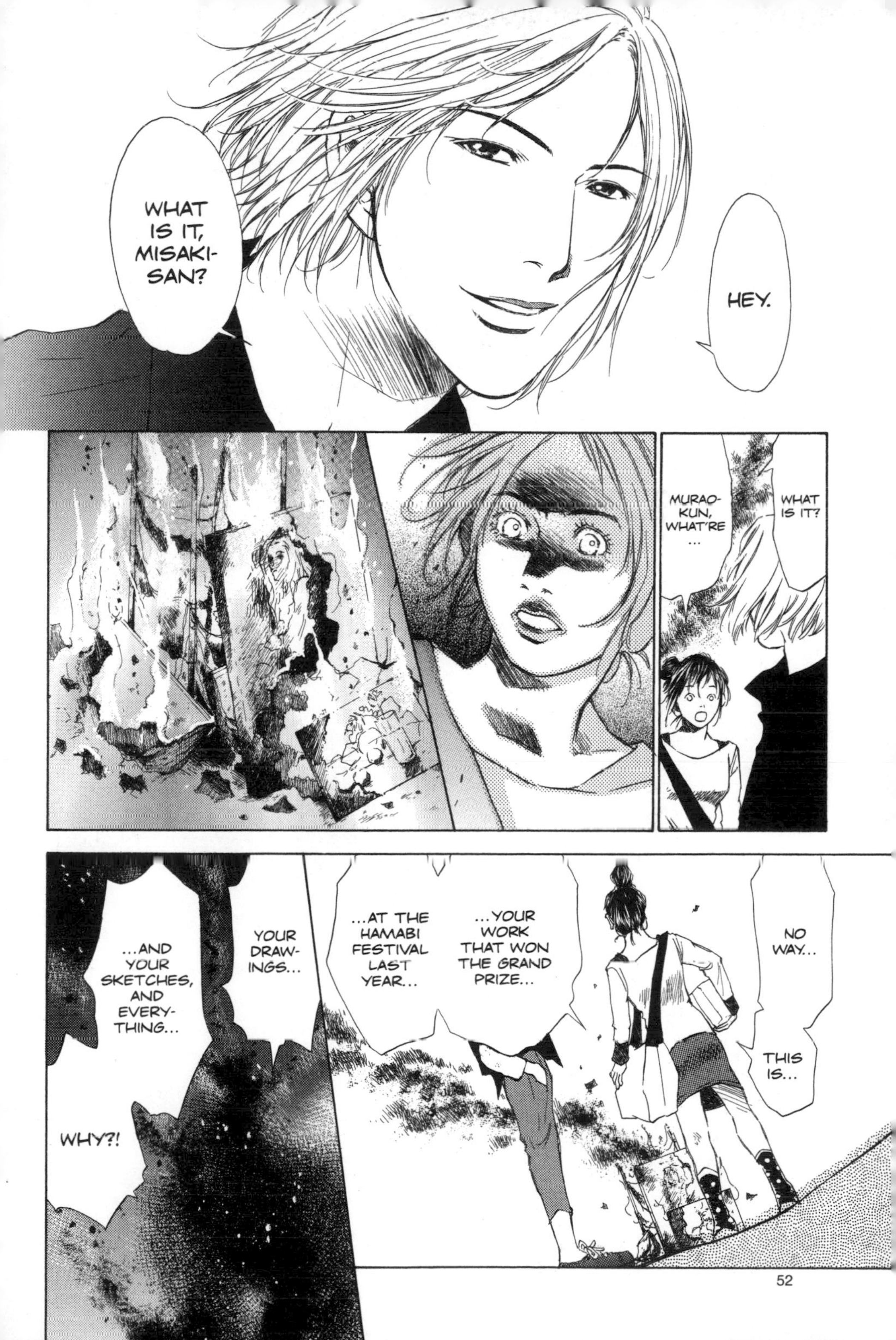
HEY.
WHAT IS IT, MISAKI-SAN?
WHAT IS IT?
MURAO-KUN, WHAT'RE ...
NO WAY...
THIS IS...
...YOUR WORK THAT WON THE GRAND PRIZE...
...AT THE HAMABI FESTIVAL LAST YEAR...
YOUR DRAWINGS...
...AND YOUR SKETCHES, AND EVERYTHING...
WHY?!

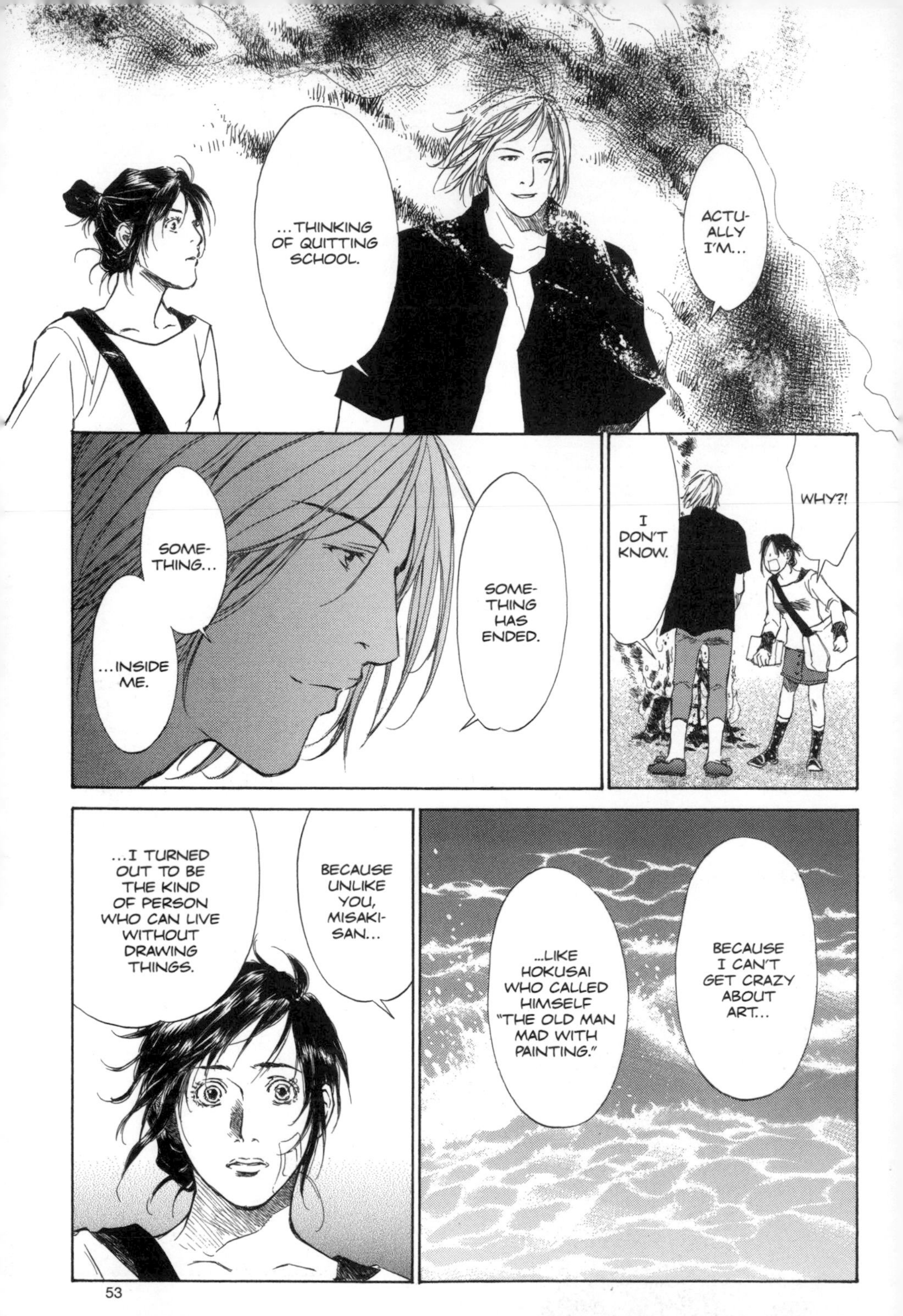
ACTU-ALLY I'M...
...THINKING OF QUITTING SCHOOL.
WHY?!
I DON'T KNOW.
SOME-THING HAS ENDED.
SOME-THING...
...INSIDE ME.
BECAUSE I CAN'T GET CRAZY ABOUT ART...
...LIKE HOKUSAI WHO CALLED HIMSELF "THE OLD MAN MAD WITH PAINTING."
BECAUSE UNLIKE YOU, MISAKI-SAN...
...I TURNED OUT TO BE THE KIND OF PERSON WHO CAN LIVE WITHOUT DRAWING THINGS.

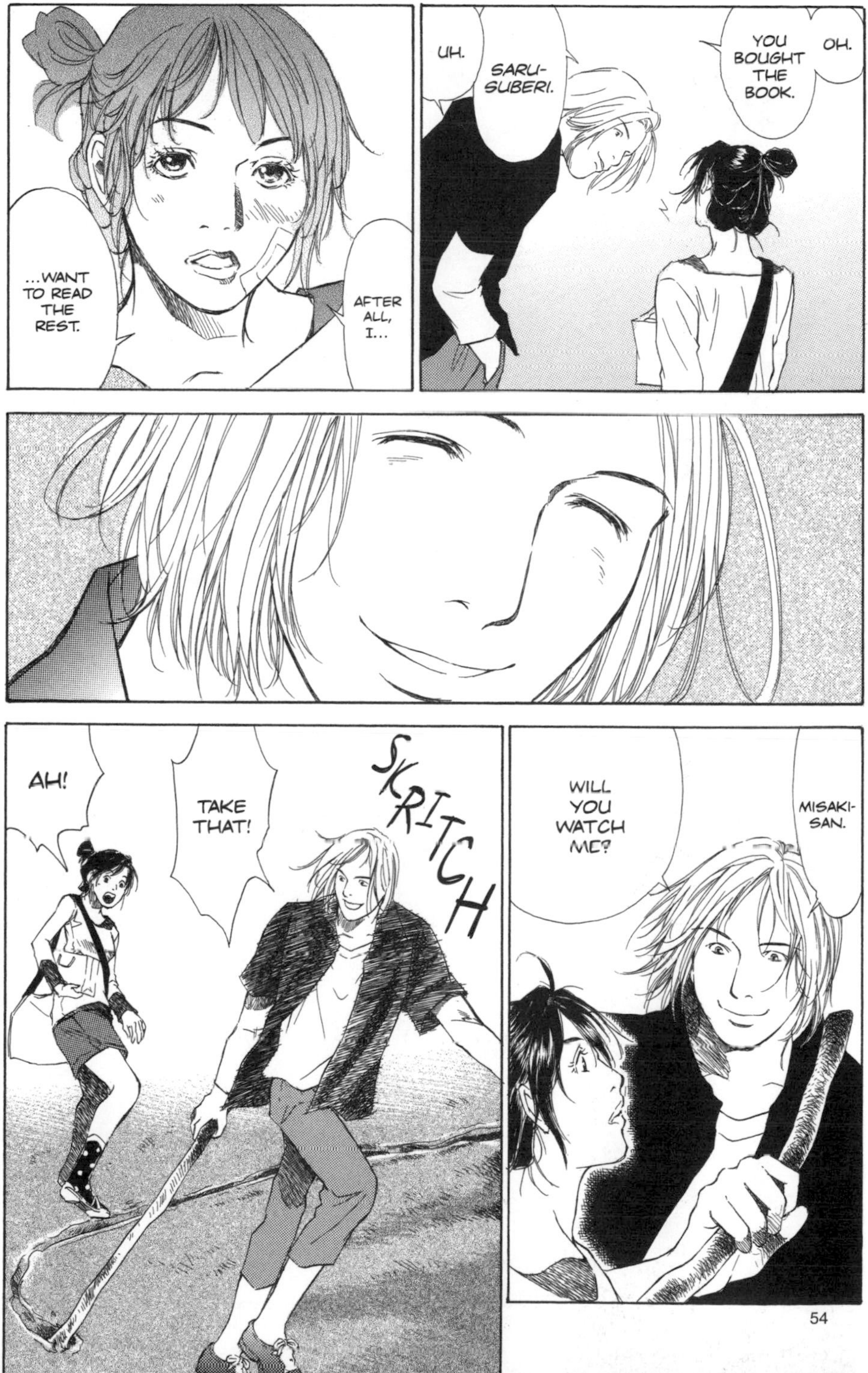
OH.
YOU BOUGHT THE BOOK.
SARU-SUBERI.
UH.
AFTER ALL, I...
...WANT TO READ THE REST.
MISAKI-SAN.
WILL YOU WATCH ME?
SKRITCH
TAKE THAT!
AH!

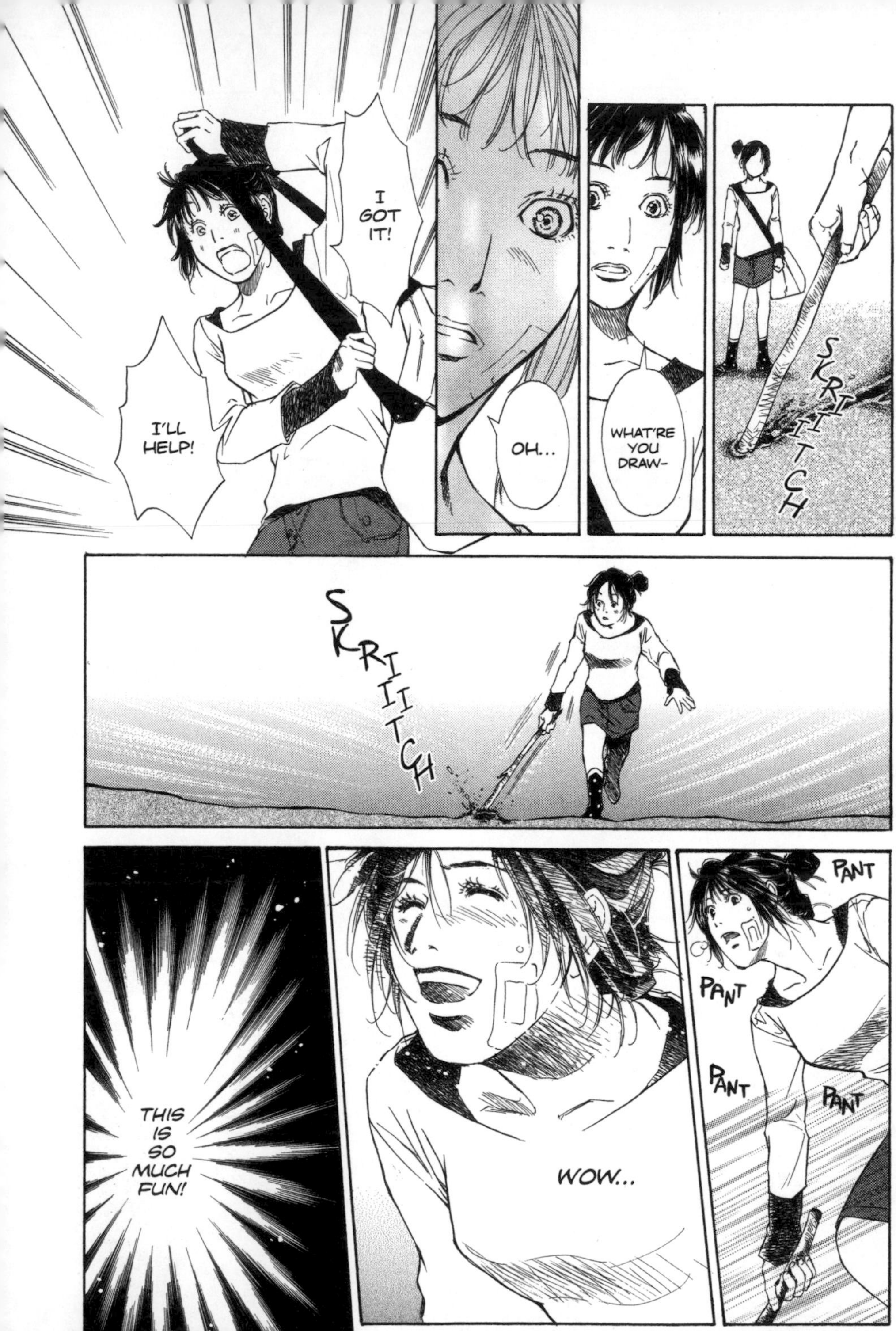
SKRIITCH
WHAT'RE YOU DRAW-
OH...
I GOT IT!
I'LL HELP!
SKRIIITCH
PANT
PANT
PANT
PANT
WOW...
THIS IS SO MUCH FUN!

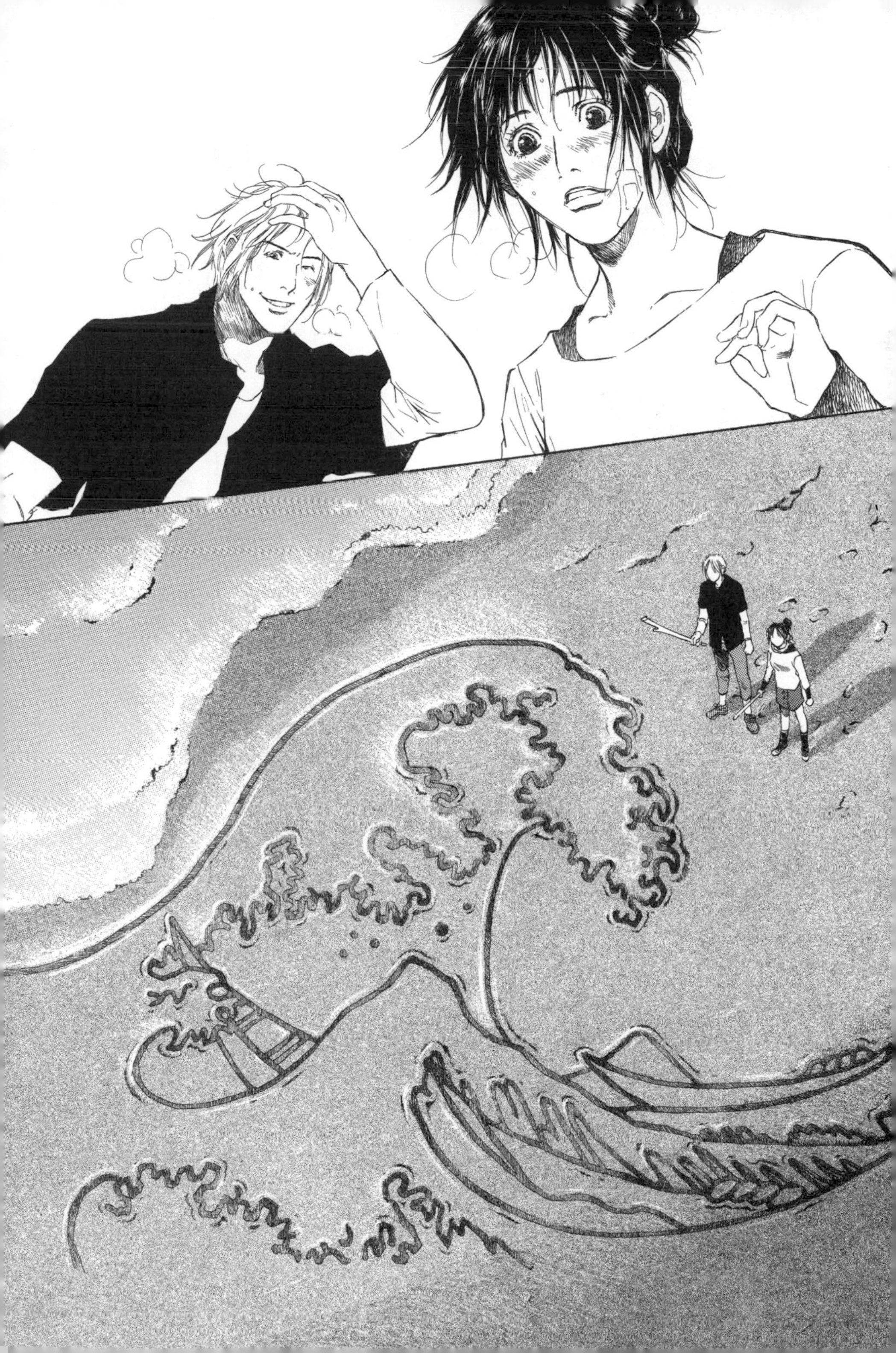

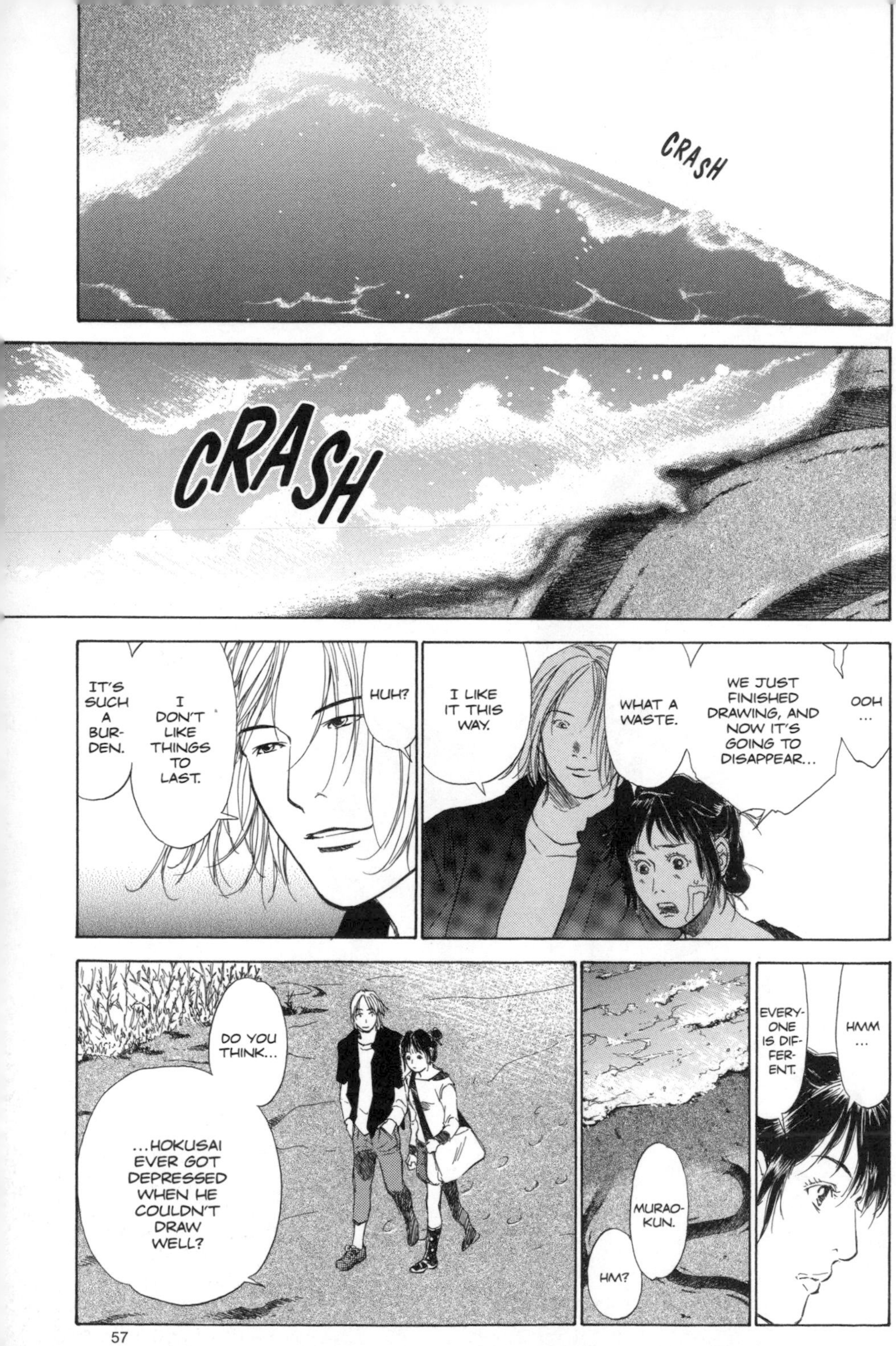
CRASH
CRASH
OOH...
WE JUST FINISHED DRAWING, AND NOW IT'S GOING TO DISAPPEAR...
WHAT A WASTE.
I LIKE IT THIS WAY.
HUH?
I DON'T LIKE THINGS TO LAST.
IT'S SUCH A BURDEN.
HMM...
EVERYONE IS DIFFERENT.
MURAO-KUN.
HM?
DO YOU THINK...
...HOKUSAI EVER GOT DEPRESSED WHEN HE COULDN'T DRAW WELL?

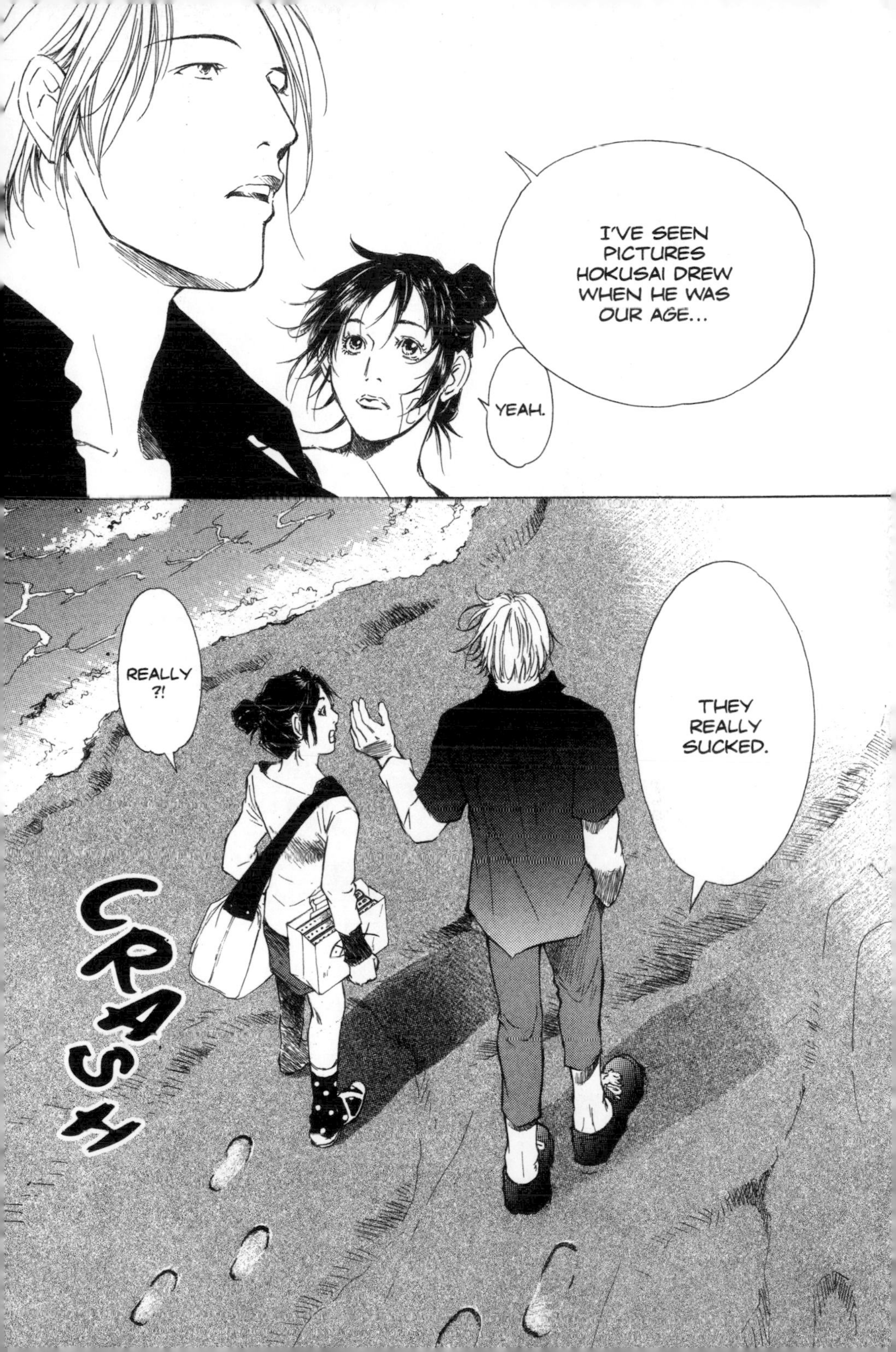
I'VE SEEN PICTURES HOKUSAI DREW WHEN HE WAS OUR AGE...
YEAH.
THEY REALLY SUCKED.
REALLY ?!
CRASH

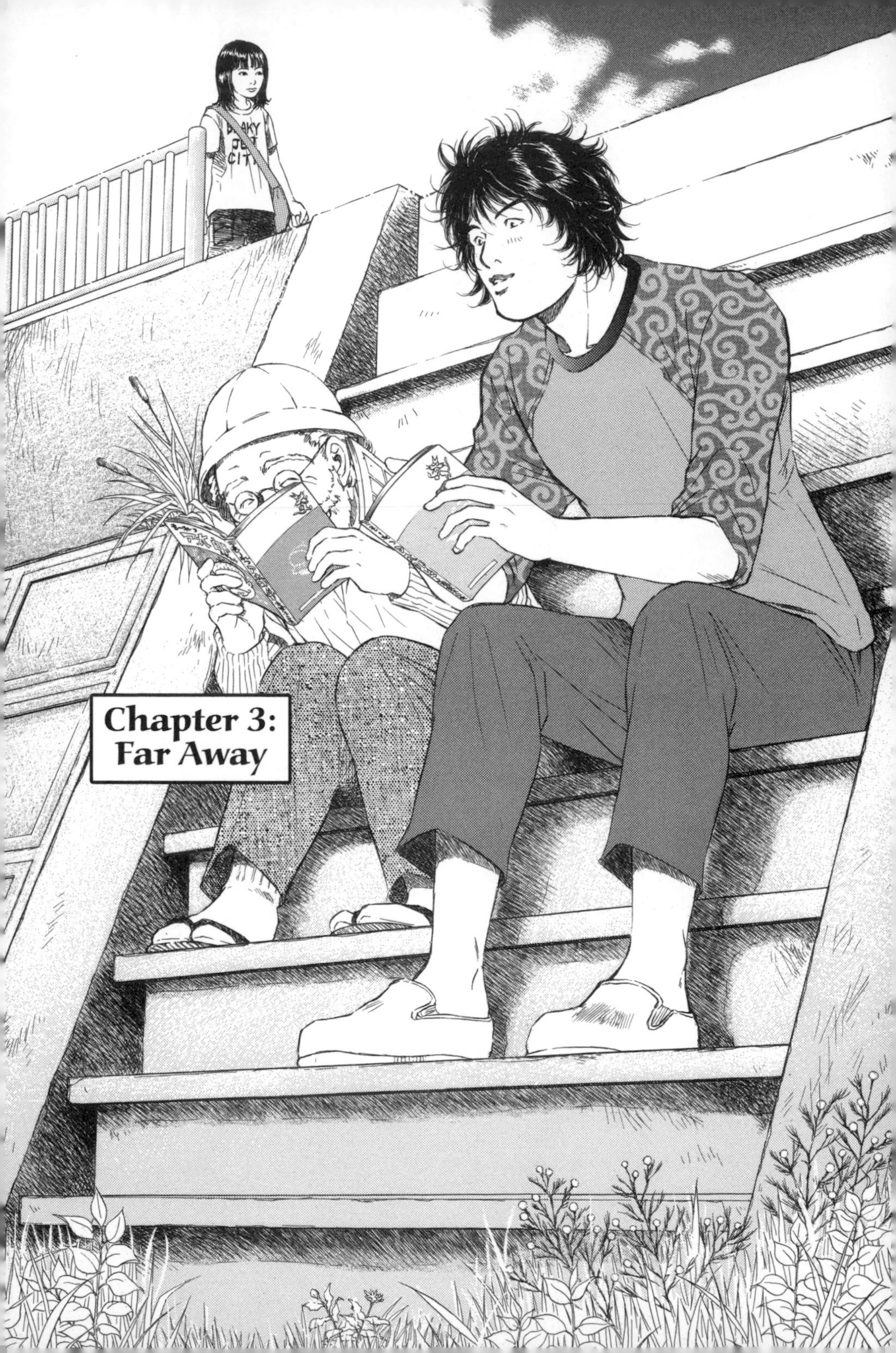

Chapter 3: Far Away

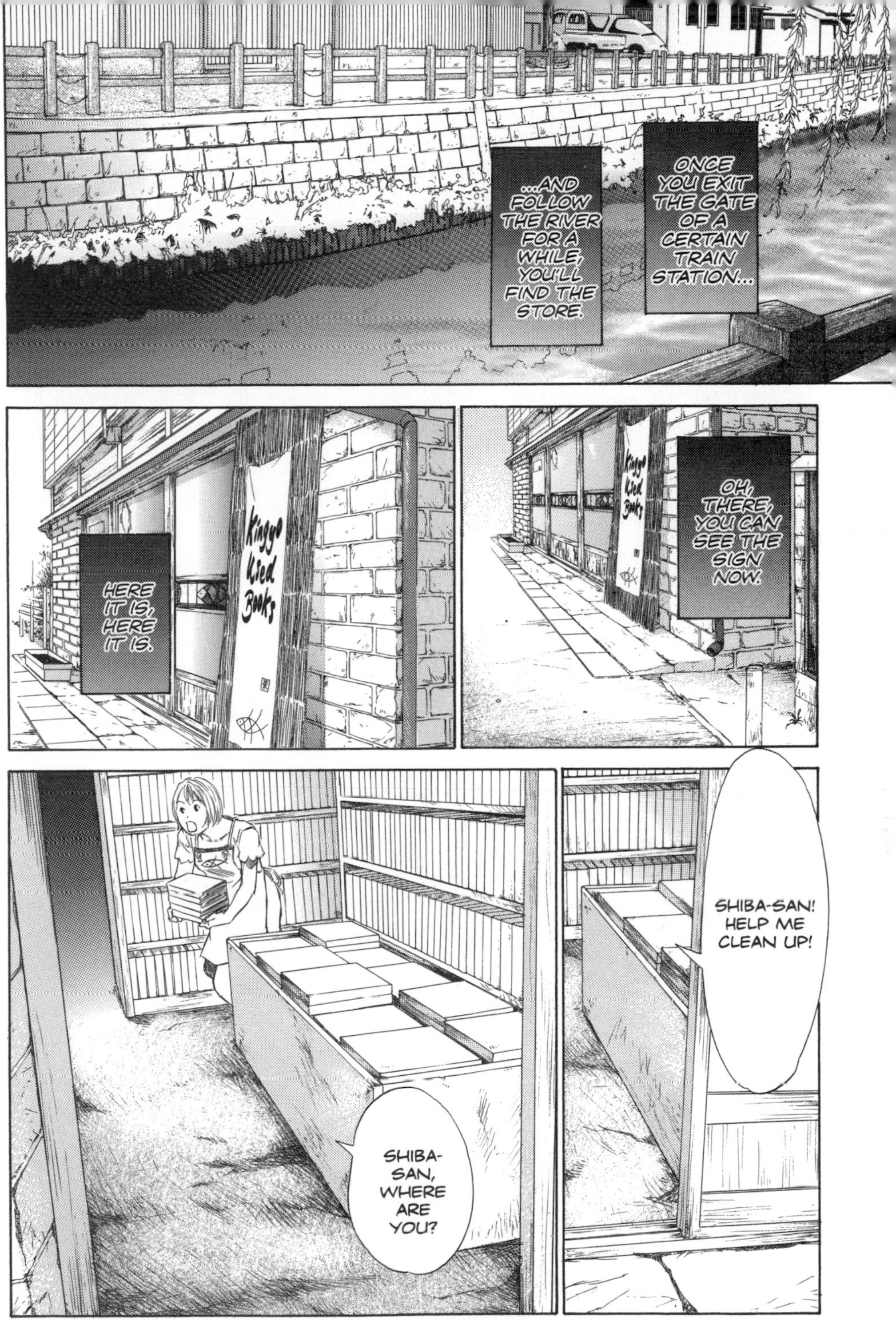
ONCE YOU EXIT THE GATE OF A CERTAIN TRAIN STATION...
...AND FOLLOW THE RIVER FOR A WHILE, YOU'LL FIND THE STORE.
Kingyo Used Books
OH, THERE, YOU CAN SEE THE SIGN NOW.
Kingyo Used Books
HERE IT IS, HERE IT IS.
SHIBA-SAN! HELP ME CLEAN UP!
SHIBA-SAN, WHERE ARE YOU?

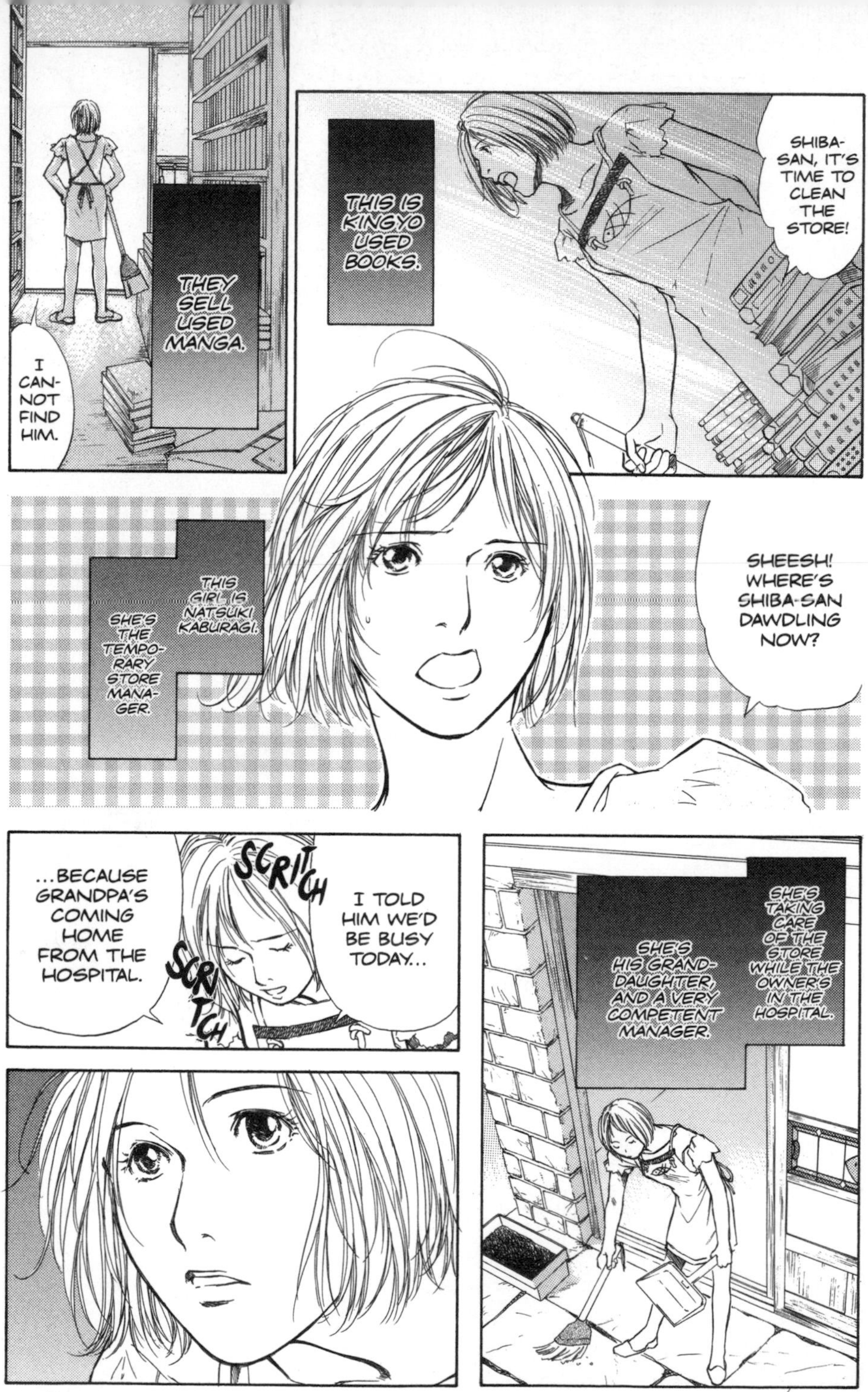
SHIBA-SAN, IT'S TIME TO CLEAN THE STORE!
THIS IS KINGYO USED BOOKS.
THEY SELL USED MANGA.
I CANNOT FIND HIM.
SHEESH! WHERE'S SHIBA-SAN DAWDLING NOW?
THIS GIRL IS NATSUKI KABURAGI.
SHE'S THE TEMPORARY STORE MANAGER.
SHE'S TAKING CARE OF THE STORE WHILE THE OWNER'S IN THE HOSPITAL.
SHE'S HIS GRANDDAUGHTER, AND A VERY COMPETENT MANAGER.
I TOLD HIM WE'D BE BUSY TODAY...
SCRITCH
...BECAUSE GRANDPA'S COMING HOME FROM THE HOSPITAL.
SCRITCH

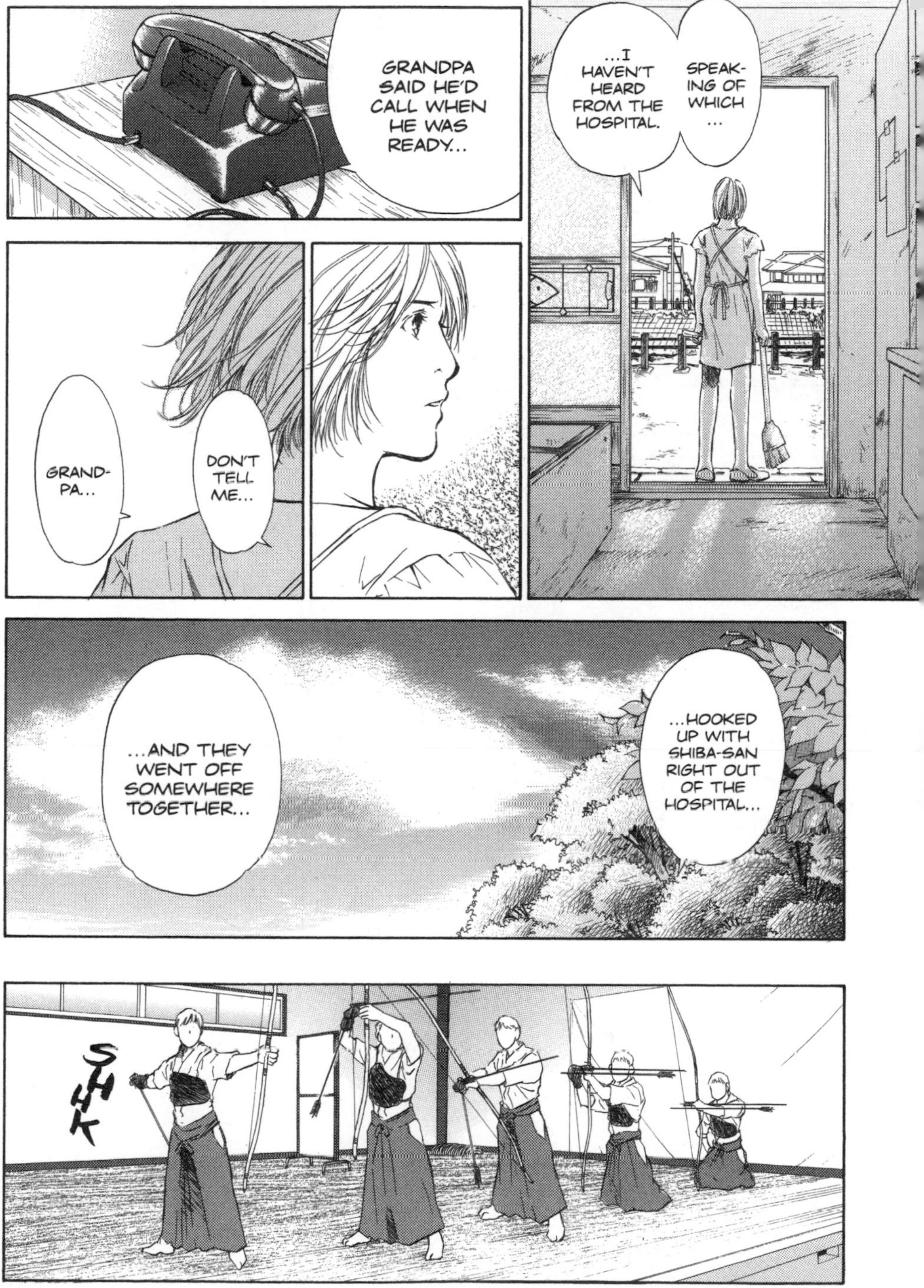
SPEAK-ING OF WHICH ...
...I HAVEN'T HEARD FROM THE HOSPITAL.
GRANDPA SAID HE'D CALL WHEN HE WAS READY...
DON'T TELL ME...
GRAND-PA...
...HOOKED UP WITH SHIBA-SAN RIGHT OUT OF THE HOSPITAL...
...AND THEY WENT OFF SOMEWHERE TOGETHER...
SHK

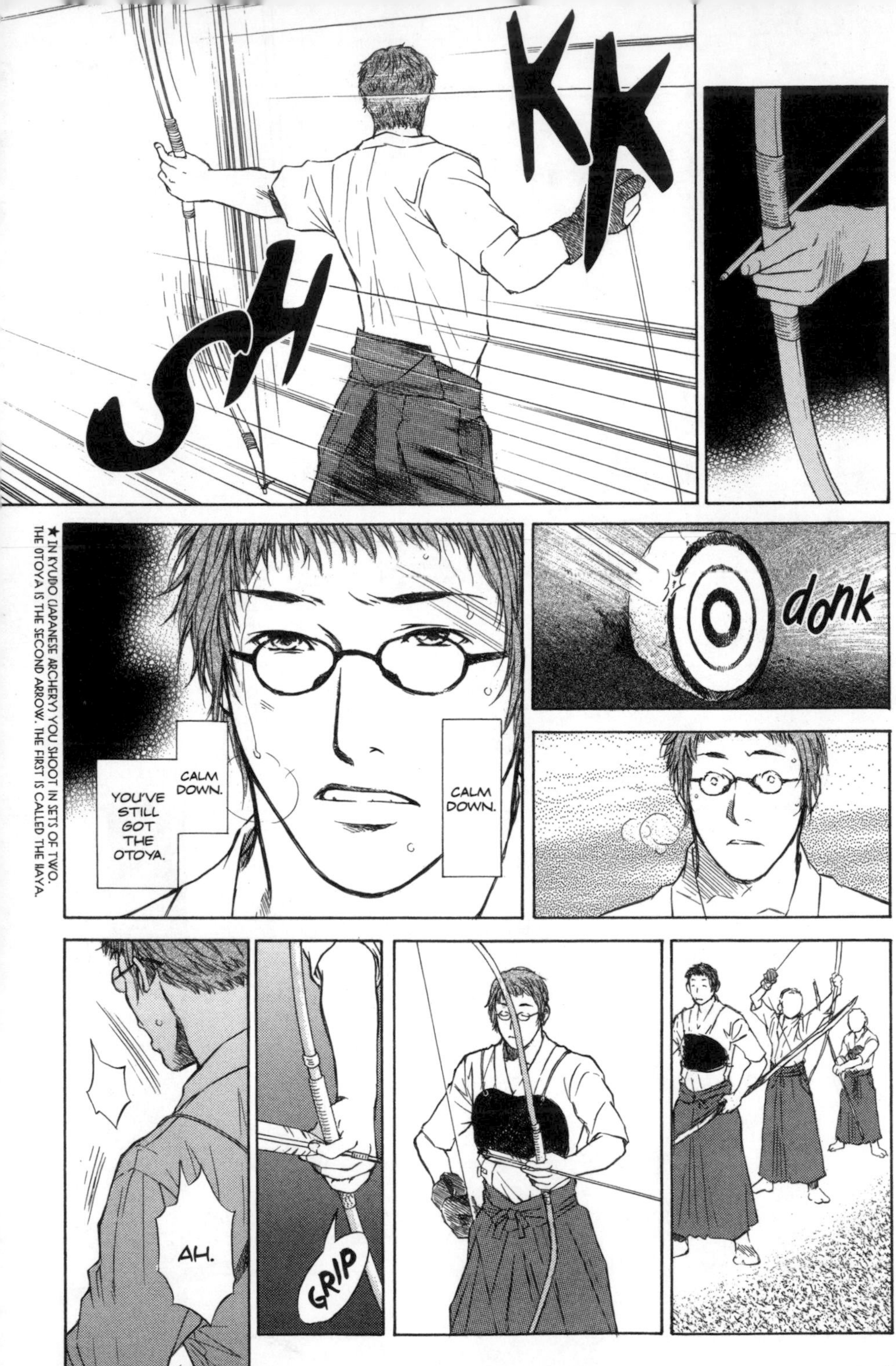
KK
SH
donk
CALM DOWN.
CALM DOWN.
YOU'VE STILL GOT THE OTOYA.
GRIP
AH.

★ IN KYUDO (JAPANESE ARCHERY) YOU SHOOT IN SETS OF TWO. THE OTOYA IS THE SECOND ARROW. THE FIRST IS CALLED THE HAYA.

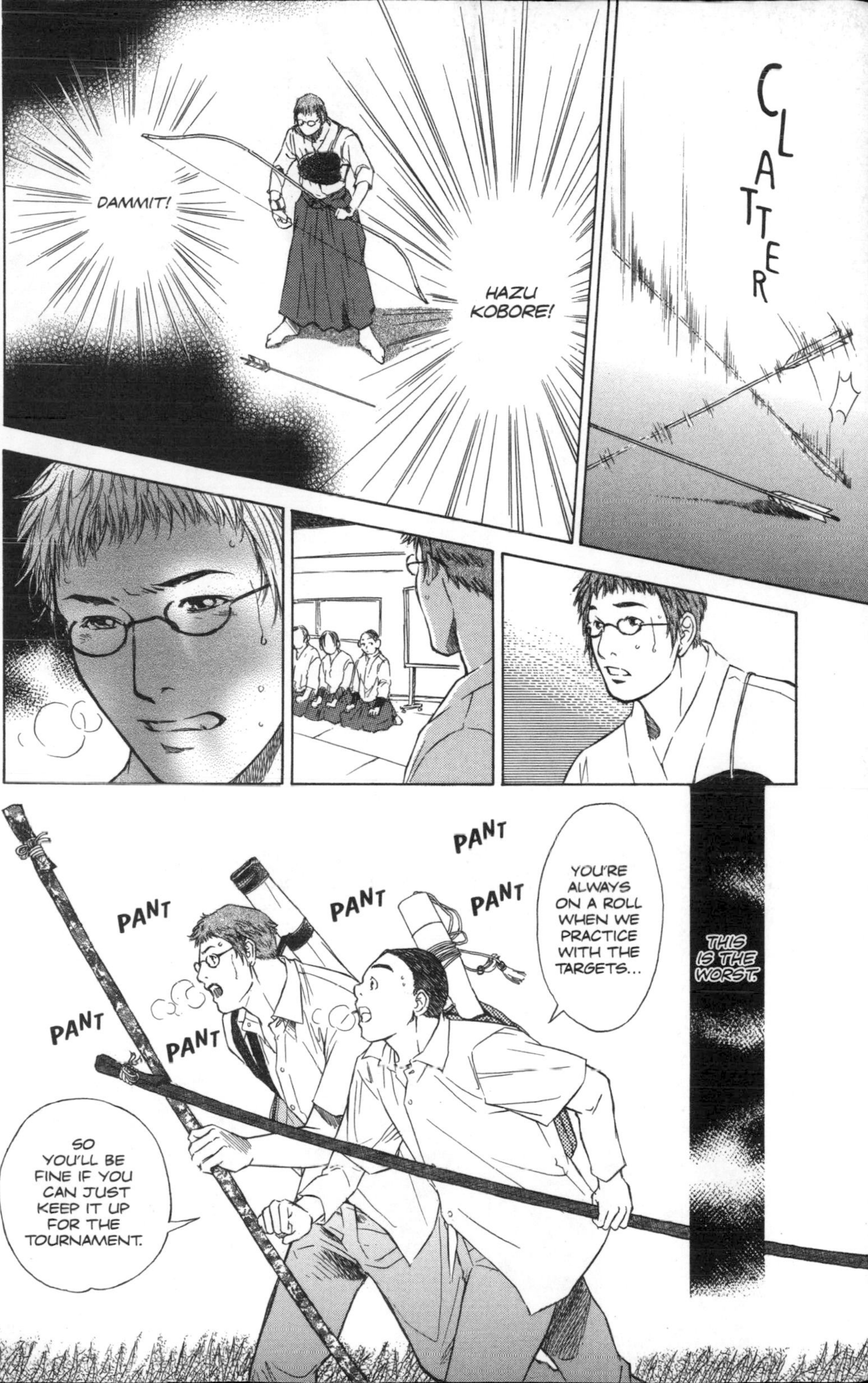
CLATTER
HAZU KOBORE!
DAMMIT!
THIS IS THE WORST.
PANT
PANT
YOU'RE ALWAYS ON A ROLL WHEN WE PRACTICE WITH THE TARGETS...
PANT
PANT
PANT
PANT
SO YOU'LL BE FINE IF YOU CAN JUST KEEP IT UP FOR THE TOURNAMENT.

★THE HAZU IS THE PART WHERE THE STRING IS ATTACHED TO THE BOW. HAZU KOBORE IS WHEN THE ARROW LIFTS FROM THE STRING OF THE BOW AND FALLS TO THE GROUND. THIS WOULD BE A FAILURE IN A COMPETITION.

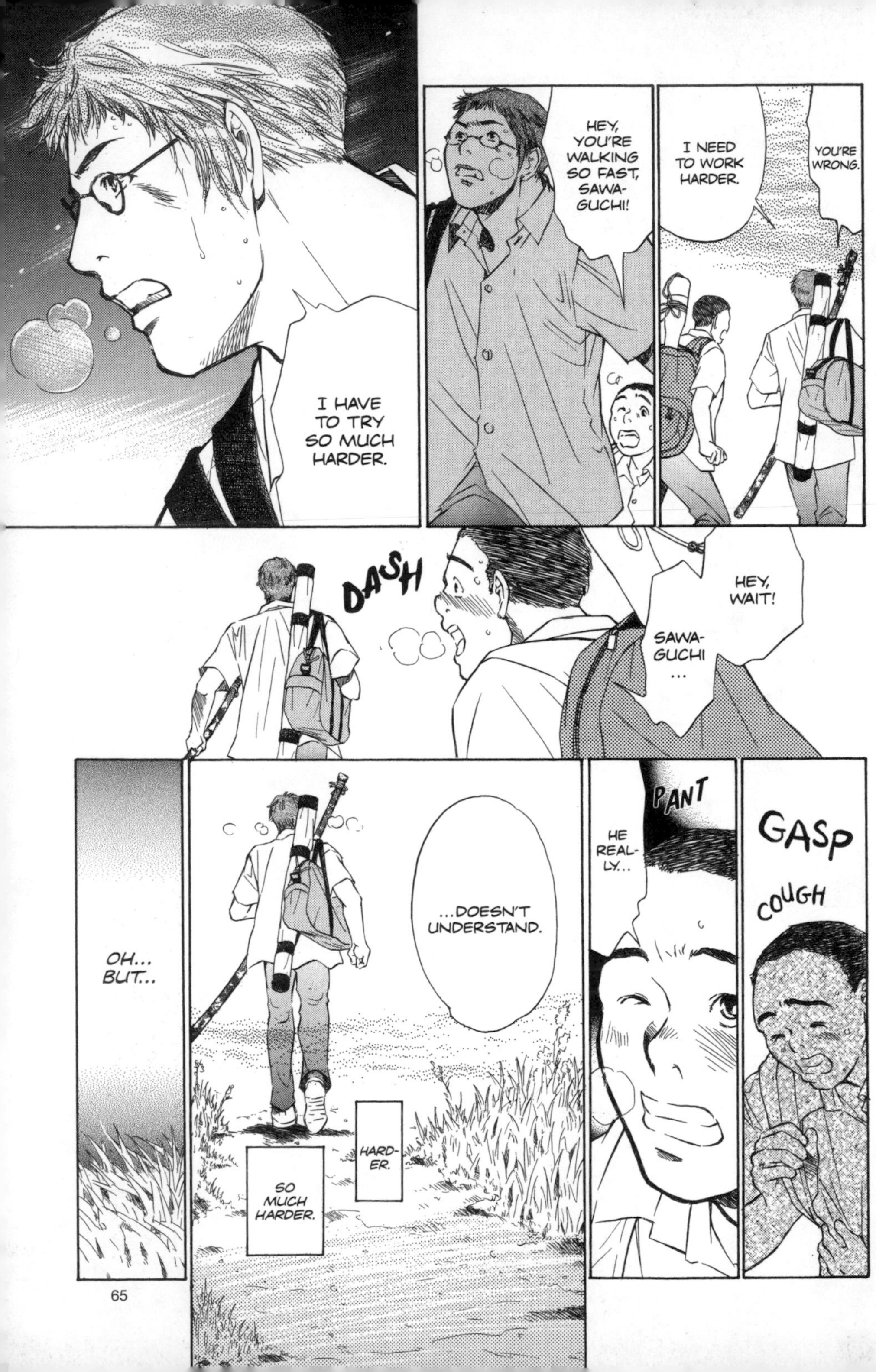
YOU'RE WRONG.
I NEED TO WORK HARDER.
HEY, YOU'RE WALKING SO FAST, SAWA-GUCHI!
I HAVE TO TRY SO MUCH HARDER.
HEY, WAIT!
SAWA-GUCHI ...
DASH
GASP
COUGH
PANT
HE REAL-LY...
...DOESN'T UNDERSTAND.
HARD-ER.
SO MUCH HARDER.
OH... BUT...

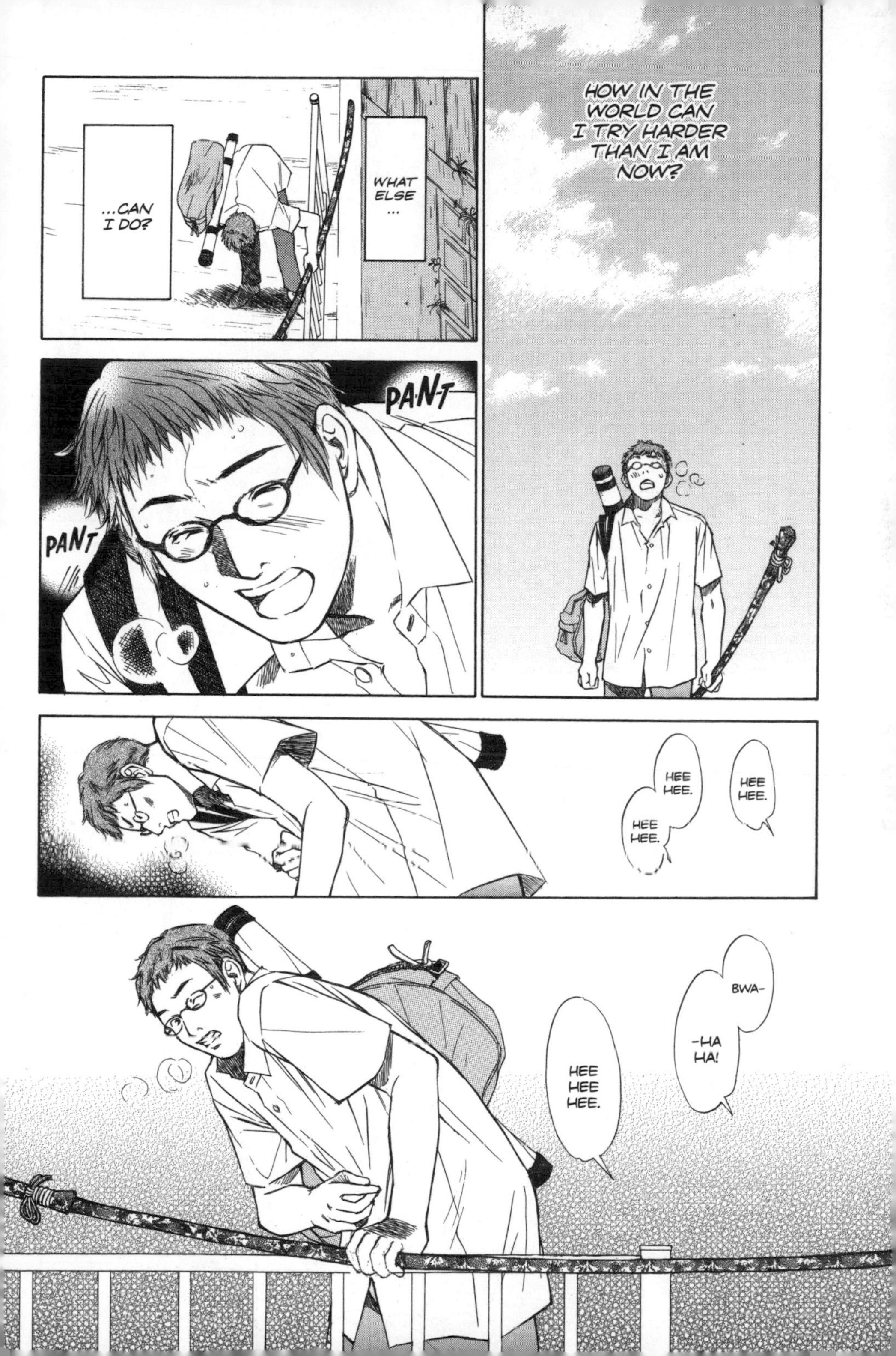
HOW IN THE WORLD CAN I TRY HARDER THAN I AM NOW?
WHAT ELSE ...
...CAN I DO?
PA-N-T
PANT
HEE HEE.
HEE HEE.
HEE HEE.
BWA-
-HA HA!
HEE HEE HEE.

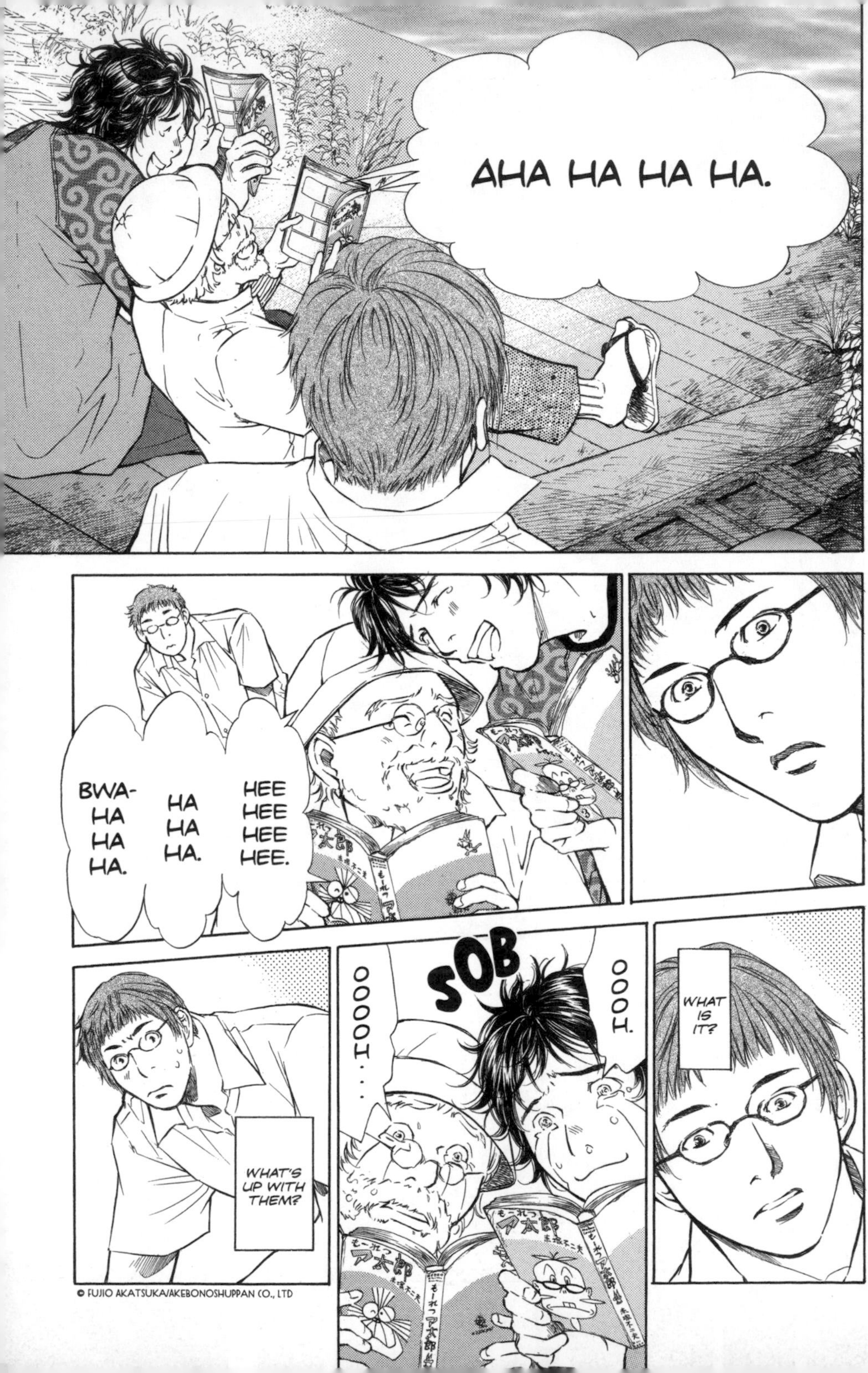
AHA HA HA HA.
BWA-HA HA HA.
HA HA HA.
HEE HEE HEE HEE.
WHAT IS IT?
OOOH.
SOB
OOOOOH...
WHAT'S UP WITH THEM?

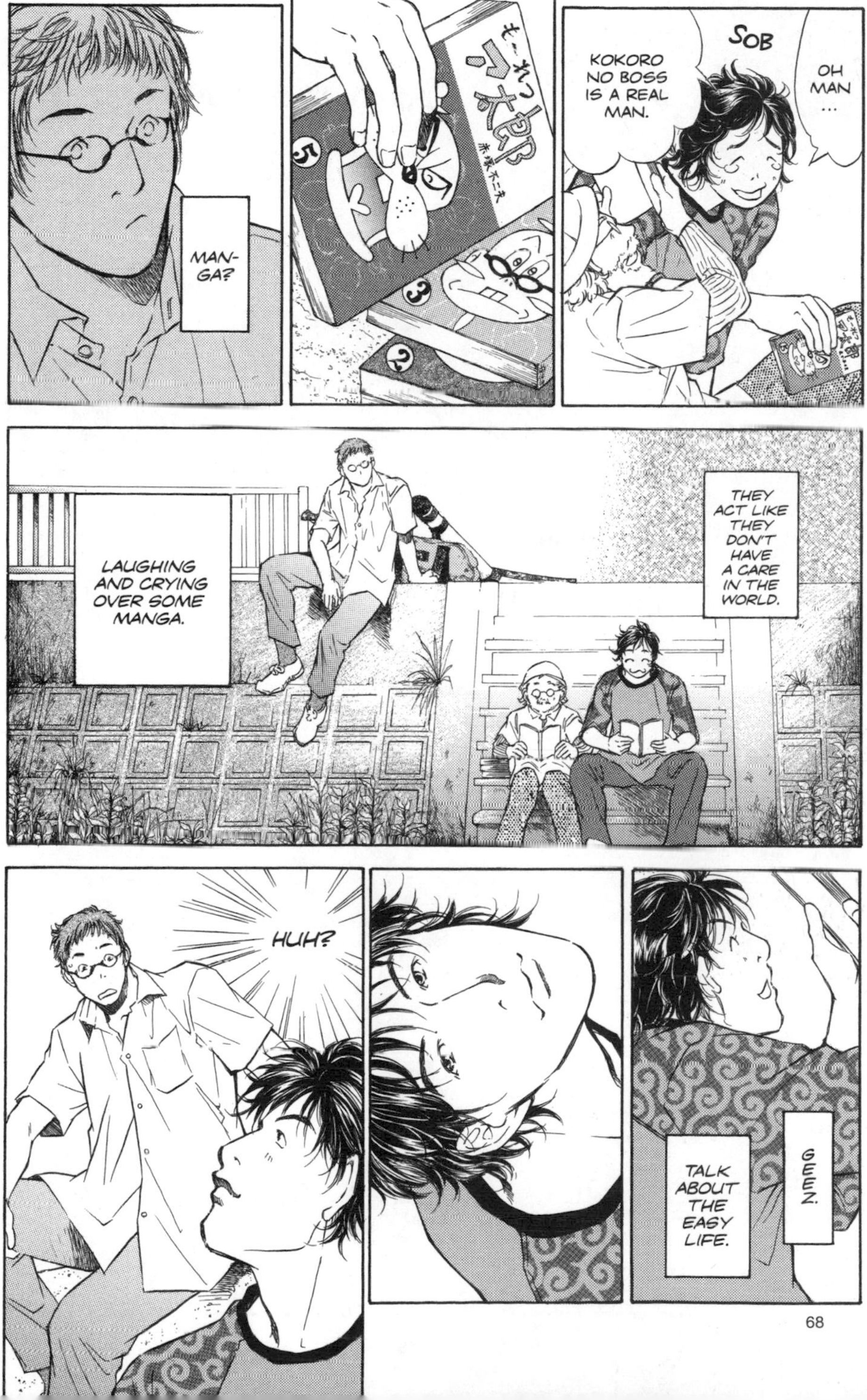
OH MAN ...
SOB
KOKORO NO BOSS IS A REAL MAN.
MAN-GA?
THEY ACT LIKE THEY DON'T HAVE A CARE IN THE WORLD.
LAUGHING AND CRYING OVER SOME MANGA.
GEEZ.
TALK ABOUT THE EASY LIFE.
HUH?

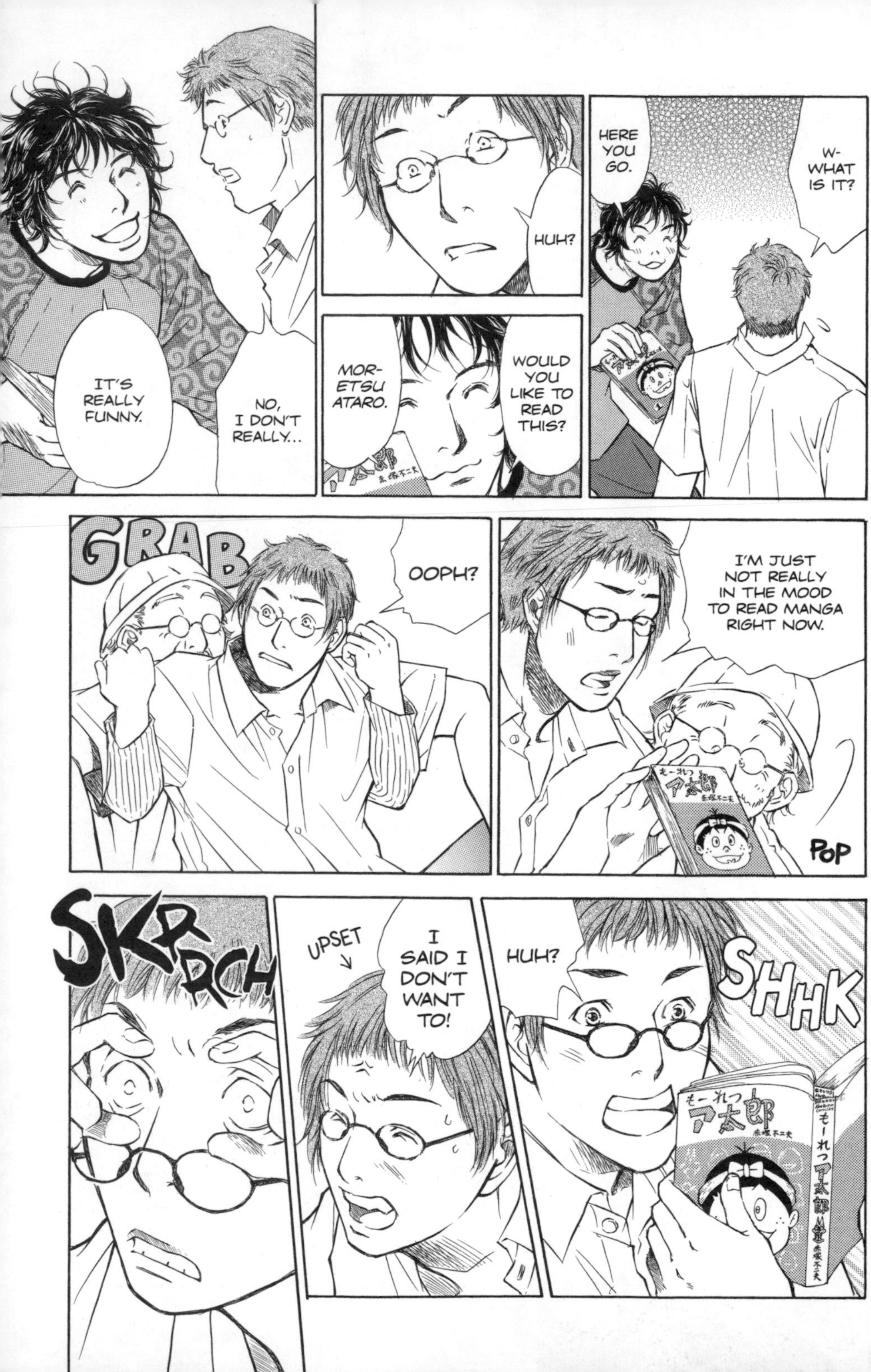
HERE YOU GO.
W- WHAT IS IT?
HUH?
WOULD YOU LIKE TO READ THIS?
MORETSU ATARO.
NO, I DON'T REALLY...
IT'S REALLY FUNNY.
I'M JUST NOT REALLY IN THE MOOD TO READ MANGA RIGHT NOW.
POP
GRAB
OOPH?
SHHK
HUH?
もーれつ ア太郎 赤塚不二夫
I SAID I DON'T WANT TO!
UPSET
SKRRCH

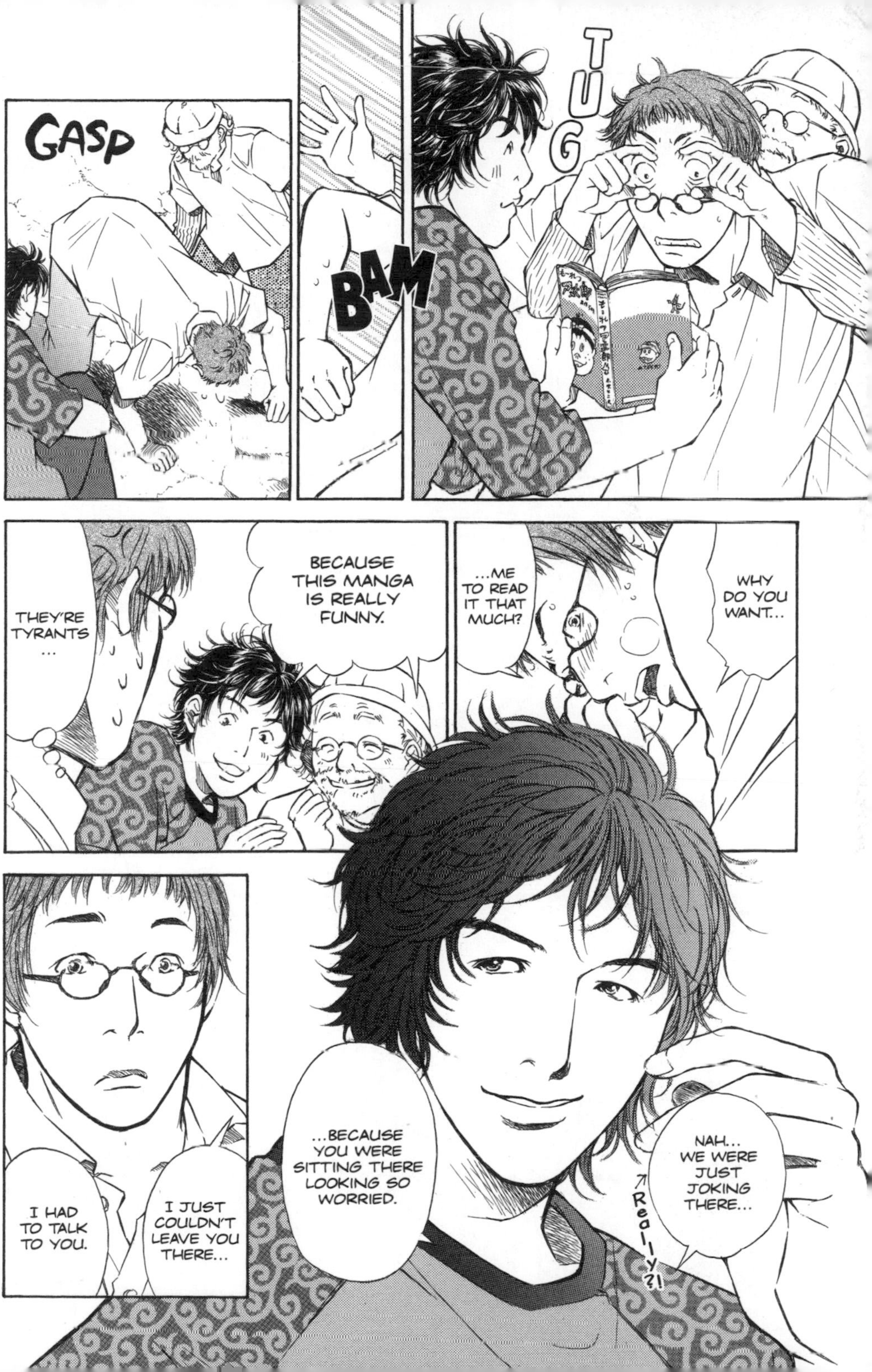
TUG
BAM
GASP
WHY DO YOU WANT...
...ME TO READ IT THAT MUCH?
BECAUSE THIS MANGA IS REALLY FUNNY.
THEY'RE TYRANTS ...
NAH... WE WERE JUST JOKING THERE...
Really?!
...BECAUSE YOU WERE SITTING THERE LOOKING SO WORRIED.
I JUST COULDN'T LEAVE YOU THERE...
I HAD TO TALK TO YOU.

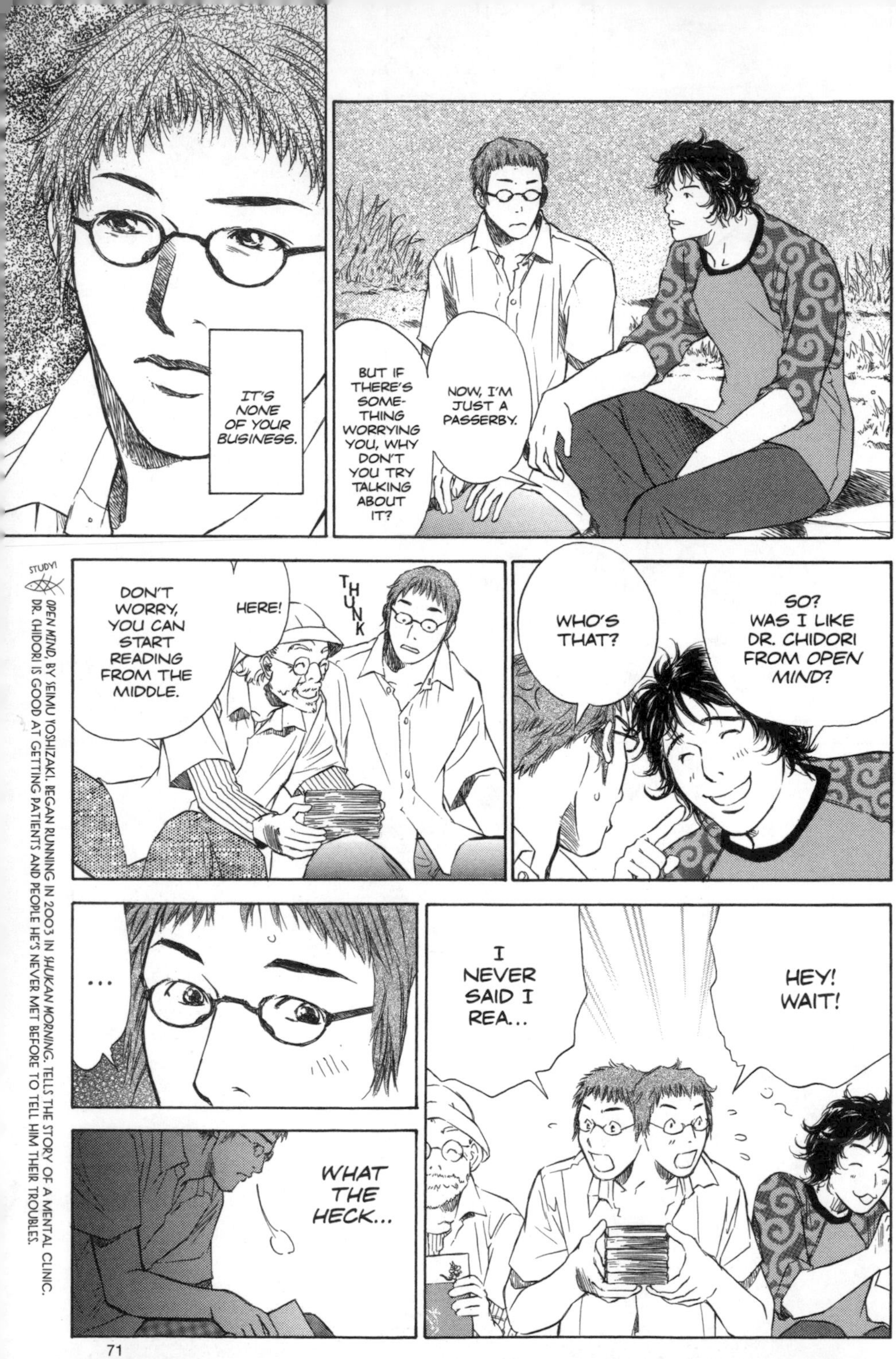
NOW, I'M JUST A PASSERBY.
BUT IF THERE'S SOME-THING WORRYING YOU, WHY DON'T YOU TRY TALKING ABOUT IT?
IT'S NONE OF YOUR BUSINESS.
SO? WAS I LIKE DR. CHIDORI FROM OPEN MIND?
WHO'S THAT?
THUNK
HERE!
DON'T WORRY, YOU CAN START READING FROM THE MIDDLE.
HEY! WAIT!
I NEVER SAID I REA...
...
WHAT THE HECK...

STUDY!

OPEN MIND, BY SEIMU YOSHIZAKI, BEGAN RUNNING IN 2003 IN *SHUKAN MORNING*. TELLS THE STORY OF A MENTAL CLINIC. DR. CHIDORI IS GOOD AT GETTING PATIENTS AND PEOPLE HE'S NEVER MET BEFORE TO TELL HIM THEIR TROUBLES.

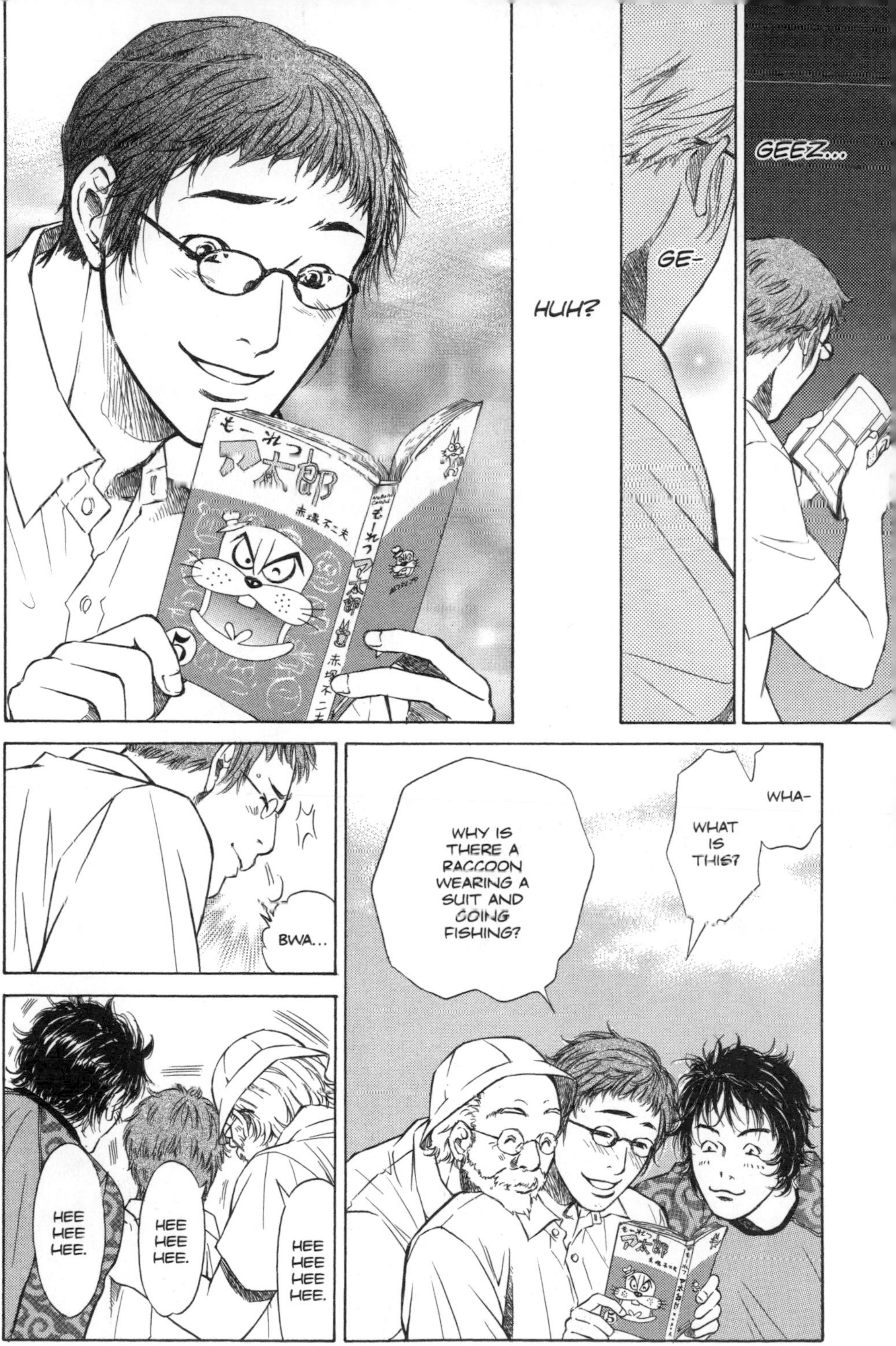

GEEZ...
GE-
HUH?
WHA-
WHAT IS THIS?
WHY IS THERE A RACCOON WEARING A SUIT AND GOING FISHING?
BWA...
HEE HEE HEE HEE.
HEE HEE HEE.
HEE HEE HEE.

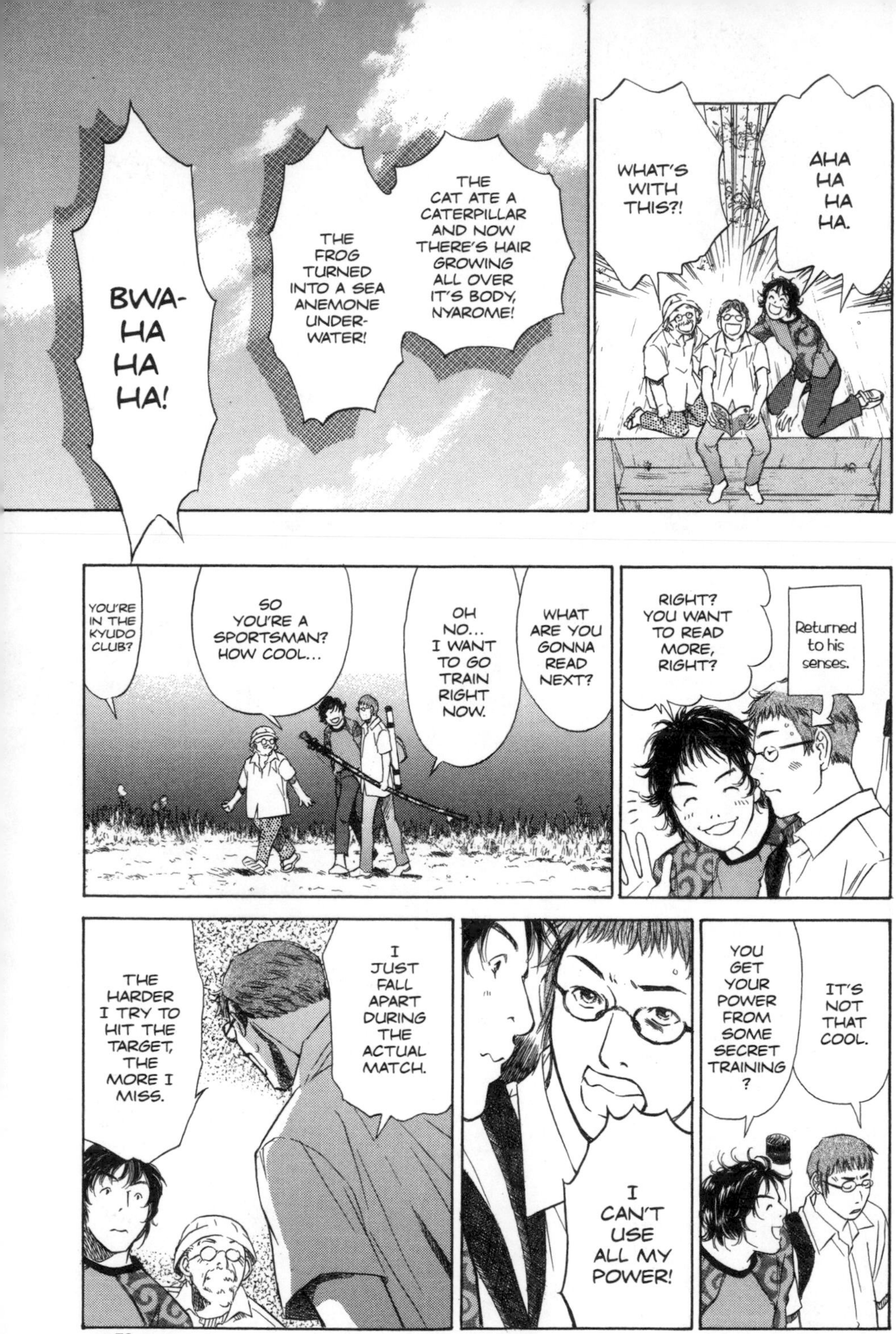
AHA HA HA HA.
WHAT'S WITH THIS?!
THE CAT ATE A CATERPILLAR AND NOW THERE'S HAIR GROWING ALL OVER IT'S BODY, NYAROME!
THE FROG TURNED INTO A SEA ANEMONE UNDER-WATER!
BWA-HA HA HA!
Returned to his senses.
RIGHT? YOU WANT TO READ MORE, RIGHT?
WHAT ARE YOU GONNA READ NEXT?
OH NO... I WANT TO GO TRAIN RIGHT NOW.
SO YOU'RE A SPORTSMAN? HOW COOL...
YOU'RE IN THE KYUDO CLUB?
IT'S NOT THAT COOL.
YOU GET YOUR POWER FROM SOME SECRET TRAINING?
I CAN'T USE ALL MY POWER!
I JUST FALL APART DURING THE ACTUAL MATCH.
THE HARDER I TRY TO HIT THE TARGET, THE MORE I MISS.

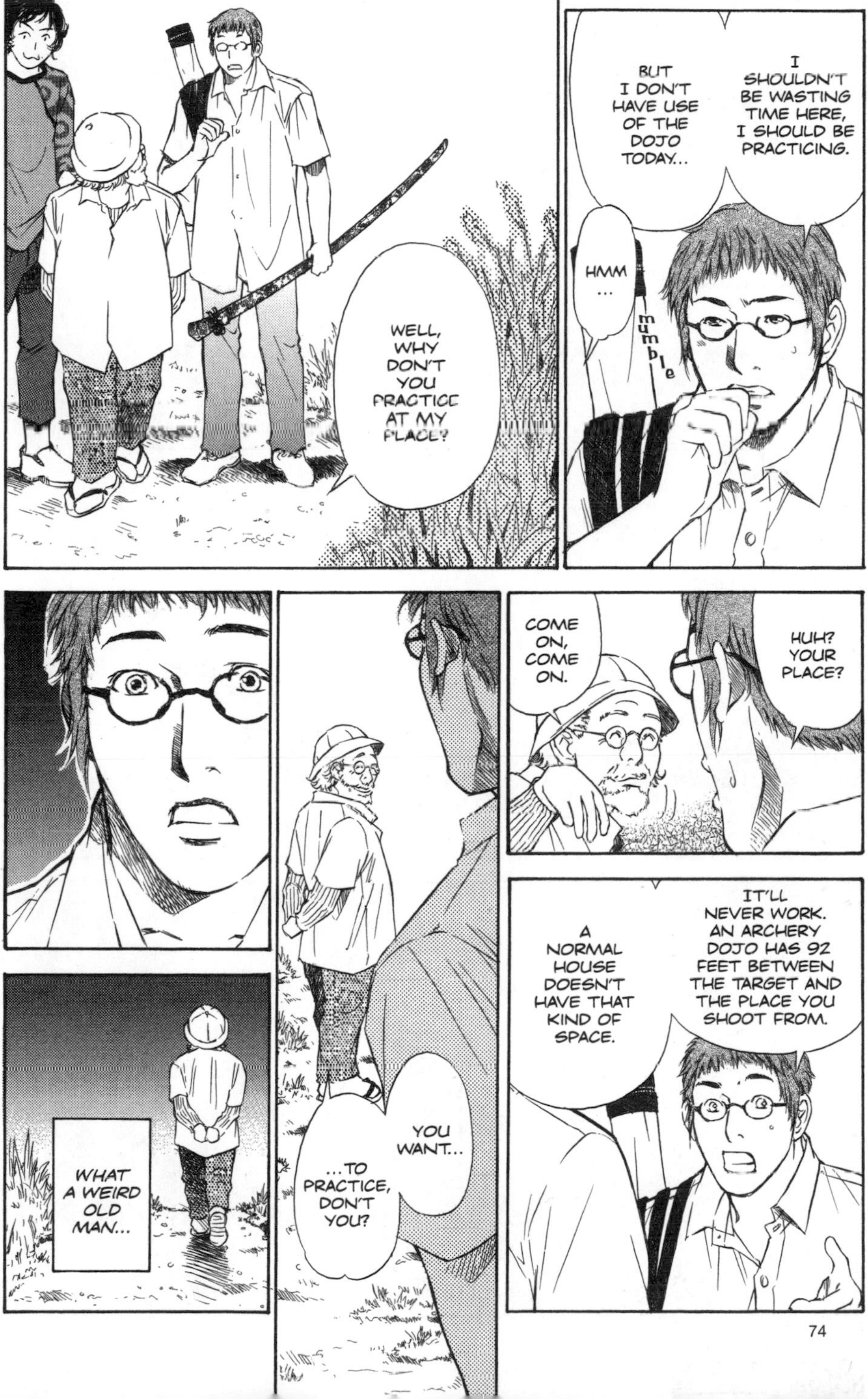
I SHOULDN'T BE WASTING TIME HERE, I SHOULD BE PRACTICING.
BUT I DON'T HAVE USE OF THE DOJO TODAY...
HMM...
mumble
WELL, WHY DON'T YOU PRACTICE AT MY PLACE?
HUH? YOUR PLACE?
COME ON, COME ON.
IT'LL NEVER WORK. AN ARCHERY DOJO HAS 92 FEET BETWEEN THE TARGET AND THE PLACE YOU SHOOT FROM.
A NORMAL HOUSE DOESN'T HAVE THAT KIND OF SPACE.
YOU WANT...
...TO PRACTICE, DON'T YOU?
WHAT A WEIRD OLD MAN...

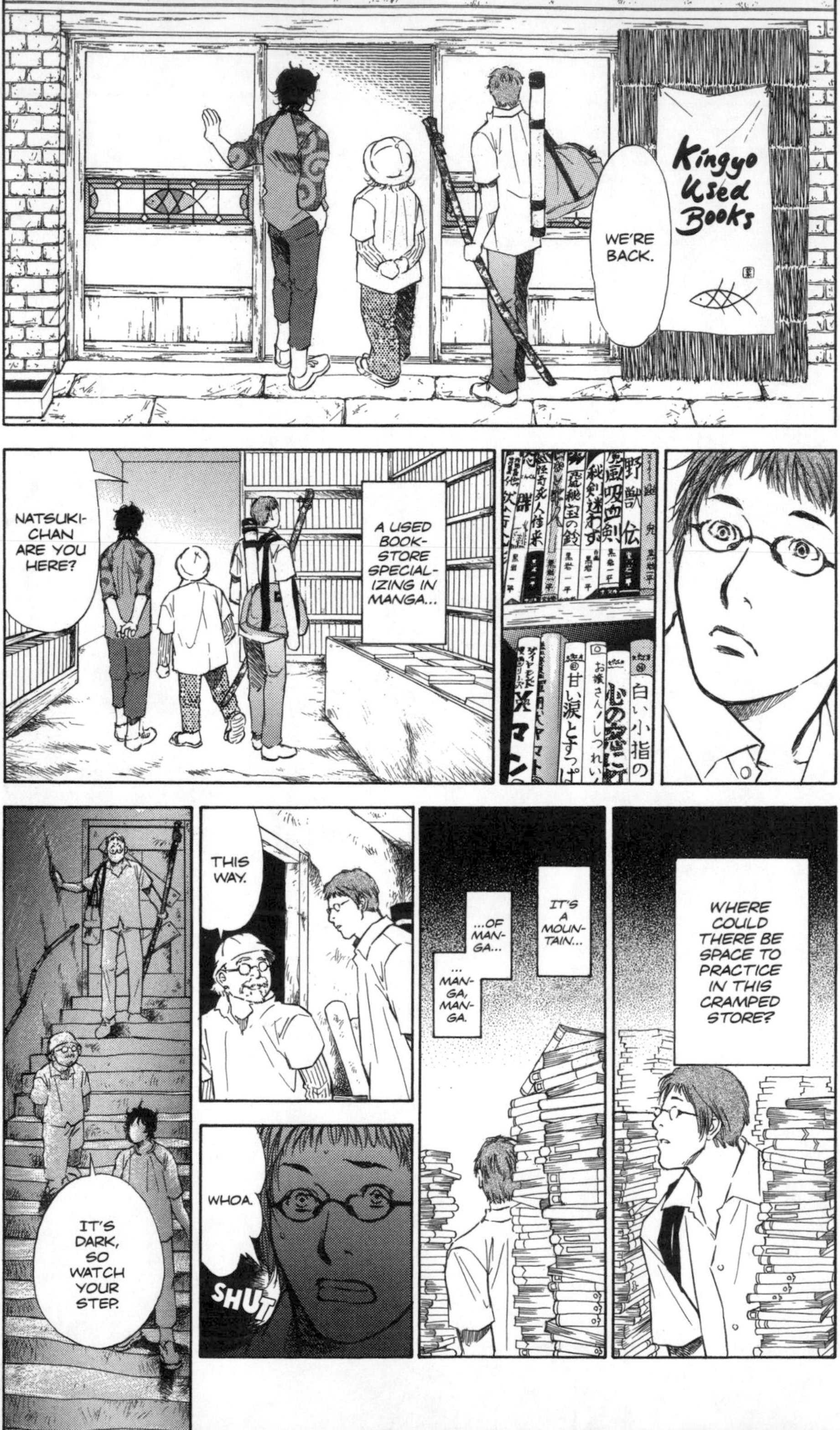
Kingyo Used Books
WE'RE BACK.
A USED BOOKSTORE SPECIALIZING IN MANGA...
NATSUKI-CHAN ARE YOU HERE?
WHERE COULD THERE BE SPACE TO PRACTICE IN THIS CRAMPED STORE?
IT'S A MOUNTAIN...
...OF MANGA...
...MANGA, MANGA.
THIS WAY.
WHOA.
SHUT
IT'S DARK, SO WATCH YOUR STEP.

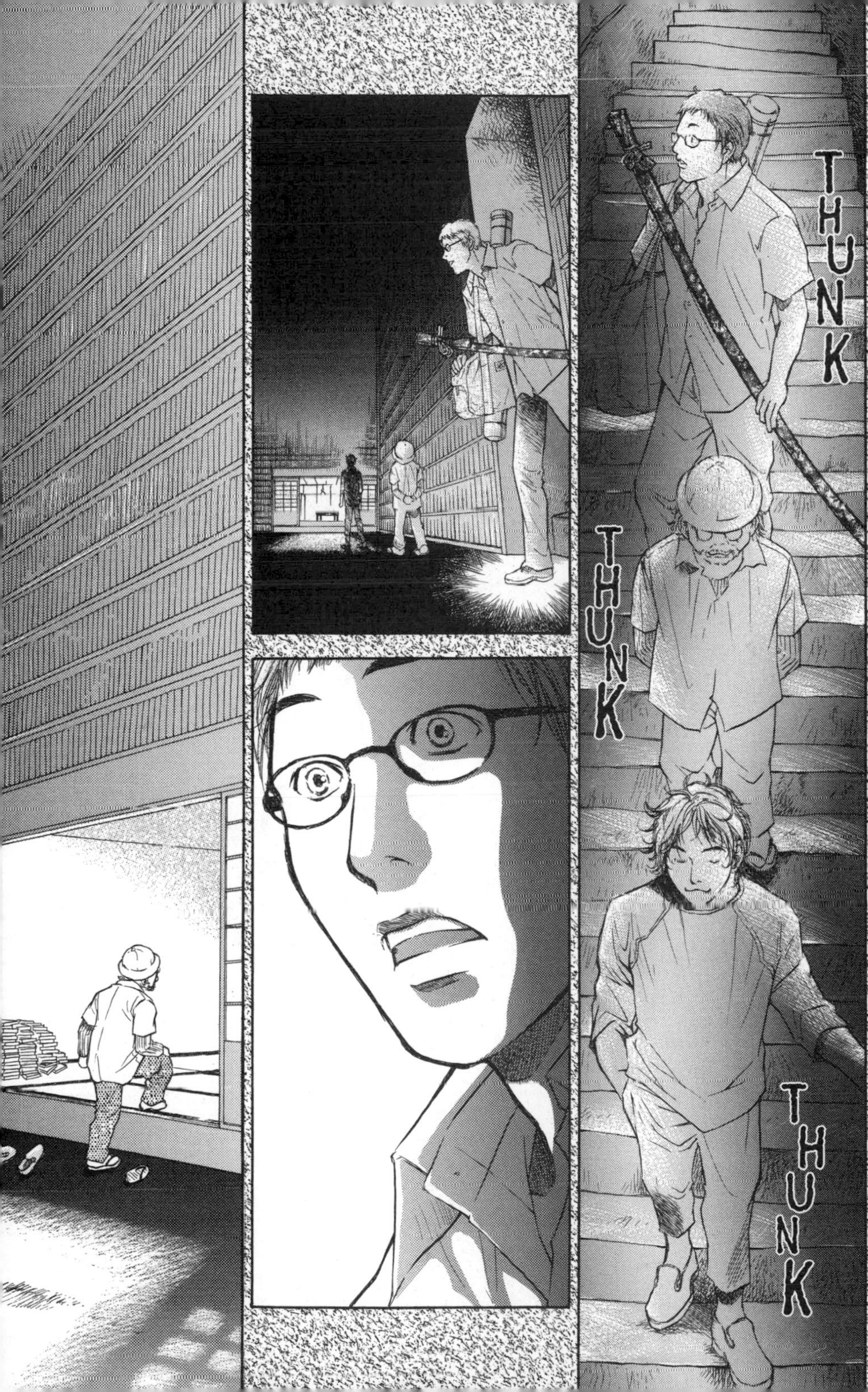
THUNK
THUNK
THUNK

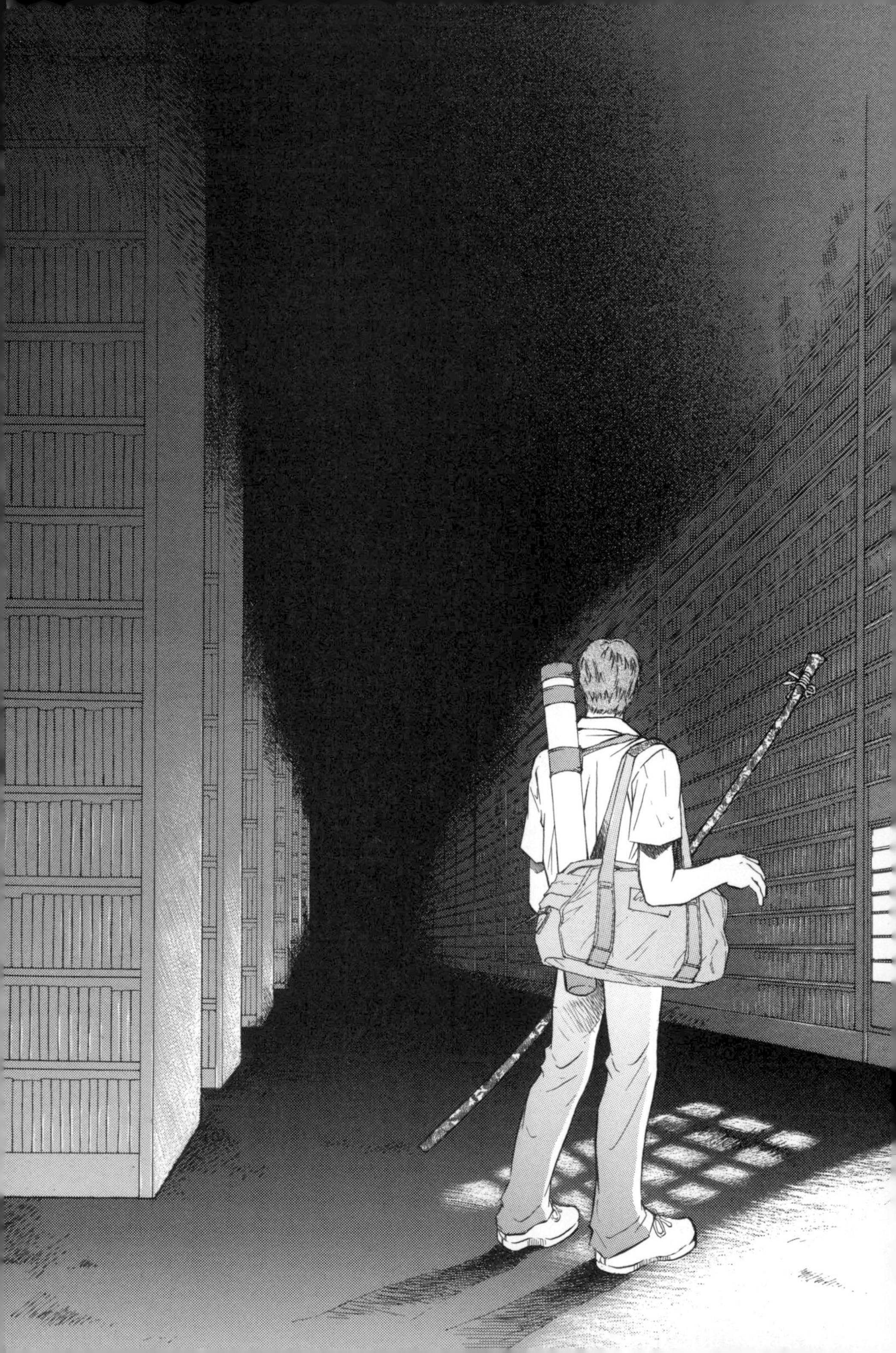

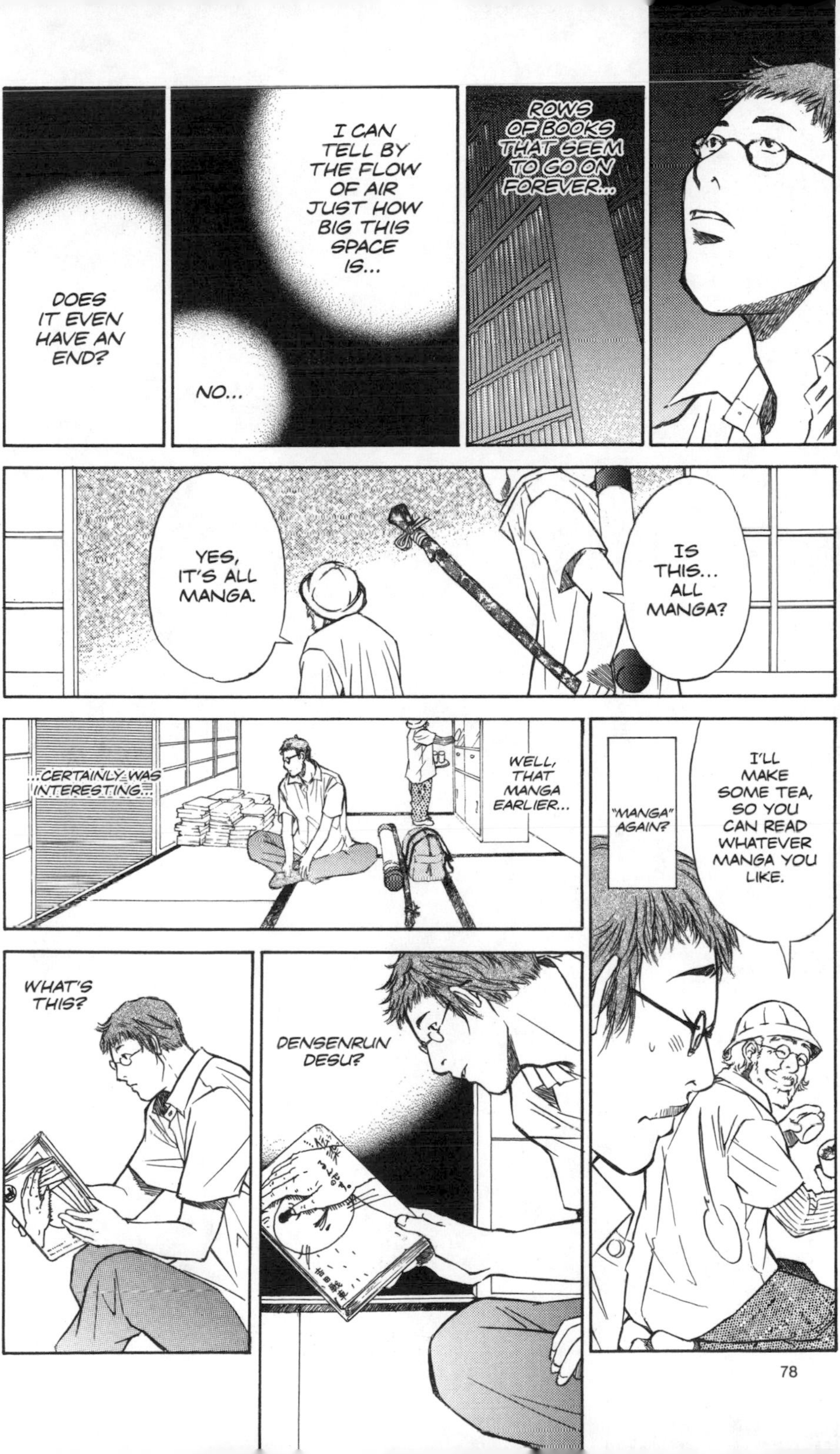
ROWS OF BOOKS THAT SEEM TO GO ON FOREVER...
I CAN TELL BY THE FLOW OF AIR JUST HOW BIG THIS SPACE IS...
NO...
DOES IT EVEN HAVE AN END?
IS THIS... ALL MANGA?
YES, IT'S ALL MANGA.
I'LL MAKE SOME TEA, SO YOU CAN READ WHATEVER MANGA YOU LIKE.
"MANGA" AGAIN?
WELL, THAT MANGA EARLIER...
...CERTAINLY WAS INTERESTING...
DENSENRUN DESU?
WHAT'S THIS?

STUDY!

DENSENRUN' DESU: SHOULD BE READ AS *UTSURUN' DESU* (LIT. IT'S CONTAGIOUS), BY SENSHA YOSHIDA. PUBLISHED IN 1989 BY *BIG COMIC SPIRITS*. A NONSENSICAL GAG MANGA FULL OF PECULIAR CHARACTERS SUCH AS THE JEALOUS KAWAUSO-KUN AND THE VIOLENT SHIITAKE MUSHROOM, AND SAITO-SAN (A BEETLE) WHO'S TRYING TO FIND A JOB. GREAT CARE WAS TAKEN IN THE CONSTRUCTION OF THE TANKOBON. THE JACKETS WERE DESIGNED BY SOBUE, WHO ALSO OVERSEES THE COVER DESIGNS OF *IKKI* (THE MAGAZINE IN WHICH KINGYO USED BOOKS IS PUBLISHED). CURRENTLY ALL FIVE VOLUMES ARE AVAILABLE.

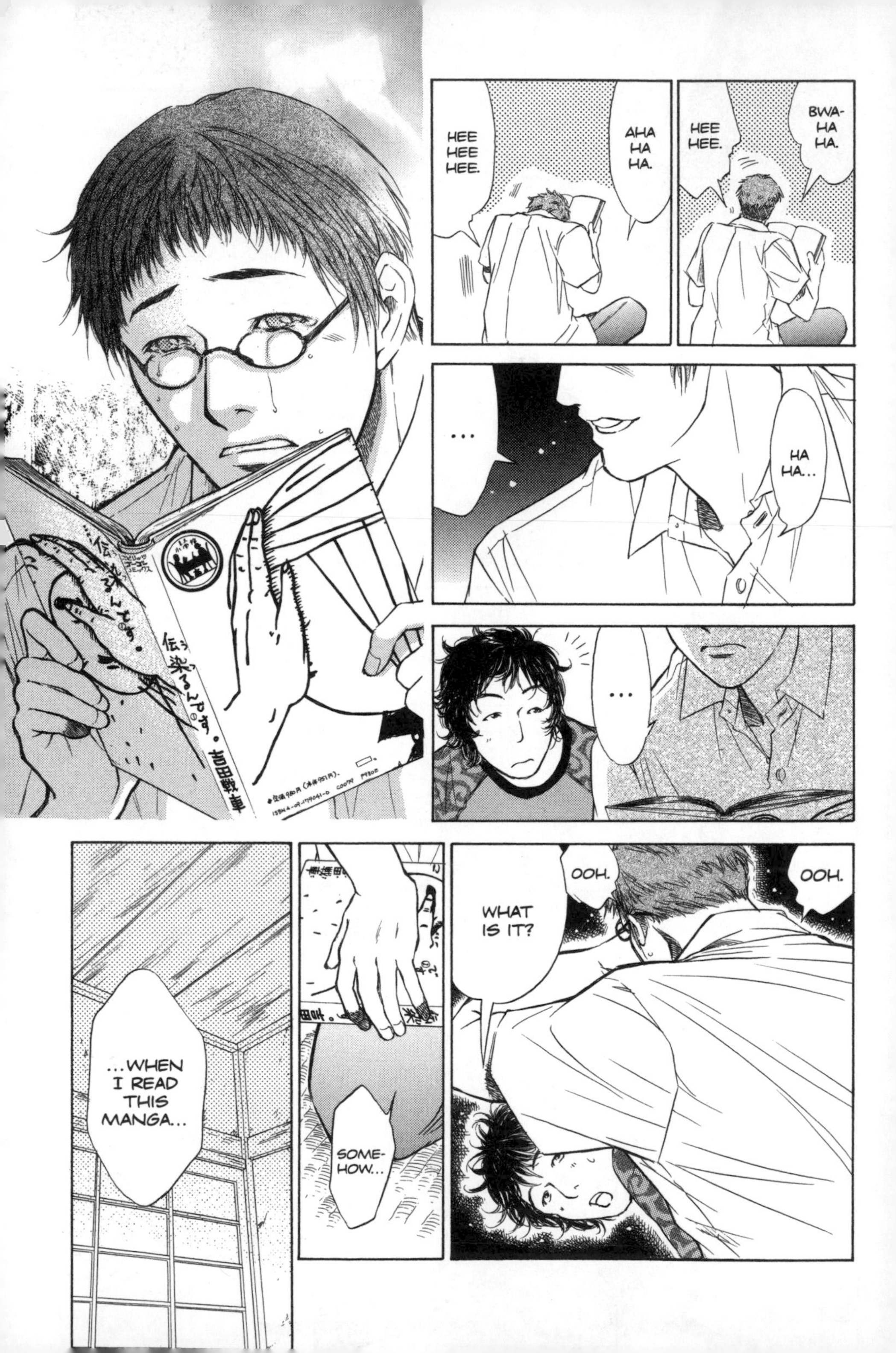
BWA-HA HA.
HEE HEE.
AHA HA HA.
HEE HEE HEE.
HA HA...
...
...
伝染るんです。
吉田戦車
OOH.
OOH.
WHAT IS IT?
SOME-HOW...
...WHEN I READ THIS MANGA...

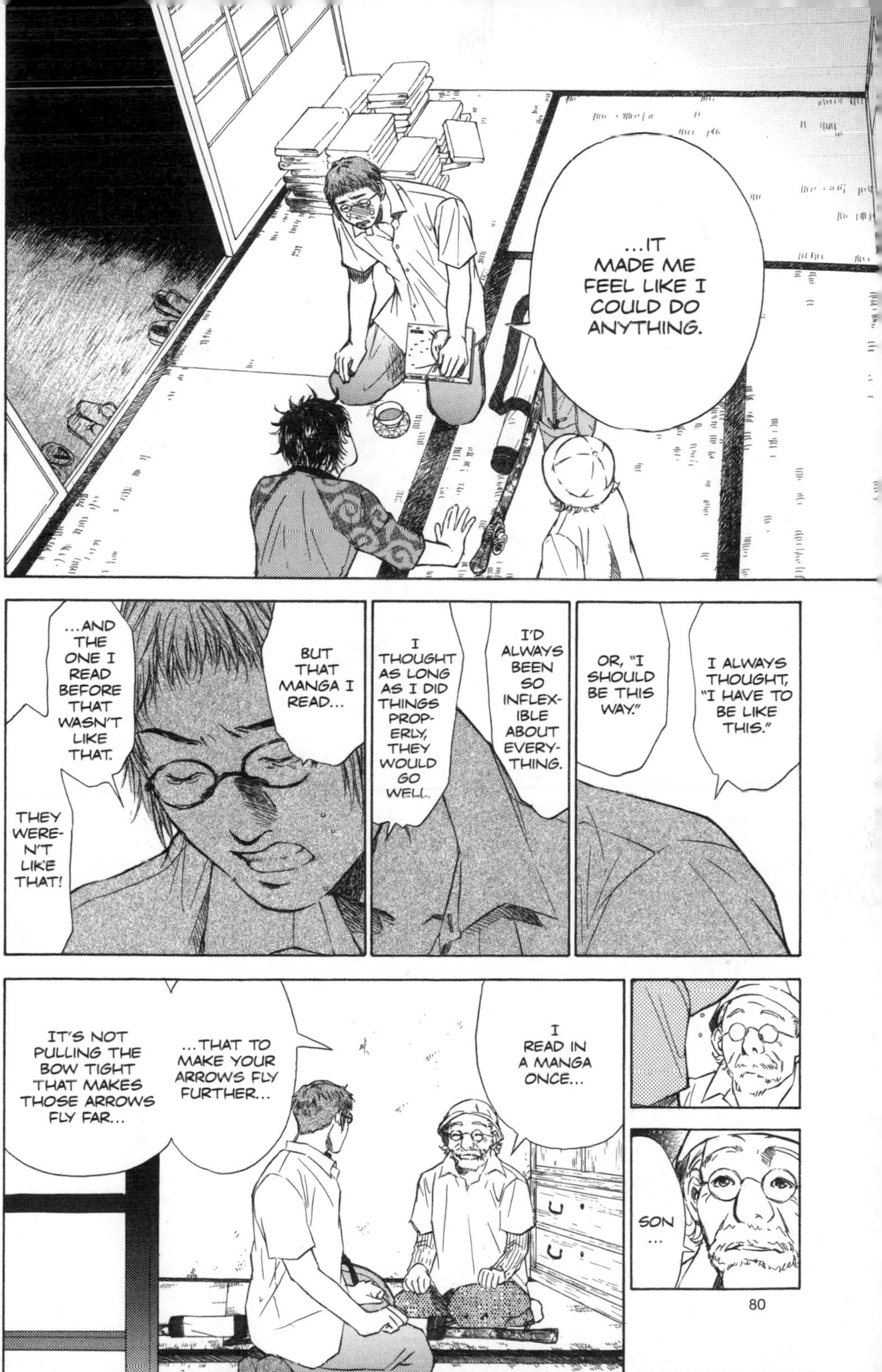
...IT MADE ME FEEL LIKE I COULD DO ANYTHING.
I ALWAYS THOUGHT, "I HAVE TO BE LIKE THIS."
OR, "I SHOULD BE THIS WAY."
I'D ALWAYS BEEN SO INFLEXIBLE ABOUT EVERYTHING.
I THOUGHT AS LONG AS I DID THINGS PROPERLY, THEY WOULD GO WELL.
BUT THAT MANGA I READ...
...AND THE ONE I READ BEFORE THAT WASN'T LIKE THAT.
THEY WEREN'T LIKE THAT!
SON ...
I READ IN A MANGA ONCE...
...THAT TO MAKE YOUR ARROWS FLY FURTHER...
IT'S NOT PULLING THE BOW TIGHT THAT MAKES THOSE ARROWS FLY FAR...

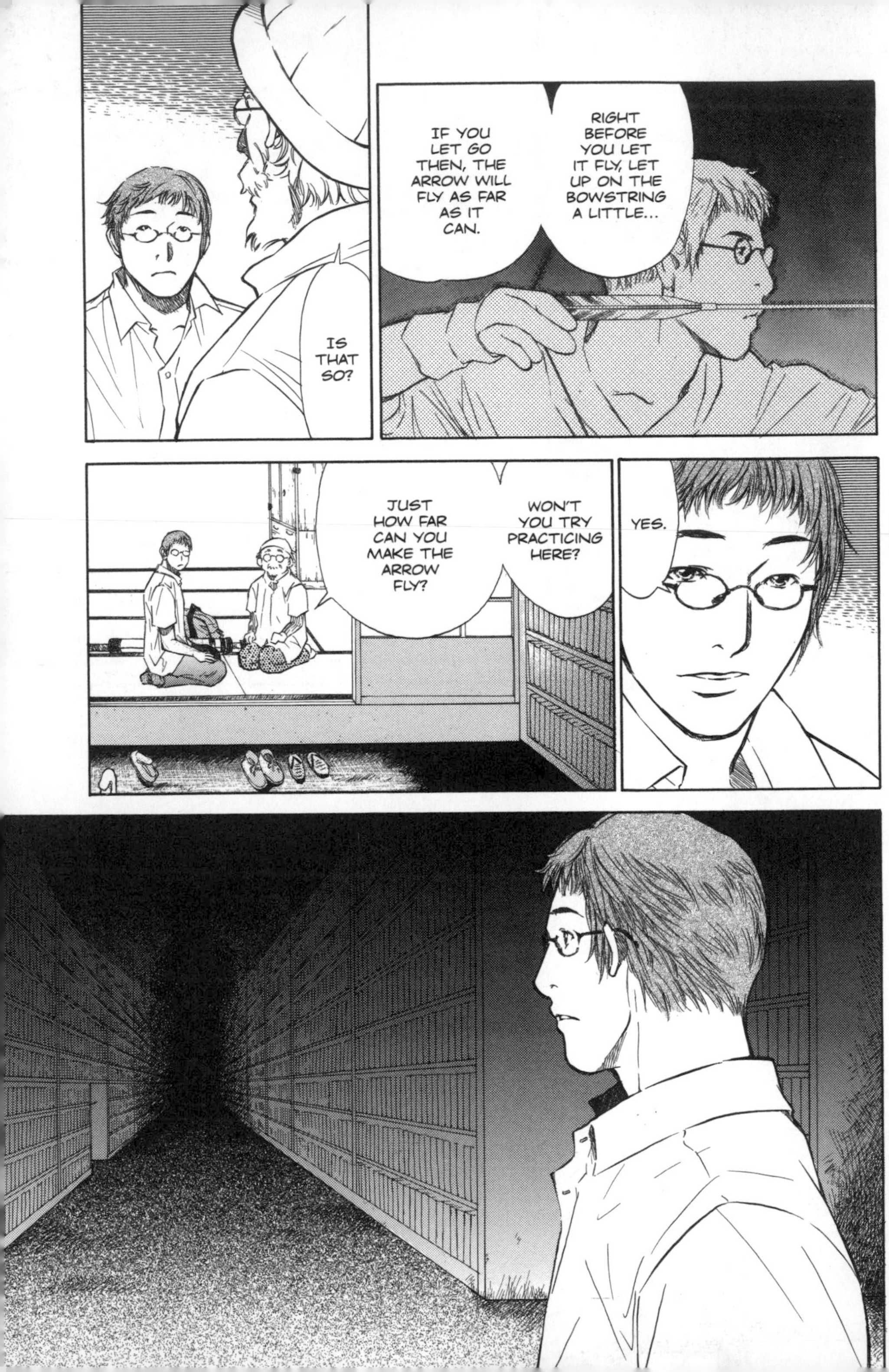
RIGHT BEFORE YOU LET IT FLY, LET UP ON THE BOWSTRING A LITTLE...
IF YOU LET GO THEN, THE ARROW WILL FLY AS FAR AS IT CAN.
IS THAT SO?
YES.
WON'T YOU TRY PRACTICING HERE?
JUST HOW FAR CAN YOU MAKE THE ARROW FLY?

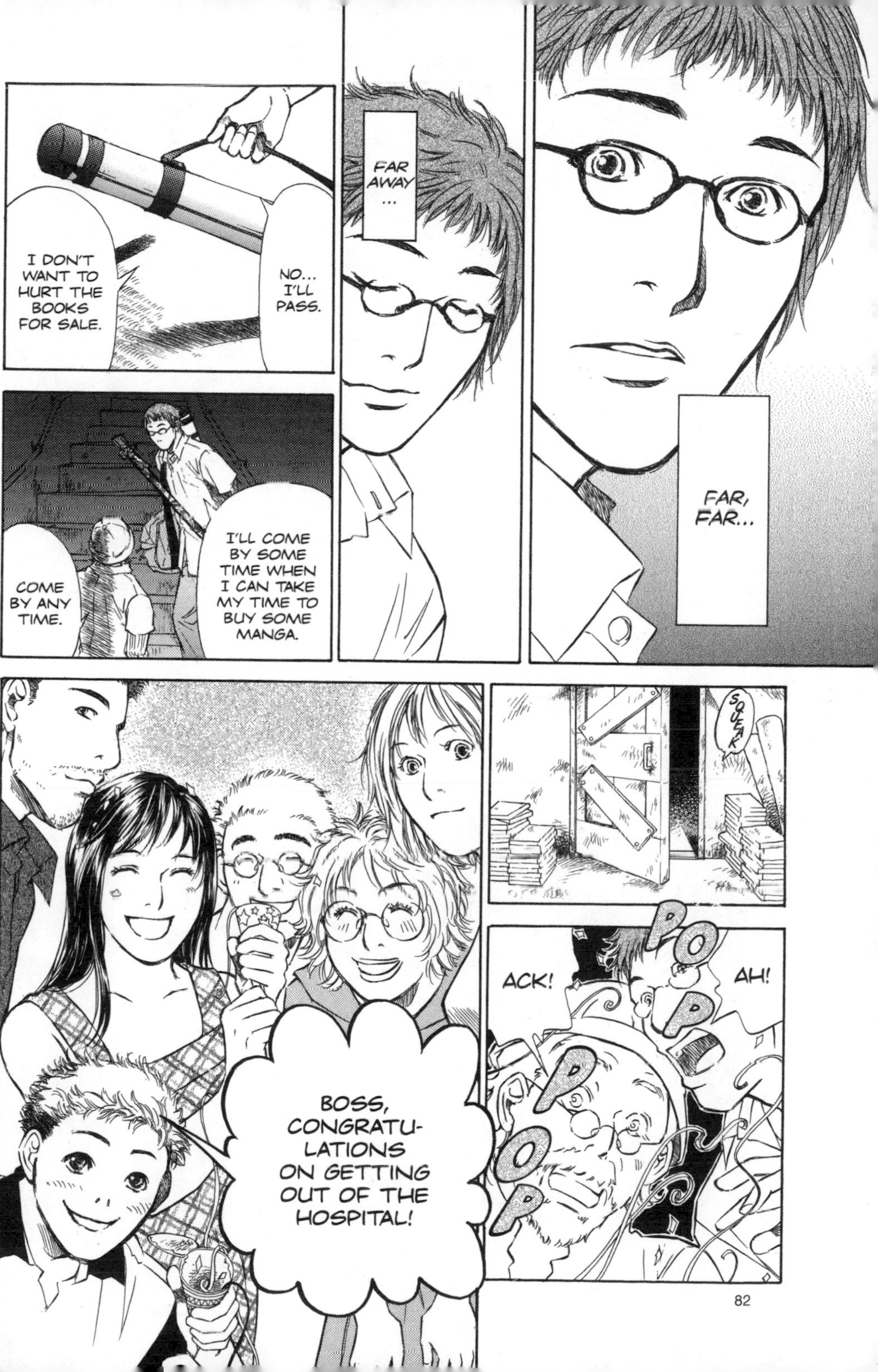
FAR, FAR...
FAR AWAY ...
NO... I'LL PASS.
I DON'T WANT TO HURT THE BOOKS FOR SALE.
I'LL COME BY SOME TIME WHEN I CAN TAKE MY TIME TO BUY SOME MANGA.
COME BY ANY TIME.
SQUEAK
POP
AH!
ACK!
POP
BOSS, CONGRATULATIONS ON GETTING OUT OF THE HOSPITAL!

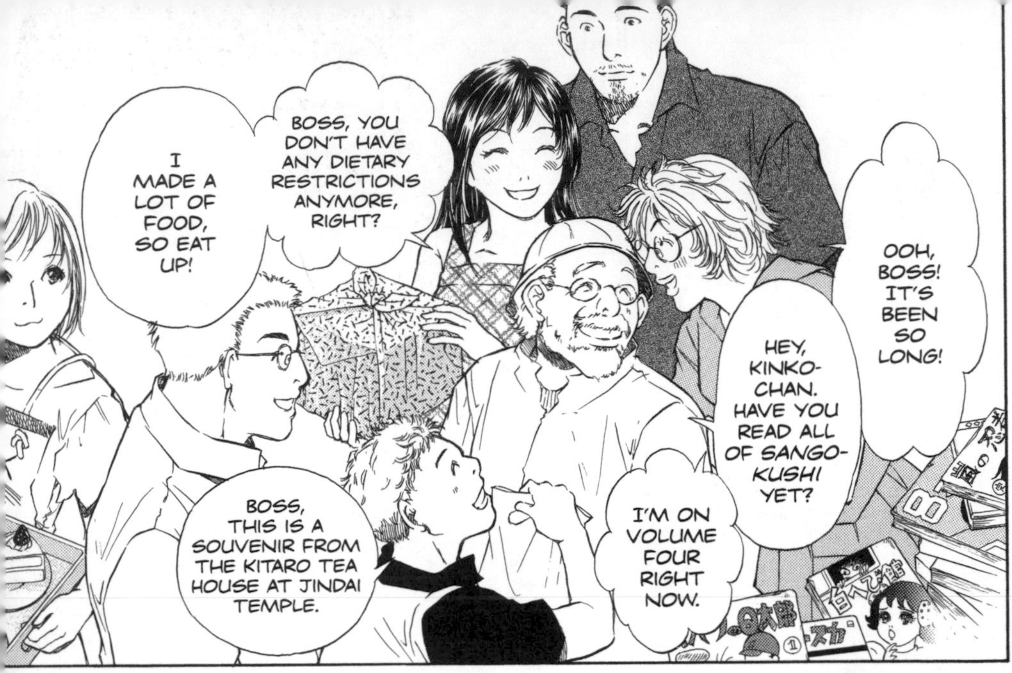
OOH, BOSS! IT'S BEEN SO LONG!
HEY, KINKO-CHAN. HAVE YOU READ ALL OF SANGO-KUSHI YET?
BOSS, YOU DON'T HAVE ANY DIETARY RESTRICTIONS ANYMORE, RIGHT?
I MADE A LOT OF FOOD, SO EAT UP!
I'M ON VOLUME FOUR RIGHT NOW.
BOSS, THIS IS A SOUVENIR FROM THE KITARO TEA HOUSE AT JINDAI TEMPLE.

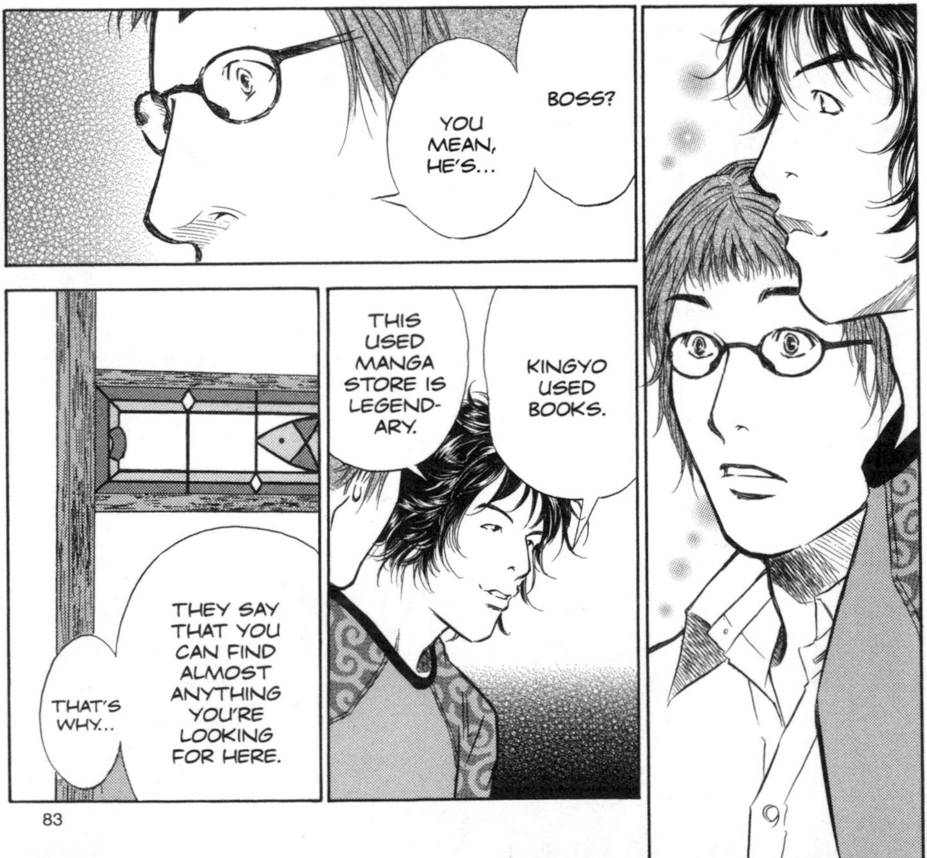
BOSS?
YOU MEAN, HE'S...
KINGYO USED BOOKS.
THIS USED MANGA STORE IS LEGEND-ARY.
THEY SAY THAT YOU CAN FIND ALMOST ANYTHING YOU'RE LOOKING FOR HERE.
THAT'S WHY...

STUDY!

SANGOKUSHI, BY MITSUTERU YOKOYAMA. PUBLISHED IN 1971 IN *KIBO NO TOMO*. *USHIO SHUPPAN* THE SERIES RECOUNTS CHINESE HISTORY, AND CONTINUED RUNNING THROUGH SEVERAL DIFFERENT MAGAZINES FOR 15 YEARS. CURRENTLY AVAILABLE FROM KIBO COMICS (60 VOLUMES) AND *USHIO BUNKO* (30 VOLUMES).

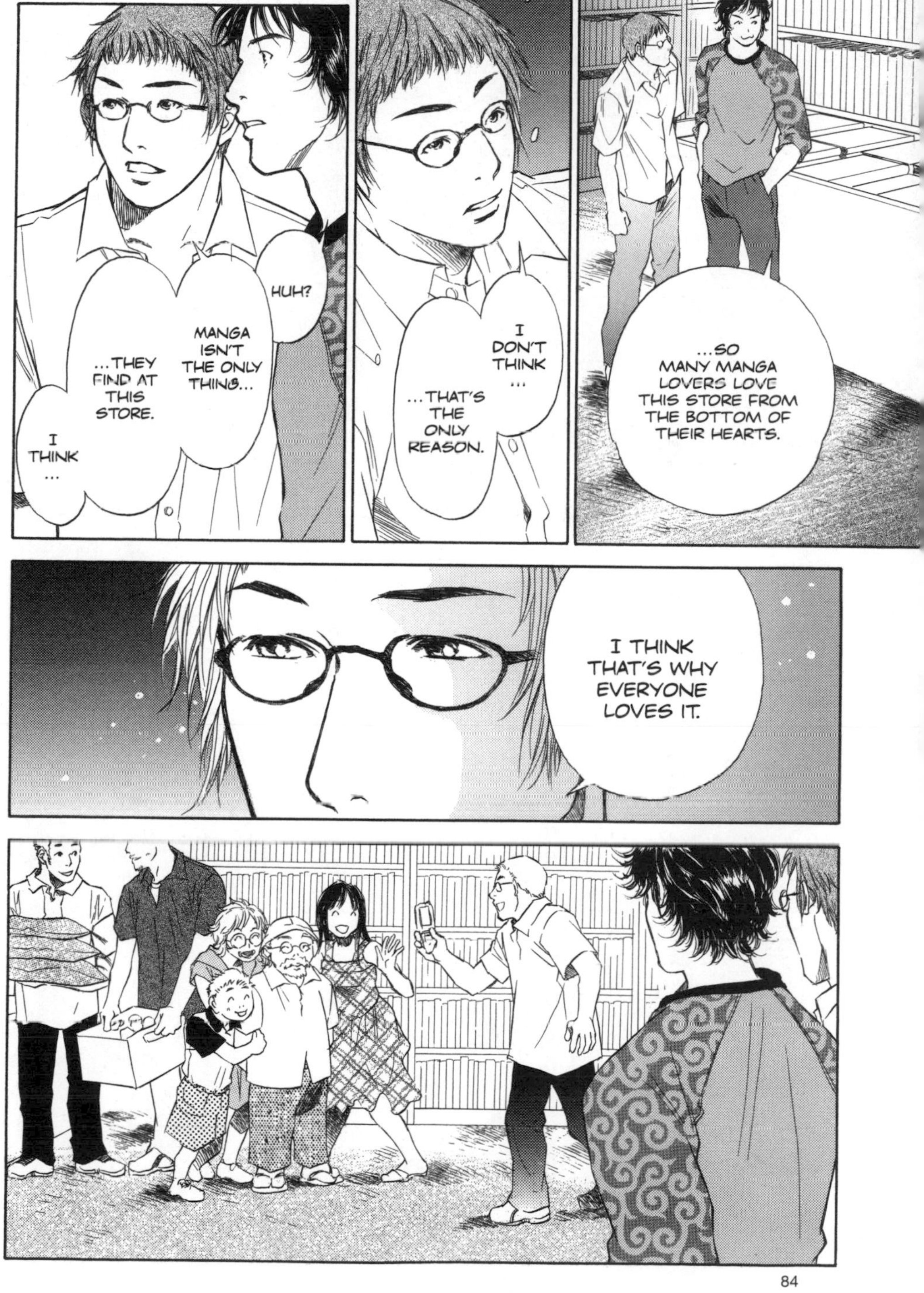
...SO MANY MANGA LOVERS LOVE THIS STORE FROM THE BOTTOM OF THEIR HEARTS.
I DON'T THINK ...
...THAT'S THE ONLY REASON.
HUH?
MANGA ISN'T THE ONLY THING...
...THEY FIND AT THIS STORE.
I THINK ...
I THINK THAT'S WHY EVERYONE LOVES IT.

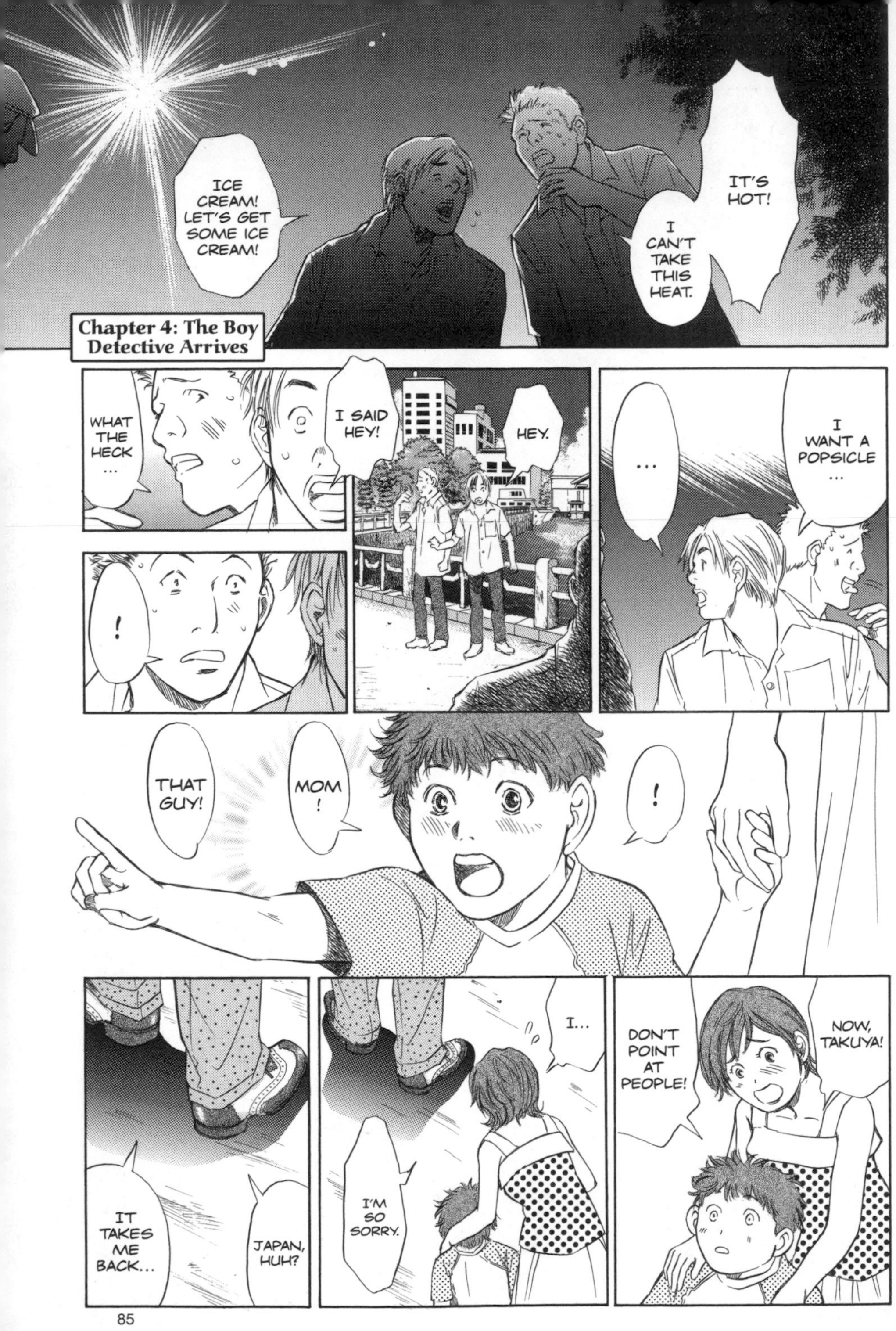
IT'S HOT!
I CAN'T TAKE THIS HEAT.
ICE CREAM! LET'S GET SOME ICE CREAM!
Chapter 4: The Boy Detective Arrives
I WANT A POPSICLE...
...
HEY.
I SAID HEY!
WHAT THE HECK...
!
!
MOM!
THAT GUY!
NOW, TAKUYA!
DON'T POINT AT PEOPLE!
I...
I'M SO SORRY.
JAPAN, HUH?
IT TAKES ME BACK...

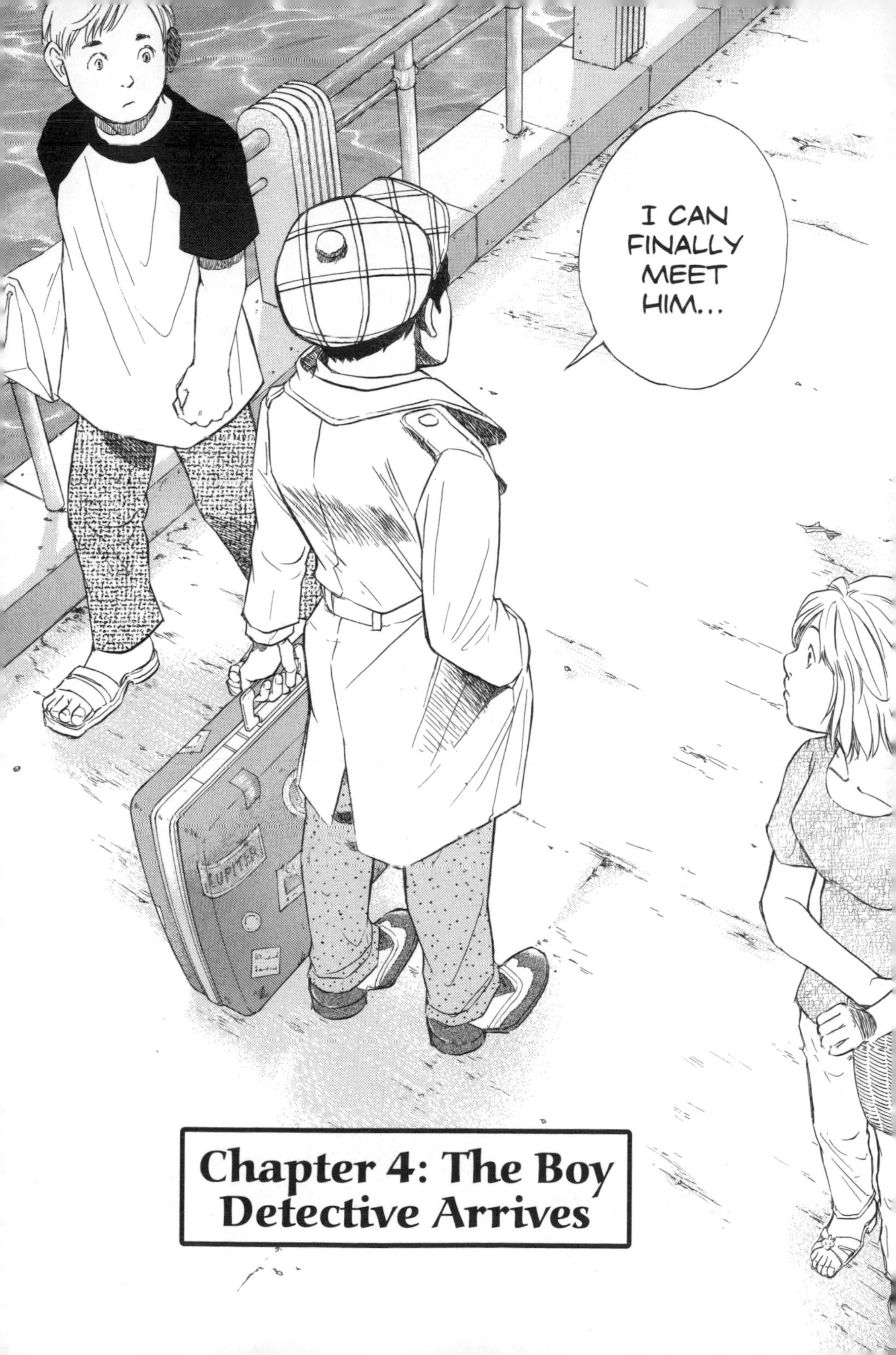
I CAN FINALLY MEET HIM...

Chapter 4: The Boy Detective Arrives

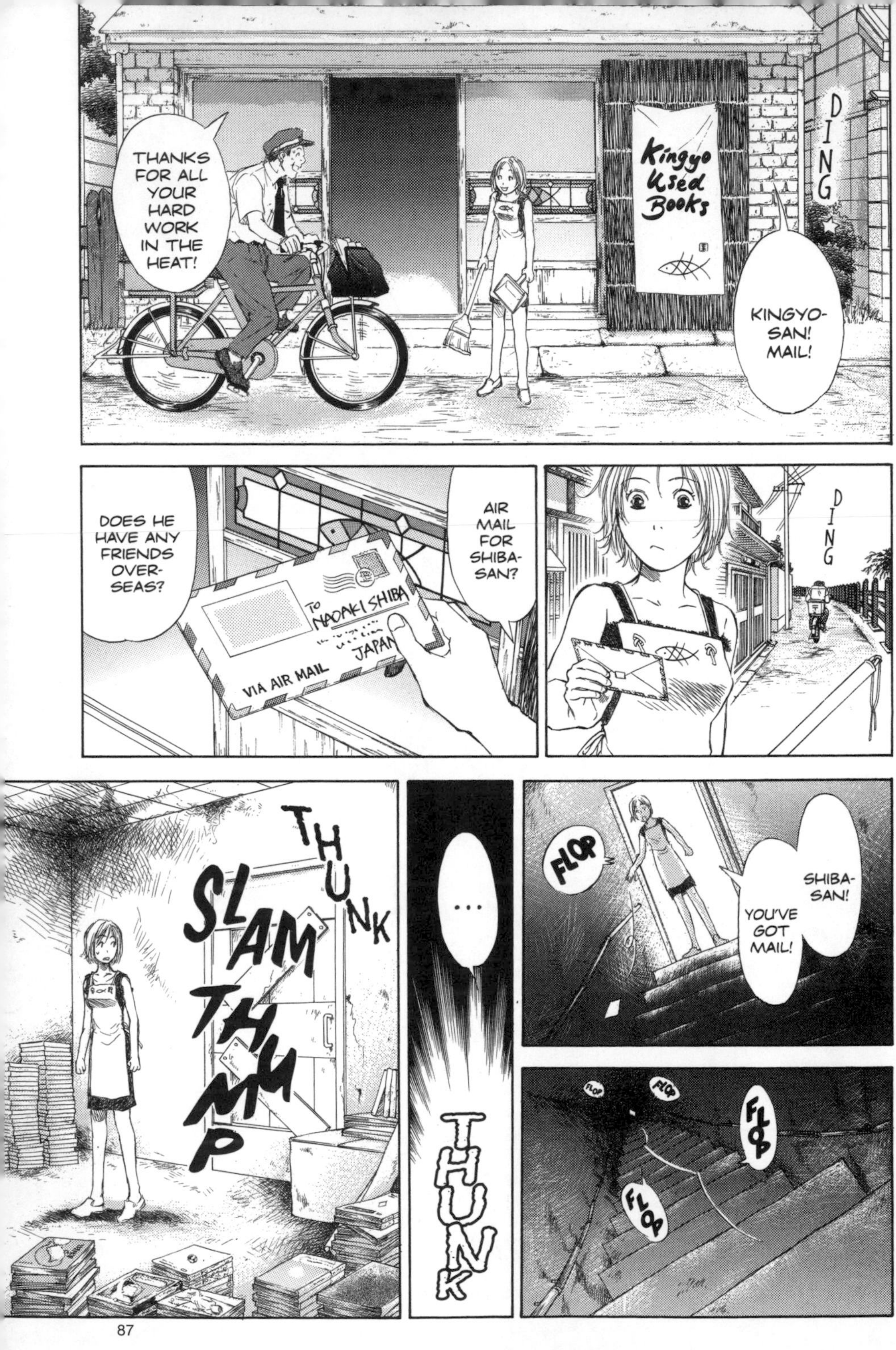
DING
KINGYO-SAN! MAIL!
Kingyo Used Books
THANKS FOR ALL YOUR HARD WORK IN THE HEAT!
DING
AIR MAIL FOR SHIBA-SAN?
DOES HE HAVE ANY FRIENDS OVER-SEAS?
TO NAOAKI SHIBA
JAPAN
VIA AIR MAIL
SHIBA-SAN!
YOU'VE GOT MAIL!
FLOP
FLOP
FLOP
FLOP
FLOP
...
THUNK
THUNK
SLAM
THUMP

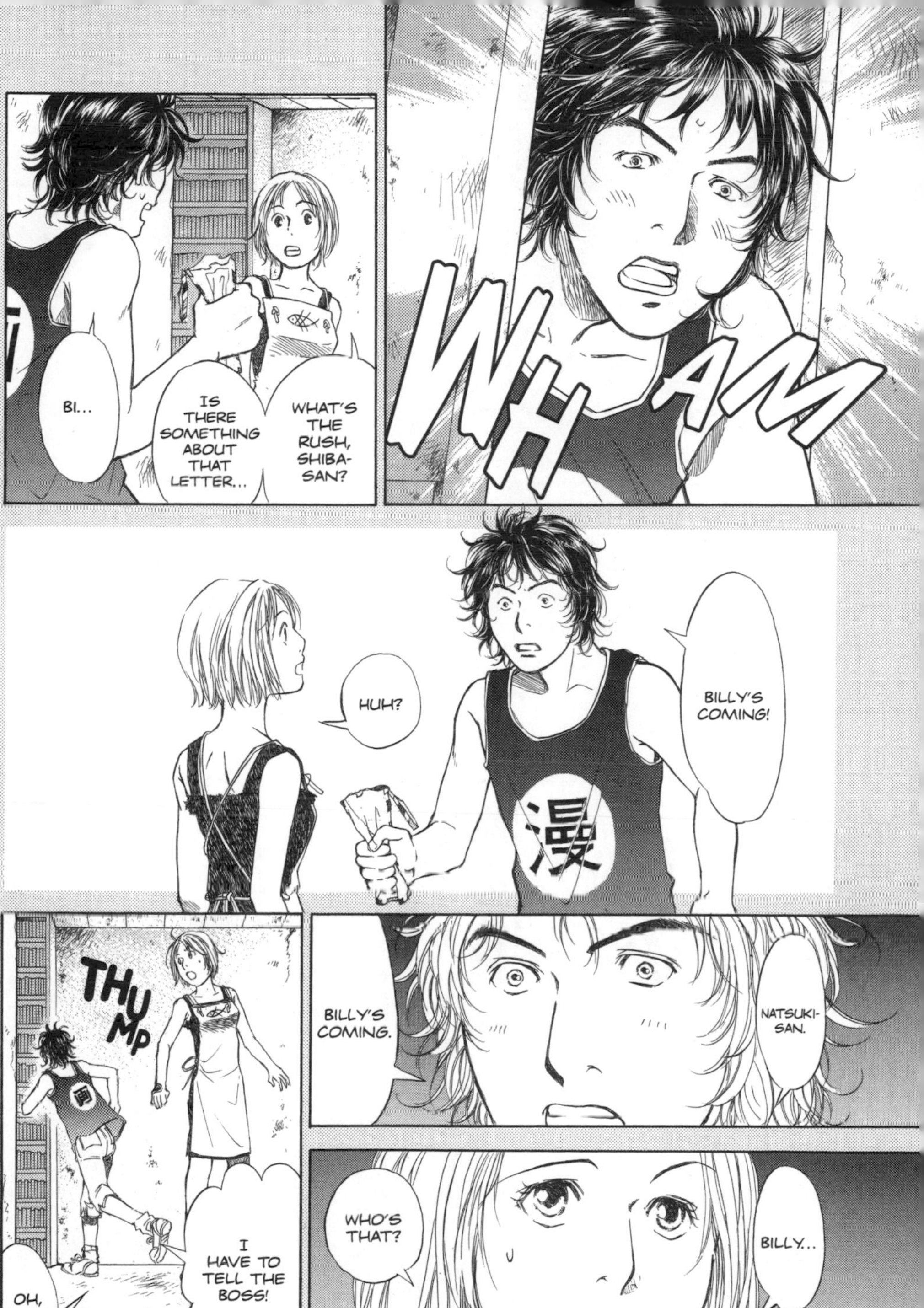
WHAM
WHAT'S THE RUSH, SHIBA-SAN?
IS THERE SOMETHING ABOUT THAT LETTER...
BI...
BILLY'S COMING!
HUH?
漫
NATSUKI-SAN.
BILLY'S COMING.
BILLY...
WHO'S THAT?
THUMP
I HAVE TO TELL THE BOSS!
OH, HEY!

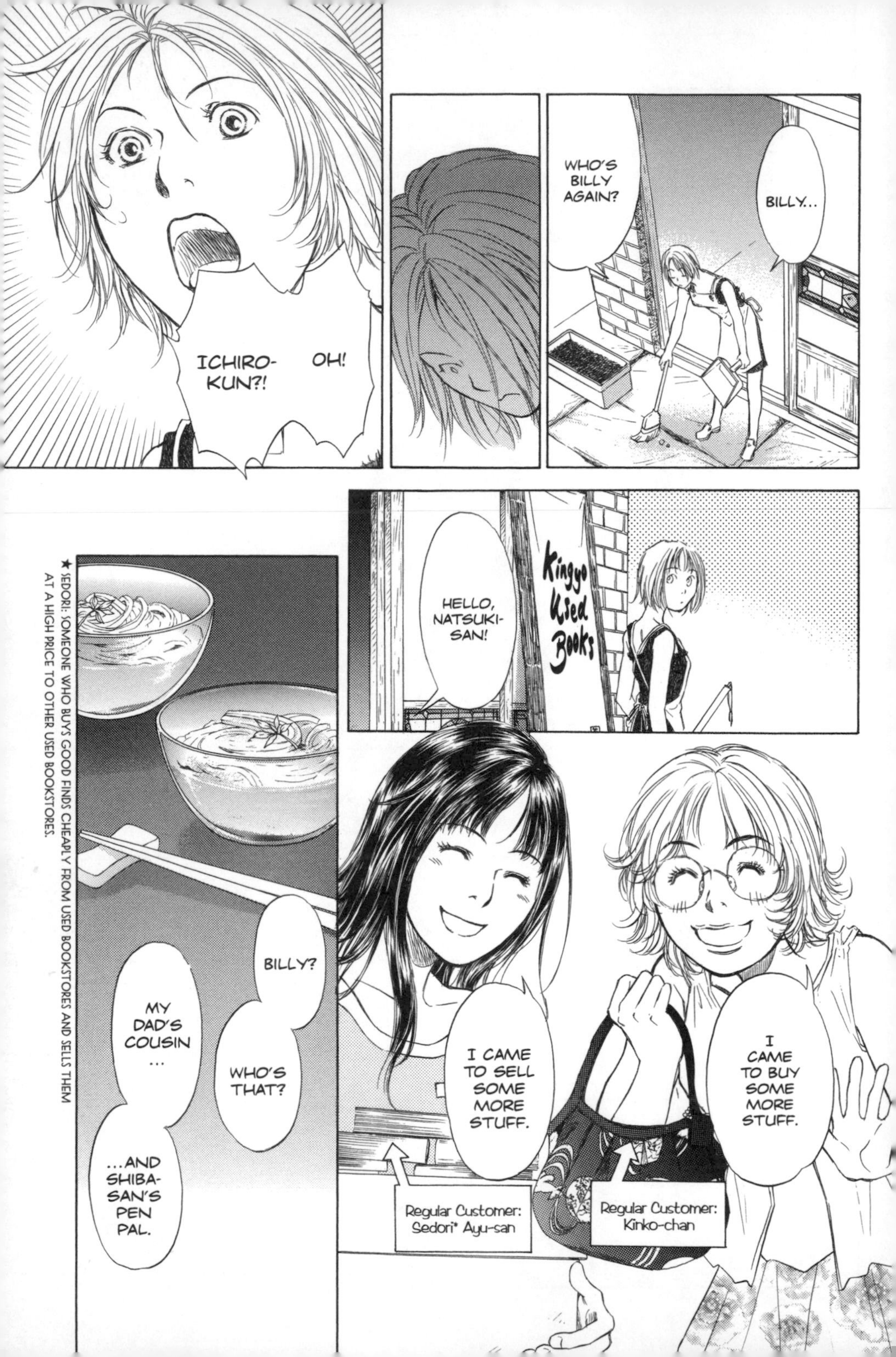
BILLY...
WHO'S BILLY AGAIN?
OH! ICHIRO-KUN?!
HELLO, NATSUKI-SAN!
Kingyo Used Books
I CAME TO BUY SOME MORE STUFF.
I CAME TO SELL SOME MORE STUFF.
Regular Customer: Kinko-chan
Regular Customer: Sedori* Ayu-san
BILLY?
WHO'S THAT?
MY DAD'S COUSIN ...
...AND SHIBA-SAN'S PEN PAL.

★ SEDORI: SOMEONE WHO BUYS GOOD FINDS CHEAPLY FROM USED BOOKSTORES AND SELLS THEM AT A HIGH PRICE TO OTHER USED BOOKSTORES.

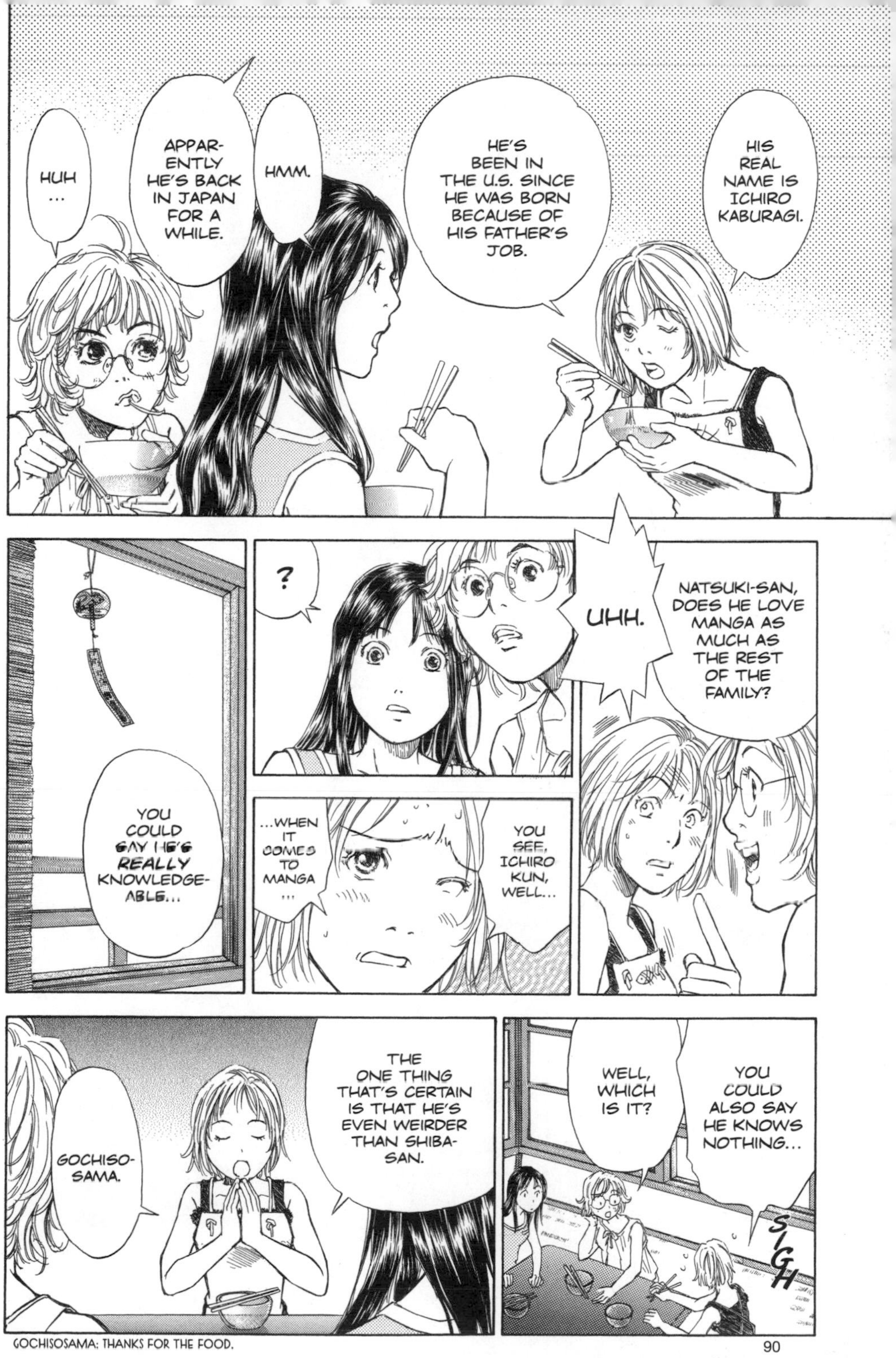
HIS REAL NAME IS ICHIRO KABURAGI.
HE'S BEEN IN THE U.S. SINCE HE WAS BORN BECAUSE OF HIS FATHER'S JOB.
HMM.
APPAR-ENTLY HE'S BACK IN JAPAN FOR A WHILE.
HUH ...
NATSUKI-SAN, DOES HE LOVE MANGA AS MUCH AS THE REST OF THE FAMILY?
UHH.
?
YOU SEE, ICHIRO KUN, WELL...
...WHEN IT COMES TO MANGA ...
YOU COULD SAY HE'S *REALLY* KNOWLEDGE-ABLE...
YOU COULD ALSO SAY HE KNOWS NOTHING...
WELL, WHICH IS IT?
SIGH
THE ONE THING THAT'S CERTAIN IS THAT HE'S EVEN WEIRDER THAN SHIBA-SAN.
GOCHISO-SAMA.

GOCHISOSAMA: THANKS FOR THE FOOD.

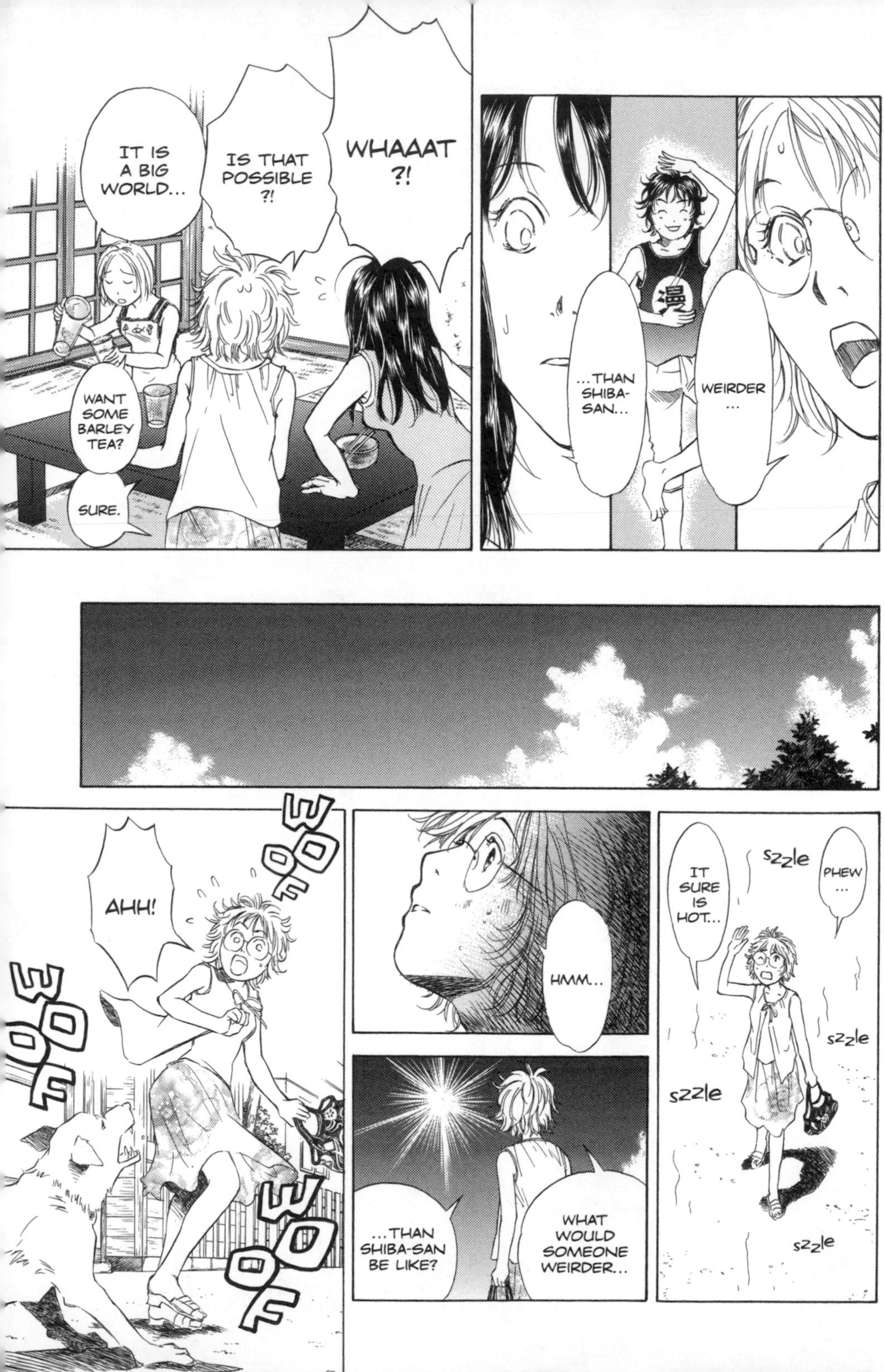
WEIRDER...
...THAN SHIBA-SAN...
WHAAAT?!
IS THAT POSSIBLE?!
IT IS A BIG WORLD...
WANT SOME BARLEY TEA?
SURE.
PHEW...
szzle
IT SURE IS HOT...
szzle
szzle
szzle
HMM...
WHAT WOULD SOMEONE WEIRDER...
...THAN SHIBA-SAN BE LIKE?
WOOF
AHH!
WOOF
WOOF

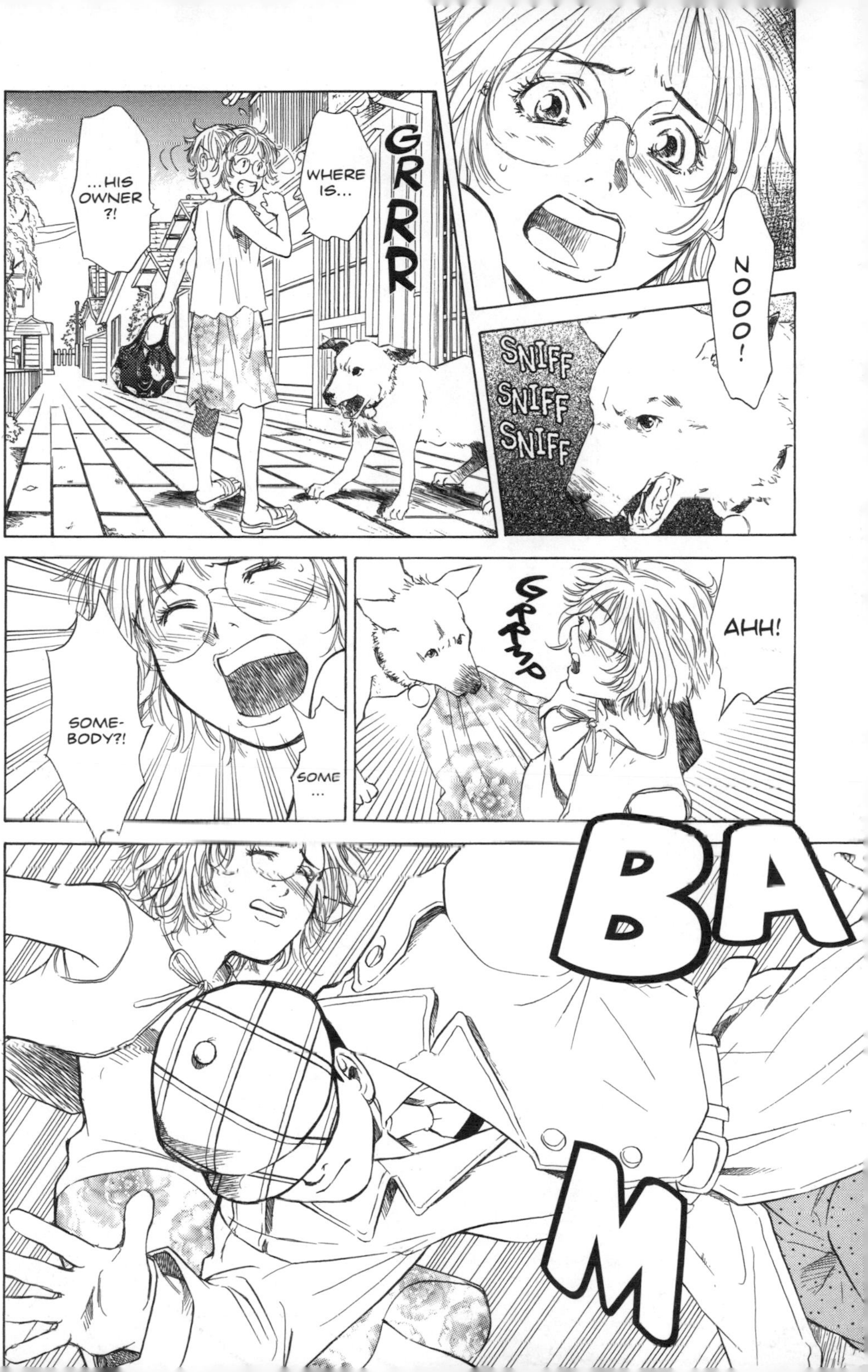
NOOOO!
SNIFF SNIFF SNIFF
GRRR
WHERE IS...
...HIS OWNER?!
AHH!
GRRMP
SOME...
SOME-BODY?!
BAM

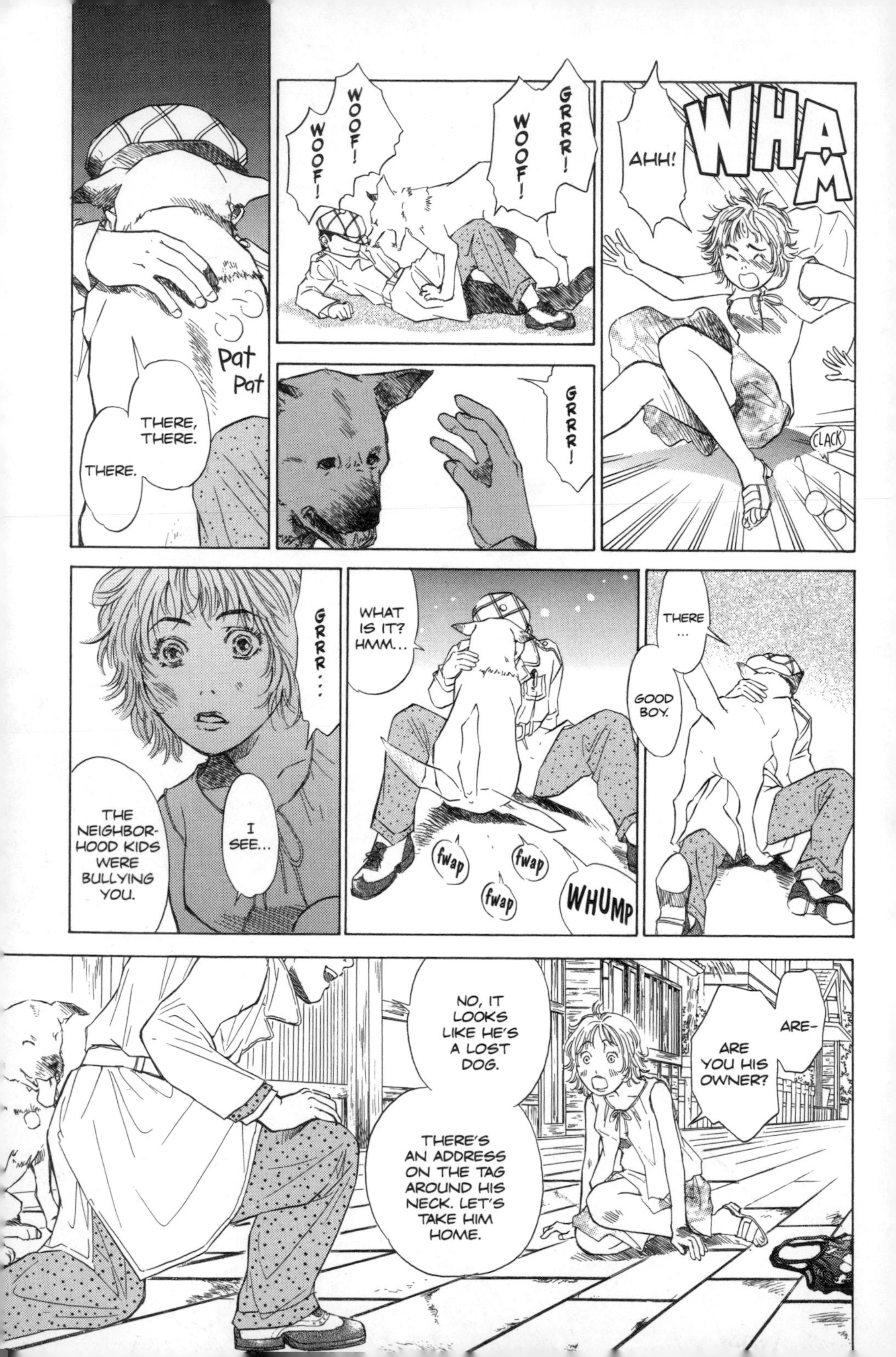
WHAM
AHH!
CLACK
GRRR! WOOF!
WOOF! WOOF!
GRRR!
Pat Pat
THERE, THERE.
THERE.
THERE...
GOOD BOY.
WHAT IS IT? HMM...
fwap
fwap
fwap
WHUMP
GRRR...
I SEE...
THE NEIGHBOR-HOOD KIDS WERE BULLYING YOU.
ARE-
ARE YOU HIS OWNER?
NO, IT LOOKS LIKE HE'S A LOST DOG.
THERE'S AN ADDRESS ON THE TAG AROUND HIS NECK. LET'S TAKE HIM HOME.

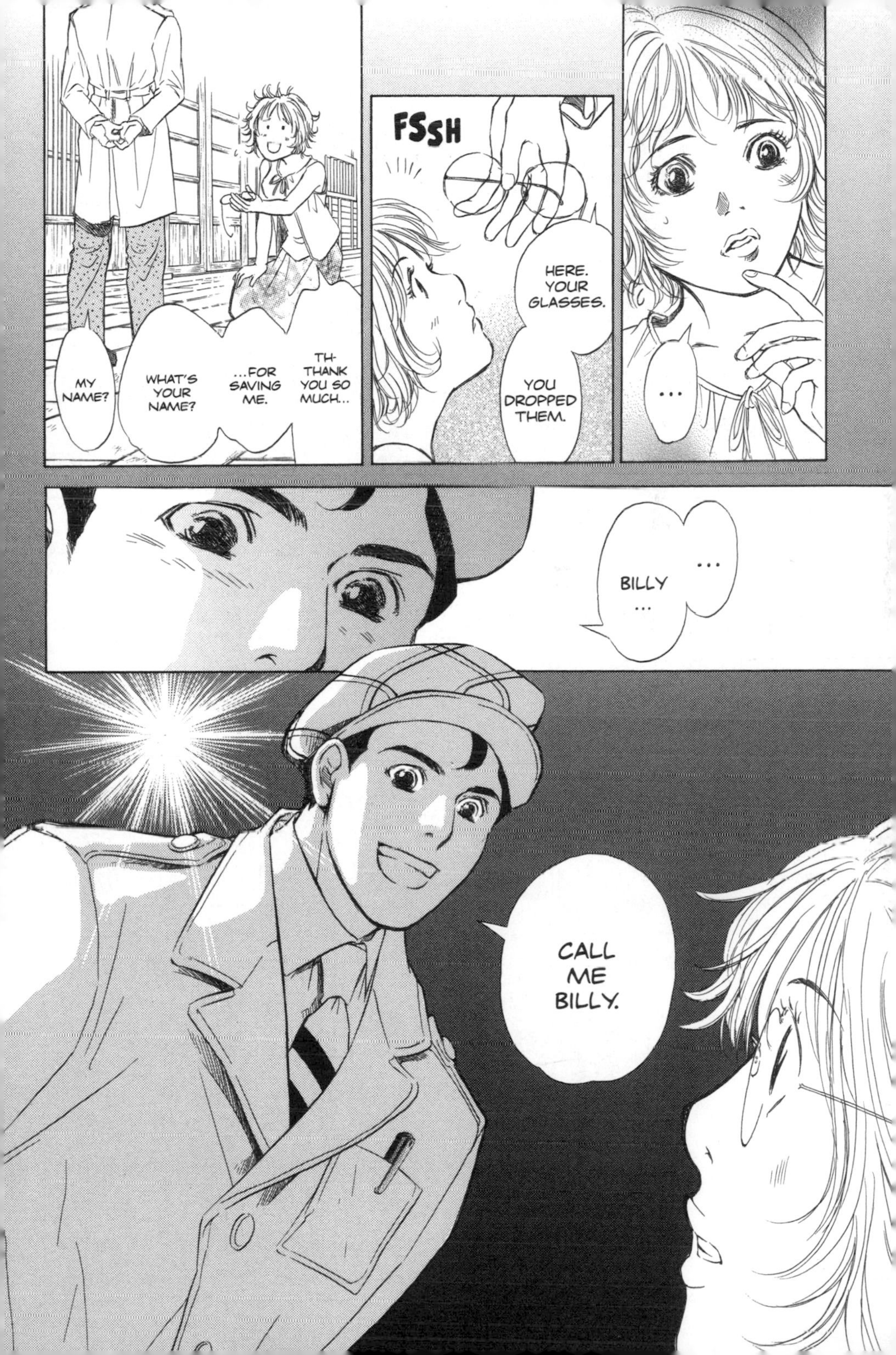
...
FSSH
HERE. YOUR GLASSES.
YOU DROPPED THEM.
TH-THANK YOU SO MUCH...
...FOR SAVING ME.
WHAT'S YOUR NAME?
MY NAME?
... BILLY ...
CALL ME BILLY.

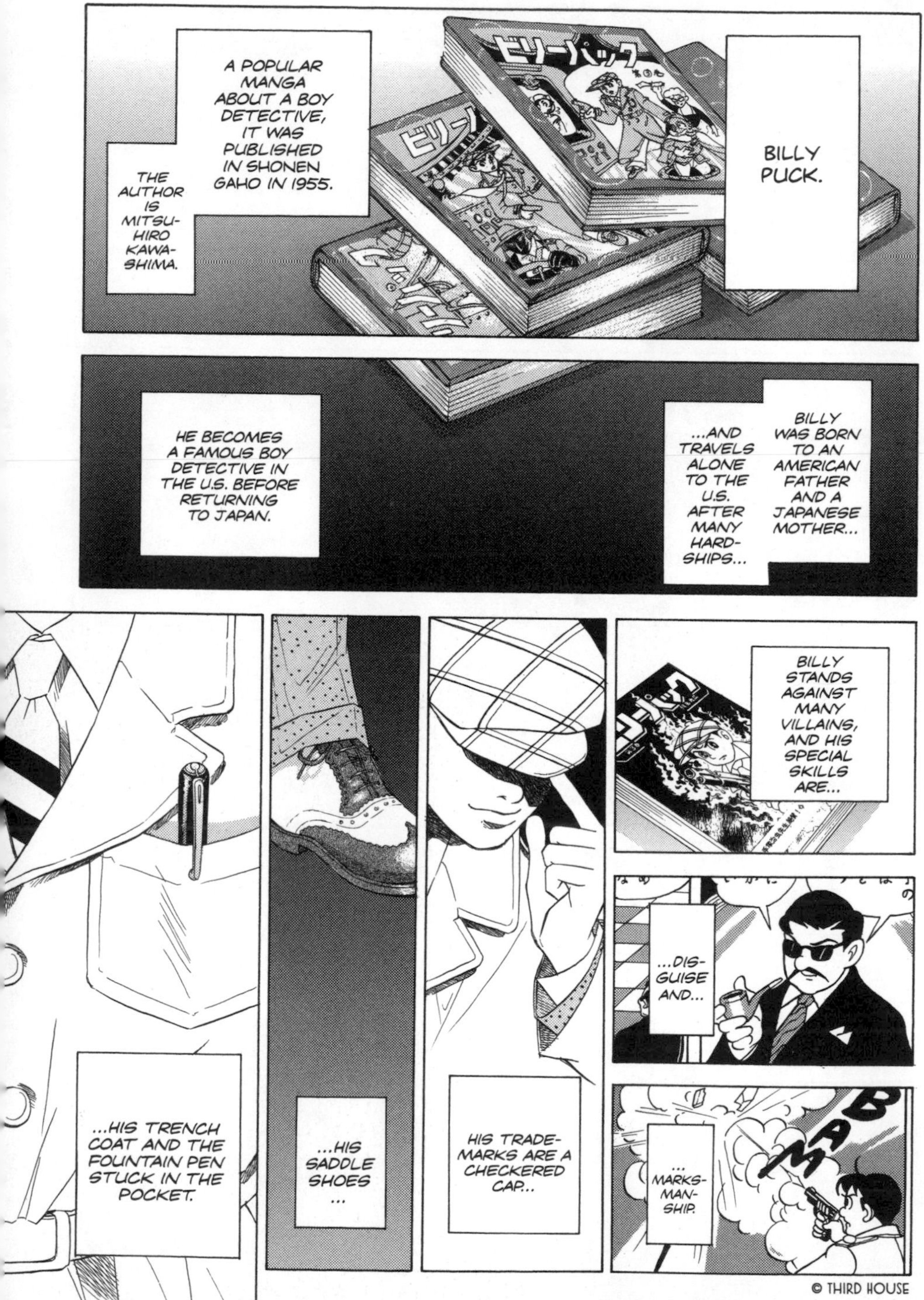
BILLY PUCK.
A POPULAR MANGA ABOUT A BOY DETECTIVE, IT WAS PUBLISHED IN SHONEN GAHO IN 1955.
THE AUTHOR IS MITSU-HIRO KAWA-SHIMA.
ビリーパック
BILLY WAS BORN TO AN AMERICAN FATHER AND A JAPANESE MOTHER...
...AND TRAVELS ALONE TO THE U.S. AFTER MANY HARD-SHIPS...
HE BECOMES A FAMOUS BOY DETECTIVE IN THE U.S. BEFORE RETURNING TO JAPAN.
BILLY STANDS AGAINST MANY VILLAINS, AND HIS SPECIAL SKILLS ARE...
...DIS-GUISE AND...
... MARKS-MAN-SHIP.
BAM
HIS TRADE-MARKS ARE A CHECKERED CAP...
...HIS SADDLE SHOES ...
...HIS TRENCH COAT AND THE FOUNTAIN PEN STUCK IN THE POCKET.

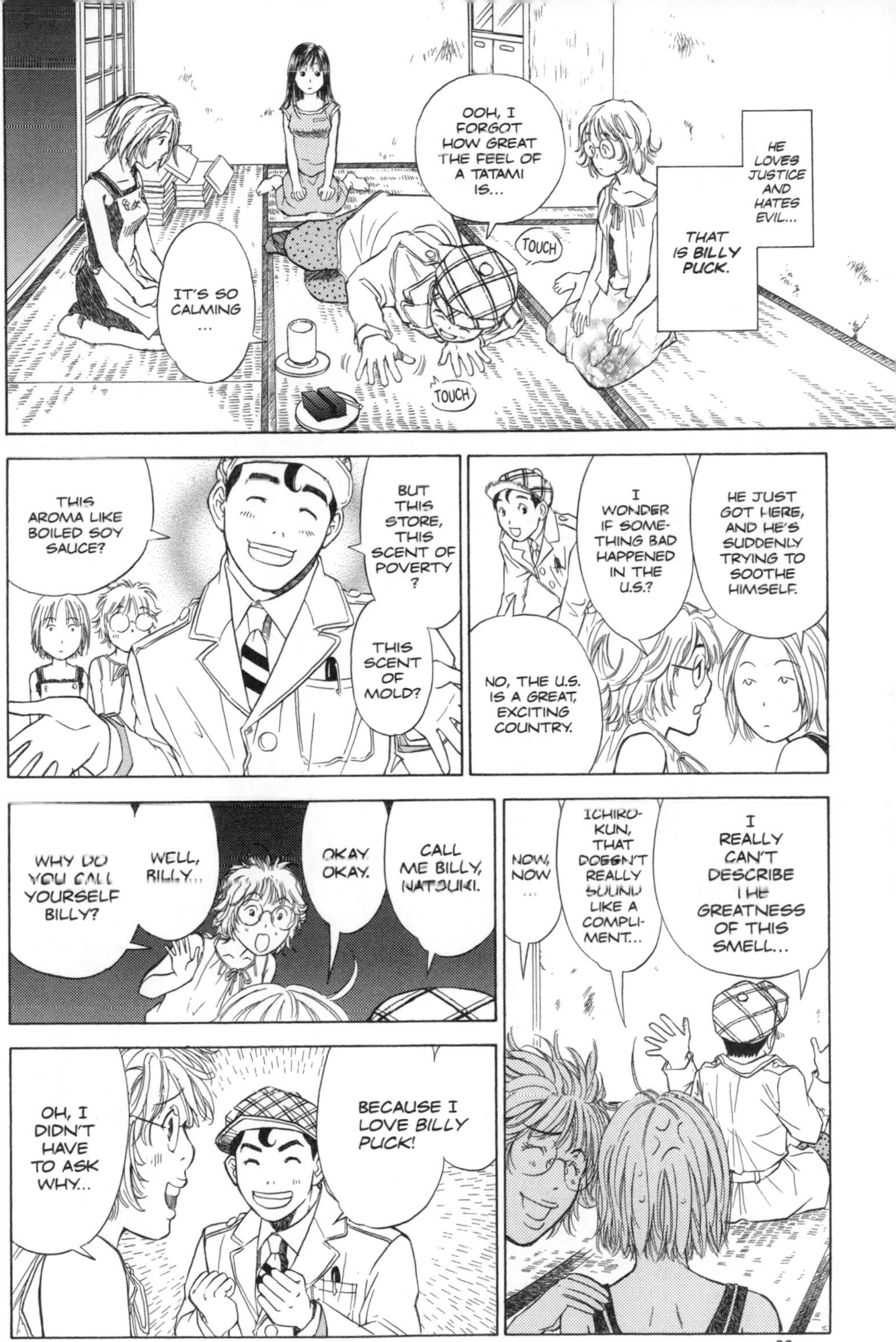
HE LOVES JUSTICE AND HATES EVIL...
THAT IS BILLY PUCK.
OOH, I FORGOT HOW GREAT THE FEEL OF A TATAMI IS...
TOUCH
IT'S SO CALMING ...
TOUCH
HE JUST GOT HERE, AND HE'S SUDDENLY TRYING TO SOOTHE HIMSELF.
I WONDER IF SOMETHING BAD HAPPENED IN THE U.S.?
NO, THE U.S. IS A GREAT, EXCITING COUNTRY.
BUT THIS STORE, THIS SCENT OF POVERTY?
THIS SCENT OF MOLD?
THIS AROMA LIKE BOILED SOY SAUCE?
I REALLY CAN'T DESCRIBE THE GREATNESS OF THIS SMELL...
ICHIRO-KUN, THAT DOESN'T REALLY SOUND LIKE A COMPLIMENT...
NOW, NOW ...
CALL ME BILLY, NATSUKI.
OKAY. OKAY.
WELL, BILLY...
WHY DO YOU CALL YOURSELF BILLY?
BECAUSE I LOVE BILLY PUCK!
OH, I DIDN'T HAVE TO ASK WHY...

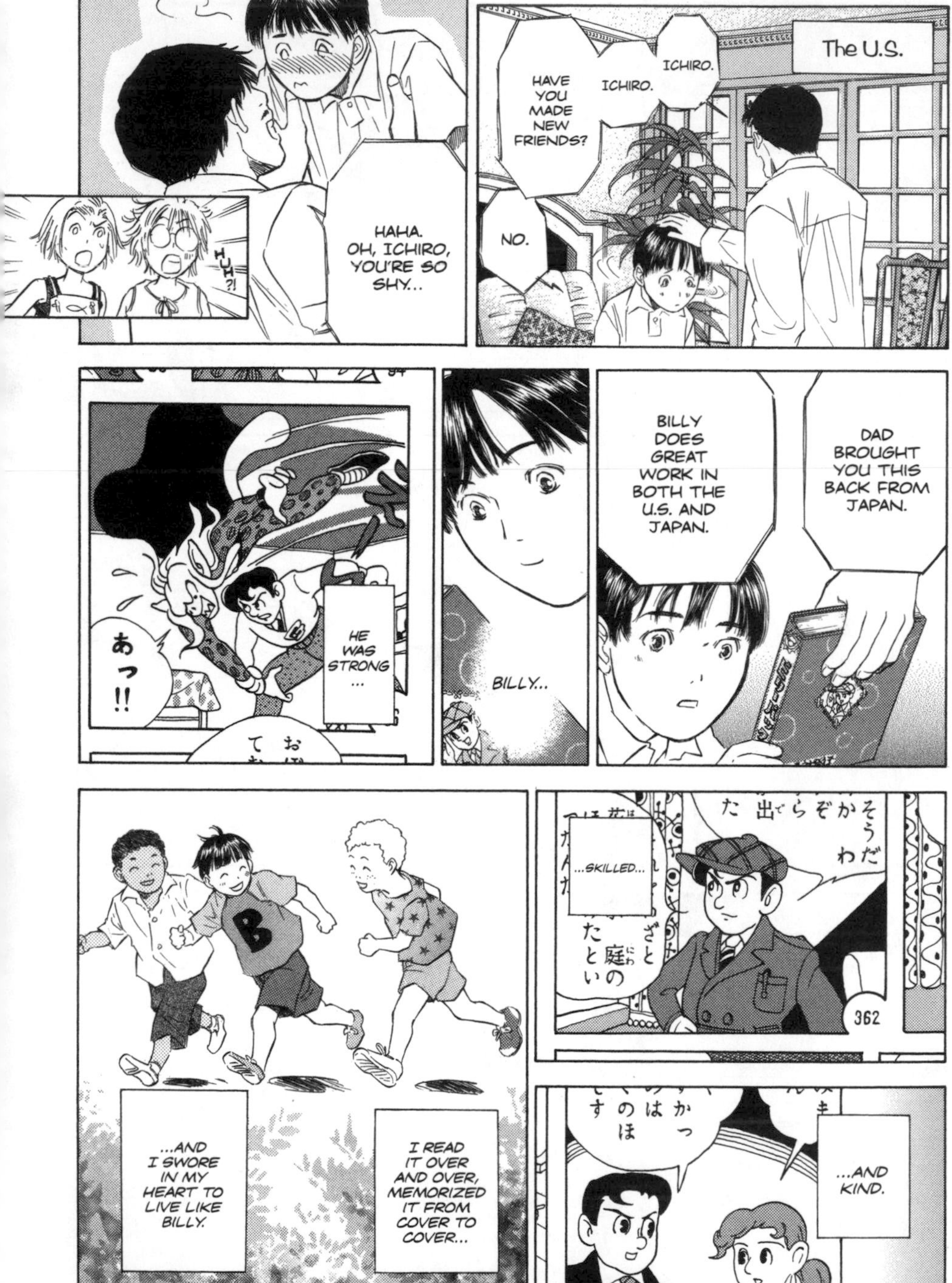

The U.S.
ICHIRO.
ICHIRO.
HAVE YOU MADE NEW FRIENDS?
NO.
HAHA. OH, ICHIRO, YOU'RE SO SHY...
HUH?!
DAD BROUGHT YOU THIS BACK FROM JAPAN.
BILLY DOES GREAT WORK IN BOTH THE U.S. AND JAPAN.
BILLY...
HE WAS STRONG...
あっ!!
...SKILLED...
362
...AND KIND.
I READ IT OVER AND OVER, MEMORIZED IT FROM COVER TO COVER...
...AND I SWORE IN MY HEART TO LIVE LIKE BILLY.

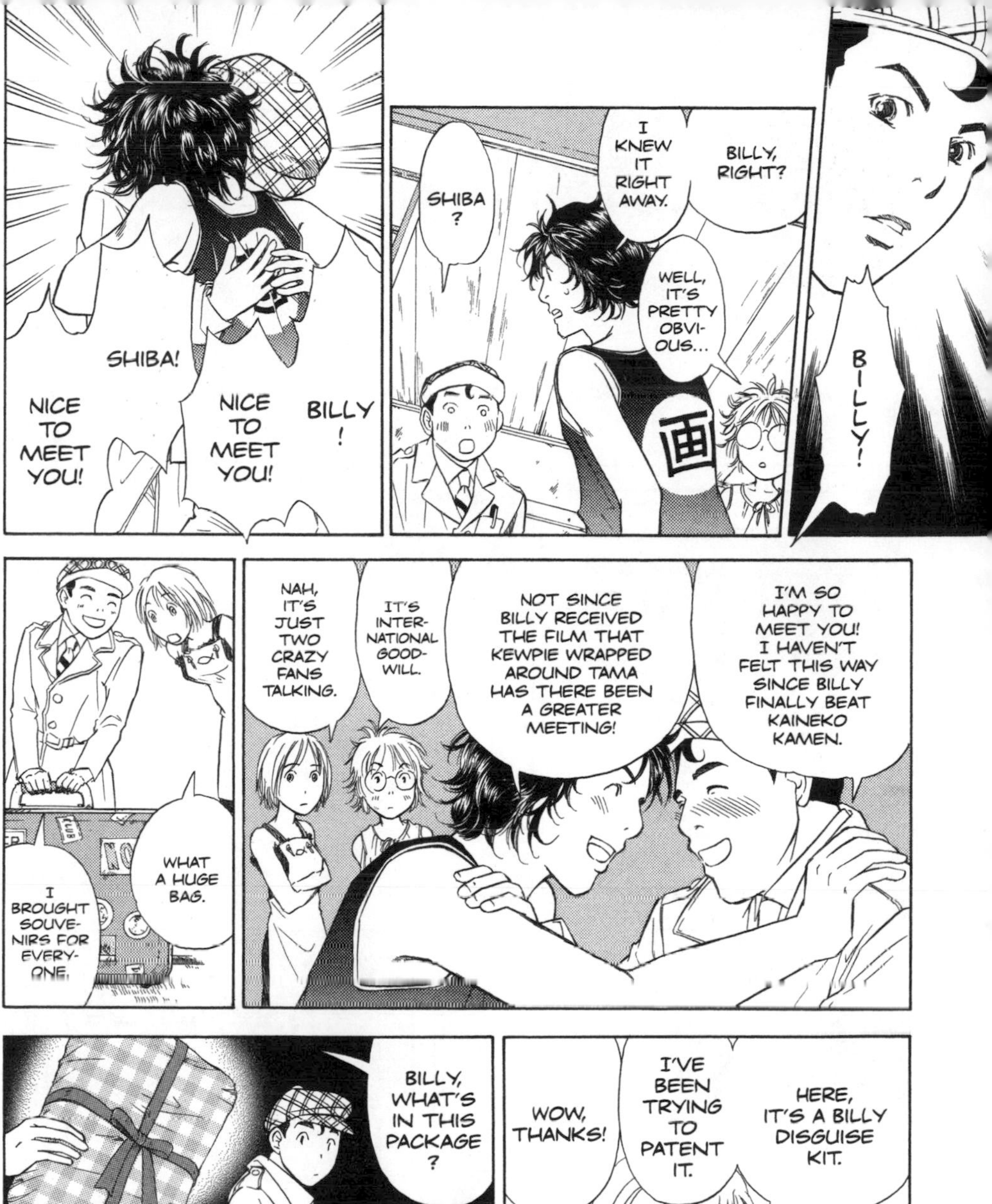

BILLY!
BILLY, RIGHT?
I KNEW IT RIGHT AWAY.
WELL, IT'S PRETTY OBVIOUS...
SHIBA?
BILLY!
NICE TO MEET YOU!
SHIBA!
NICE TO MEET YOU!
I'M SO HAPPY TO MEET YOU! I HAVEN'T FELT THIS WAY SINCE BILLY FINALLY BEAT KAINEKO KAMEN.
NOT SINCE BILLY RECEIVED THE FILM THAT KEWPIE WRAPPED AROUND TAMA HAS THERE BEEN A GREATER MEETING!
IT'S INTERNATIONAL GOODWILL.
NAH, IT'S JUST TWO CRAZY FANS TALKING.
WHAT A HUGE BAG.
I BROUGHT SOUVENIRS FOR EVERYONE.
HERE, IT'S A BILLY DISGUISE KIT.
I'VE BEEN TRYING TO PATENT IT.
WOW, THANKS!
BILLY, WHAT'S IN THIS PACKAGE?
RUSTLE
IT'S A SECRET.

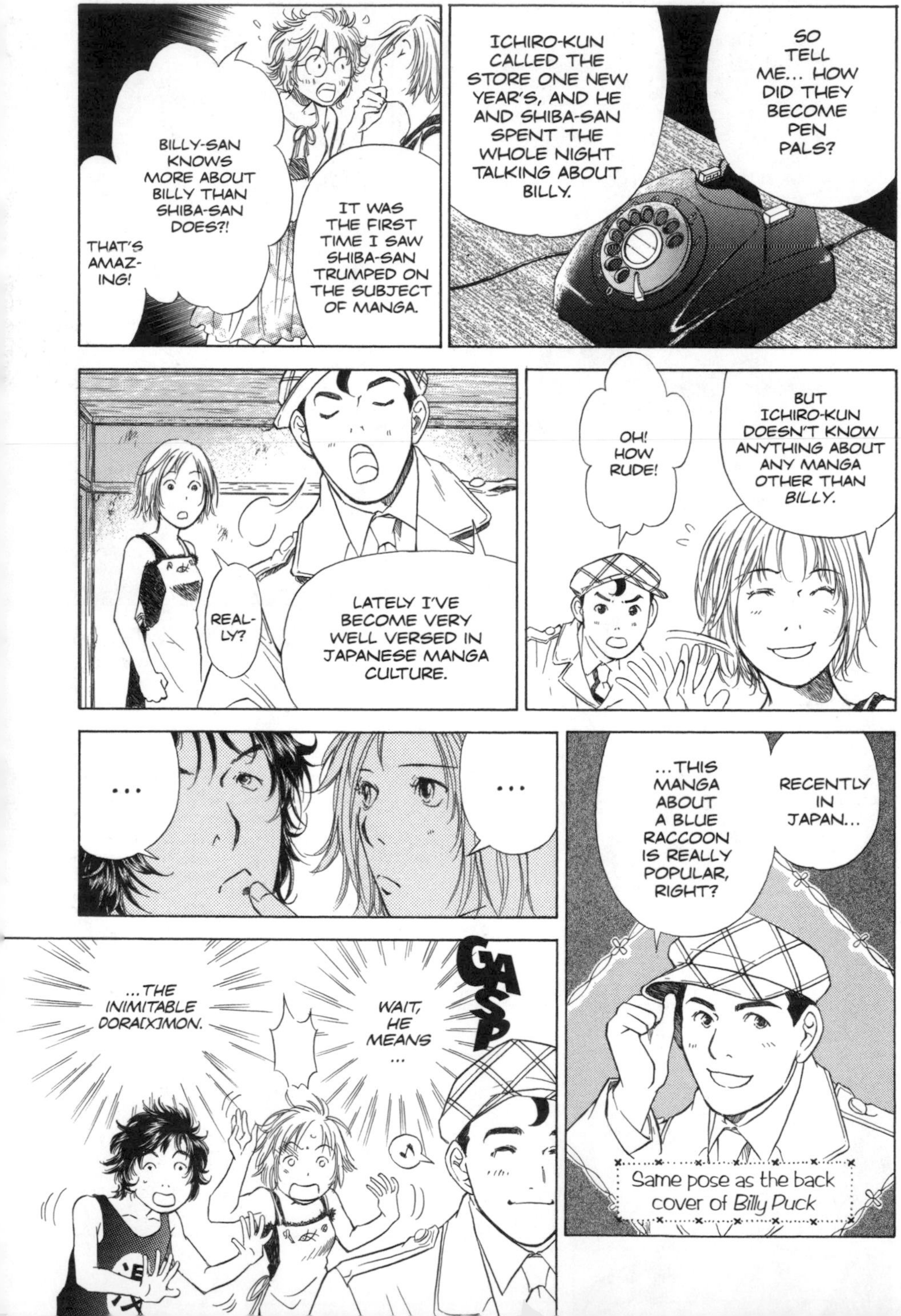
SO TELL ME... HOW DID THEY BECOME PEN PALS?
ICHIRO-KUN CALLED THE STORE ONE NEW YEAR'S, AND HE AND SHIBA-SAN SPENT THE WHOLE NIGHT TALKING ABOUT BILLY.
IT WAS THE FIRST TIME I SAW SHIBA-SAN TRUMPED ON THE SUBJECT OF MANGA.
BILLY-SAN KNOWS MORE ABOUT BILLY THAN SHIBA-SAN DOES?!
THAT'S AMAZ-ING!
BUT ICHIRO-KUN DOESN'T KNOW ANYTHING ABOUT ANY MANGA OTHER THAN BILLY.
OH! HOW RUDE!
LATELY I'VE BECOME VERY WELL VERSED IN JAPANESE MANGA CULTURE.
REAL-LY?
RECENTLY IN JAPAN...
...THIS MANGA ABOUT A BLUE RACCOON IS REALLY POPULAR, RIGHT?
Same pose as the back cover of *Billy Puck*
...
...
GASP
WAIT, HE MEANS ...
...THE INIMITABLE DORA[X]MON.

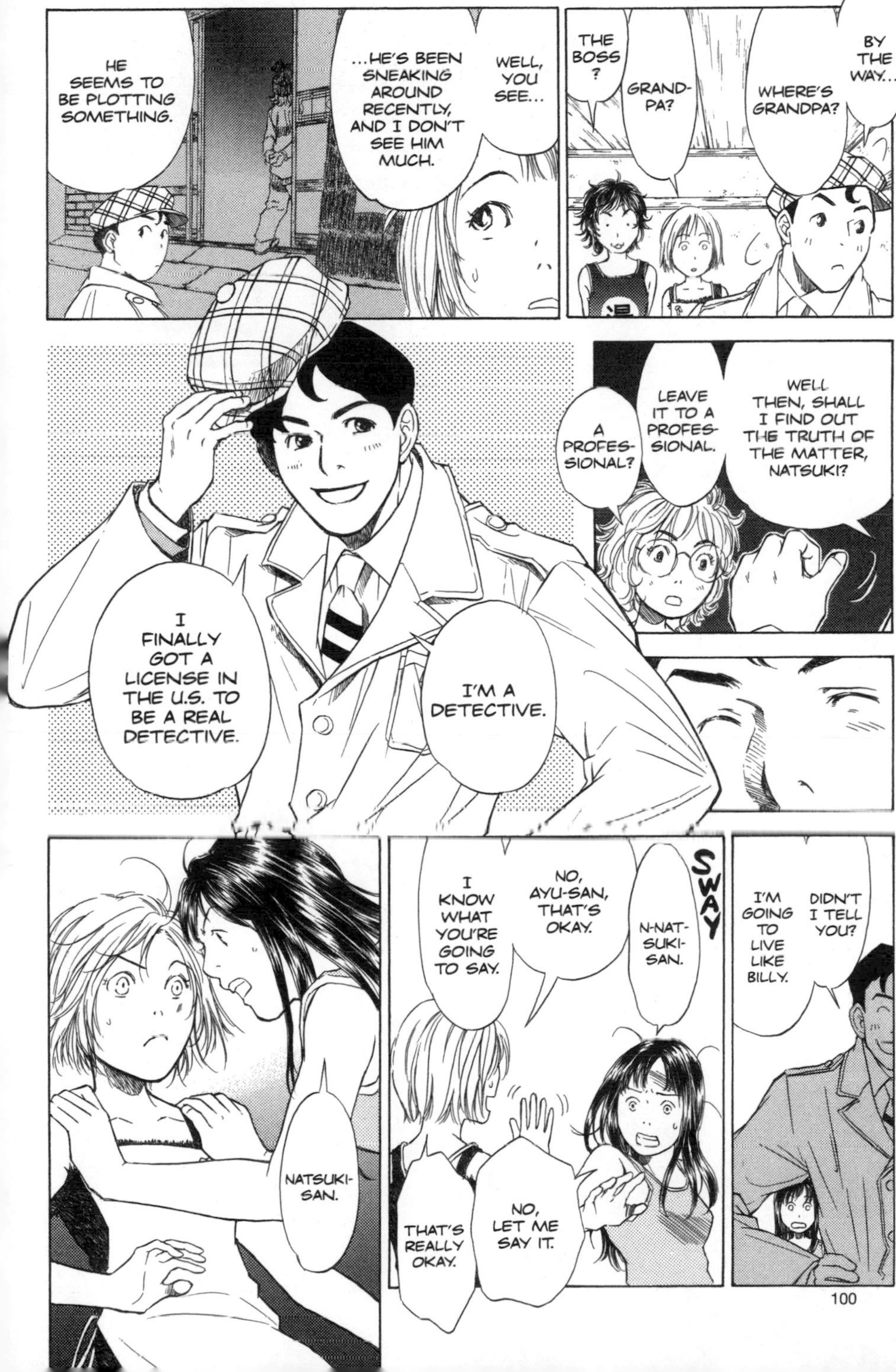
BY THE WAY...
WHERE'S GRANDPA?
GRAND-PA?
THE BOSS?
WELL, YOU SEE...
...HE'S BEEN SNEAKING AROUND RECENTLY, AND I DON'T SEE HIM MUCH.
HE SEEMS TO BE PLOTTING SOMETHING.
WELL THEN, SHALL I FIND OUT THE TRUTH OF THE MATTER, NATSUKI?
LEAVE IT TO A PROFES-SIONAL.
A PROFES-SIONAL?
I'M A DETECTIVE.
I FINALLY GOT A LICENSE IN THE U.S. TO BE A REAL DETECTIVE.
DIDN'T I TELL YOU?
I'M GOING TO LIVE LIKE BILLY.
SWAY
N-NAT-SUKI-SAN.
NO, AYU-SAN, THAT'S OKAY.
I KNOW WHAT YOU'RE GOING TO SAY.
NO, LET ME SAY IT.
THAT'S REALLY OKAY.
NATSUKI-SAN.

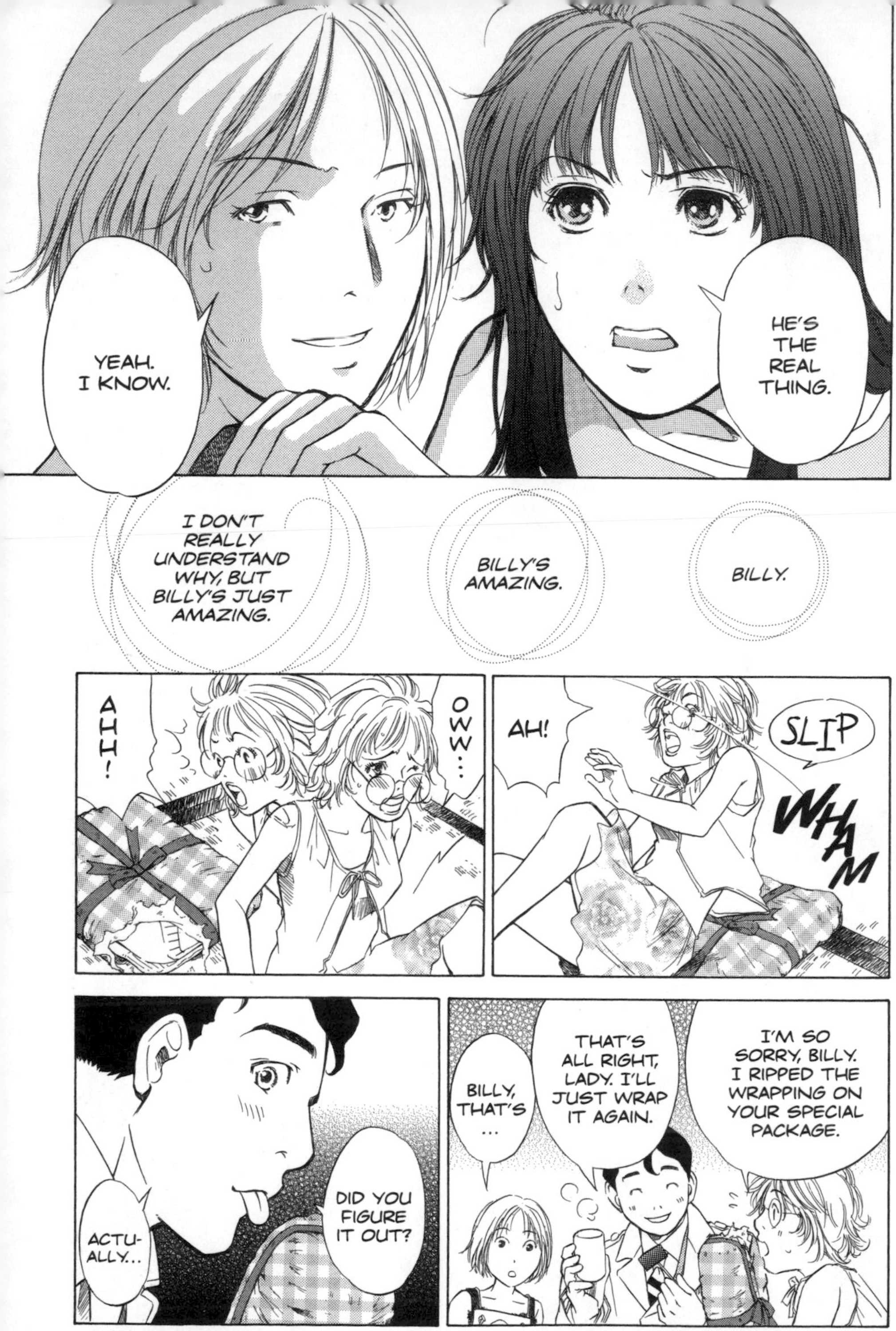
HE'S THE REAL THING.
YEAH. I KNOW.
BILLY.
BILLY'S AMAZING.
I DON'T REALLY UNDERSTAND WHY, BUT BILLY'S JUST AMAZING.
SLIP
WHAM
AH!
OWW...
AHH!
I'M SO SORRY, BILLY. I RIPPED THE WRAPPING ON YOUR SPECIAL PACKAGE.
THAT'S ALL RIGHT, LADY. I'LL JUST WRAP IT AGAIN.
BILLY, THAT'S ...
DID YOU FIGURE IT OUT?
ACTU-ALLY...

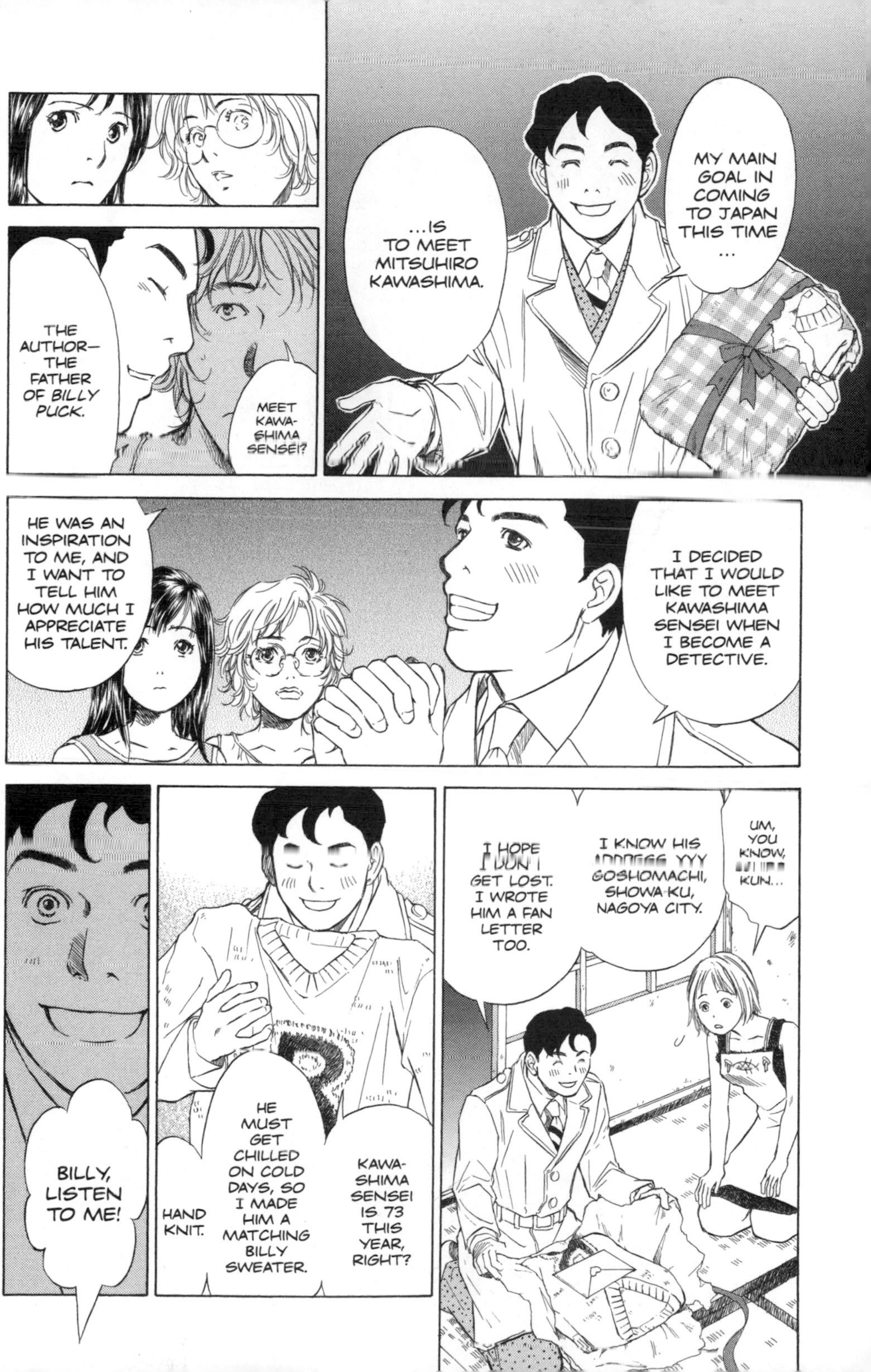
MY MAIN GOAL IN COMING TO JAPAN THIS TIME ...
...IS TO MEET MITSUHIRO KAWASHIMA.
MEET KAWA-SHIMA SENSEI?
THE AUTHOR— THE FATHER OF BILLY PUCK.
I DECIDED THAT I WOULD LIKE TO MEET KAWASHIMA SENSEI WHEN I BECOME A DETECTIVE.
HE WAS AN INSPIRATION TO ME, AND I WANT TO TELL HIM HOW MUCH I APPRECIATE HIS TALENT.
UM, YOU KNOW, KUN...
I KNOW HIS GOSHOMACHI, SHOWA-KU, NAGOYA CITY.
I HOPE GET LOST. I WROTE HIM A FAN LETTER TOO.
KAWA-SHIMA SENSEI IS 73 THIS YEAR, RIGHT?
HE MUST GET CHILLED ON COLD DAYS, SO I MADE HIM A MATCHING BILLY SWEATER.
HAND KNIT.
BILLY, LISTEN TO ME!

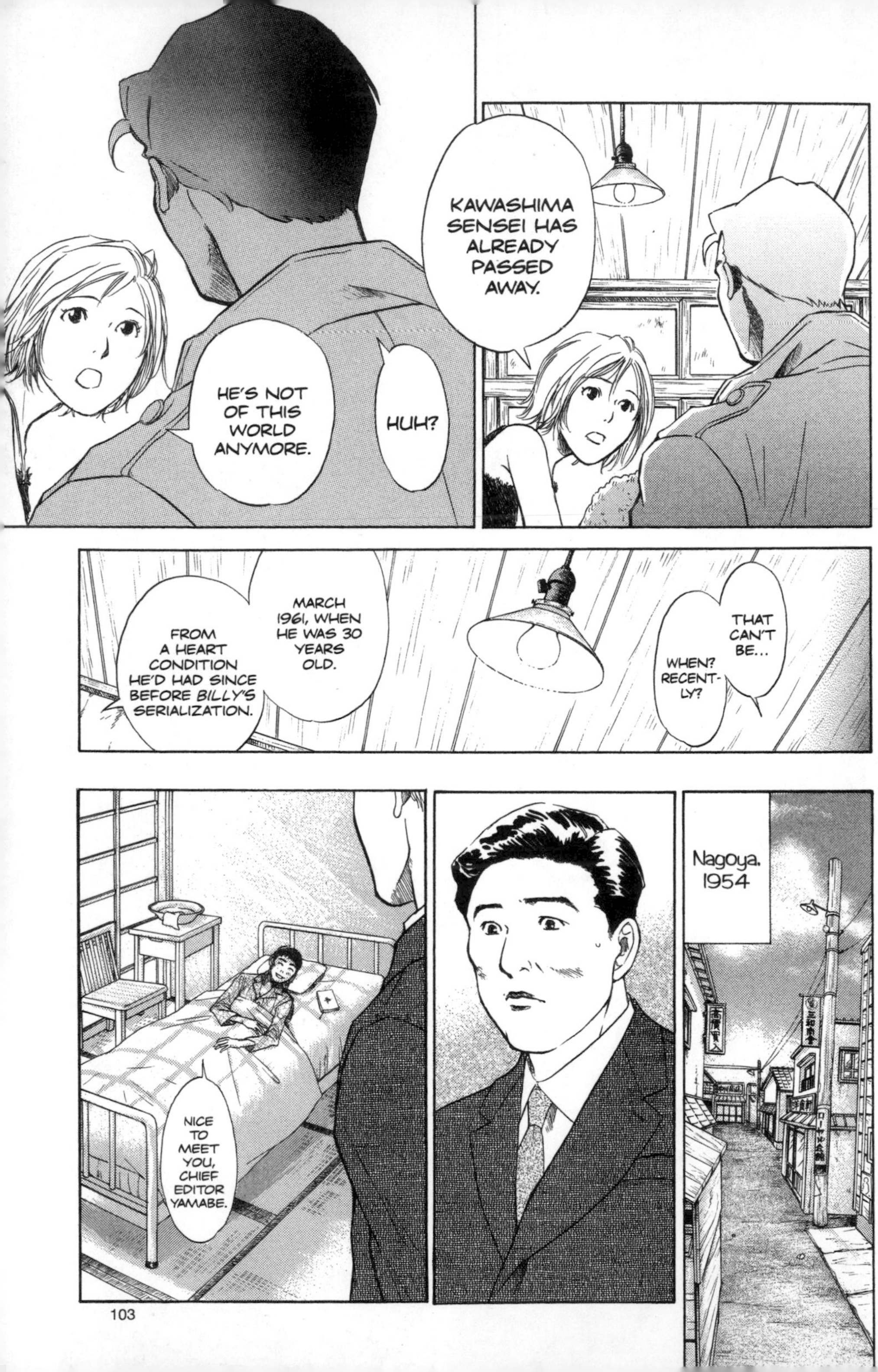
KAWASHIMA SENSEI HAS ALREADY PASSED AWAY.
HUH?
HE'S NOT OF THIS WORLD ANYMORE.
THAT CAN'T BE...
WHEN? RECENT-LY?
MARCH 1961, WHEN HE WAS 30 YEARS OLD.
FROM A HEART CONDITION HE'D HAD SINCE BEFORE *BILLY'S* SERIALIZATION.
Nagoya. 1954
NICE TO MEET YOU, CHIEF EDITOR YAMABE.

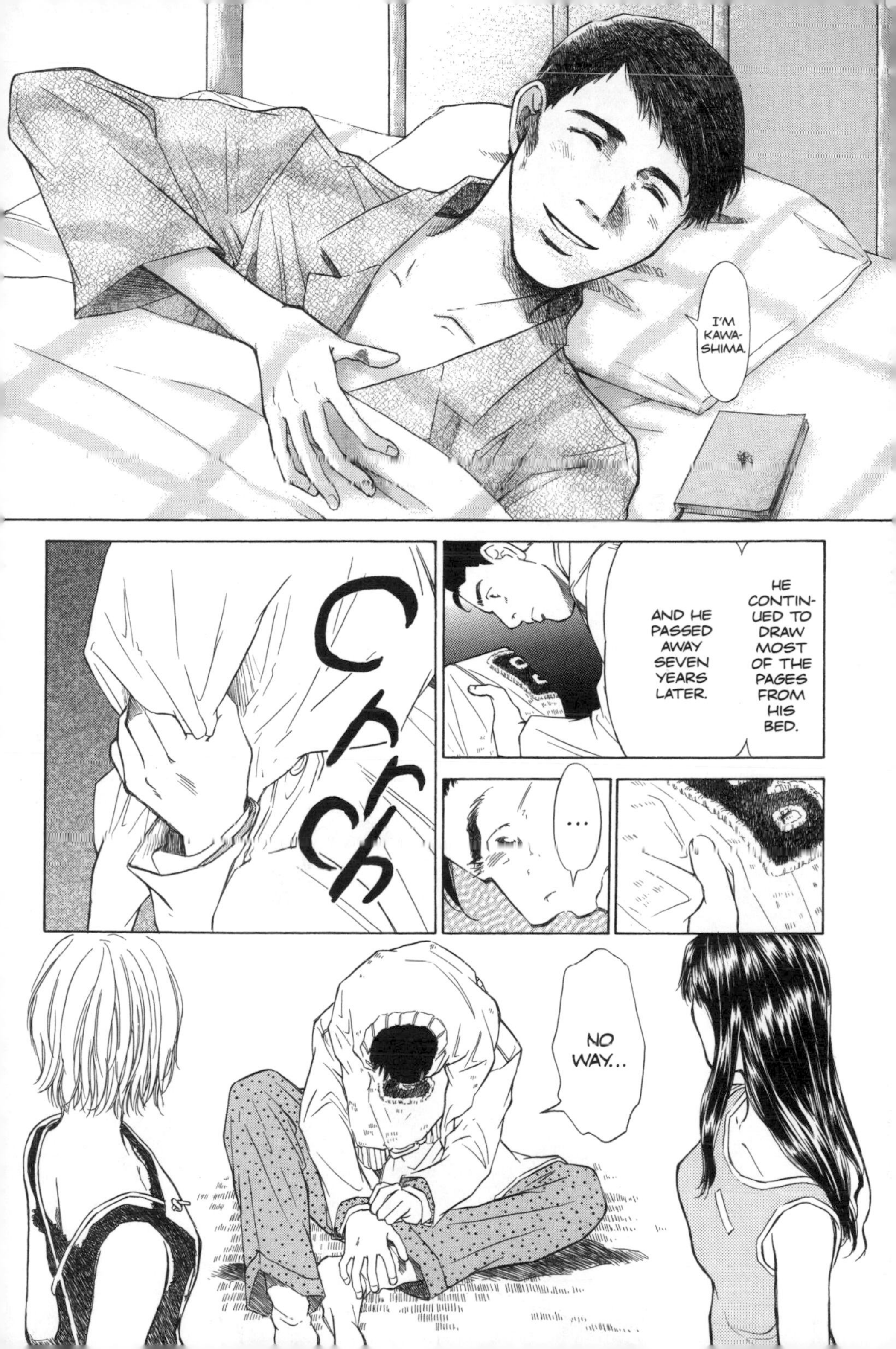
I'M KAWA-SHIMA.
HE CONTIN-UED TO DRAW MOST OF THE PAGES FROM HIS BED.
AND HE PASSED AWAY SEVEN YEARS LATER.
...
Crrch
NO WAY...

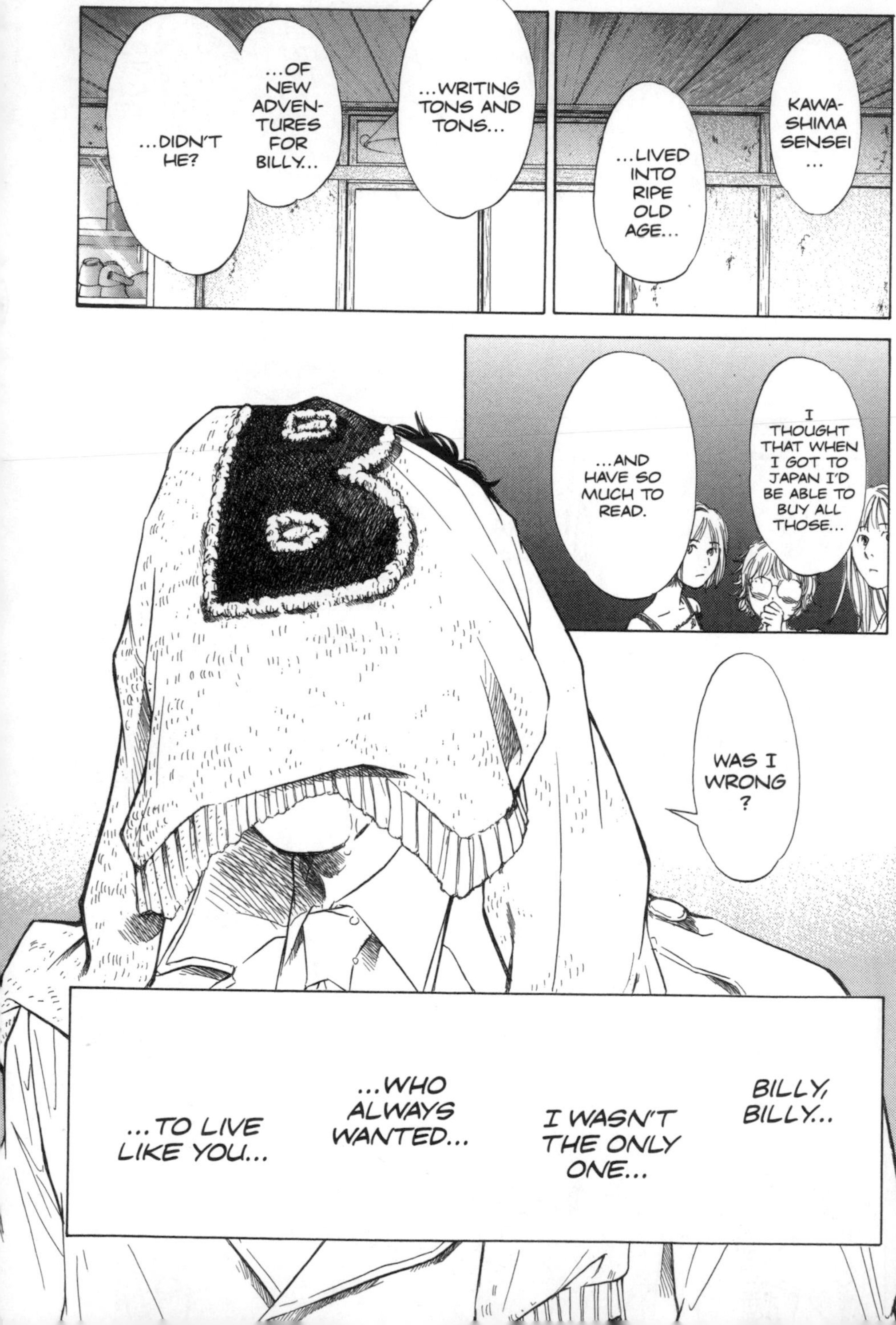
KAWA-SHIMA SENSEI...
...LIVED INTO RIPE OLD AGE...
...WRITING TONS AND TONS...
...OF NEW ADVENTURES FOR BILLY...
...DIDN'T HE?
I THOUGHT THAT WHEN I GOT TO JAPAN I'D BE ABLE TO BUY ALL THOSE...
...AND HAVE SO MUCH TO READ.
WAS I WRONG?
BILLY, BILLY...
I WASN'T THE ONLY ONE...
...WHO ALWAYS WANTED...
...TO LIVE LIKE YOU...

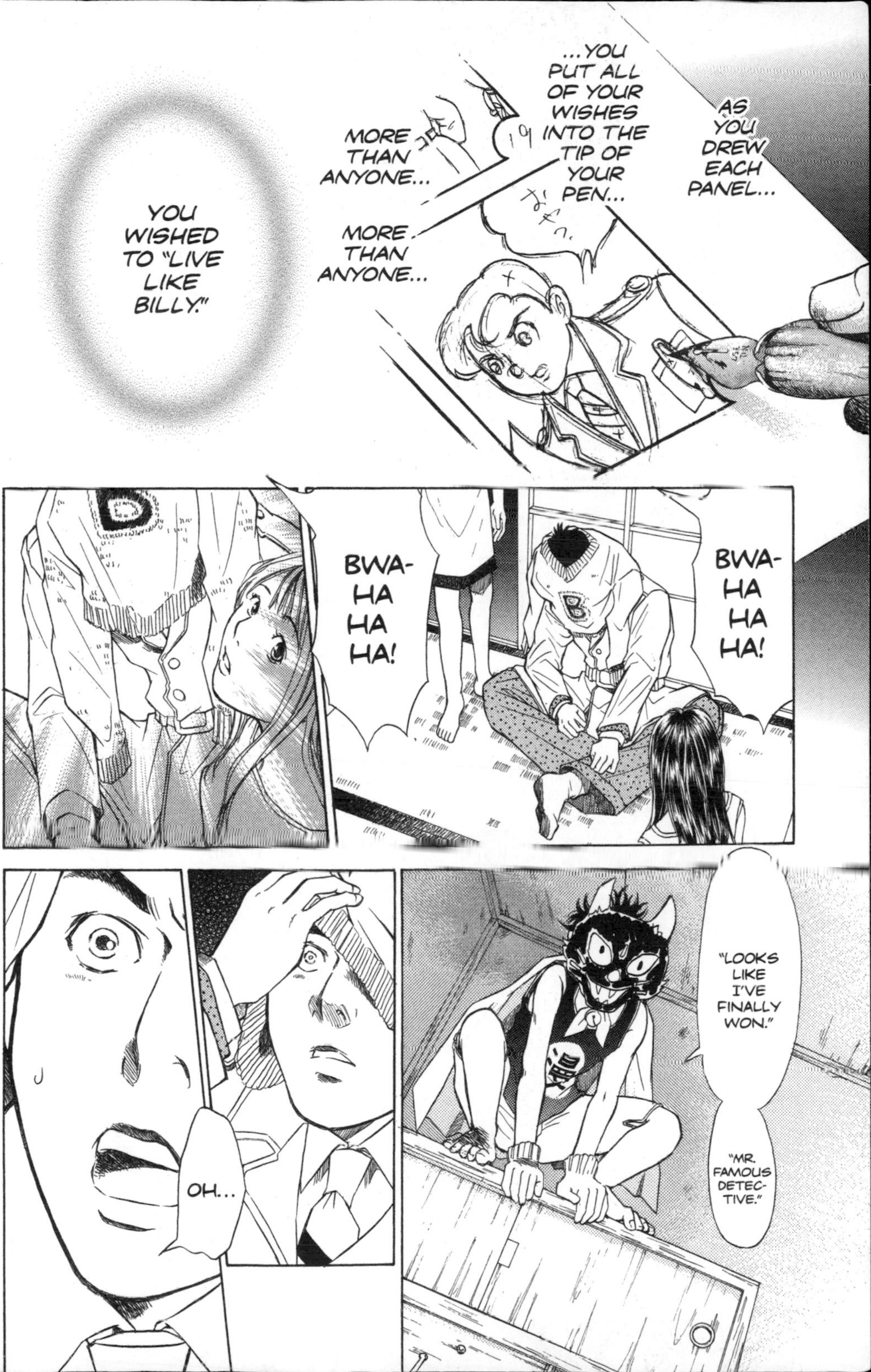
AS YOU DREW EACH PANEL...
...YOU PUT ALL OF YOUR WISHES INTO THE TIP OF YOUR PEN...
MORE THAN ANYONE...
MORE THAN ANYONE...
YOU WISHED TO "LIVE LIKE BILLY."
BWA-HA HA HA!
BWA-HA HA HA!
"LOOKS LIKE I'VE FINALLY WON."
"MR. FAMOUS DETECTIVE."
OH...

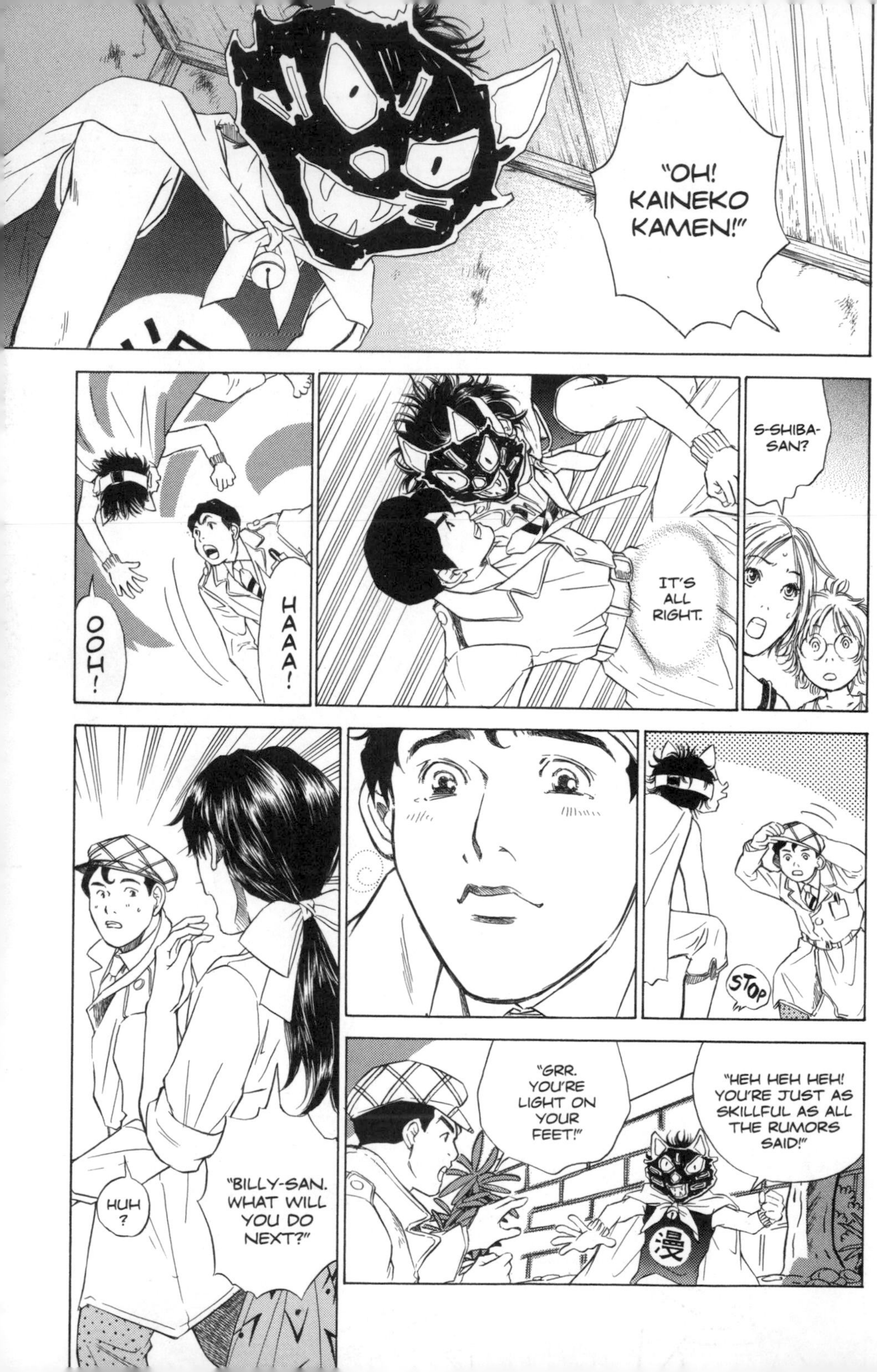
"OH! KAINEKO KAMEN!"
S-SHIBA-SAN?
IT'S ALL RIGHT.
HAAAA!
OOH!
STOP
"HEH HEH HEH! YOU'RE JUST AS SKILLFUL AS ALL THE RUMORS SAID!"
"GRR. YOU'RE LIGHT ON YOUR FEET!"
"BILLY-SAN. WHAT WILL YOU DO NEXT?"
HUH?

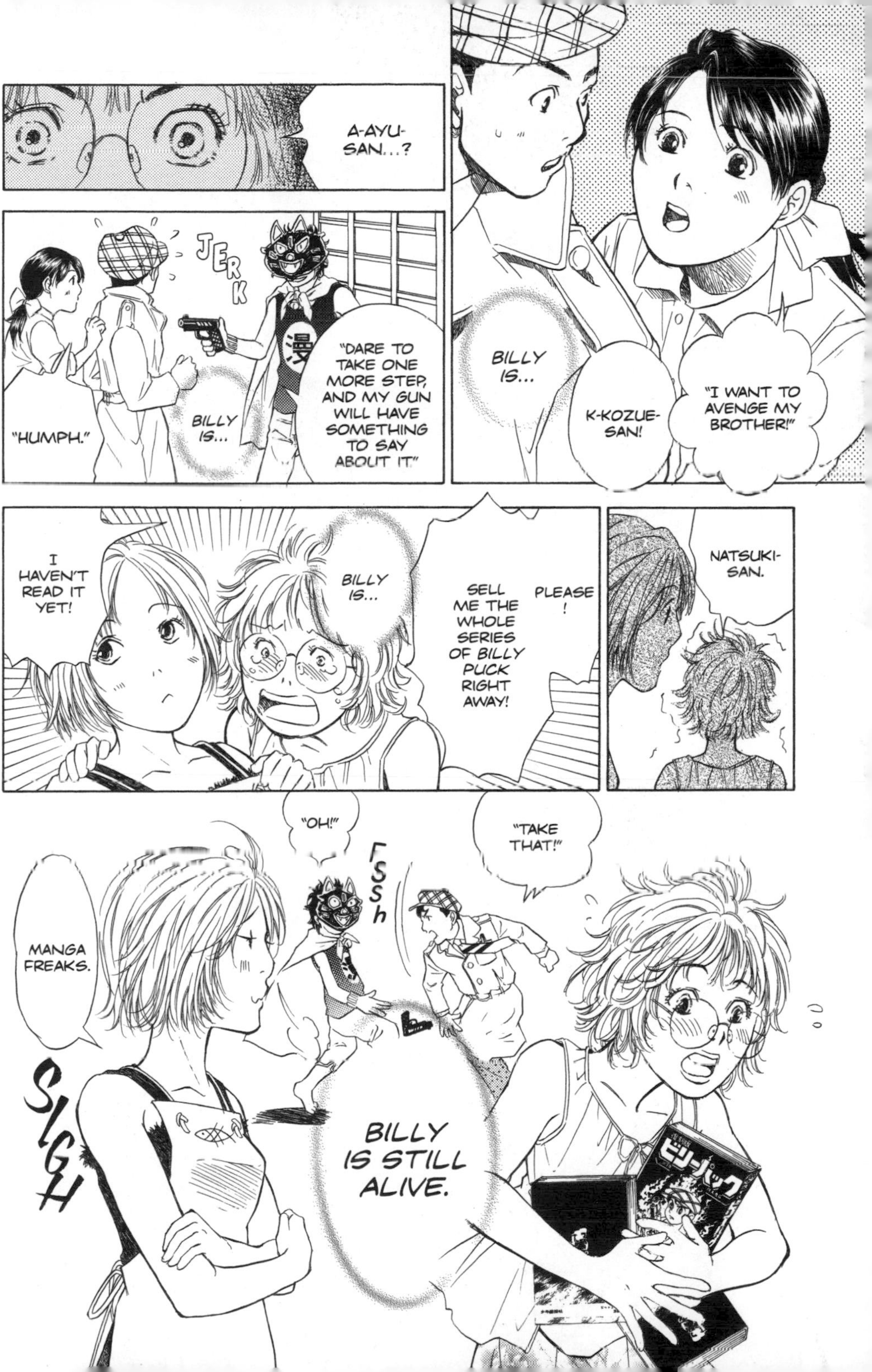
"I WANT TO AVENGE MY BROTHER!"
K-KOZUE-SAN!
BILLY IS...
A-AYU-SAN...?
JERK
"DARE TO TAKE ONE MORE STEP, AND MY GUN WILL HAVE SOMETHING TO SAY ABOUT IT."
BILLY IS...
"HUMPH."
NATSUKI-SAN.
PLEASE!
SELL ME THE WHOLE SERIES OF BILLY PUCK RIGHT AWAY!
BILLY IS...
I HAVEN'T READ IT YET!
"TAKE THAT!"
FSSh
"OH!"
MANGA FREAKS.
BILLY IS STILL ALIVE.
SIGH

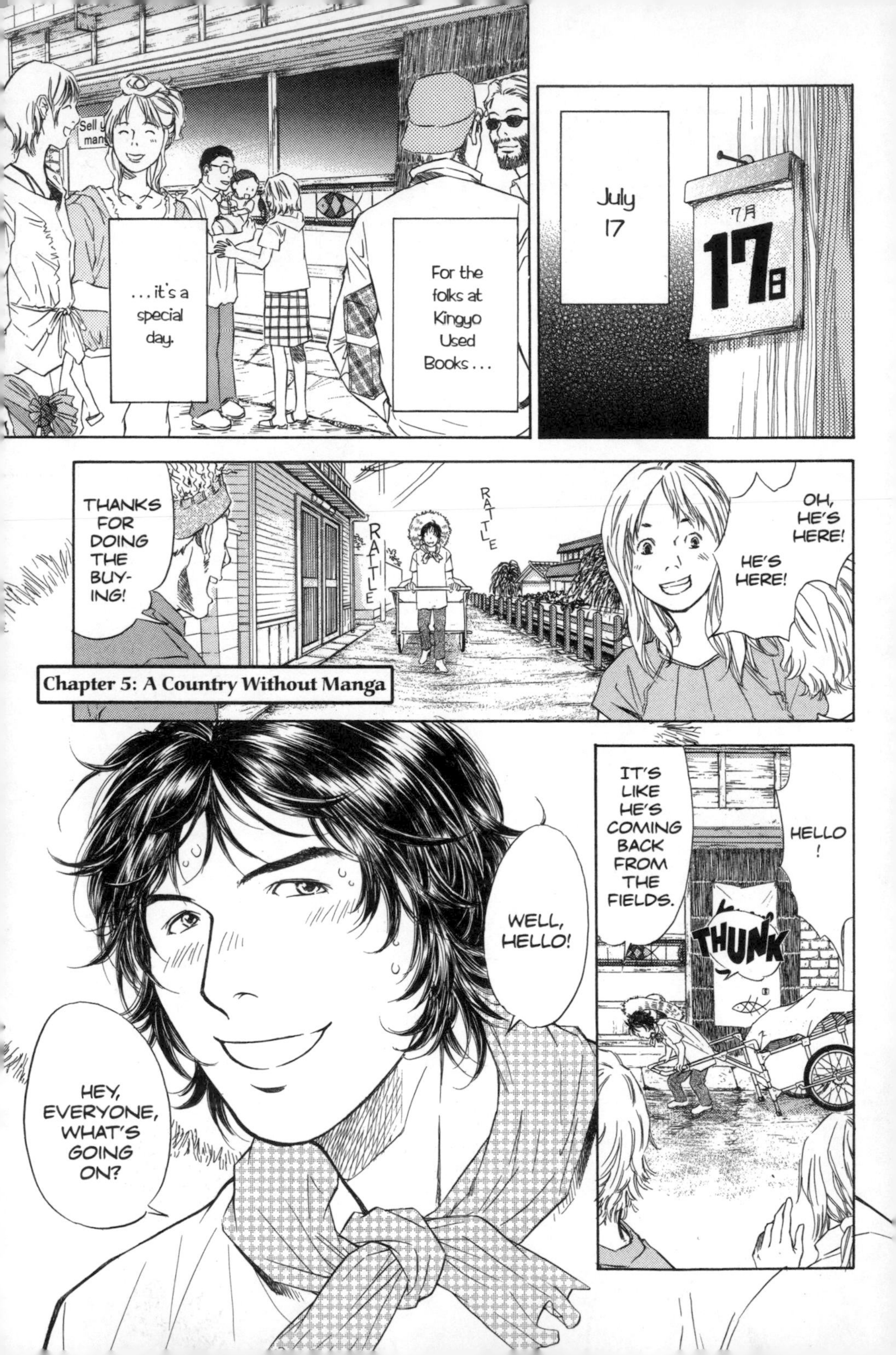

July 17
7月
17日
For the folks at Kingyo Used Books . . .
. . . it's a special day.
OH, HE'S HERE!
HE'S HERE!
RATTLE
RATTLE
THANKS FOR DOING THE BUY-ING!
Chapter 5: A Country Without Manga
HELLO!
IT'S LIKE HE'S COMING BACK FROM THE FIELDS.
THUNK
WELL, HELLO!
HEY, EVERYONE, WHAT'S GOING ON?

Chapter 5: A Country Without Manga

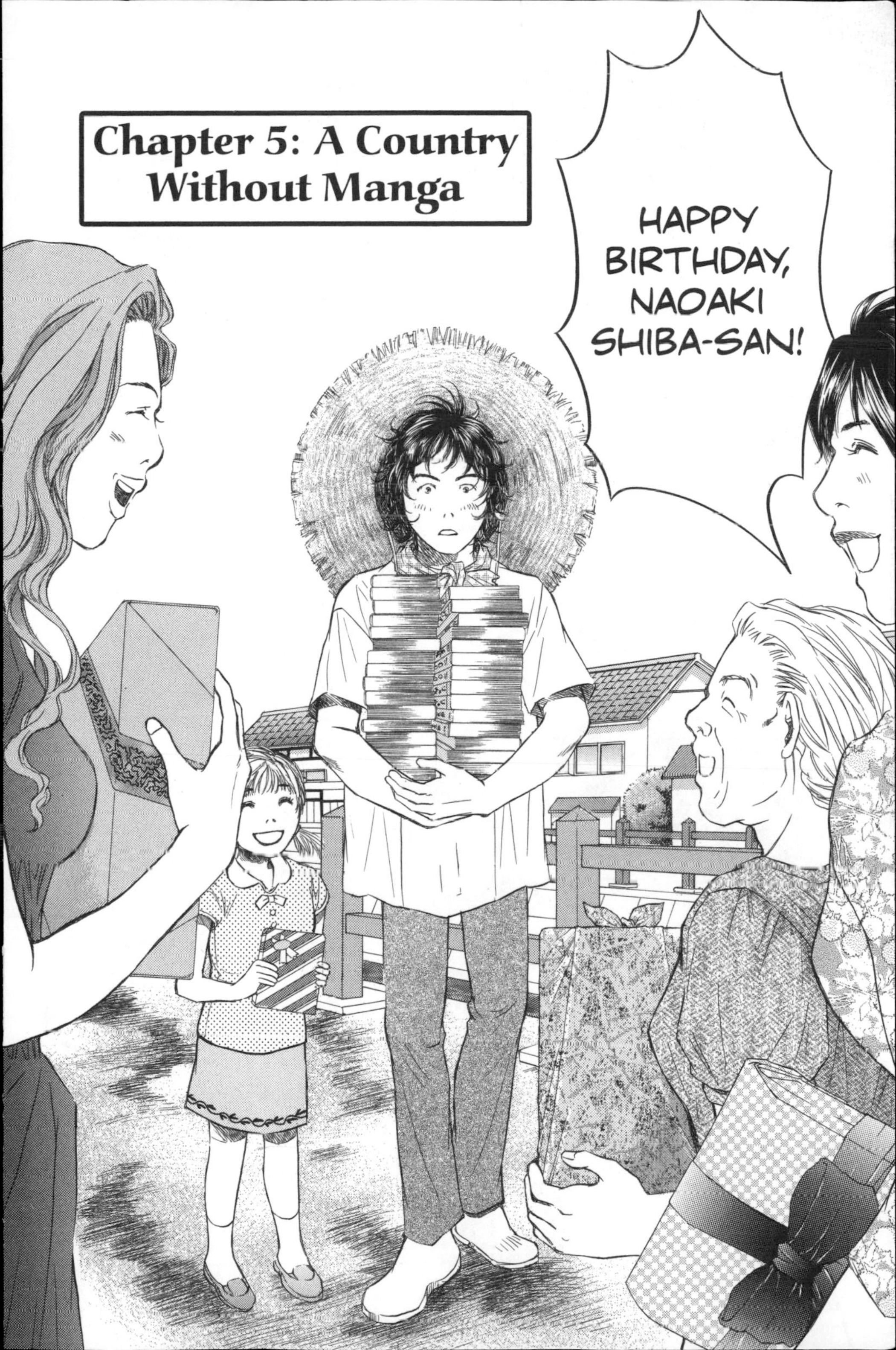
HAPPY BIRTHDAY, NAOAKI SHIBA-SAN!

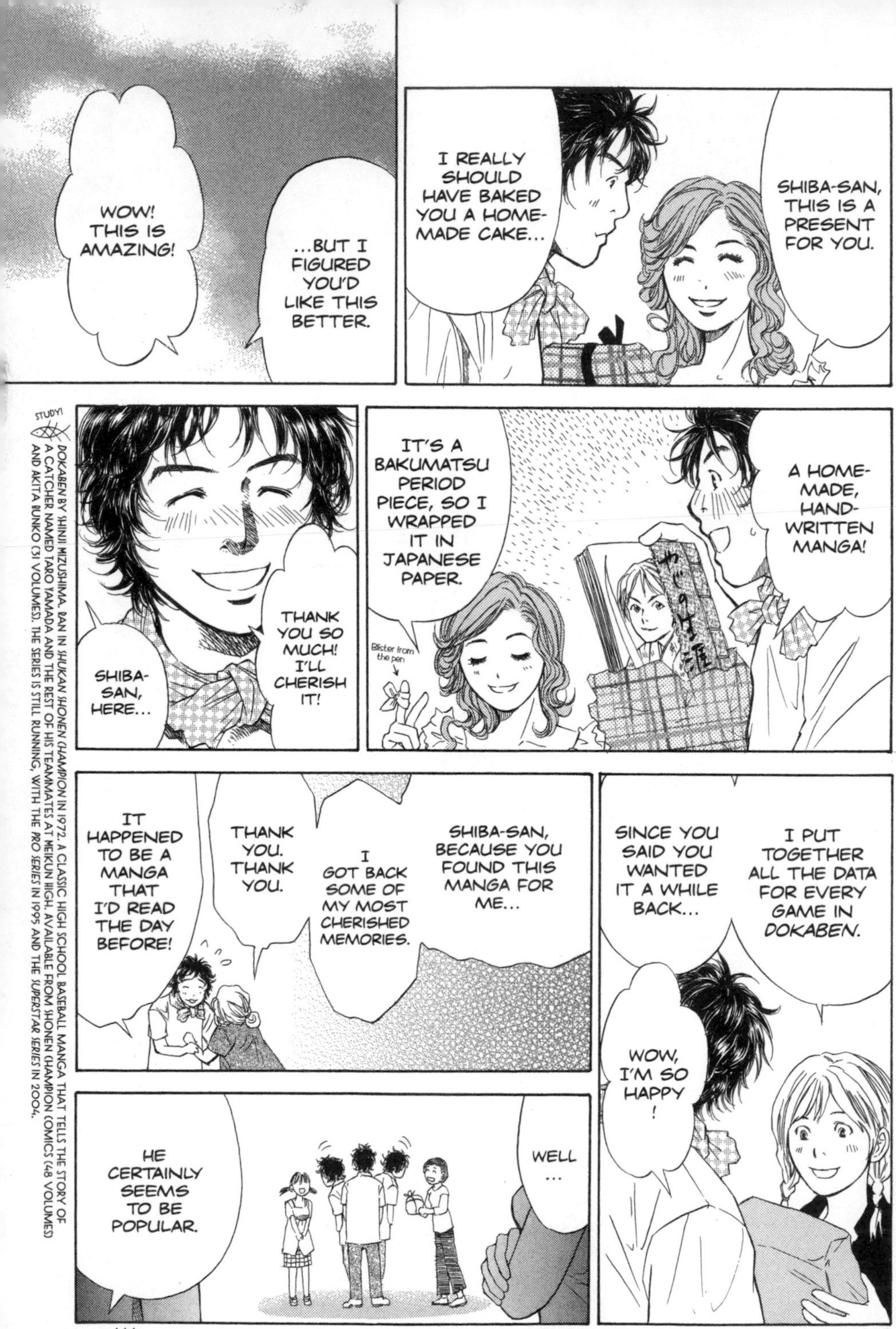
SHIBA-SAN, THIS IS A PRESENT FOR YOU.
I REALLY SHOULD HAVE BAKED YOU A HOME-MADE CAKE...
...BUT I FIGURED YOU'D LIKE THIS BETTER.
WOW! THIS IS AMAZING!
A HOME-MADE, HAND-WRITTEN MANGA!
IT'S A BAKUMATSU PERIOD PIECE, SO I WRAPPED IT IN JAPANESE PAPER.
Blister from the pen
THANK YOU SO MUCH! I'LL CHERISH IT!
SHIBA-SAN, HERE...
I PUT TOGETHER ALL THE DATA FOR EVERY GAME IN DOKABEN.
SINCE YOU SAID YOU WANTED IT A WHILE BACK...
WOW, I'M SO HAPPY!
SHIBA-SAN, BECAUSE YOU FOUND THIS MANGA FOR ME...
I GOT BACK SOME OF MY MOST CHERISHED MEMORIES.
THANK YOU. THANK YOU.
IT HAPPENED TO BE A MANGA THAT I'D READ THE DAY BEFORE!
WELL...
HE CERTAINLY SEEMS TO BE POPULAR.

STUDY!

DOKABEN BY SHINJI MIZUSHIMA. RAN IN *SHUKAN SHONEN CHAMPION* IN 1972. A CLASSIC HIGH SCHOOL BASEBALL MANGA THAT TELLS THE STORY OF A CATCHER NAMED TARO YAMADA AND THE REST OF HIS TEAMMATES AT MEIKUN HIGH. AVAILABLE FROM SHONEN CHAMPION COMICS (48 VOLUMES) AND AKITA BUNKO (31 VOLUMES). THE SERIES IS STILL RUNNING, WITH THE *PRO SERIES* IN 1995 AND THE *SUPERSTAR SERIES* IN 2004.

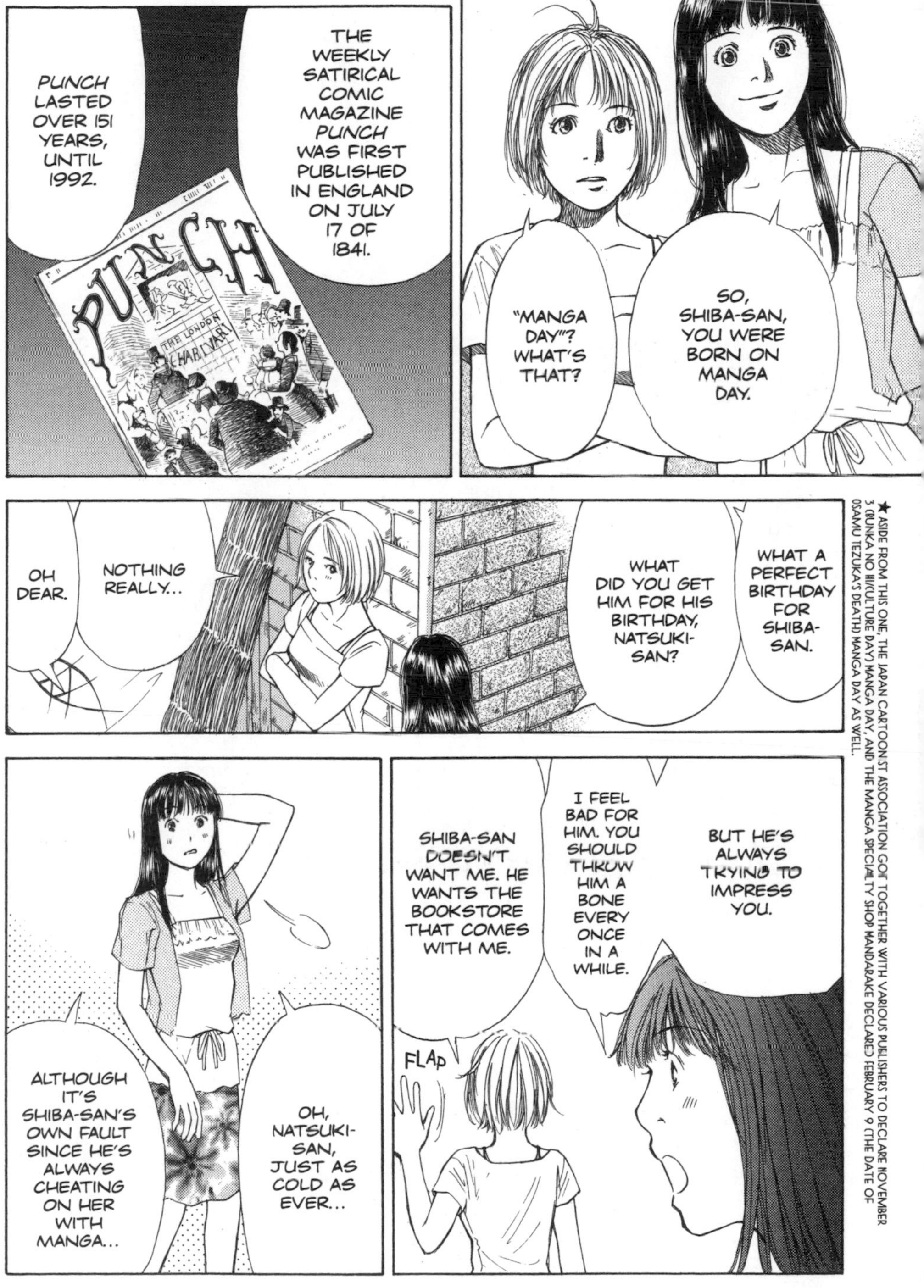
SO, SHIBA-SAN, YOU WERE BORN ON MANGA DAY.
"MANGA DAY"? WHAT'S THAT?
THE WEEKLY SATIRICAL COMIC MAGAZINE PUNCH WAS FIRST PUBLISHED IN ENGLAND ON JULY 17 OF 1841.
PUNCH LASTED OVER 151 YEARS, UNTIL 1992.
PUNCH
THE LONDON CHARIVARI
WHAT A PERFECT BIRTHDAY FOR SHIBA-SAN.
WHAT DID YOU GET HIM FOR HIS BIRTHDAY, NATSUKI-SAN?
NOTHING REALLY...
OH DEAR.
BUT HE'S ALWAYS TRYING TO IMPRESS YOU.
I FEEL BAD FOR HIM. YOU SHOULD THROW HIM A BONE EVERY ONCE IN A WHILE.
SHIBA-SAN DOESN'T WANT ME. HE WANTS THE BOOKSTORE THAT COMES WITH ME.
FLAP
OH, NATSUKI-SAN, JUST AS COLD AS EVER...
ALTHOUGH IT'S SHIBA-SAN'S OWN FAULT SINCE HE'S ALWAYS CHEATING ON HER WITH MANGA...

★ ASIDE FROM THIS ONE, THE JAPAN CARTOONIST ASSOCIATION GOT TOGETHER WITH VARIOUS PUBLISHERS TO DECLARE NOVEMBER 3 (BUNKA NO HI(CULTURE DAY) MANGA DAY, AND THE MANGA SPECIALTY SHOP MANDARAKE DECLARED FEBRUARY 9 (THE DATE OF OSAMU TEZUKA'S DEATH) MANGA DAY AS WELL.

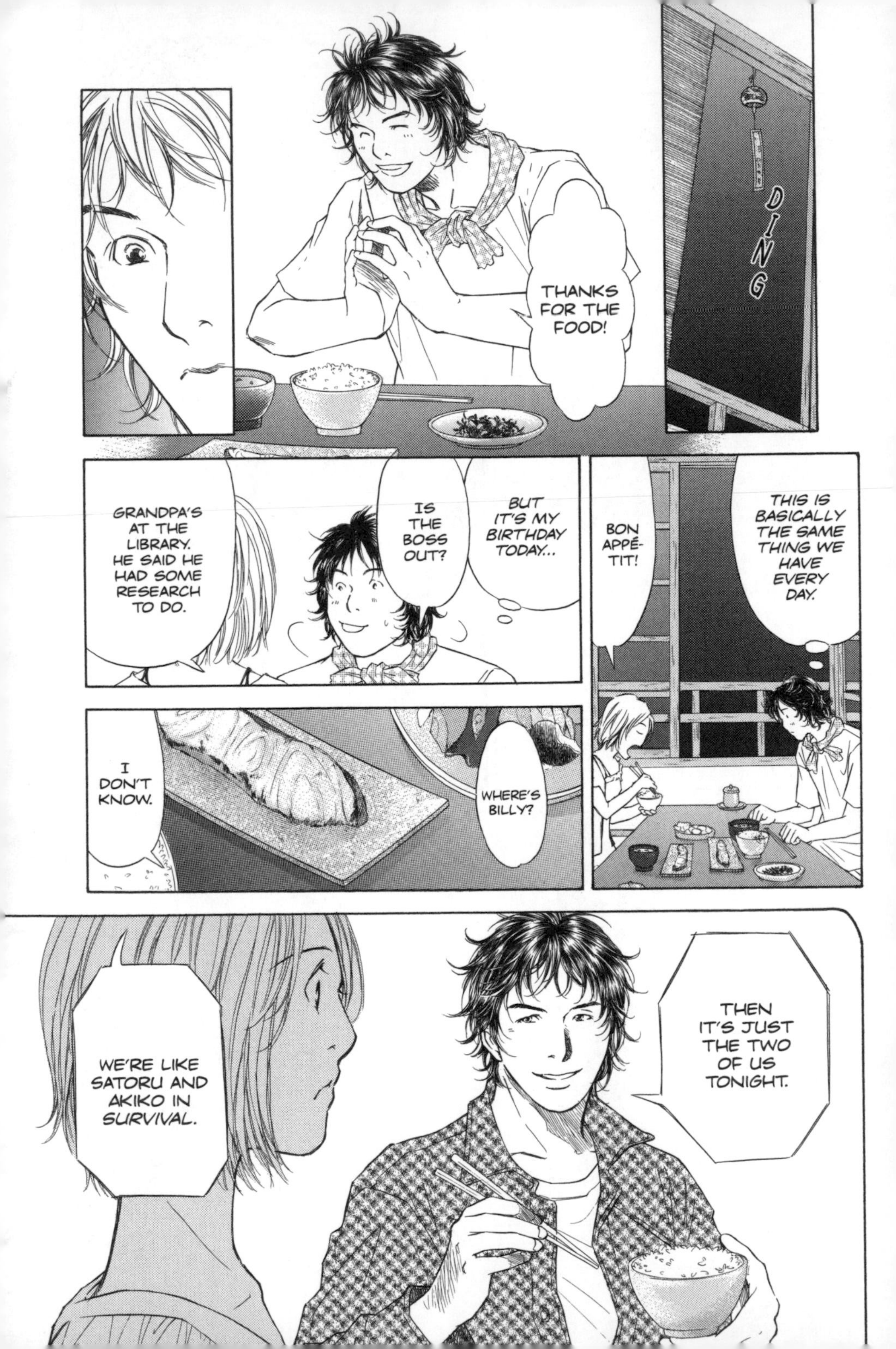
DING
THANKS FOR THE FOOD!
THIS IS BASICALLY THE SAME THING WE HAVE EVERY DAY.
BON APPÉTIT!
BUT IT'S MY BIRTHDAY TODAY...
IS THE BOSS OUT?
GRANDPA'S AT THE LIBRARY. HE SAID HE HAD SOME RESEARCH TO DO.
WHERE'S BILLY?
I DON'T KNOW.
THEN IT'S JUST THE TWO OF US TONIGHT.
WE'RE LIKE SATORU AND AKIKO IN SURVIVAL.

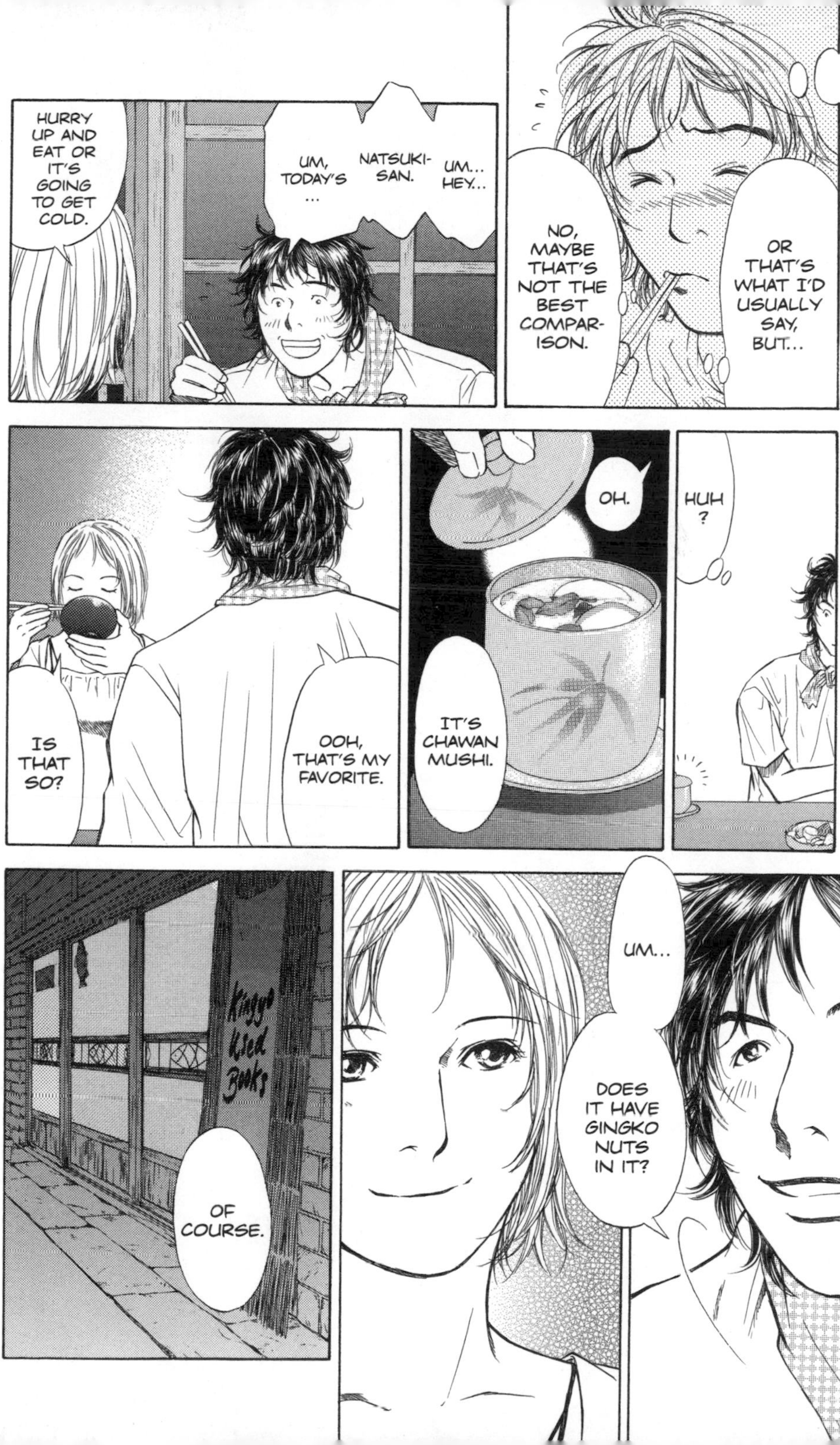
OR THAT'S WHAT I'D USUALLY SAY, BUT...
NO, MAYBE THAT'S NOT THE BEST COMPARISON.
UM... HEY...
NATSUKI-SAN.
UM, TODAY'S...
HURRY UP AND EAT OR IT'S GOING TO GET COLD.
HUH?
OH.
IT'S CHAWAN MUSHI.
OOH, THAT'S MY FAVORITE.
IS THAT SO?
UM...
DOES IT HAVE GINGKO NUTS IN IT?
Kingyo Used Books
OF COURSE.

STUDY!

SURVIVAL BY TAKAO SAITO, SHUKAN SHONEN, 1976. SATORU, THE LONE SURVIVOR OF A GREAT EARTHQUAKE, FINDS HIMSELF ON A DESERTED ISLAND. LATER, A WOMAN NAMED AKIKO DRIFTS ASHORE, AND THEY LIVE TOGETHER. AVAILABLE FROM LEED BUNKO (TEN VOLUMES).

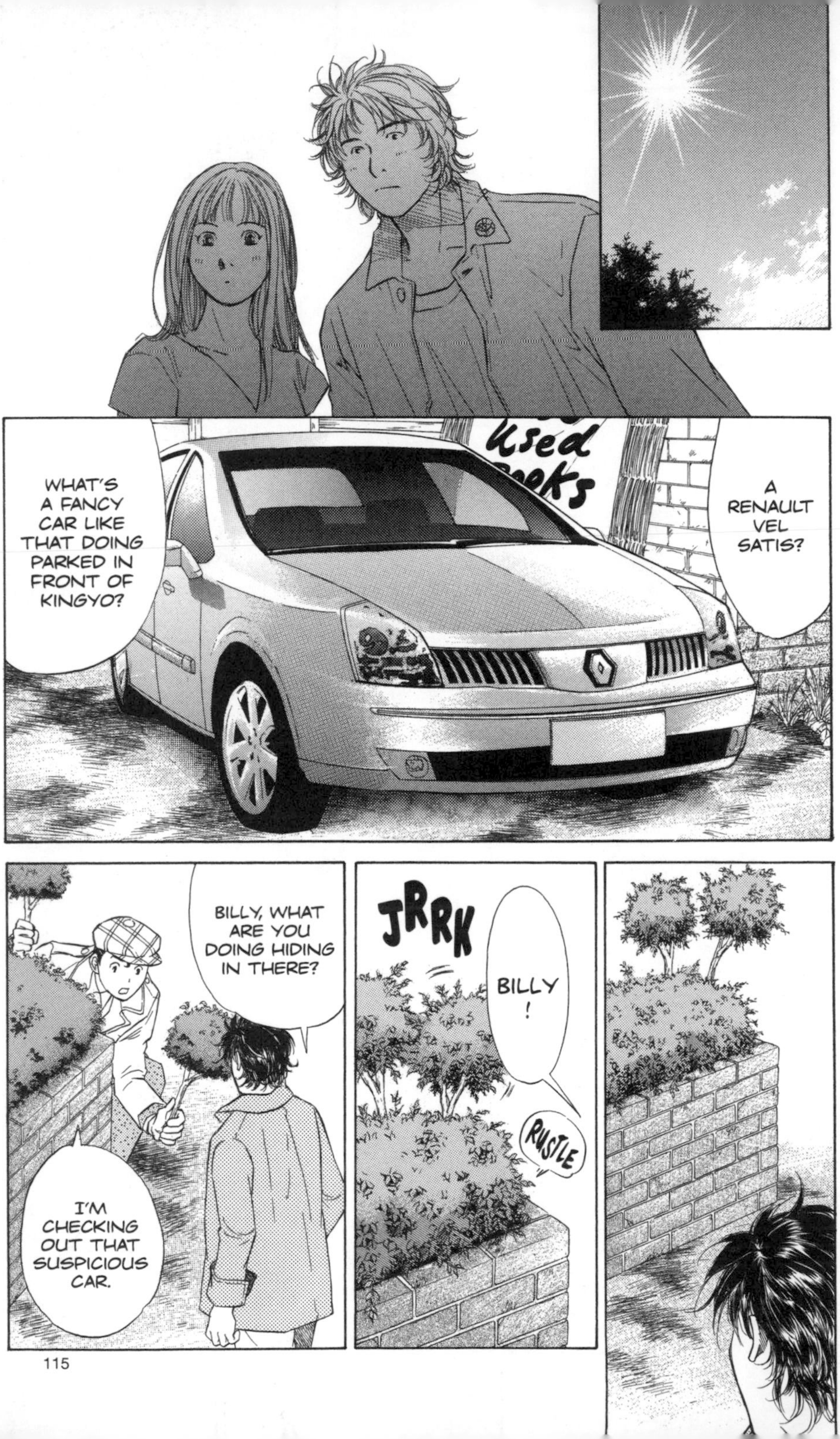
A RENAULT VEL SATIS?
Used
WHAT'S A FANCY CAR LIKE THAT DOING PARKED IN FRONT OF KINGYO?
BILLY!
JRRK
RUSTLE
BILLY, WHAT ARE YOU DOING HIDING IN THERE?
I'M CHECKING OUT THAT SUSPICIOUS CAR.

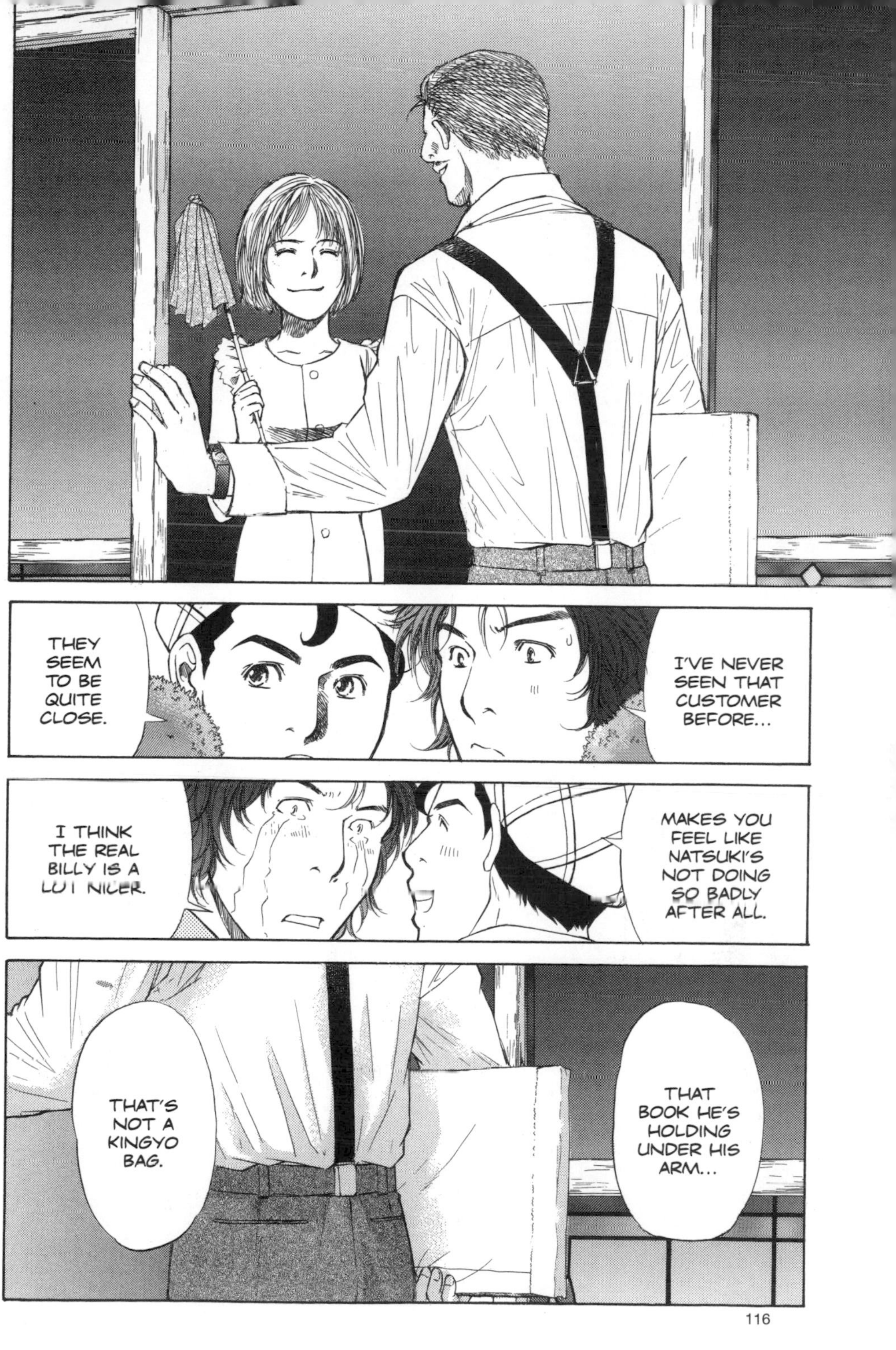
I'VE NEVER SEEN THAT CUSTOMER BEFORE...
THEY SEEM TO BE QUITE CLOSE.
MAKES YOU FEEL LIKE NATSUKI'S NOT DOING SO BADLY AFTER ALL.
I THINK THE REAL BILLY IS A LOT NICER.
THAT BOOK HE'S HOLDING UNDER HIS ARM...
THAT'S NOT A KINGYO BAG.

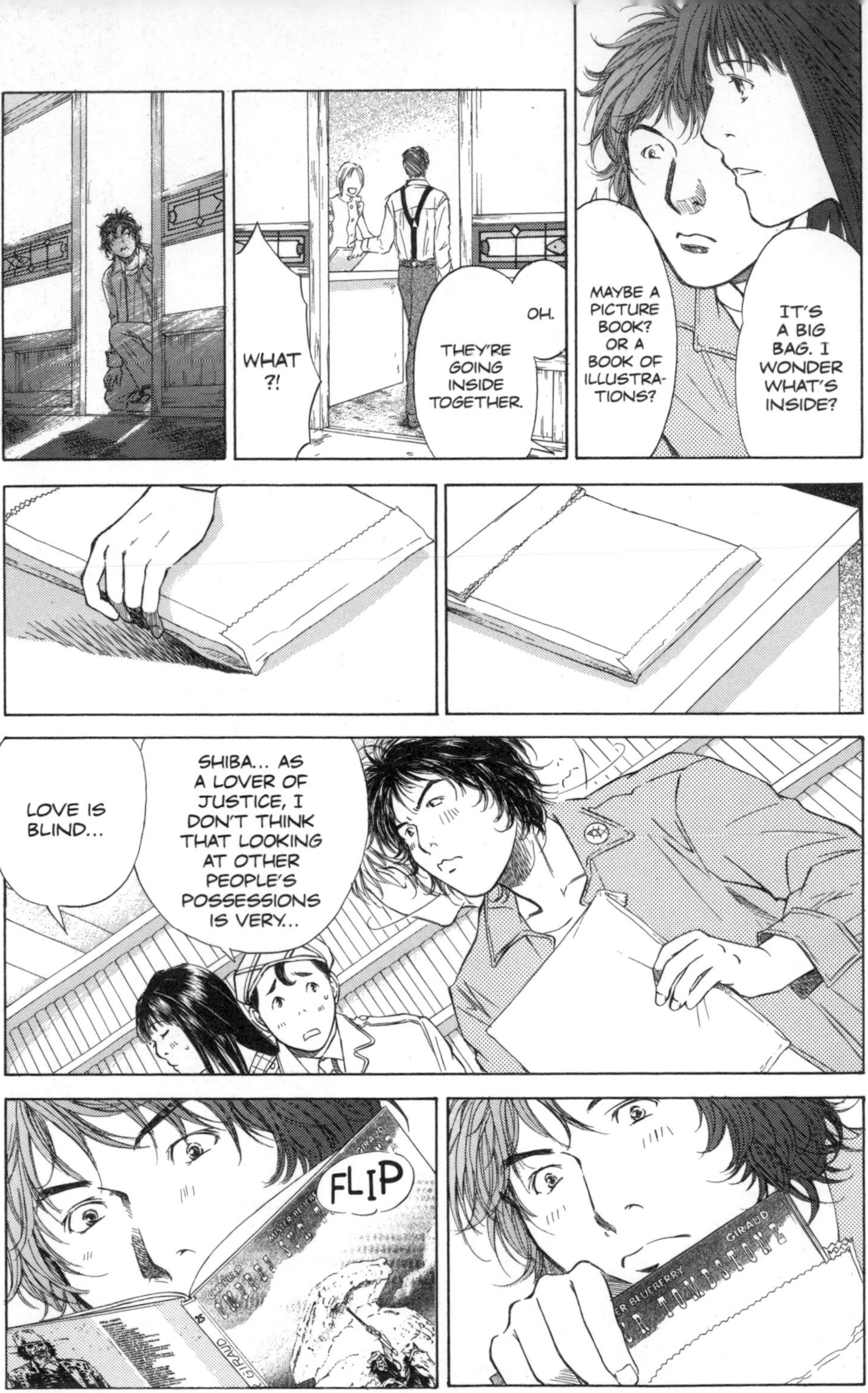
IT'S A BIG BAG. I WONDER WHAT'S INSIDE?
MAYBE A PICTURE BOOK? OR A BOOK OF ILLUSTRATIONS?
OH.
THEY'RE GOING INSIDE TOGETHER.
WHAT ?!
SHIBA... AS A LOVER OF JUSTICE, I DON'T THINK THAT LOOKING AT OTHER PEOPLE'S POSSESSIONS IS VERY...
LOVE IS BLIND...
FLIP

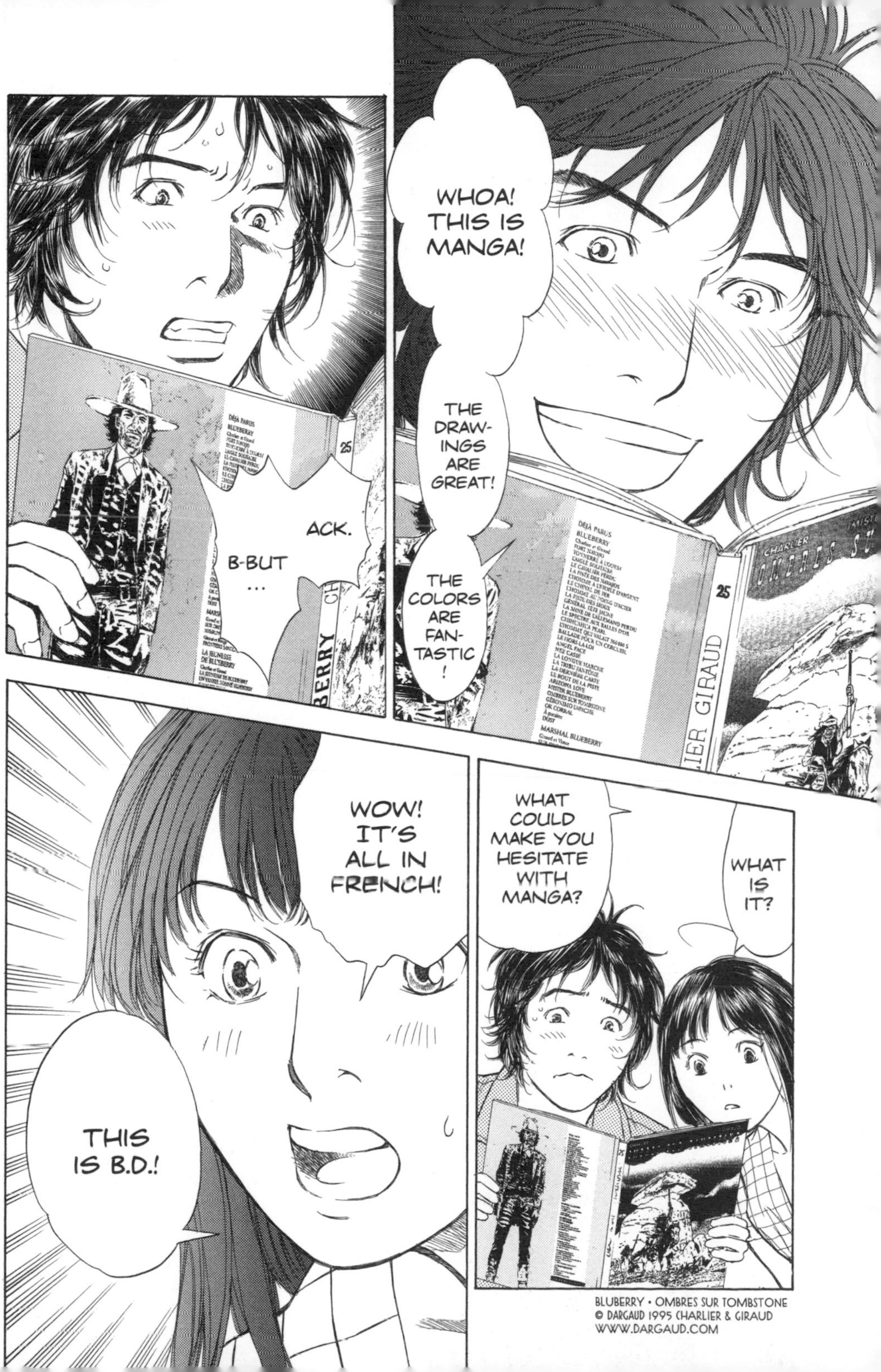
WHOA! THIS IS MANGA!
THE DRAW- INGS ARE GREAT!
THE COLORS ARE FAN- TASTIC!
ACK.
B-BUT ...
WHAT IS IT?
WHAT COULD MAKE YOU HESITATE WITH MANGA?
WOW! IT'S ALL IN FRENCH!
THIS IS B.D.!

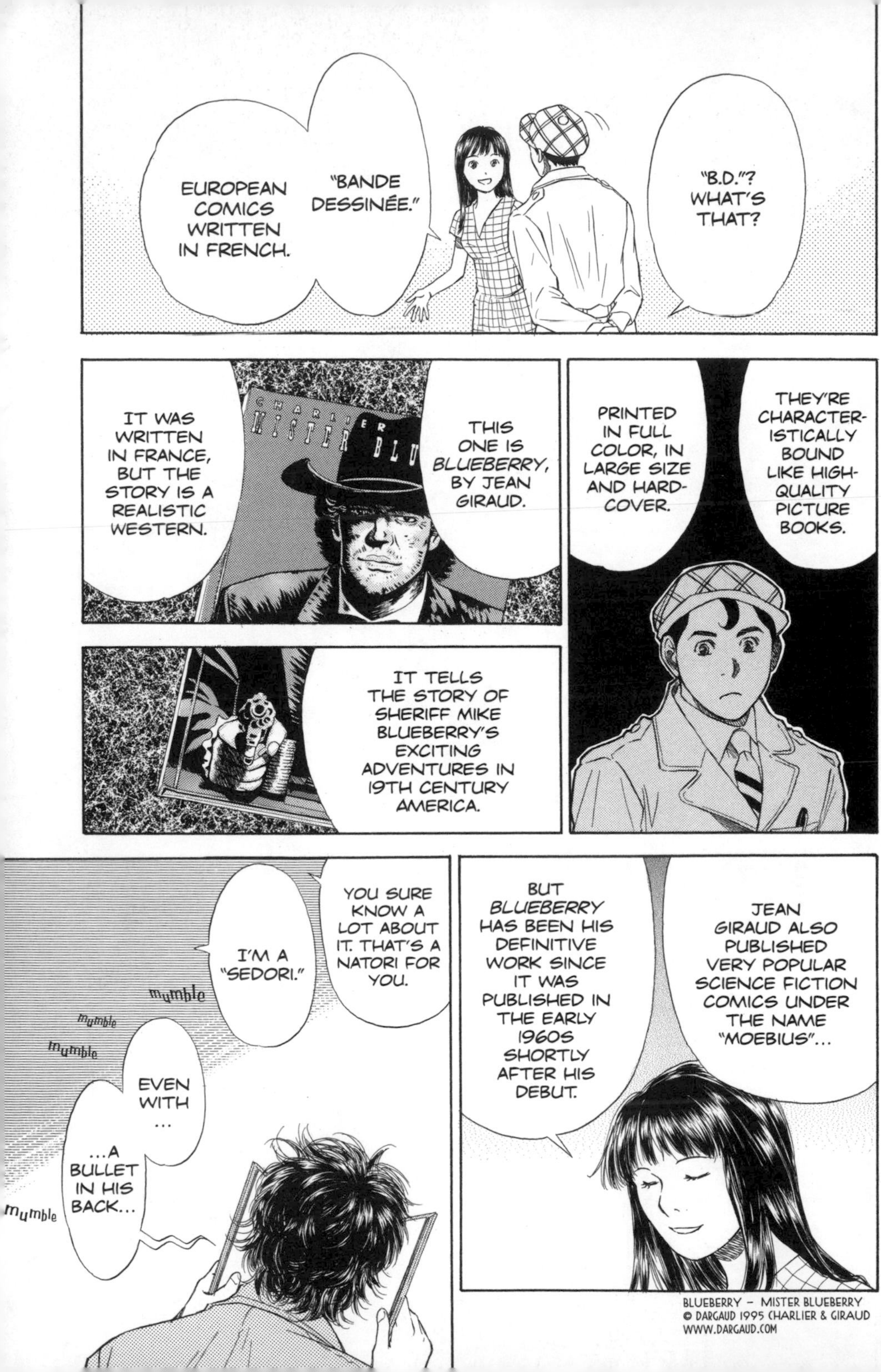
"B.D."? WHAT'S THAT?
"BANDE DESSINÉE."
EUROPEAN COMICS WRITTEN IN FRENCH.
THEY'RE CHARACTER-ISTICALLY BOUND LIKE HIGH-QUALITY PICTURE BOOKS.
PRINTED IN FULL COLOR, IN LARGE SIZE AND HARD-COVER.
THIS ONE IS *BLUEBERRY*, BY JEAN GIRAUD.
IT WAS WRITTEN IN FRANCE, BUT THE STORY IS A REALISTIC WESTERN.
IT TELLS THE STORY OF SHERIFF MIKE BLUEBERRY'S EXCITING ADVENTURES IN 19TH CENTURY AMERICA.
JEAN GIRAUD ALSO PUBLISHED VERY POPULAR SCIENCE FICTION COMICS UNDER THE NAME "MOEBIUS"...
BUT *BLUEBERRY* HAS BEEN HIS DEFINITIVE WORK SINCE IT WAS PUBLISHED IN THE EARLY 1960S SHORTLY AFTER HIS DEBUT.
YOU SURE KNOW A LOT ABOUT IT. THAT'S A NATORI FOR YOU.
I'M A "SEDORI."
mumble
mumble
mumble
EVEN WITH...
...A BULLET IN HIS BACK...
mumble

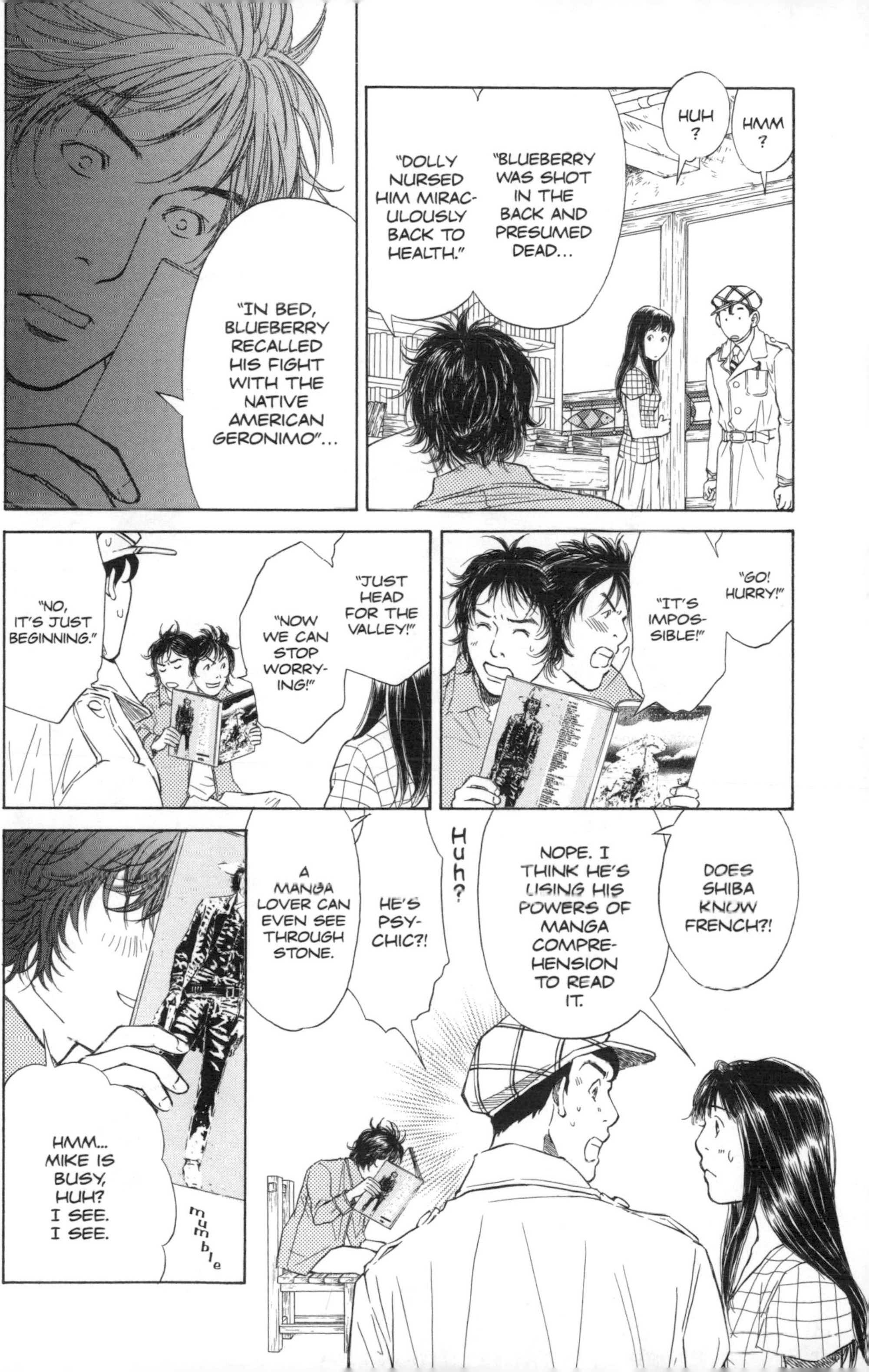
HMM ?
HUH ?
"BLUEBERRY WAS SHOT IN THE BACK AND PRESUMED DEAD...
"DOLLY NURSED HIM MIRAC-ULOUSLY BACK TO HEALTH."
"IN BED, BLUEBERRY RECALLED HIS FIGHT WITH THE NATIVE AMERICAN GERONIMO"...
"GO! HURRY!"
"IT'S IMPOS-SIBLE!"
"JUST HEAD FOR THE VALLEY!"
"NOW WE CAN STOP WORRY-ING!"
"NO, IT'S JUST BEGINNING."
DOES SHIBA KNOW FRENCH?!
NOPE. I THINK HE'S USING HIS POWERS OF MANGA COMPRE-HENSION TO READ IT.
Huh?
HE'S PSY-CHIC?!
A MANGA LOVER CAN EVEN SEE THROUGH STONE.
HMM... MIKE IS BUSY, HUH? I SEE. I SEE.
mumble

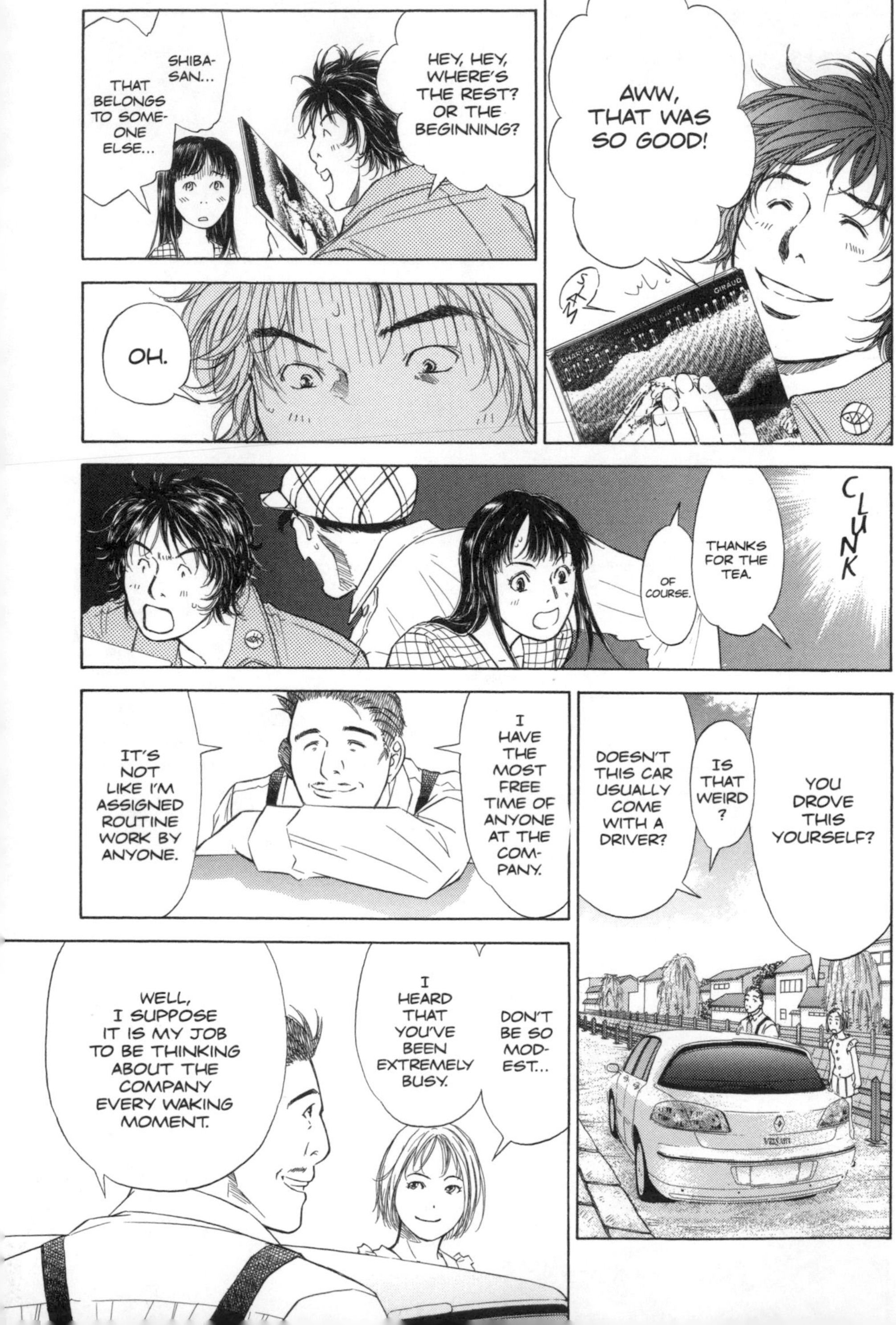
AWW, THAT WAS SO GOOD!
HEY, HEY, WHERE'S THE REST? OR THE BEGINNING?
SHIBA-SAN...
THAT BELONGS TO SOME-ONE ELSE...
OH.
CLUNK
THANKS FOR THE TEA.
OF COURSE.
YOU DROVE THIS YOURSELF?
IS THAT WEIRD?
DOESN'T THIS CAR USUALLY COME WITH A DRIVER?
I HAVE THE MOST FREE TIME OF ANYONE AT THE COM-PANY.
IT'S NOT LIKE I'M ASSIGNED ROUTINE WORK BY ANYONE.
DON'T BE SO MOD-EST...
I HEARD THAT YOU'VE BEEN EXTREMELY BUSY.
WELL, I SUPPOSE IT IS MY JOB TO BE THINKING ABOUT THE COMPANY EVERY WAKING MOMENT.

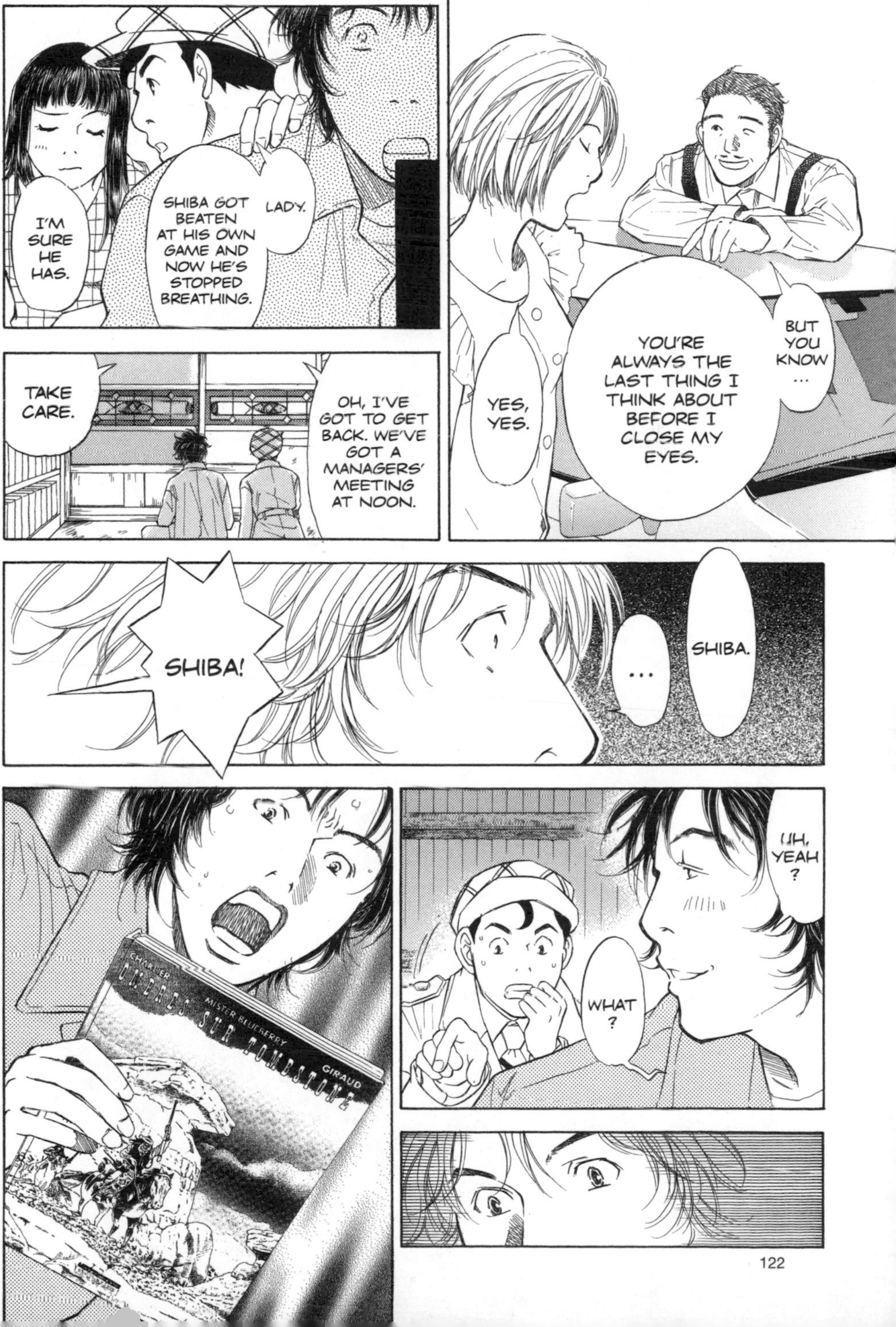
BUT YOU KNOW ...
YOU'RE ALWAYS THE LAST THING I THINK ABOUT BEFORE I CLOSE MY EYES.
YES, YES.
LADY.
SHIBA GOT BEATEN AT HIS OWN GAME AND NOW HE'S STOPPED BREATHING.
I'M SURE HE HAS.
OH, I'VE GOT TO GET BACK. WE'VE GOT A MANAGERS' MEETING AT NOON.
TAKE CARE.
SHIBA.
...
SHIBA!
UH, YEAH ?
WHAT ?
CHARLIER
MISTER BLUEBERRY
GIRAUD
OMBRES SUR TOMBSTONE

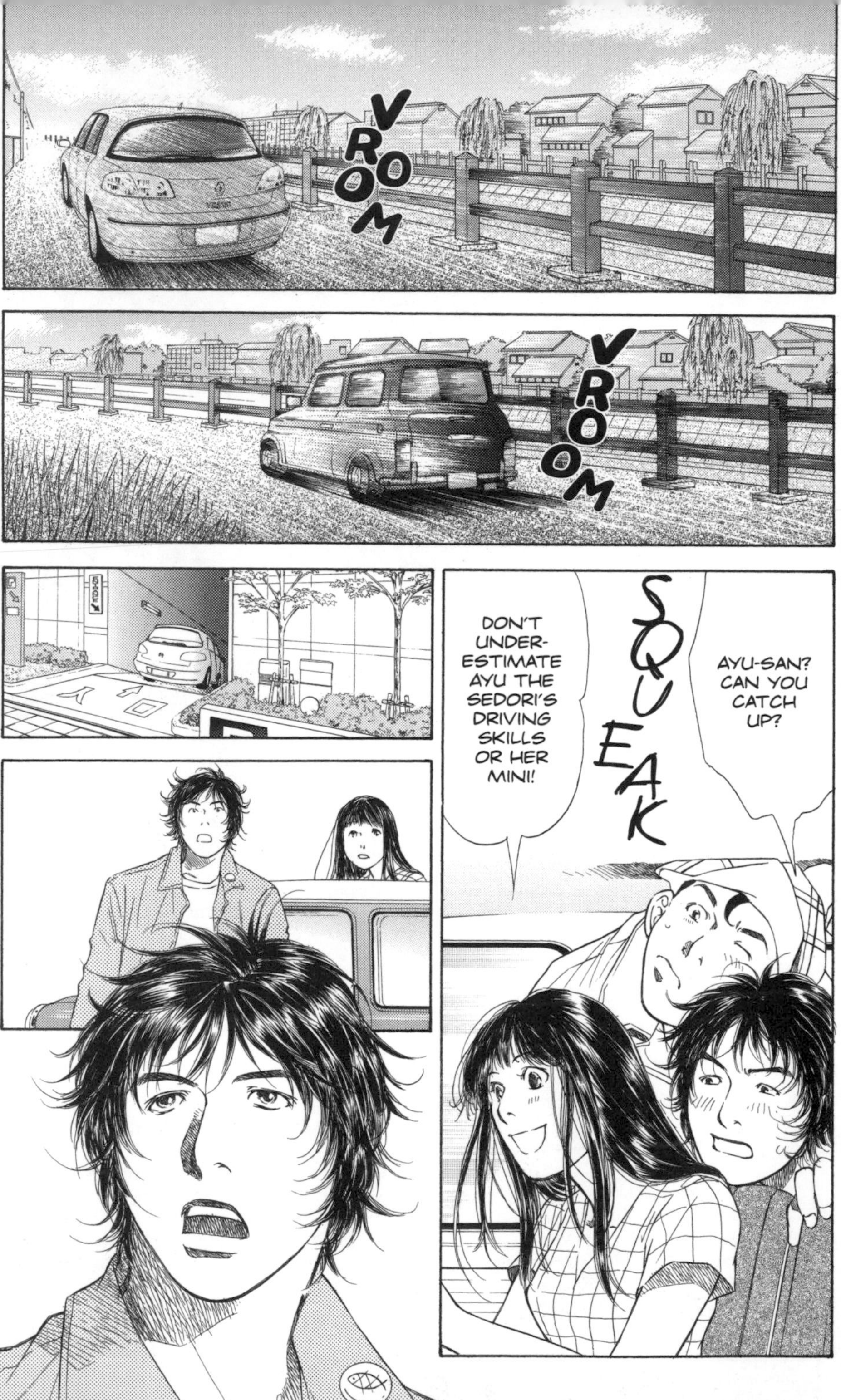
VROOM
VROOM
AYU-SAN? CAN YOU CATCH UP?
SQUEAK
DON'T UNDER-ESTIMATE AYU THE SEDORI'S DRIVING SKILLS OR HER MINI!

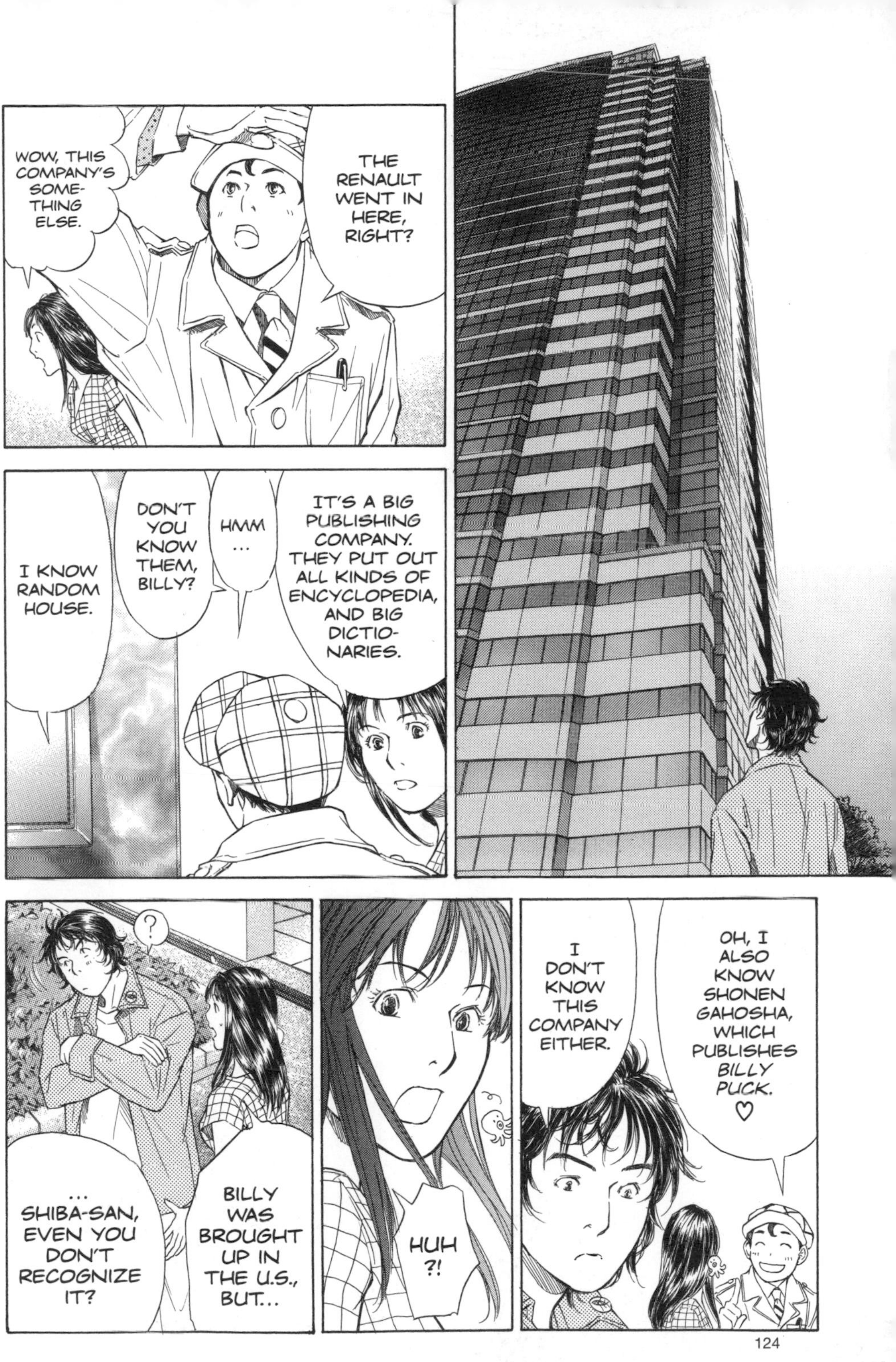
THE RENAULT WENT IN HERE, RIGHT?
WOW, THIS COMPANY'S SOMETHING ELSE.
IT'S A BIG PUBLISHING COMPANY. THEY PUT OUT ALL KINDS OF ENCYCLOPEDIA, AND BIG DICTIONARIES.
HMM ...
DON'T YOU KNOW THEM, BILLY?
I KNOW RANDOM HOUSE.
OH, I ALSO KNOW SHONEN GAHOSHA, WHICH PUBLISHES BILLY PUCK. ♡
I DON'T KNOW THIS COMPANY EITHER.
HUH ?!
?
BILLY WAS BROUGHT UP IN THE U.S., BUT...
... SHIBA-SAN, EVEN YOU DON'T RECOGNIZE IT?

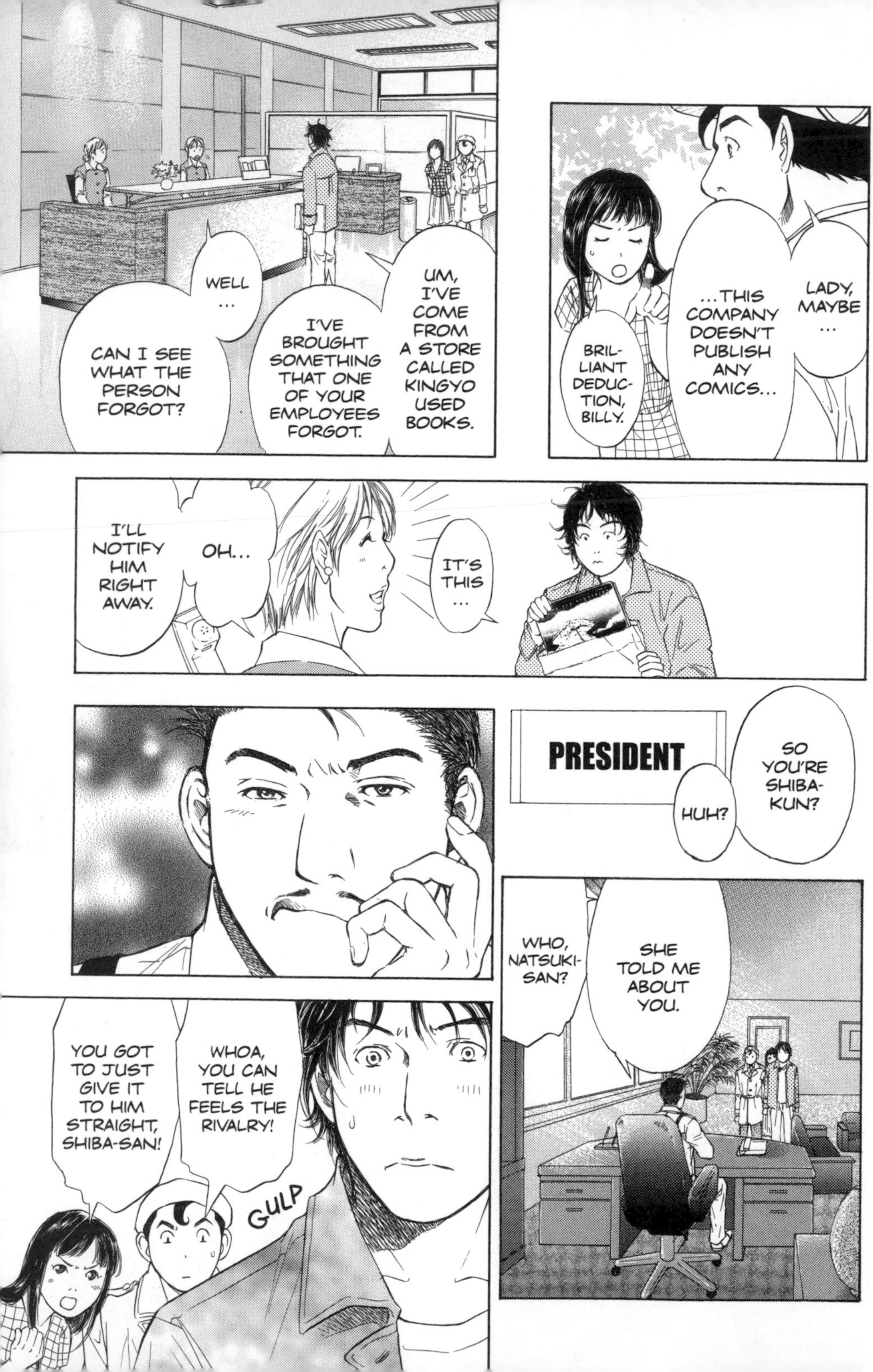
LADY, MAYBE ...
...THIS COMPANY DOESN'T PUBLISH ANY COMICS...
BRIL-LIANT DEDUC-TION, BILLY.
UM, I'VE COME FROM A STORE CALLED KINGYO USED BOOKS.
I'VE BROUGHT SOMETHING THAT ONE OF YOUR EMPLOYEES FORGOT.
WELL ...
CAN I SEE WHAT THE PERSON FORGOT?
IT'S THIS ...
OH...
I'LL NOTIFY HIM RIGHT AWAY.
PRESIDENT
SO YOU'RE SHIBA-KUN?
HUH?
SHE TOLD ME ABOUT YOU.
WHO, NATSUKI-SAN?
WHOA, YOU CAN TELL HE FEELS THE RIVALRY!
YOU GOT TO JUST GIVE IT TO HIM STRAIGHT, SHIBA-SAN!
GULP

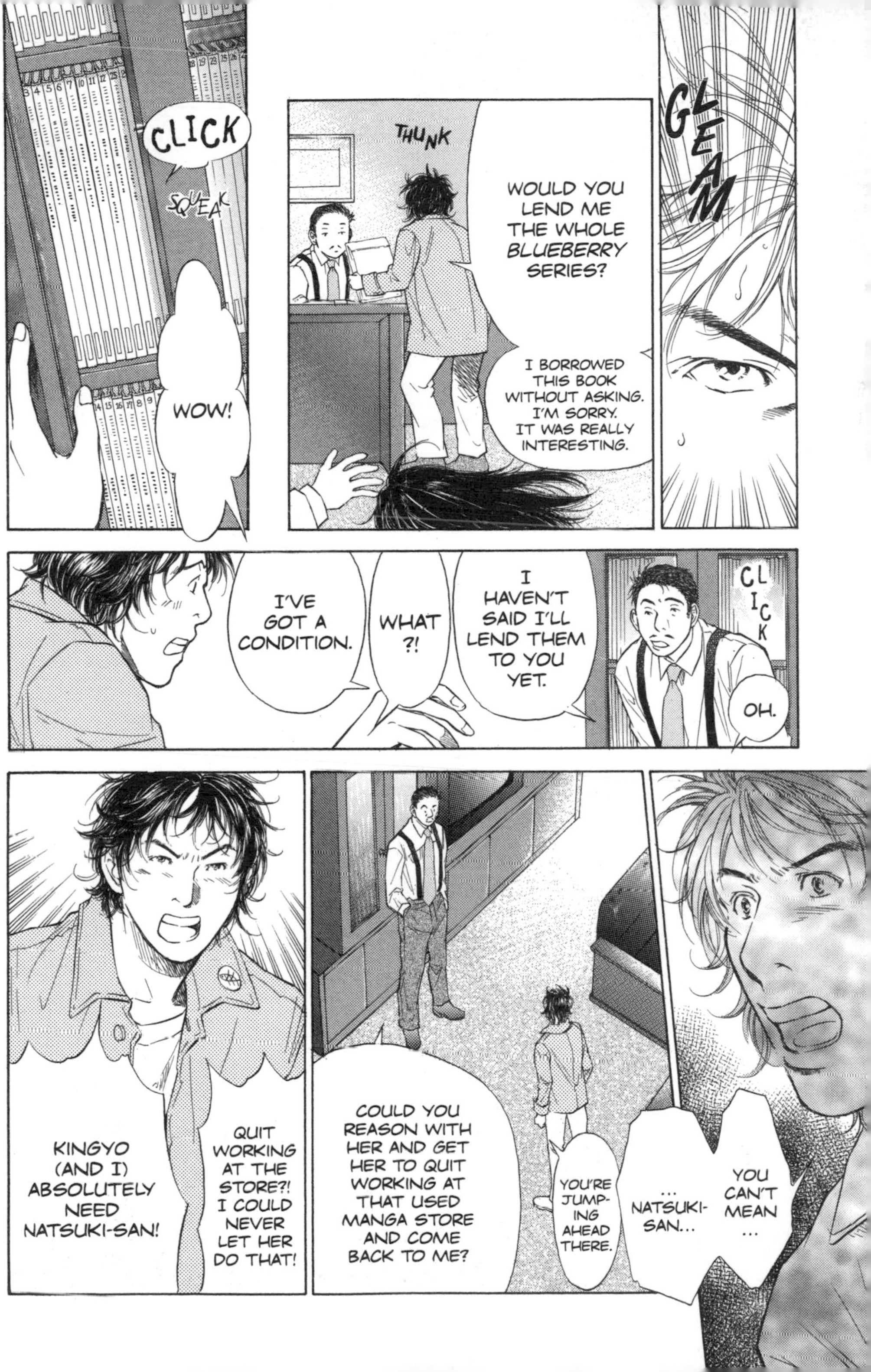
GLEAM
THUNK
WOULD YOU LEND ME THE WHOLE BLUEBERRY SERIES?
I BORROWED THIS BOOK WITHOUT ASKING. I'M SORRY. IT WAS REALLY INTERESTING.
CLICK
SQUEAK
WOW!
CLICK
OH.
I HAVEN'T SAID I'LL LEND THEM TO YOU YET.
WHAT?!
I'VE GOT A CONDITION.
YOU CAN'T MEAN...
...NATSUKI-SAN...
COULD YOU REASON WITH HER AND GET HER TO QUIT WORKING AT THAT USED MANGA STORE AND COME BACK TO ME?
YOU'RE JUMPING AHEAD THERE.
QUIT WORKING AT THE STORE?! I COULD NEVER LET HER DO THAT!
KINGYO (AND I) ABSOLUTELY NEED NATSUKI-SAN!

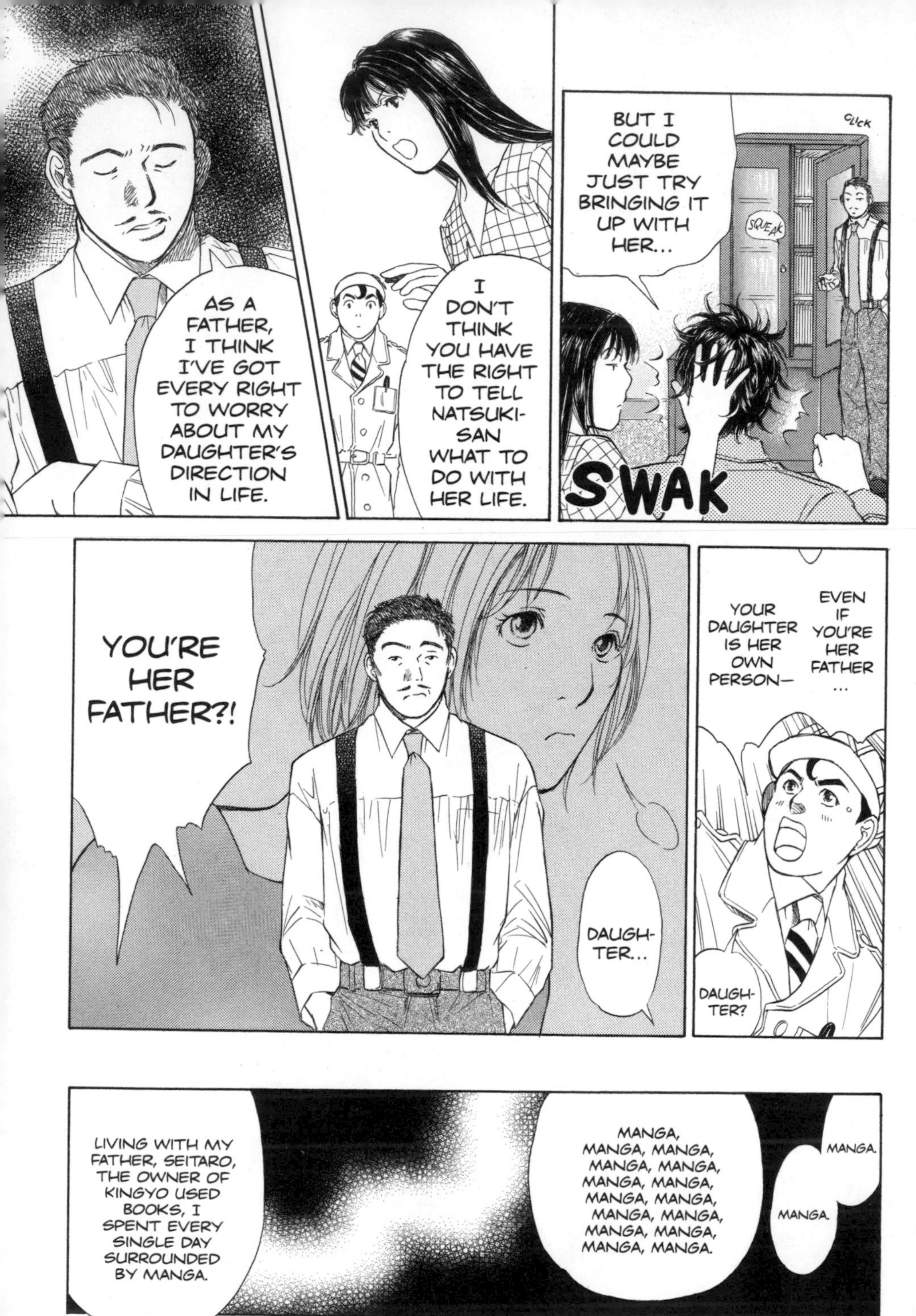
BUT I COULD MAYBE JUST TRY BRINGING IT UP WITH HER...
CLICK
SQUEAK
SWAK
I DON'T THINK YOU HAVE THE RIGHT TO TELL NATSUKI-SAN WHAT TO DO WITH HER LIFE.
AS A FATHER, I THINK I'VE GOT EVERY RIGHT TO WORRY ABOUT MY DAUGHTER'S DIRECTION IN LIFE.
EVEN IF YOU'RE HER FATHER...
YOUR DAUGHTER IS HER OWN PERSON—
DAUGH-TER?
YOU'RE HER FATHER?!
DAUGH-TER...
MANGA.
MANGA.
MANGA, MANGA, MANGA, MANGA, MANGA, MANGA, MANGA, MANGA, MANGA, MANGA, MANGA, MANGA, MANGA, MANGA, MANGA.
LIVING WITH MY FATHER, SEITARO, THE OWNER OF KINGYO USED BOOKS, I SPENT EVERY SINGLE DAY SURROUNDED BY MANGA.

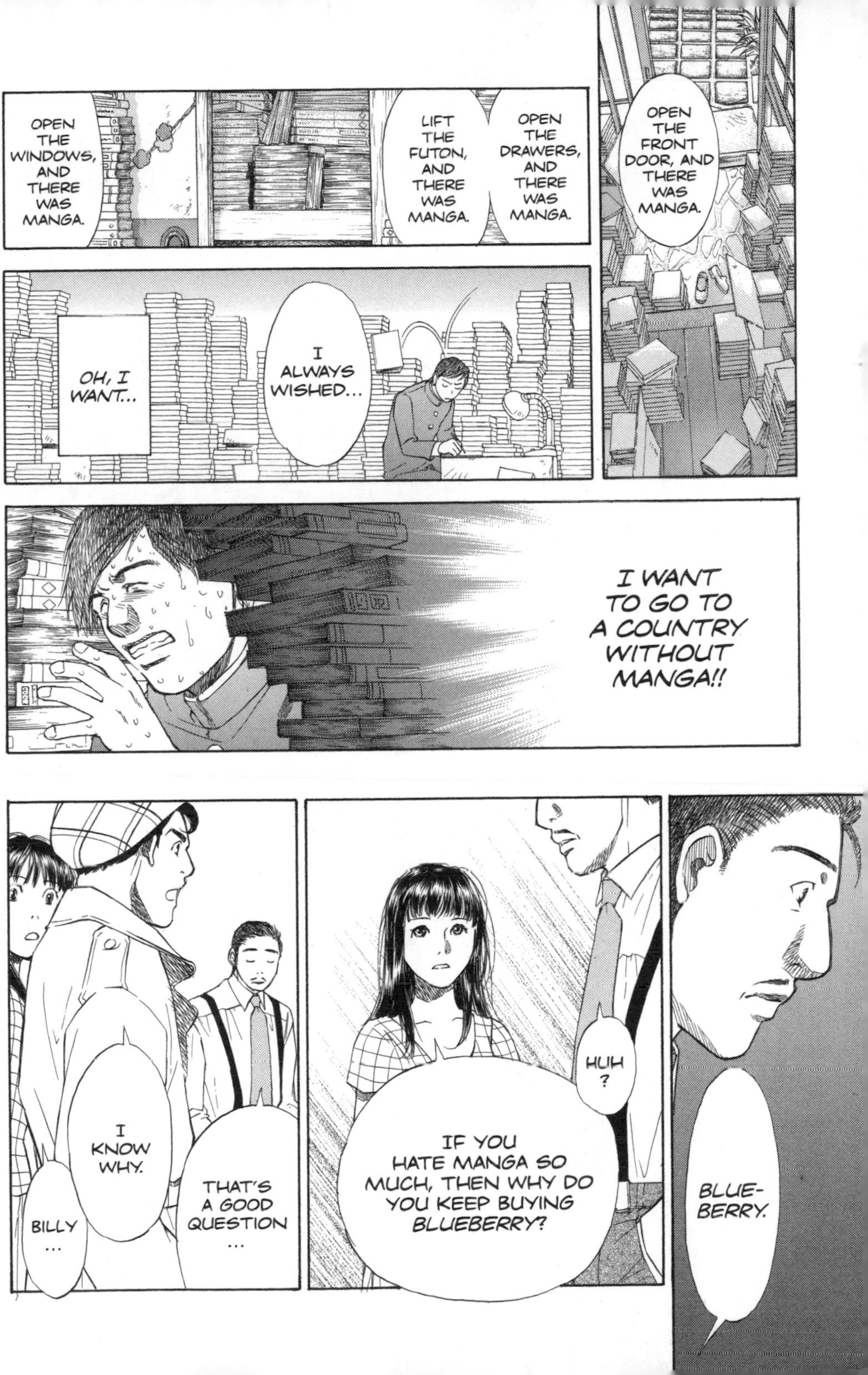
OPEN THE FRONT DOOR, AND THERE WAS MANGA.
OPEN THE DRAWERS, AND THERE WAS MANGA.
LIFT THE FUTON, AND THERE WAS MANGA.
OPEN THE WINDOWS, AND THERE WAS MANGA.
I ALWAYS WISHED...
OH, I WANT...
I WANT TO GO TO A COUNTRY WITHOUT MANGA!!
BLUE-BERRY.
HUH?
IF YOU HATE MANGA SO MUCH, THEN WHY DO YOU KEEP BUYING BLUEBERRY?
THAT'S A GOOD QUESTION...
I KNOW WHY.
BILLY...

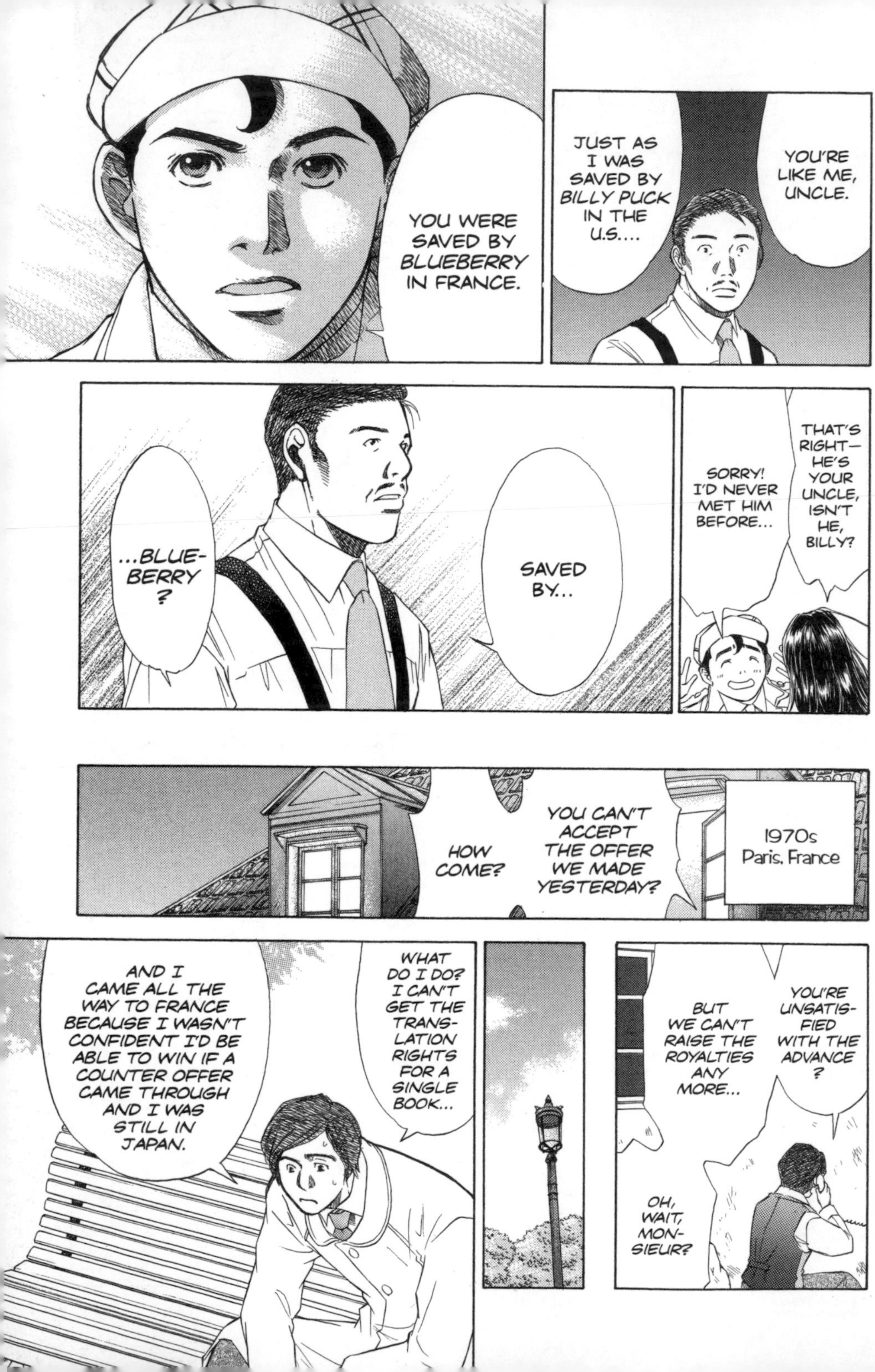
YOU'RE LIKE ME, UNCLE.
JUST AS I WAS SAVED BY BILLY PUCK IN THE U.S....
YOU WERE SAVED BY BLUEBERRY IN FRANCE.
THAT'S RIGHT— HE'S YOUR UNCLE, ISN'T HE, BILLY?
SORRY! I'D NEVER MET HIM BEFORE...
SAVED BY...
...BLUEBERRY?
1970s Paris, France
YOU CAN'T ACCEPT THE OFFER WE MADE YESTERDAY?
HOW COME?
YOU'RE UNSATISFIED WITH THE ADVANCE?
BUT WE CAN'T RAISE THE ROYALTIES ANY MORE...
OH, WAIT, MONSIEUR?
WHAT DO I DO? I CAN'T GET THE TRANSLATION RIGHTS FOR A SINGLE BOOK...
AND I CAME ALL THE WAY TO FRANCE BECAUSE I WASN'T CONFIDENT I'D BE ABLE TO WIN IF A COUNTER OFFER CAME THROUGH AND I WAS STILL IN JAPAN.

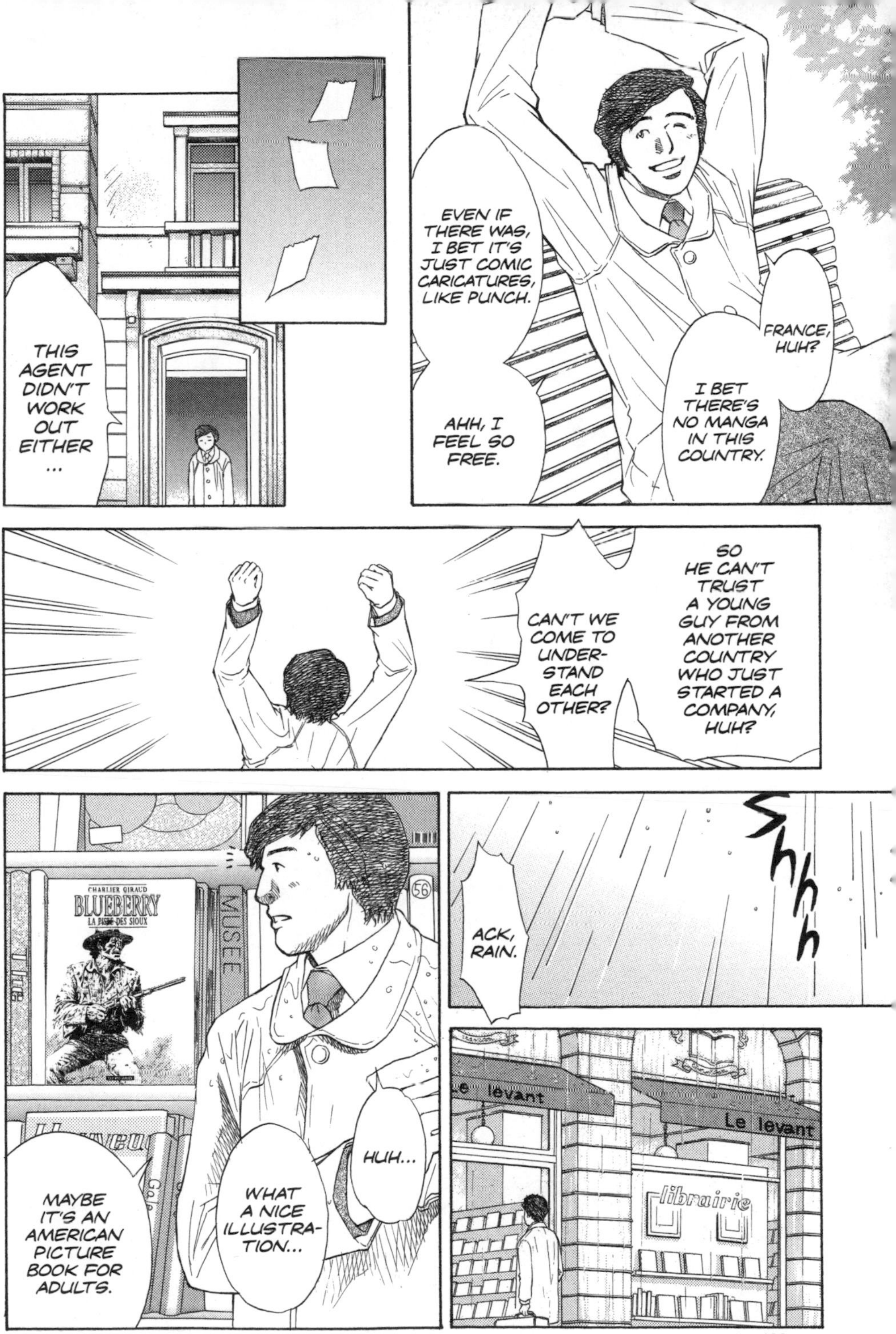
FRANCE, HUH?
I BET THERE'S NO MANGA IN THIS COUNTRY.
EVEN IF THERE WAS, I BET IT'S JUST COMIC CARICATURES, LIKE PUNCH.
AHH, I FEEL SO FREE.
THIS AGENT DIDN'T WORK OUT EITHER ...
SO HE CAN'T TRUST A YOUNG GUY FROM ANOTHER COUNTRY WHO JUST STARTED A COMPANY, HUH?
CAN'T WE COME TO UNDER-STAND EACH OTHER?
SHHH
ACK, RAIN.
Le levant
Le levant
librairie
CHARLIER GIRAUD
BLUEBERRY
LA PISTE DES SIOUX
MUSEE
56
HUH...
WHAT A NICE ILLUSTRA-TION...
MAYBE IT'S AN AMERICAN PICTURE BOOK FOR ADULTS.

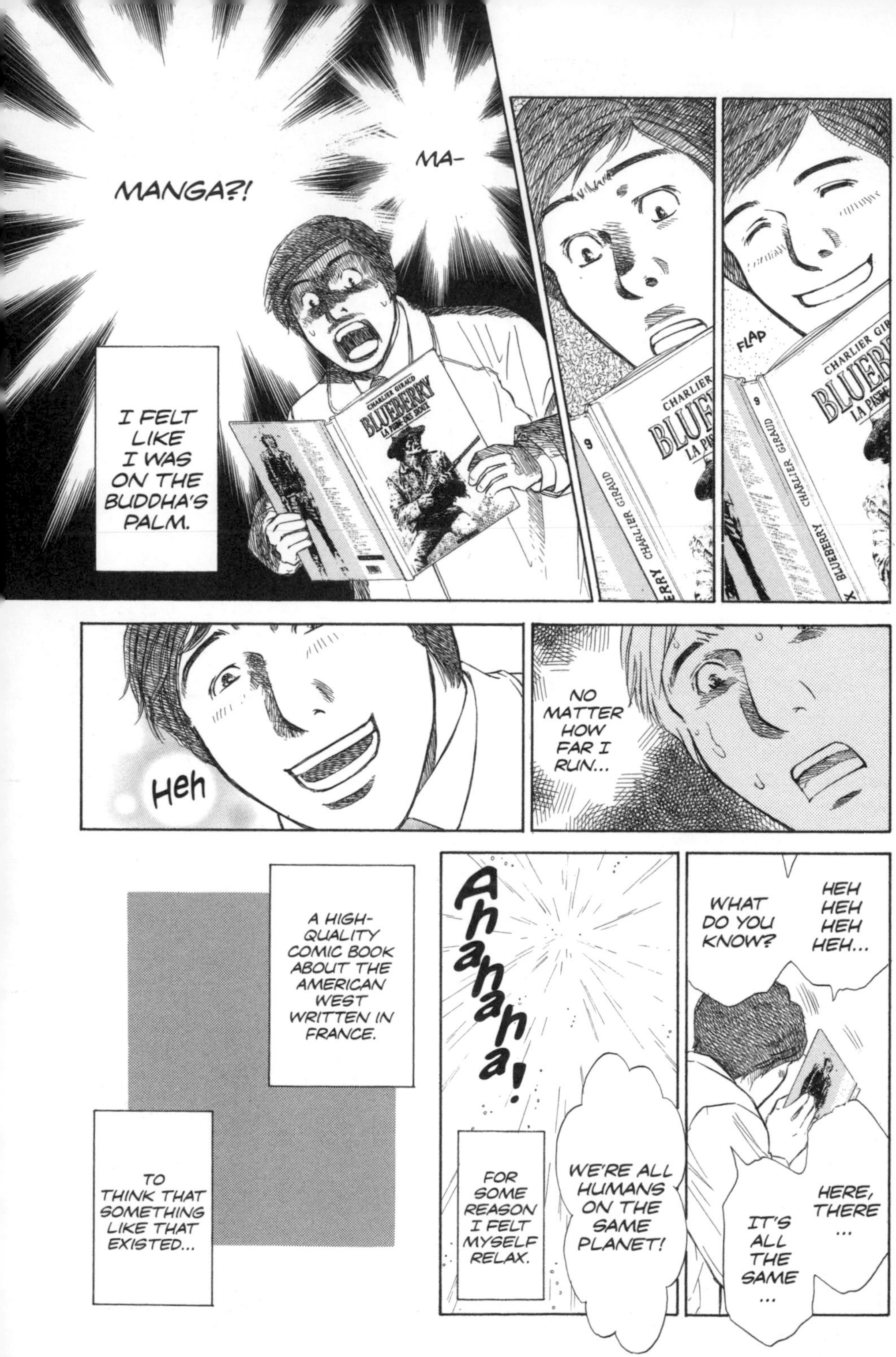
FLAP
MA-
MANGA?!
I FELT LIKE I WAS ON THE BUDDHA'S PALM.
NO MATTER HOW FAR I RUN...
Heh
HEH HEH HEH HEH...
WHAT DO YOU KNOW?
HERE, THERE...
IT'S ALL THE SAME...
Ahahaha!
WE'RE ALL HUMANS ON THE SAME PLANET!
FOR SOME REASON I FELT MYSELF RELAX.
A HIGH-QUALITY COMIC BOOK ABOUT THE AMERICAN WEST WRITTEN IN FRANCE.
TO THINK THAT SOMETHING LIKE THAT EXISTED...

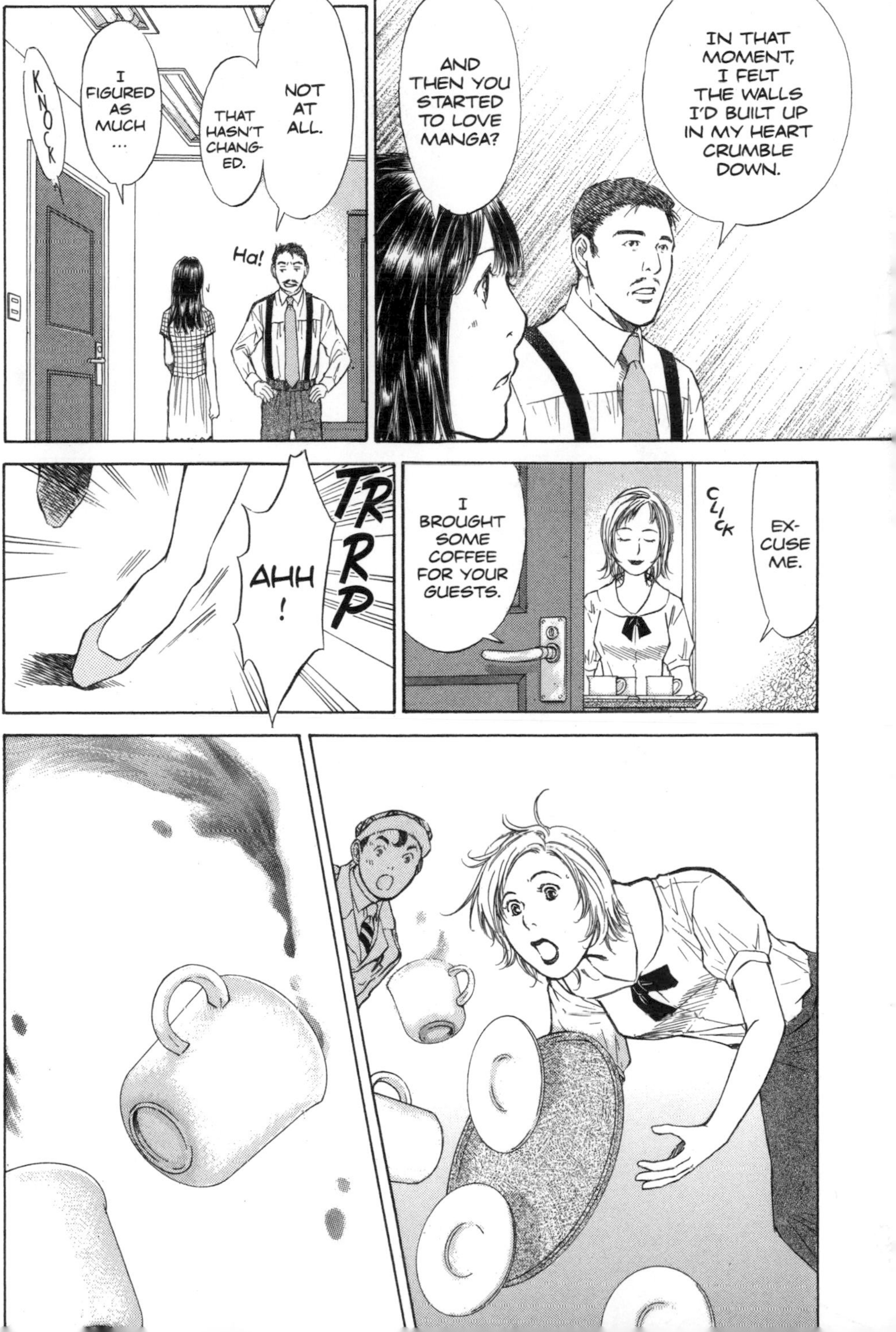
IN THAT MOMENT, I FELT THE WALLS I'D BUILT UP IN MY HEART CRUMBLE DOWN.
AND THEN YOU STARTED TO LOVE MANGA?
NOT AT ALL.
THAT HASN'T CHANG-ED.
I FIGURED AS MUCH...
KNOCK
Ha!
EX-CUSE ME.
CLICK
I BROUGHT SOME COFFEE FOR YOUR GUESTS.
TRRP
AHH!

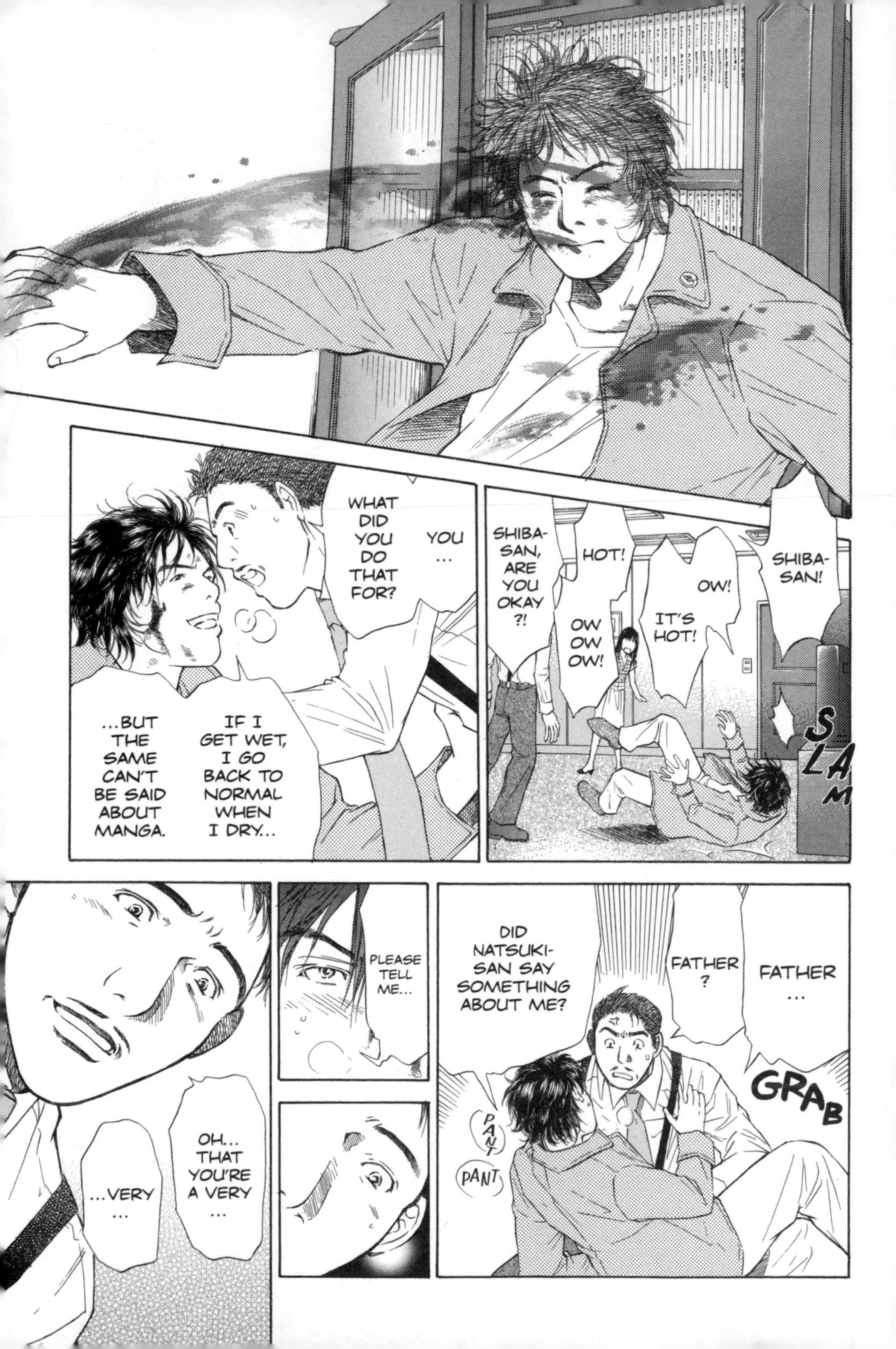
SLAM
SHIBA-SAN!
OW!
IT'S HOT!
HOT!
OW OW OW!
SHIBA-SAN, ARE YOU OKAY?!
YOU...
WHAT DID YOU DO THAT FOR?
IF I GET WET, I GO BACK TO NORMAL WHEN I DRY...
...BUT THE SAME CAN'T BE SAID ABOUT MANGA.
FATHER...
FATHER?
GRAB
DID NATSUKI-SAN SAY SOMETHING ABOUT ME?
PANT
PANT
PLEASE TELL ME...
OH... THAT YOU'RE A VERY...
...VERY...

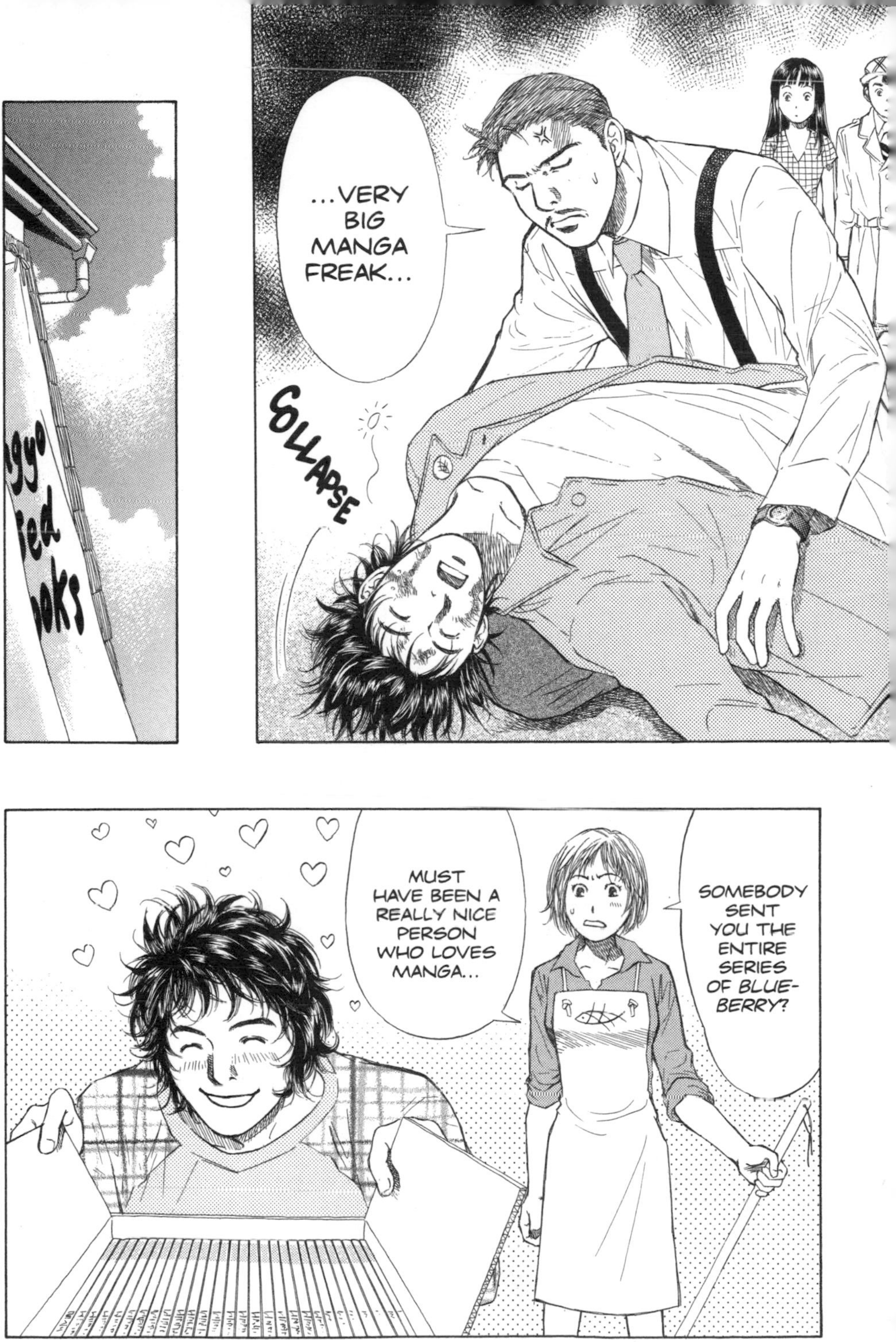
...VERY BIG MANGA FREAK...
COLLAPSE
SOMEBODY SENT YOU THE ENTIRE SERIES OF BLUE-BERRY?
MUST HAVE BEEN A REALLY NICE PERSON WHO LOVES MANGA...

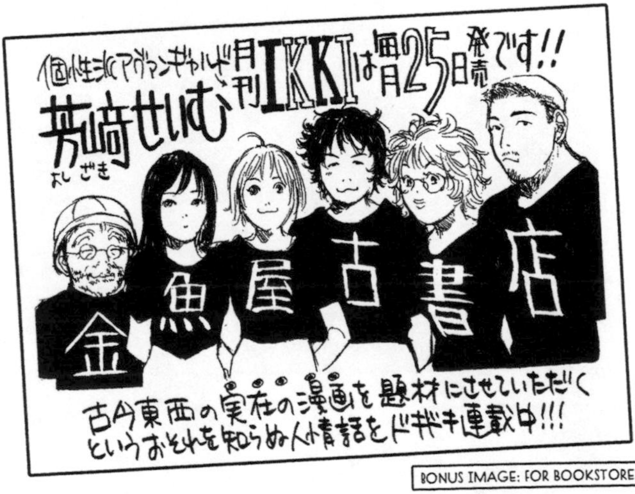

個性派アヴァンギャルド月刊IKKIは毎月25日発売です!!
芳崎せいむ
よしざき
金
魚
屋
古
書
店
古今東西の実在の漫画を題材にさせていただく
というおそれを知らぬ人情話をドキドキ連載中!!!

BONUS IMAGE: FOR BOOKSTORES

TRANSLATION OF ABOVE IMAGE:
AVANT-GARDE GEKKAN IKKI OUT ON THE 25TH OF EVERY MONTH!! — SEIMU YOSHIZAKI
NOW RUNNING THIS EXCITING HUMAN DRAMA FEARLESSLY COVERING ACTUAL MANGA NEW AND OLD, EASTERN AND WESTERN.
[SHOWN TOGETHER, THE T-SHIRTS SPELL OUT KINGYO USED BOOKS — ED.]

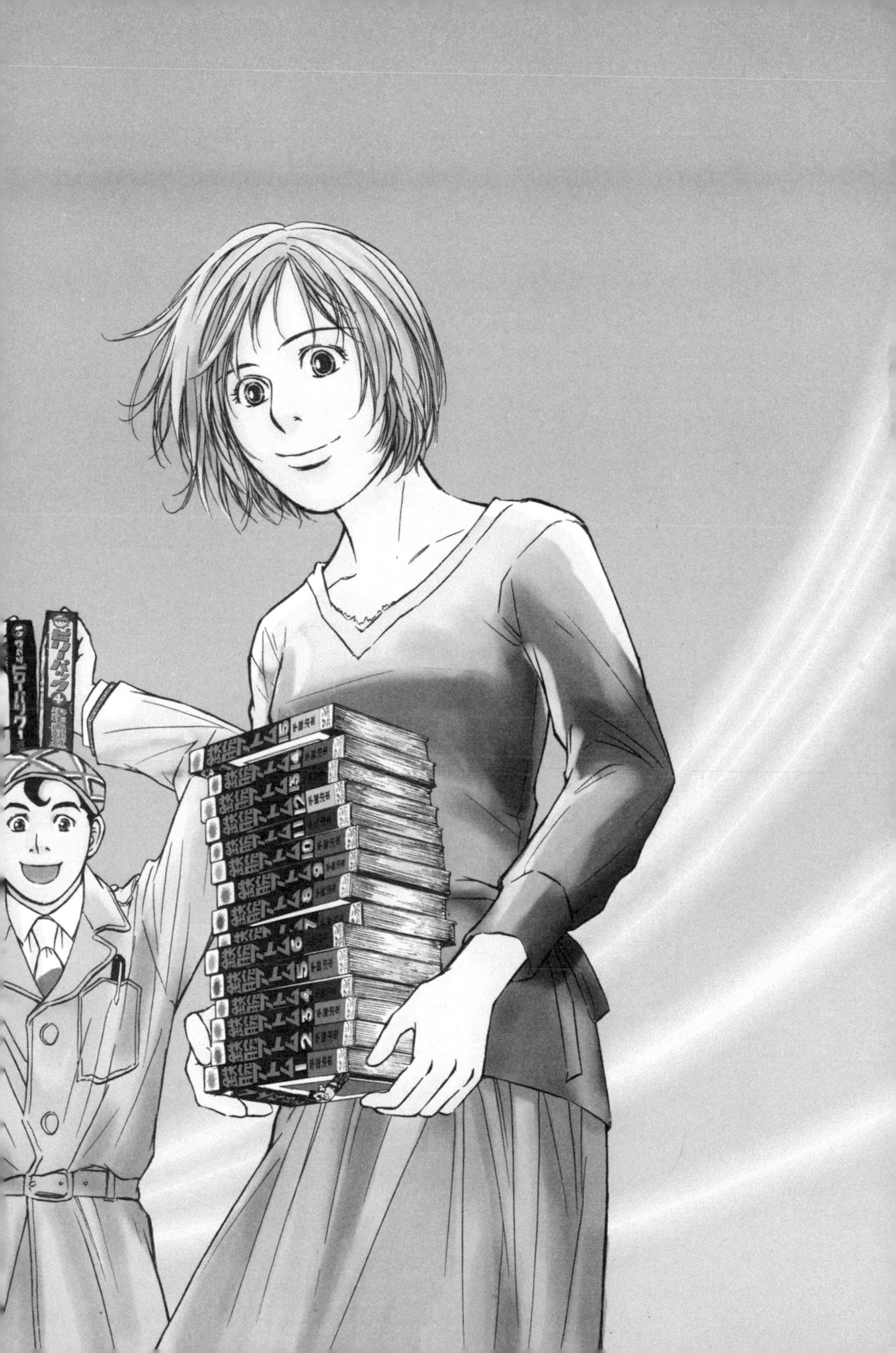

Chapter 6: Fujiomi-kun

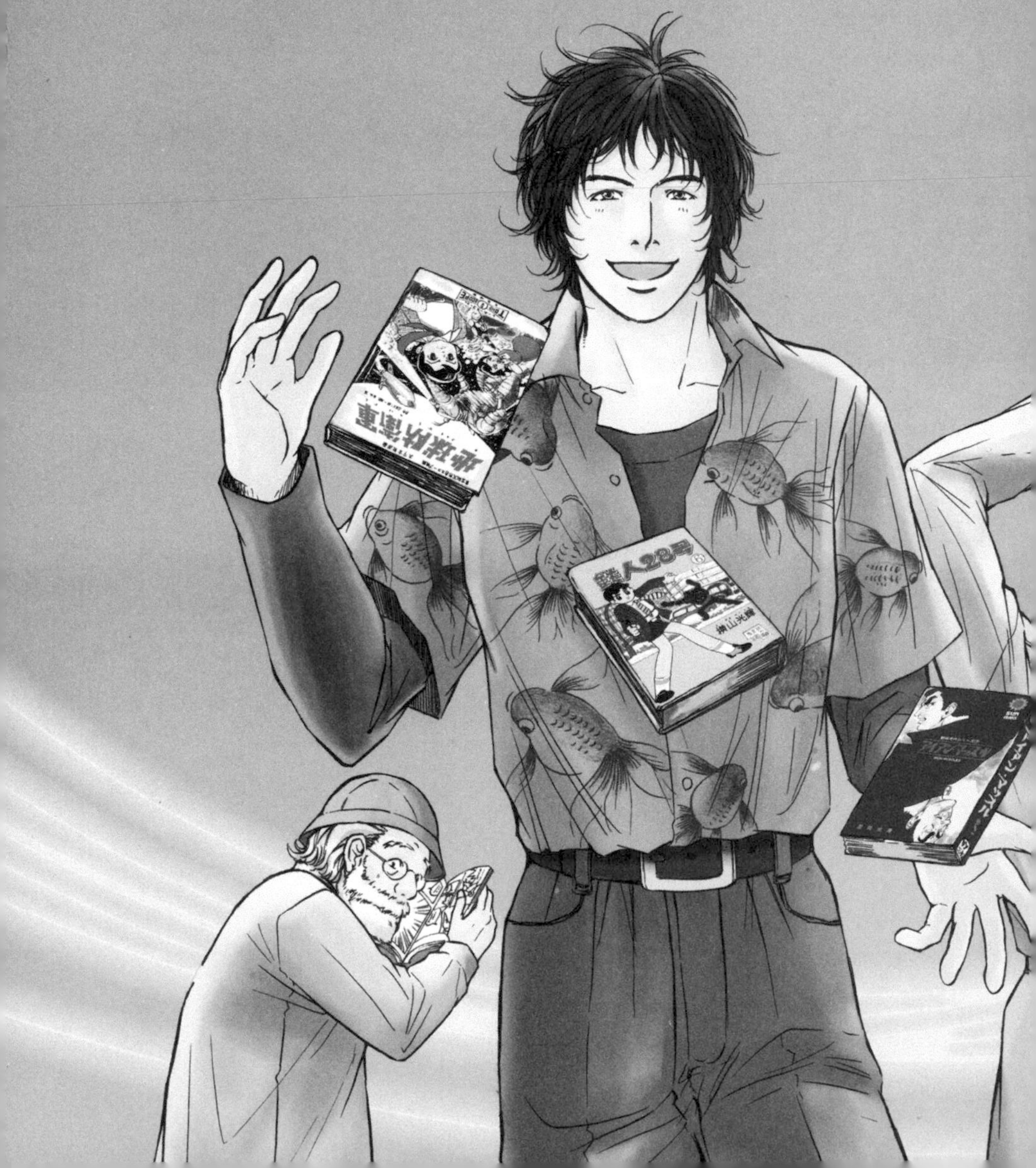
鉄人28号

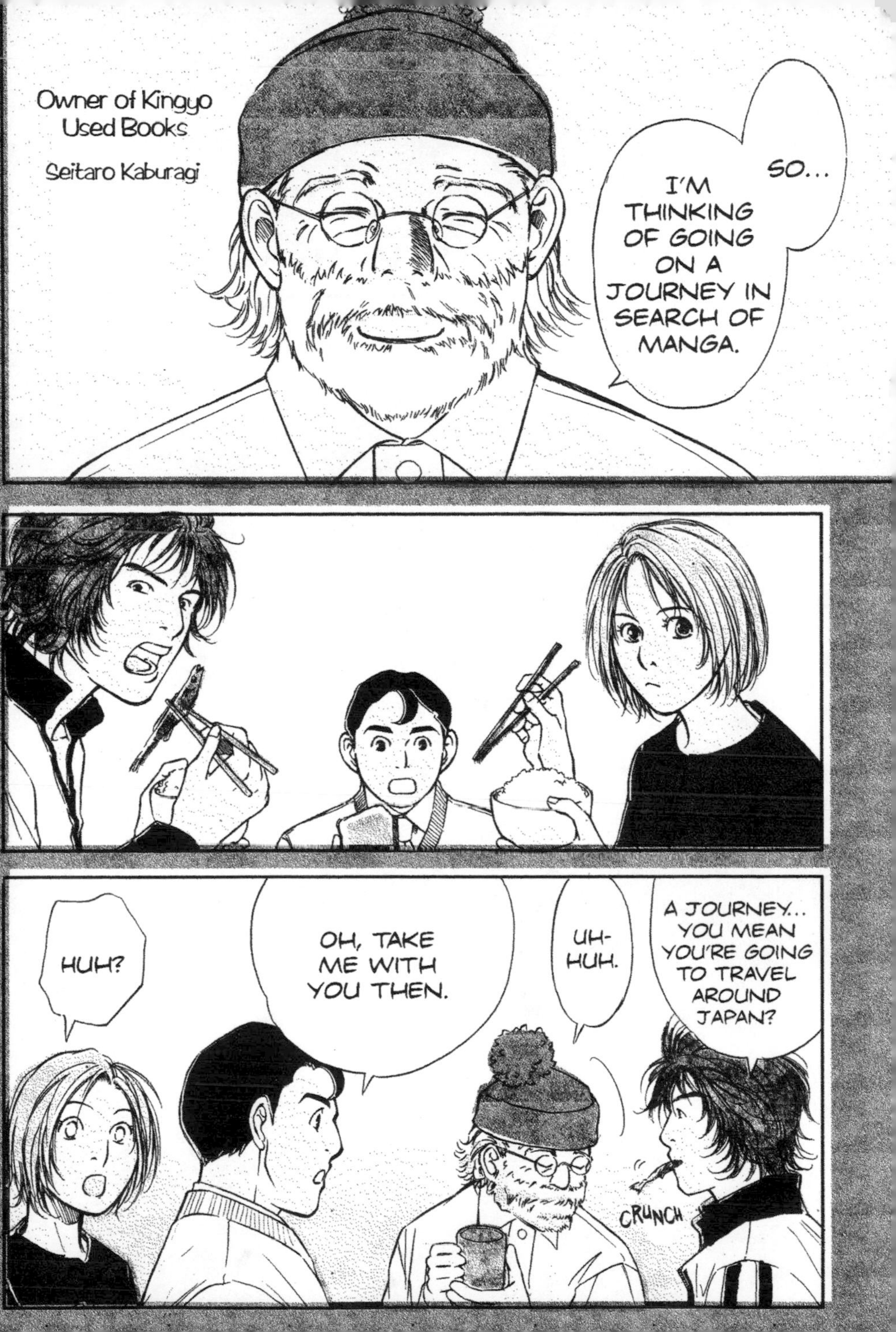
SO... I'M THINKING OF GOING ON A JOURNEY IN SEARCH OF MANGA.
Owner of Kingyo Used Books
Seitaro Kaburagi
A JOURNEY... YOU MEAN YOU'RE GOING TO TRAVEL AROUND JAPAN?
CRUNCH
UH-HUH.
OH, TAKE ME WITH YOU THEN.
HUH?

STUDY!

KASEI TANKEN BY NOBORU OHSHIRO, PUBLISHED IN 1940. OFTEN CITED AS THE FIRST LONG SCIENCE FICTION FANTASY MANGA IN THE WORLD, IT WAS PRINTED IN COLOR, WITH AN ARTISTIC "THREE-COLOR PRINTING" SCREEN AND COVER (INFO FROM SHIBA-SAN). ALL VOLUMES WERE REPUBLISHED IN JAPAN IN FEBRUARY OF 2005. THE STORY OF THE DISCOVERY OF *KASEI TANKEN* CAN BE FOUND IN THE FIRST VOLUME OF THE *KINGYO USED BOOKS NOTEBOOK*.

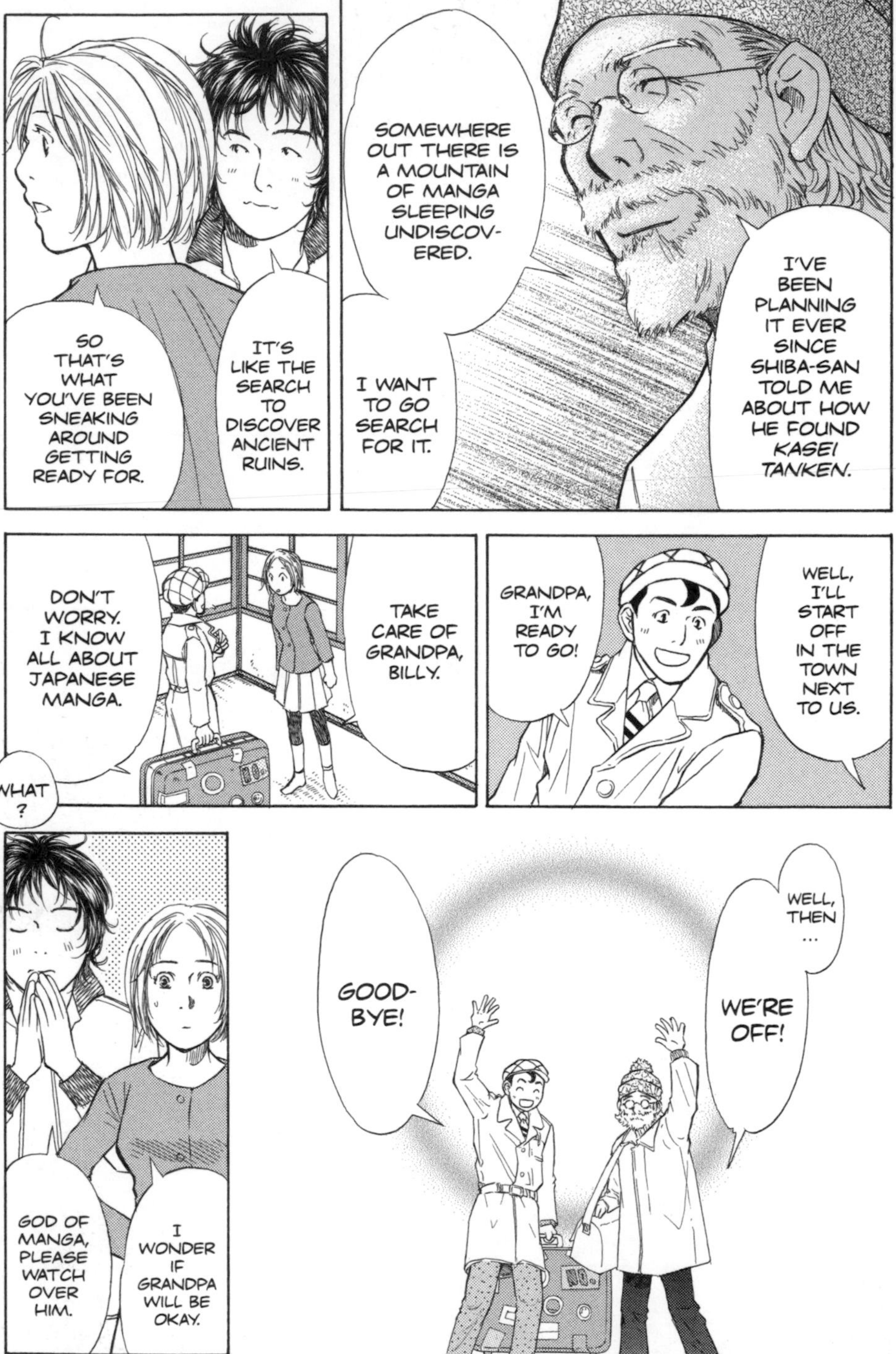

I'VE BEEN PLANNING IT EVER SINCE SHIBA-SAN TOLD ME ABOUT HOW HE FOUND *KASEI TANKEN*.
SOMEWHERE OUT THERE IS A MOUNTAIN OF MANGA SLEEPING UNDISCOV-ERED.
I WANT TO GO SEARCH FOR IT.
IT'S LIKE THE SEARCH TO DISCOVER ANCIENT RUINS.
SO THAT'S WHAT YOU'VE BEEN SNEAKING AROUND GETTING READY FOR.
WELL, I'LL START OFF IN THE TOWN NEXT TO US.
GRANDPA, I'M READY TO GO!
TAKE CARE OF GRANDPA, BILLY.
DON'T WORRY. I KNOW ALL ABOUT JAPANESE MANGA.
WHAT?
WELL, THEN...
WE'RE OFF!
GOOD-BYE!
I WONDER IF GRANDPA WILL BE OKAY.
GOD OF MANGA, PLEASE WATCH OVER HIM.

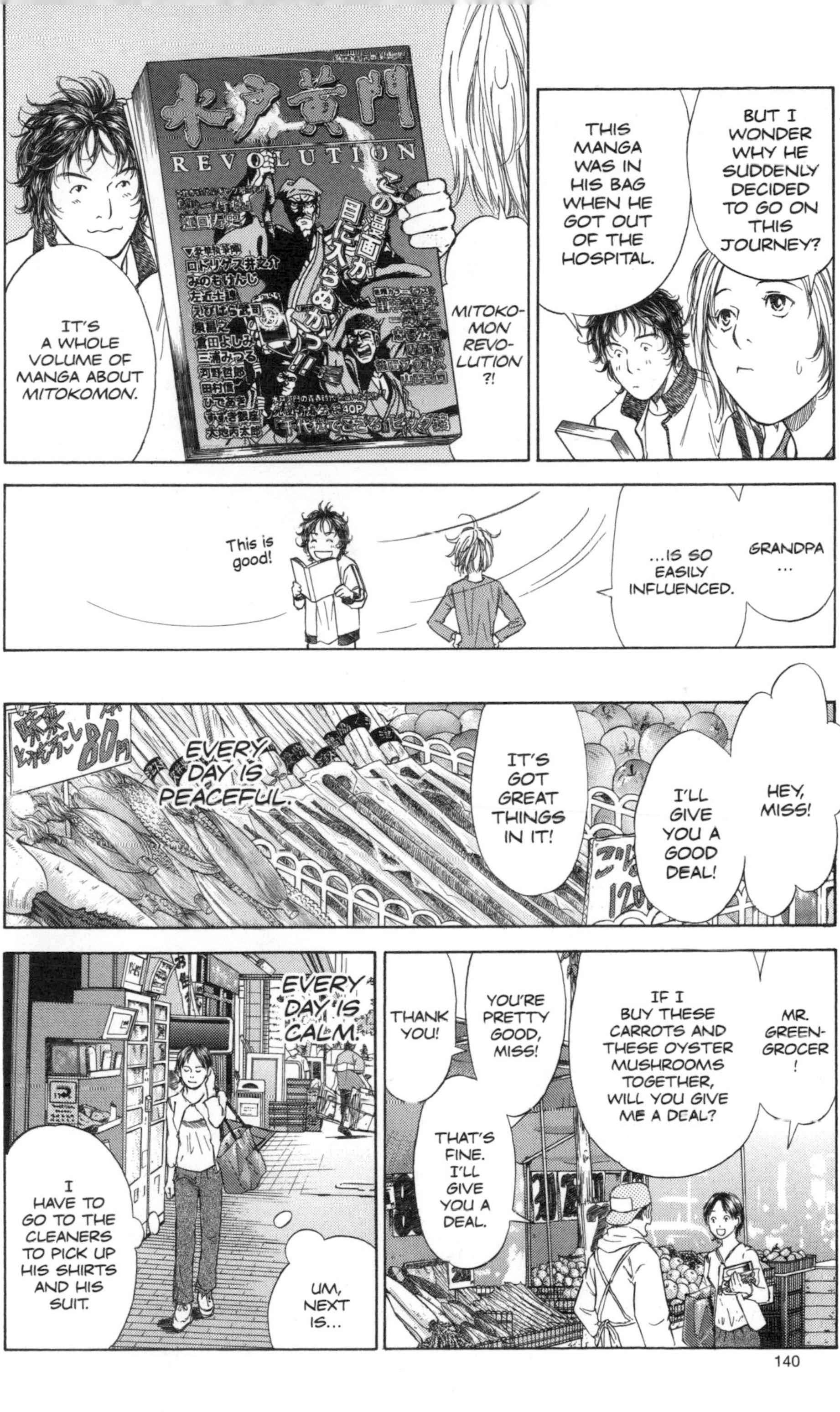
BUT I WONDER WHY HE SUDDENLY DECIDED TO GO ON THIS JOURNEY?
THIS MANGA WAS IN HIS BAG WHEN HE GOT OUT OF THE HOSPITAL.
MITOKOMON REVOLUTION ?!
IT'S A WHOLE VOLUME OF MANGA ABOUT MITOKOMON.
REVOLUTION
GRANDPA …
…IS SO EASILY INFLUENCED.
This is good!
HEY, MISS!
I'LL GIVE YOU A GOOD DEAL!
IT'S GOT GREAT THINGS IN IT!
EVERY DAY IS PEACEFUL.
MR. GREEN-GROCER !
IF I BUY THESE CARROTS AND THESE OYSTER MUSHROOMS TOGETHER, WILL YOU GIVE ME A DEAL?
YOU'RE PRETTY GOOD, MISS!
THAT'S FINE. I'LL GIVE YOU A DEAL.
THANK YOU!
EVERY DAY IS CALM.
I HAVE TO GO TO THE CLEANERS TO PICK UP HIS SHIRTS AND HIS SUIT.
UM, NEXT IS…

STUDY! *MITOKOMON REVOLUTION*: A MAGAZINE RELEASED IN 2004 TO COMMEMORATE THE 1,000TH EPISODE OF THE TV SERIES *MITOKOMON*. IT'S AN ANTHOLOGY OF STORIES AND INCLUDES WORK BY BIG JOE AND HISASHI EGUCHI.

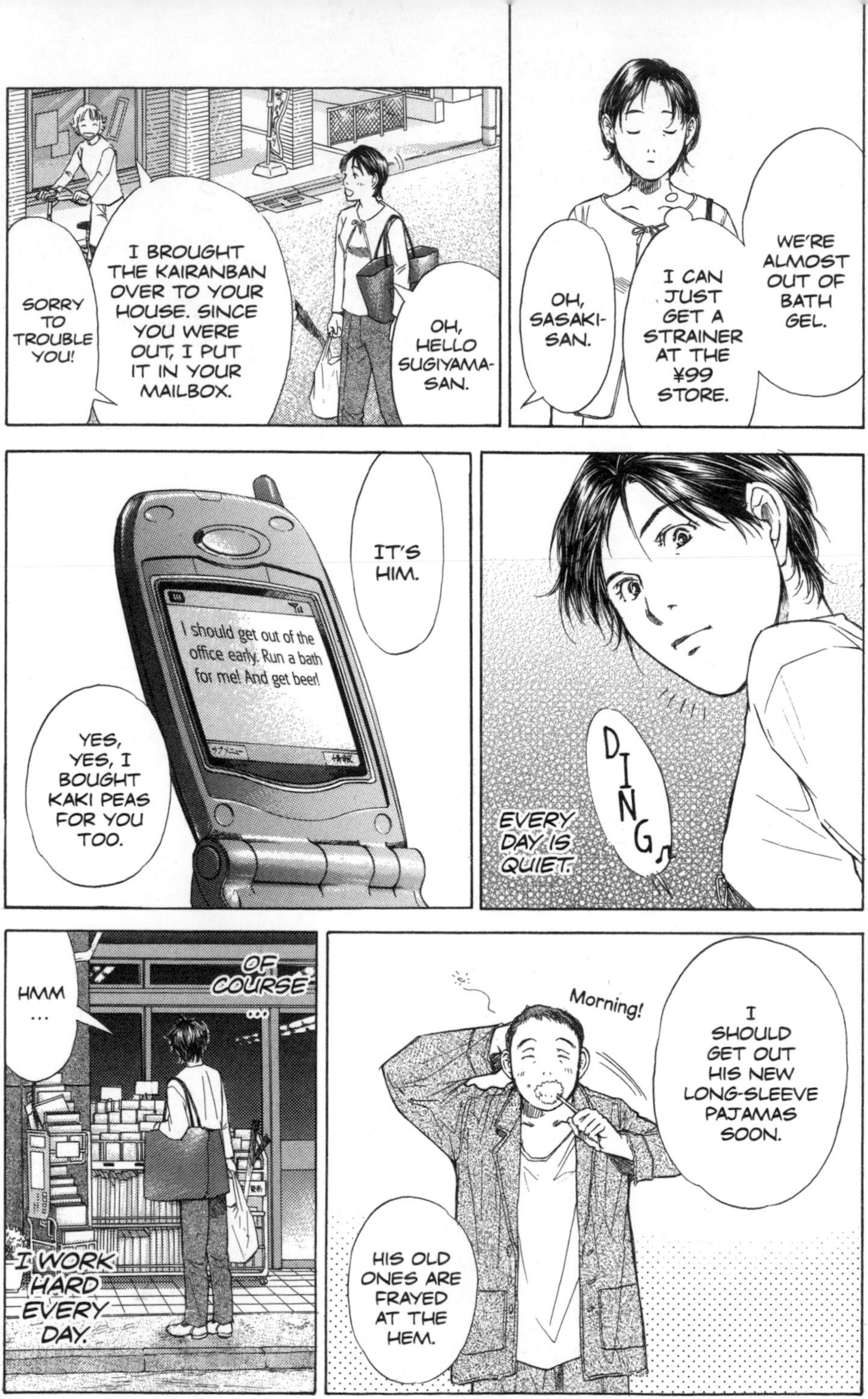
WE'RE ALMOST OUT OF BATH GEL.
I CAN JUST GET A STRAINER AT THE ¥99 STORE.
OH, SASAKI-SAN.
OH, HELLO SUGIYAMA-SAN.
I BROUGHT THE KAIRANBAN OVER TO YOUR HOUSE. SINCE YOU WERE OUT, I PUT IT IN YOUR MAILBOX.
SORRY TO TROUBLE YOU!
DING
EVERY DAY IS QUIET.
IT'S HIM.
I should get out of the office early. Run a bath for me! And get beer!
YES, YES, I BOUGHT KAKI PEAS FOR YOU TOO.
I SHOULD GET OUT HIS NEW LONG-SLEEVE PAJAMAS SOON.
Morning!
HIS OLD ONES ARE FRAYED AT THE HEM.
OF COURSE...
HMM...
I WORK HARD EVERY DAY.

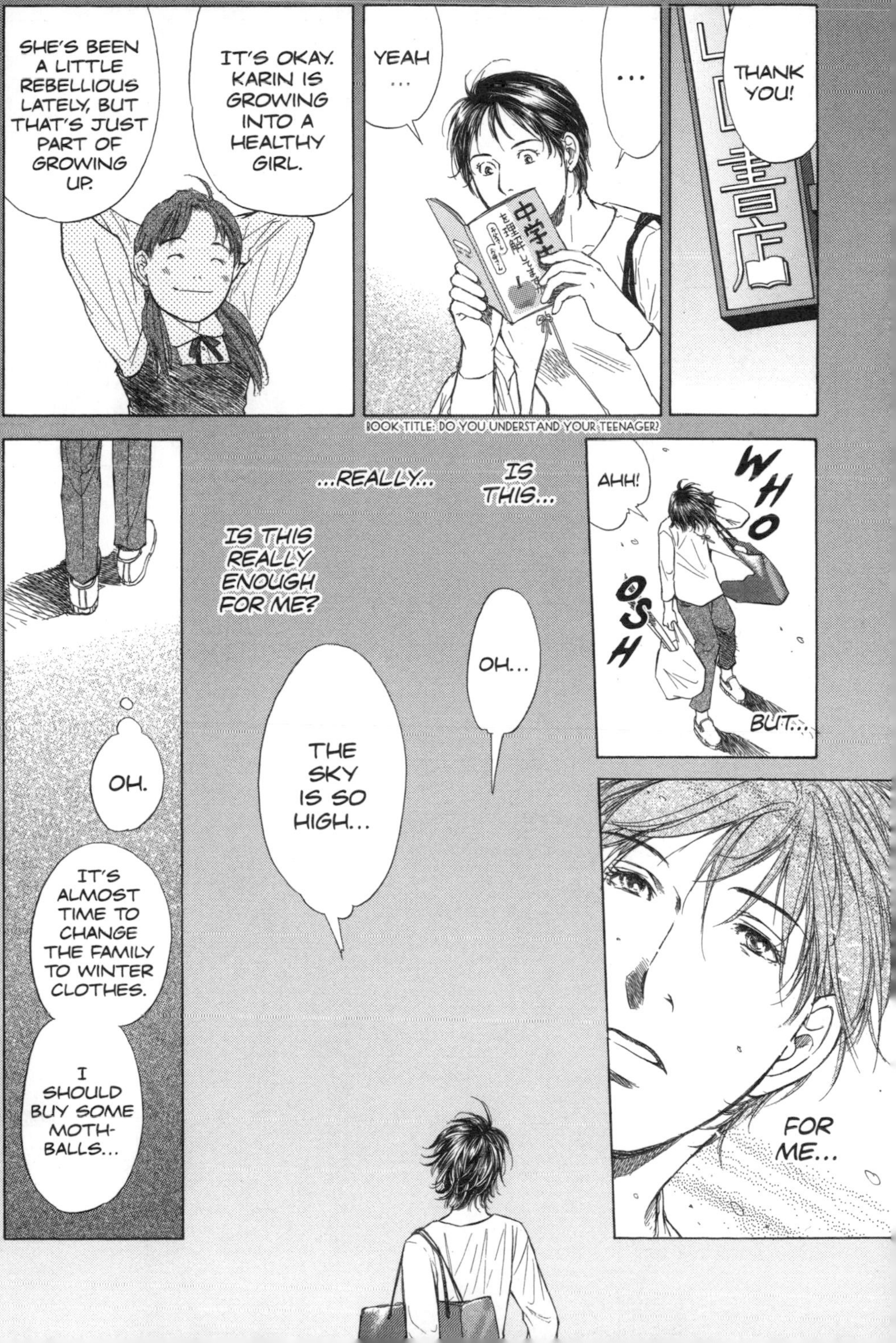
THANK YOU!
...
YEAH ...
IT'S OKAY. KARIN IS GROWING INTO A HEALTHY GIRL.
SHE'S BEEN A LITTLE REBELLIOUS LATELY, BUT THAT'S JUST PART OF GROWING UP.
BOOK TITLE: DO YOU UNDERSTAND YOUR TEENAGER?
AHH!
WHOOSH
BUT...
FOR ME...
IS THIS...
...REALLY...
IS THIS REALLY ENOUGH FOR ME?
OH...
THE SKY IS SO HIGH...
OH.
IT'S ALMOST TIME TO CHANGE THE FAMILY TO WINTER CLOTHES.
I SHOULD BUY SOME MOTH-BALLS...

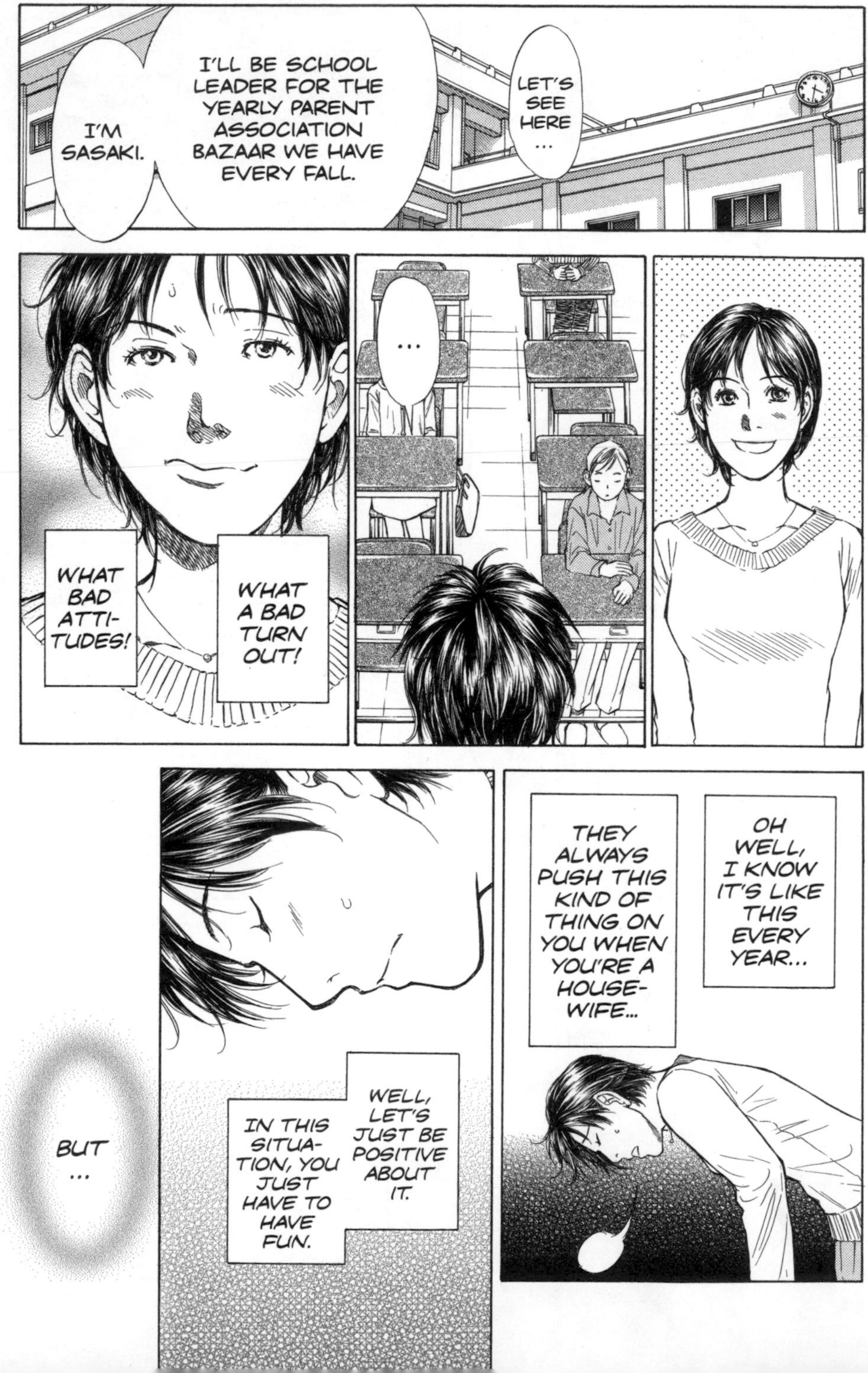
LET'S SEE HERE ...
I'LL BE SCHOOL LEADER FOR THE YEARLY PARENT ASSOCIATION BAZAAR WE HAVE EVERY FALL.
I'M SASAKI.
...
WHAT A BAD TURN OUT!
WHAT BAD ATTI-TUDES!
OH WELL, I KNOW IT'S LIKE THIS EVERY YEAR...
THEY ALWAYS PUSH THIS KIND OF THING ON YOU WHEN YOU'RE A HOUSE-WIFE...
WELL, LET'S JUST BE POSITIVE ABOUT IT.
IN THIS SITUA-TION, YOU JUST HAVE TO HAVE FUN.
BUT ...

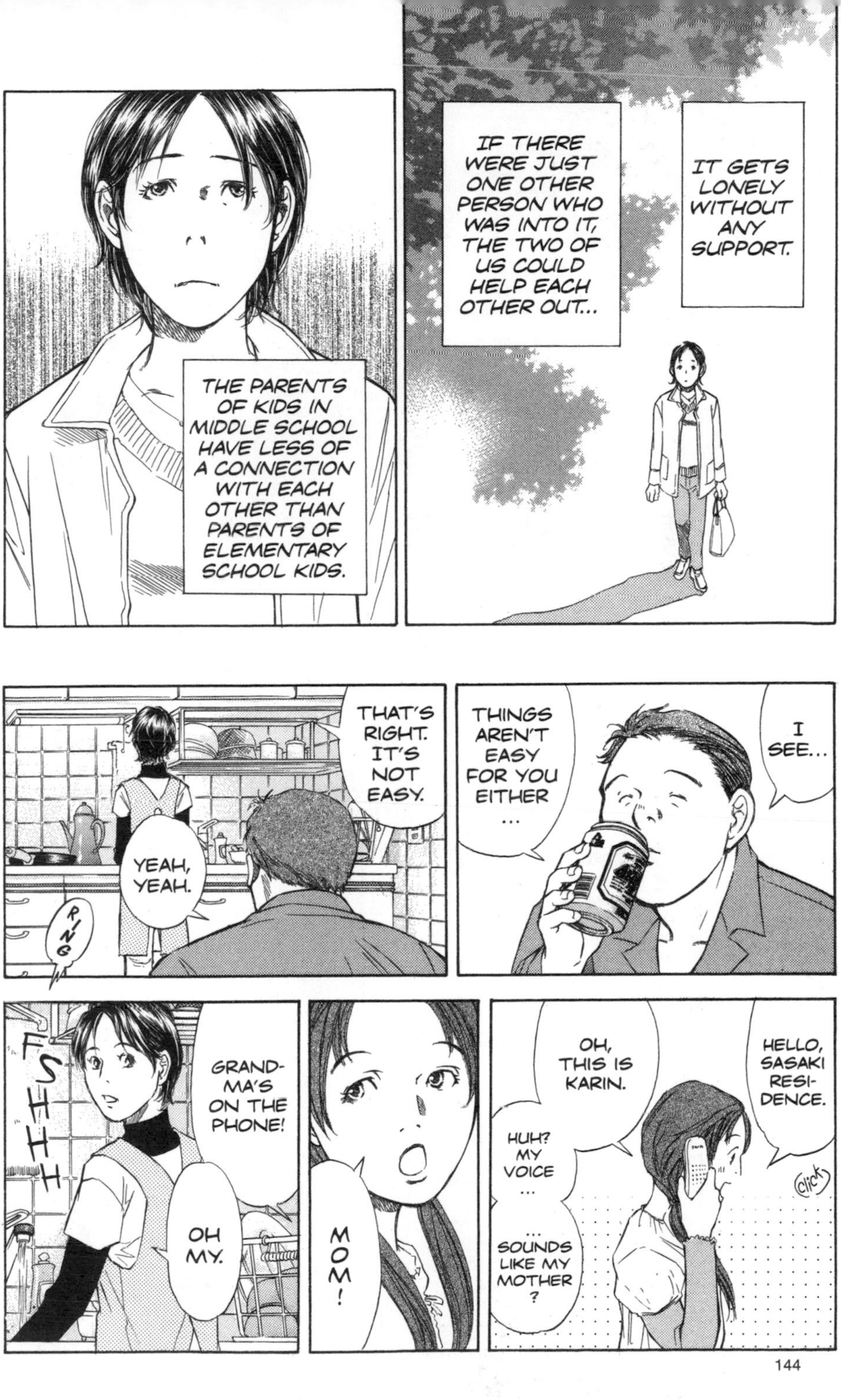
IT GETS LONELY WITHOUT ANY SUPPORT.
IF THERE WERE JUST ONE OTHER PERSON WHO WAS INTO IT, THE TWO OF US COULD HELP EACH OTHER OUT...
THE PARENTS OF KIDS IN MIDDLE SCHOOL HAVE LESS OF A CONNECTION WITH EACH OTHER THAN PARENTS OF ELEMENTARY SCHOOL KIDS.
I SEE...
THINGS AREN'T EASY FOR YOU EITHER ...
THAT'S RIGHT. IT'S NOT EASY.
YEAH, YEAH.
RING
HELLO, SASAKI RESIDENCE.
CLICK
OH, THIS IS KARIN.
HUH? MY VOICE ...
... SOUNDS LIKE MY MOTHER ?
MOM!
GRAND-MA'S ON THE PHONE!
OH MY.
FSHHH

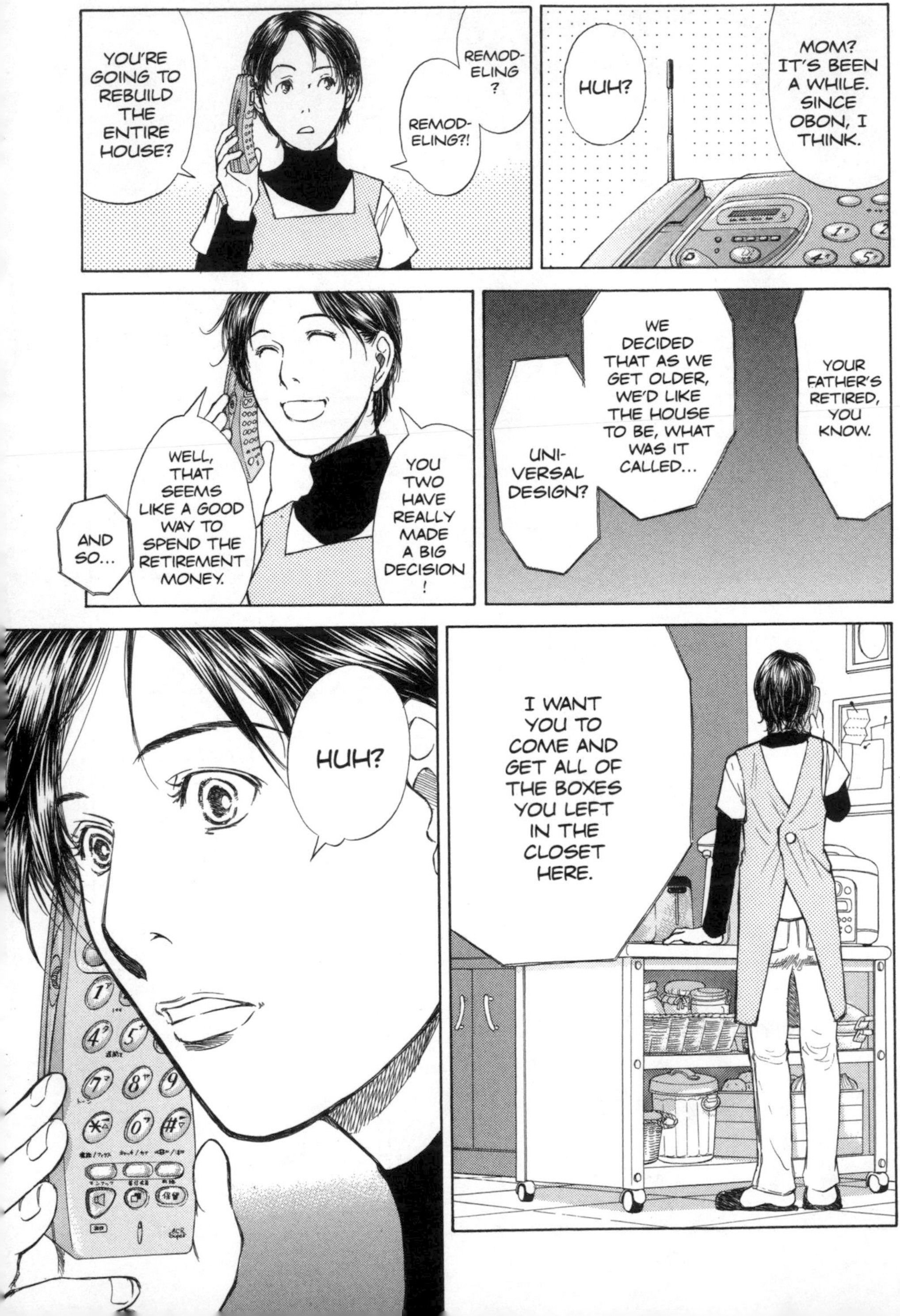
MOM? IT'S BEEN A WHILE. SINCE OBON, I THINK.
HUH?
REMODELING?
REMODELING?!
YOU'RE GOING TO REBUILD THE ENTIRE HOUSE?
YOUR FATHER'S RETIRED, YOU KNOW.
WE DECIDED THAT AS WE GET OLDER, WE'D LIKE THE HOUSE TO BE, WHAT WAS IT CALLED...
UNIVERSAL DESIGN?
YOU TWO HAVE REALLY MADE A BIG DECISION!
WELL, THAT SEEMS LIKE A GOOD WAY TO SPEND THE RETIREMENT MONEY.
AND SO...
I WANT YOU TO COME AND GET ALL OF THE BOXES YOU LEFT IN THE CLOSET HERE.
HUH?

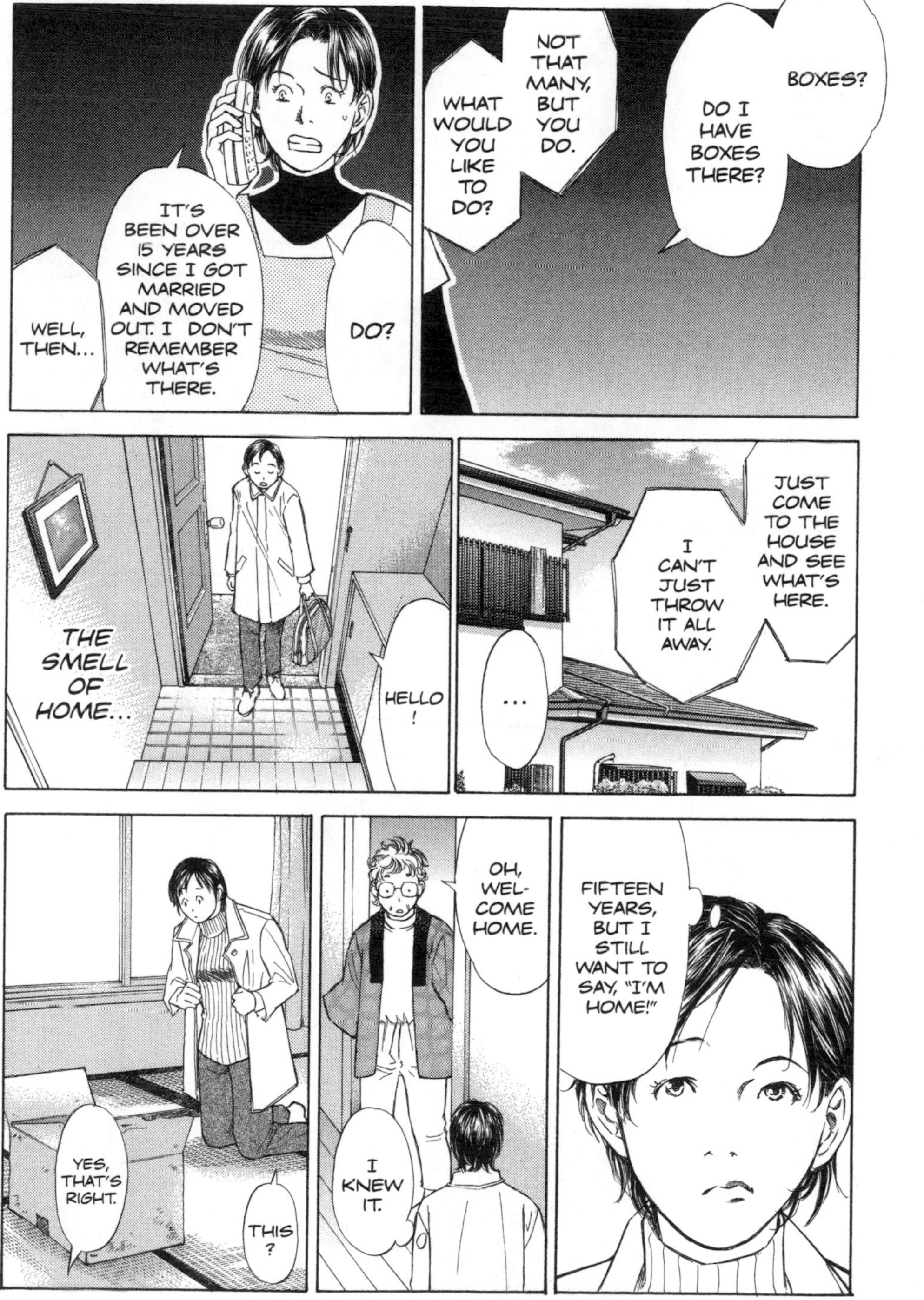
BOXES?
DO I HAVE BOXES THERE?
NOT THAT MANY, BUT YOU DO.
WHAT WOULD YOU LIKE TO DO?
DO?
IT'S BEEN OVER 15 YEARS SINCE I GOT MARRIED AND MOVED OUT. I DON'T REMEMBER WHAT'S THERE.
WELL, THEN...
JUST COME TO THE HOUSE AND SEE WHAT'S HERE.
I CAN'T JUST THROW IT ALL AWAY.
...
HELLO!
THE SMELL OF HOME...
FIFTEEN YEARS, BUT I STILL WANT TO SAY, "I'M HOME!"
OH, WEL-COME HOME.
I KNEW IT.
THIS?
YES, THAT'S RIGHT.

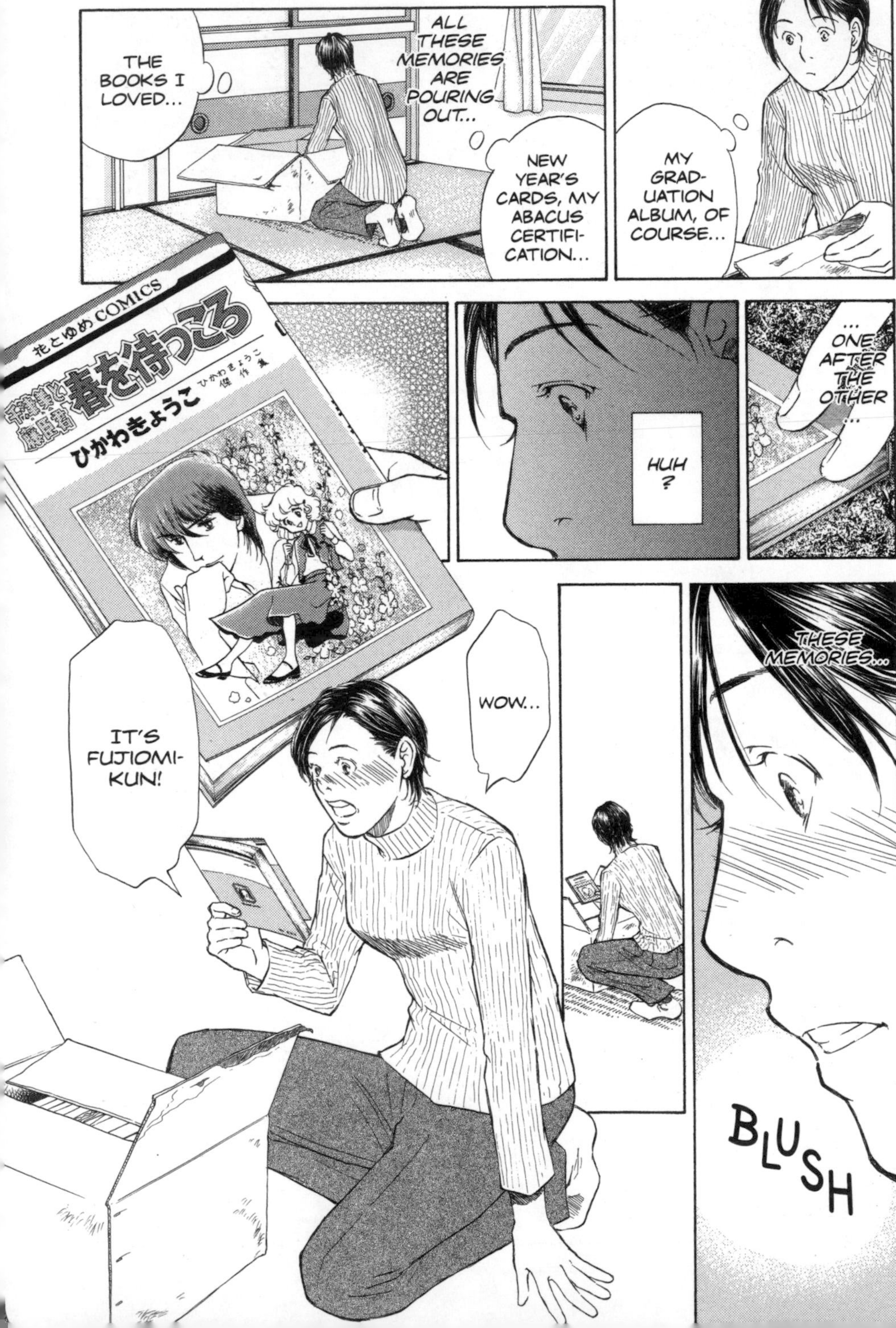
MY GRADUATION ALBUM, OF COURSE...
ALL THESE MEMORIES ARE POURING OUT...
NEW YEAR'S CARDS, MY ABACUS CERTIFICATION...
THE BOOKS I LOVED...
... ONE AFTER THE OTHER ...
HUH?
花とゆめ COMICS
千津美と藤臣君 春を待つころ
ひかわきょうこ
ひかわきょうこ 傑作集
THESE MEMORIES...
BLUSH
WOW...
IT'S FUJIOMI-KUN!

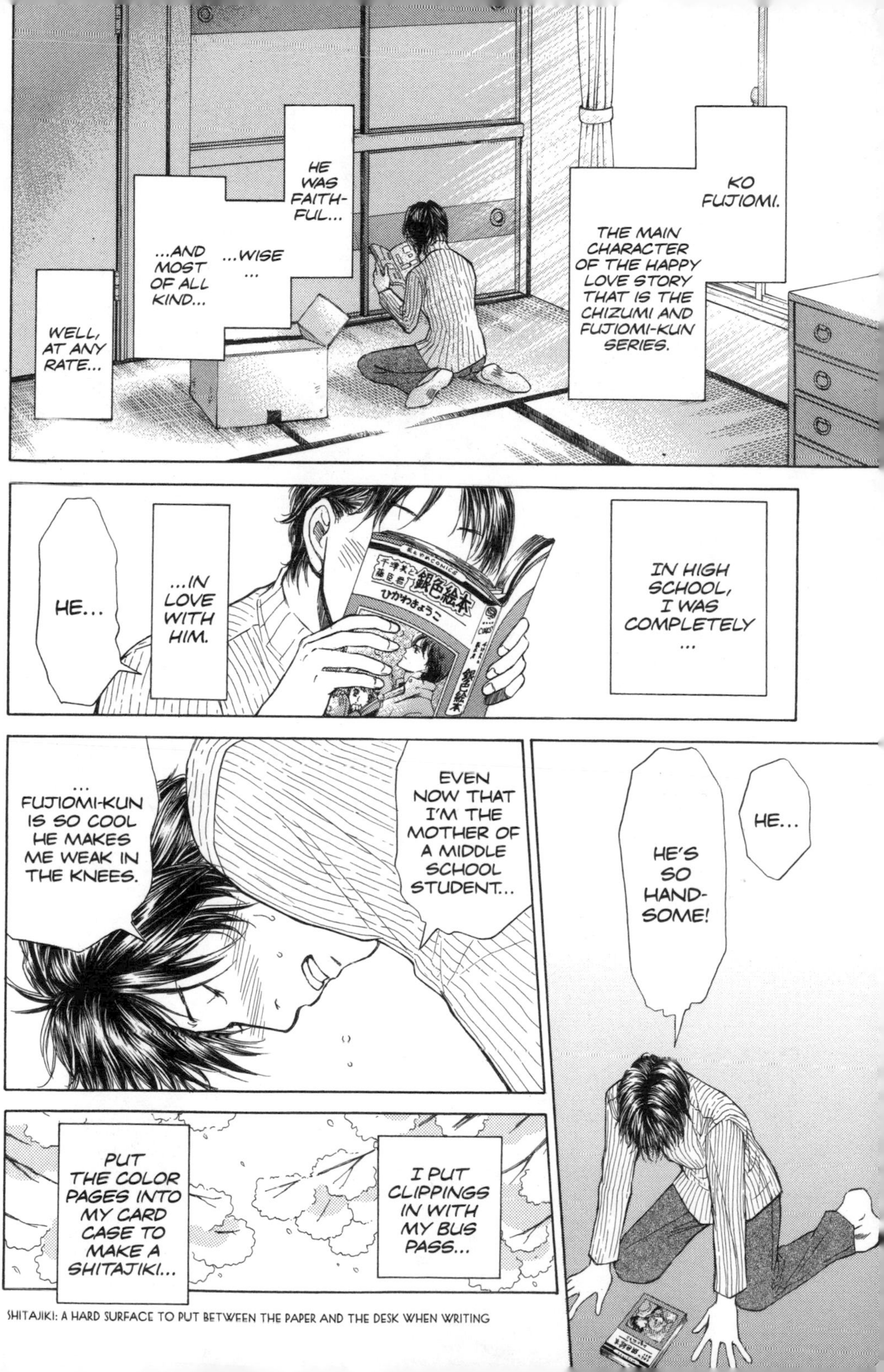
KO FUJIOMI.
THE MAIN CHARACTER OF THE HAPPY LOVE STORY THAT IS THE CHIZUMI AND FUJIOMI-KUN SERIES.
HE WAS FAITHFUL...
...WISE...
...AND MOST OF ALL KIND...
WELL, AT ANY RATE...
IN HIGH SCHOOL, I WAS COMPLETELY...
...IN LOVE WITH HIM.
HE...
HE...
HE'S SO HANDSOME!
EVEN NOW THAT I'M THE MOTHER OF A MIDDLE SCHOOL STUDENT...
...FUJIOMI-KUN IS SO COOL HE MAKES ME WEAK IN THE KNEES.
I PUT CLIPPINGS IN WITH MY BUS PASS...
PUT THE COLOR PAGES INTO MY CARD CASE TO MAKE A SHITAJIKI...

SHITAJIKI: A HARD SURFACE TO PUT BETWEEN THE PAPER AND THE DESK WHEN WRITING

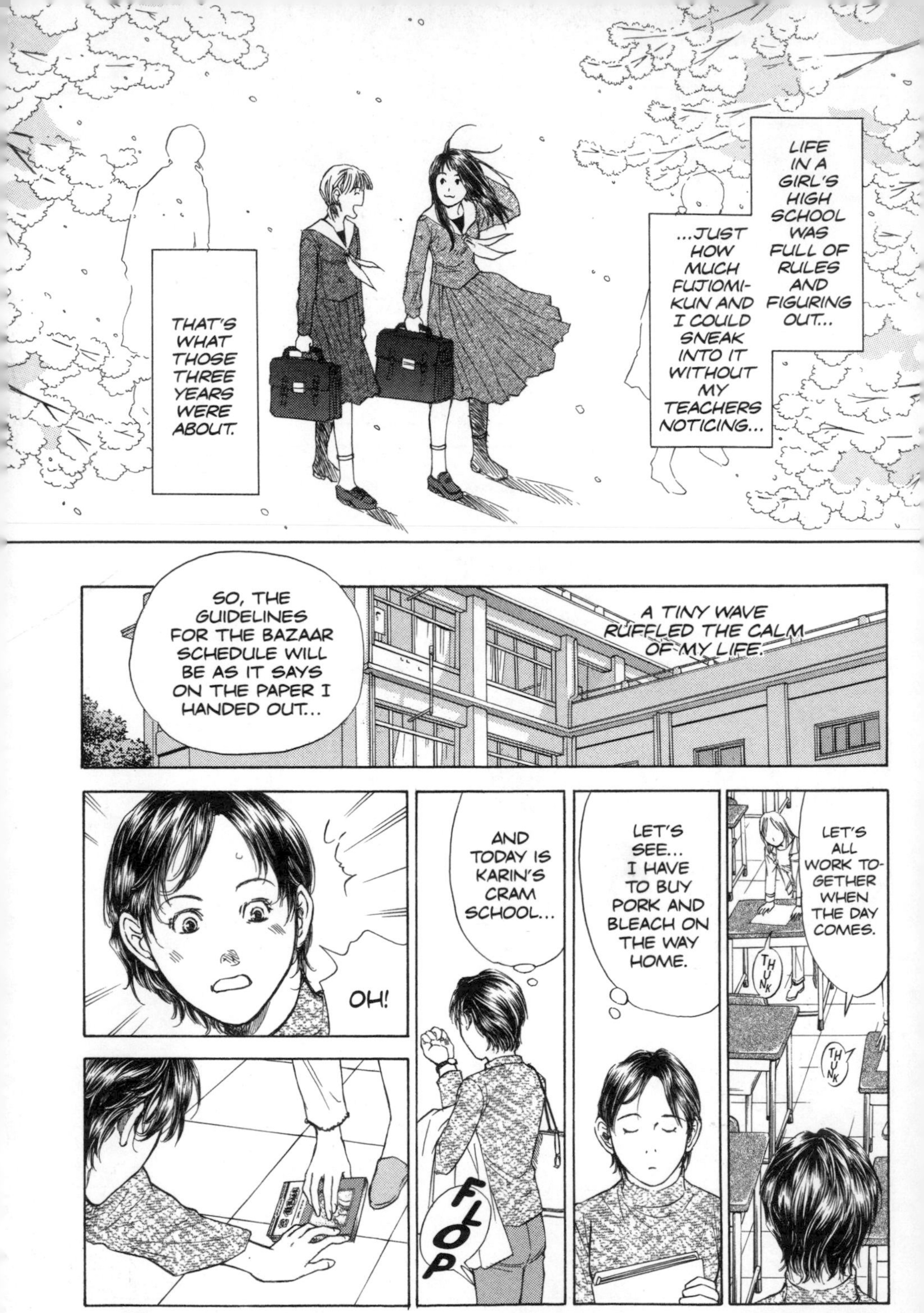
LIFE IN A GIRL'S HIGH SCHOOL WAS FULL OF RULES AND FIGURING OUT...
...JUST HOW MUCH FUJIOMI-KUN AND I COULD SNEAK INTO IT WITHOUT MY TEACHERS NOTICING...
THAT'S WHAT THOSE THREE YEARS WERE ABOUT.
A TINY WAVE RUFFLED THE CALM OF MY LIFE.
SO, THE GUIDELINES FOR THE BAZAAR SCHEDULE WILL BE AS IT SAYS ON THE PAPER I HANDED OUT...
LET'S ALL WORK TO-GETHER WHEN THE DAY COMES.
THUNK
THUNK
LET'S SEE... I HAVE TO BUY PORK AND BLEACH ON THE WAY HOME.
AND TODAY IS KARIN'S CRAM SCHOOL...
FLOP
OH!

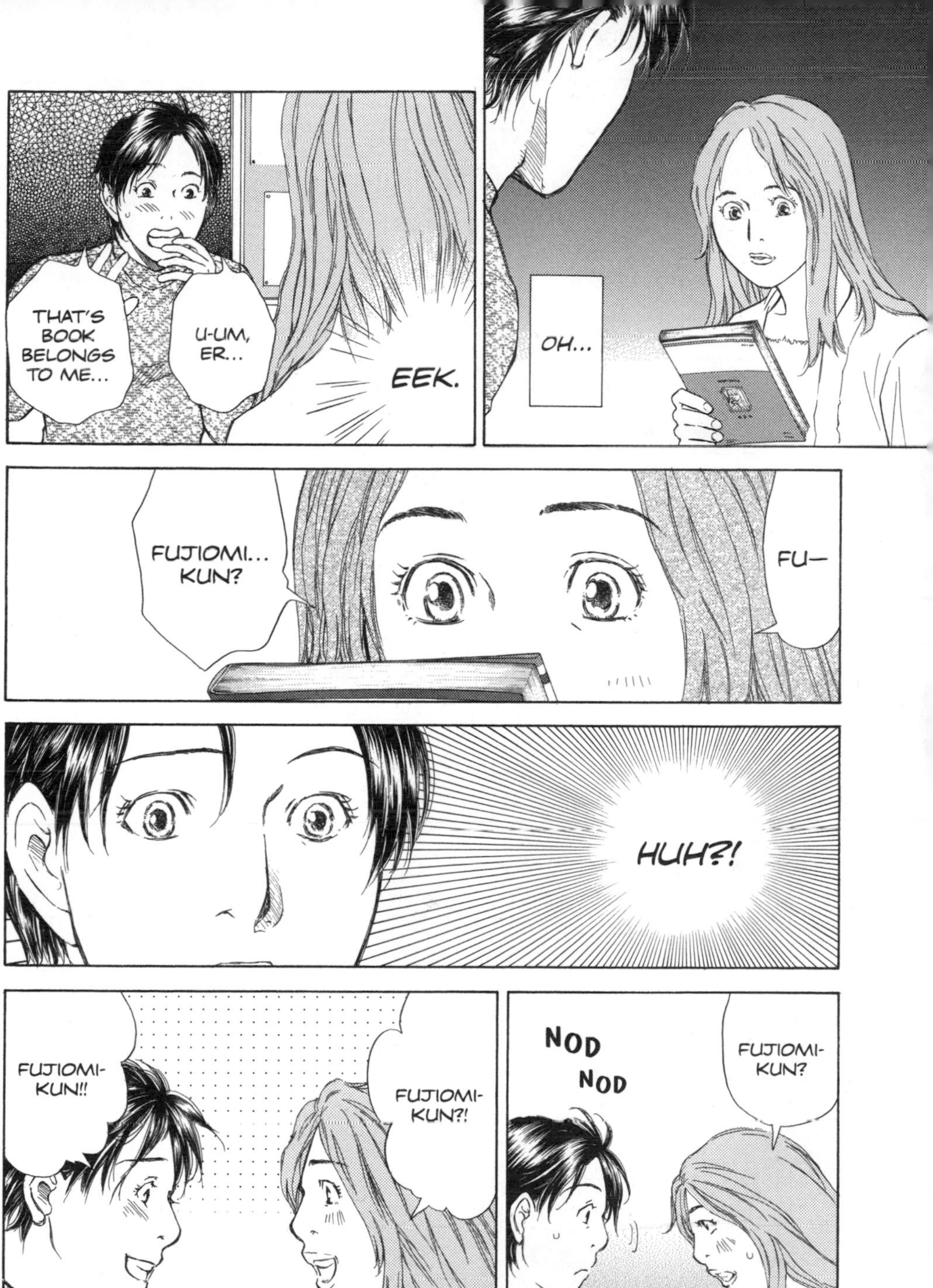
OH…
EEK.
U-UM, ER…
THAT'S BOOK BELONGS TO ME…
FU—
FUJIOMI… KUN?
HUH?!
FUJIOMI-KUN?
NOD NOD
FUJIOMI-KUN?!
FUJIOMI-KUN!!

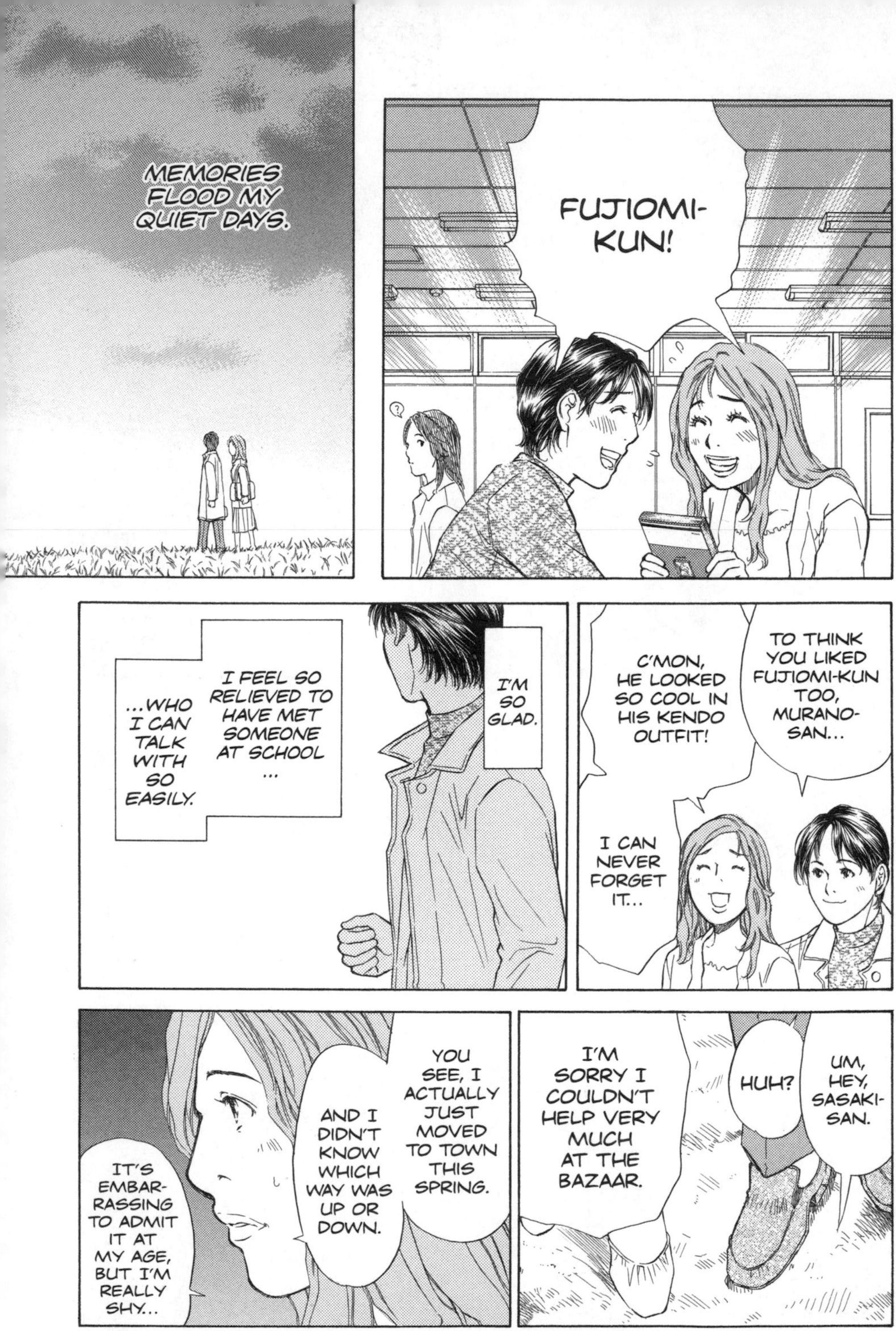
FUJIOMI-KUN!
MEMORIES FLOOD MY QUIET DAYS.
TO THINK YOU LIKED FUJIOMI-KUN TOO, MURANO-SAN...
C'MON, HE LOOKED SO COOL IN HIS KENDO OUTFIT!
I CAN NEVER FORGET IT...
I'M SO GLAD.
I FEEL SO RELIEVED TO HAVE MET SOMEONE AT SCHOOL...
...WHO I CAN TALK WITH SO EASILY.
UM, HEY, SASAKI-SAN.
HUH?
I'M SORRY I COULDN'T HELP VERY MUCH AT THE BAZAAR.
YOU SEE, I ACTUALLY JUST MOVED TO TOWN THIS SPRING.
AND I DIDN'T KNOW WHICH WAY WAS UP OR DOWN.
IT'S EMBARRASSING TO ADMIT IT AT MY AGE, BUT I'M REALLY SHY...

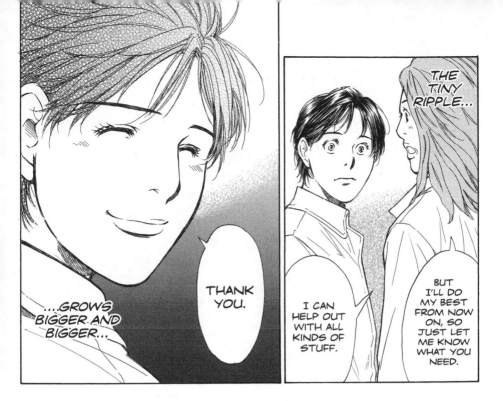

THE TINY RIPPLE...
BUT I'LL DO MY BEST FROM NOW ON, SO JUST LET ME KNOW WHAT YOU NEED.
I CAN HELP OUT WITH ALL KINDS OF STUFF.
THANK YOU.
...GROWS BIGGER AND BIGGER...
YEAH.
WITH THE TWO OF US...
WE CAN KEEP ON DOING OUR BEST.

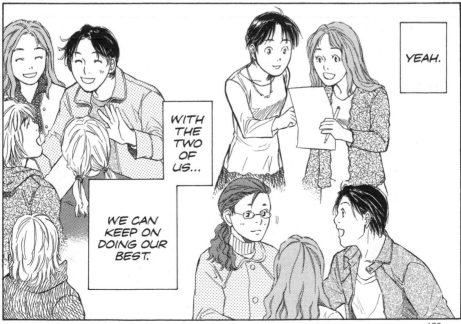

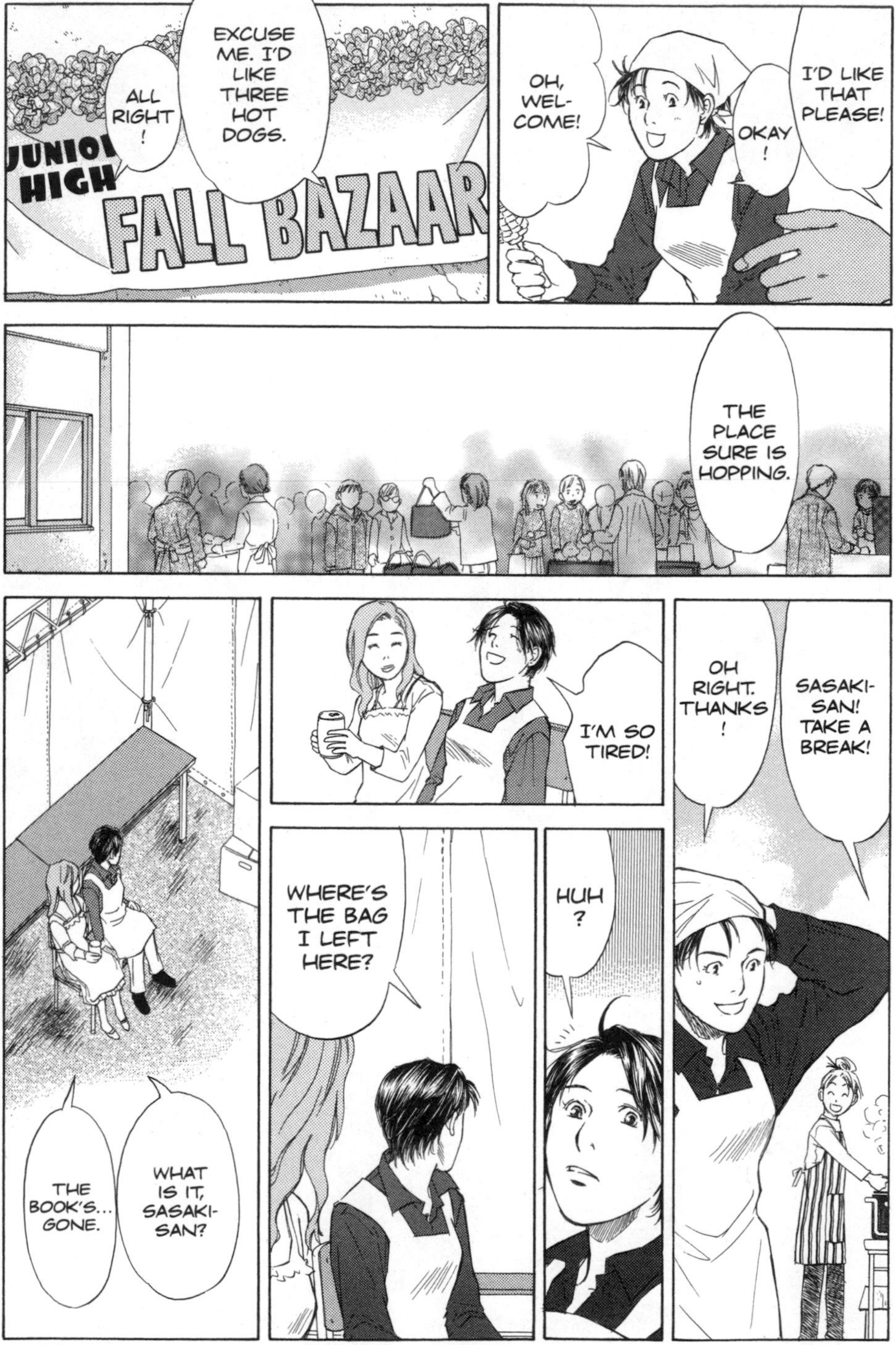
I'D LIKE THAT PLEASE!
OKAY!
OH, WELCOME!
EXCUSE ME. I'D LIKE THREE HOT DOGS.
ALL RIGHT!
HIGH
FALL BAZAAR
THE PLACE SURE IS HOPPING.
SASAKI-SAN! TAKE A BREAK!
OH RIGHT. THANKS!
I'M SO TIRED!
HUH?
WHERE'S THE BAG I LEFT HERE?
WHAT IS IT, SASAKI-SAN?
THE BOOK'S... GONE.

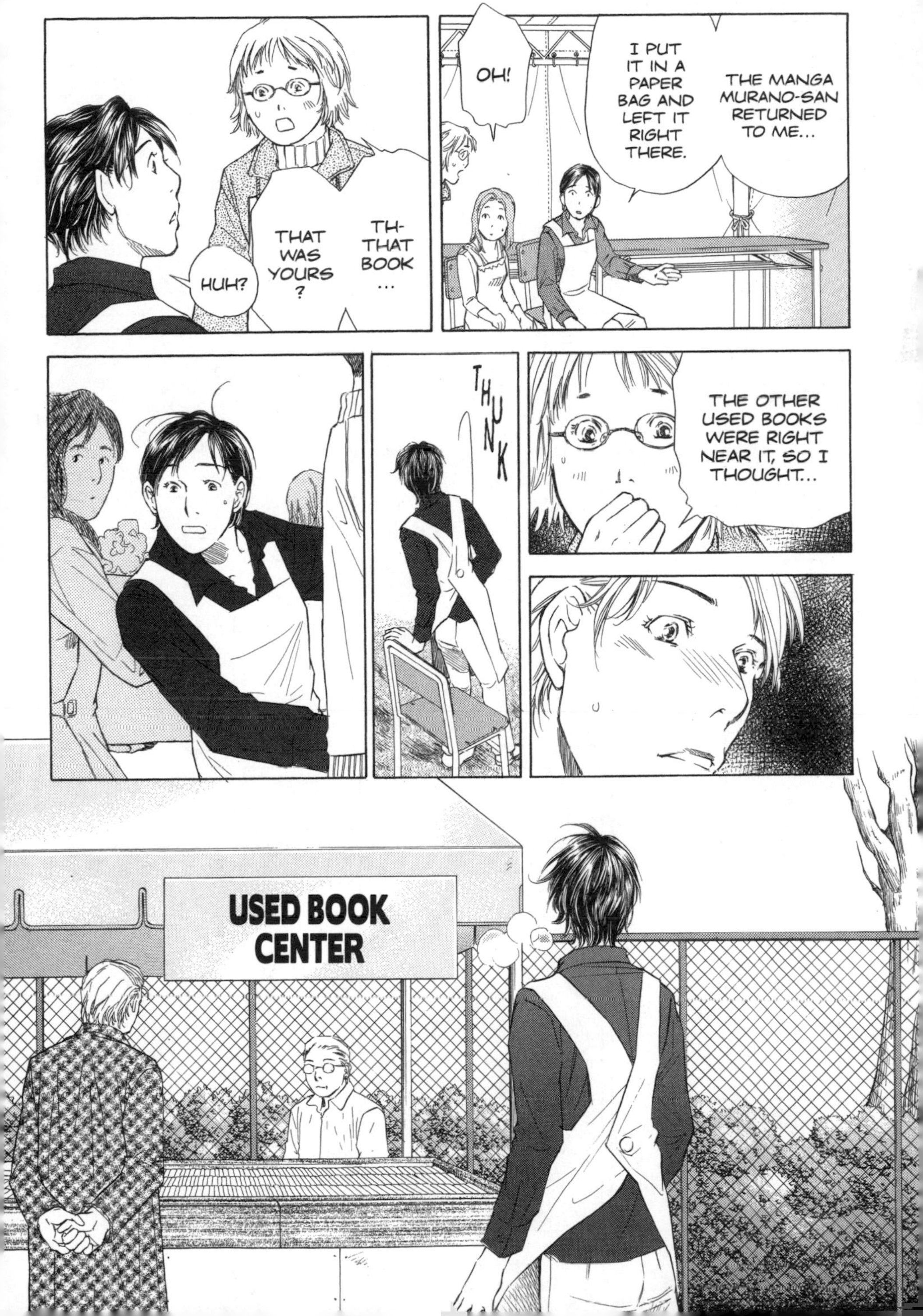
THE MANGA MURANO-SAN RETURNED TO ME...
I PUT IT IN A PAPER BAG AND LEFT IT RIGHT THERE.
OH!
TH-THAT BOOK...
THAT WAS YOURS?
HUH?
THE OTHER USED BOOKS WERE RIGHT NEAR IT, SO I THOUGHT...
THUNK
USED BOOK CENTER

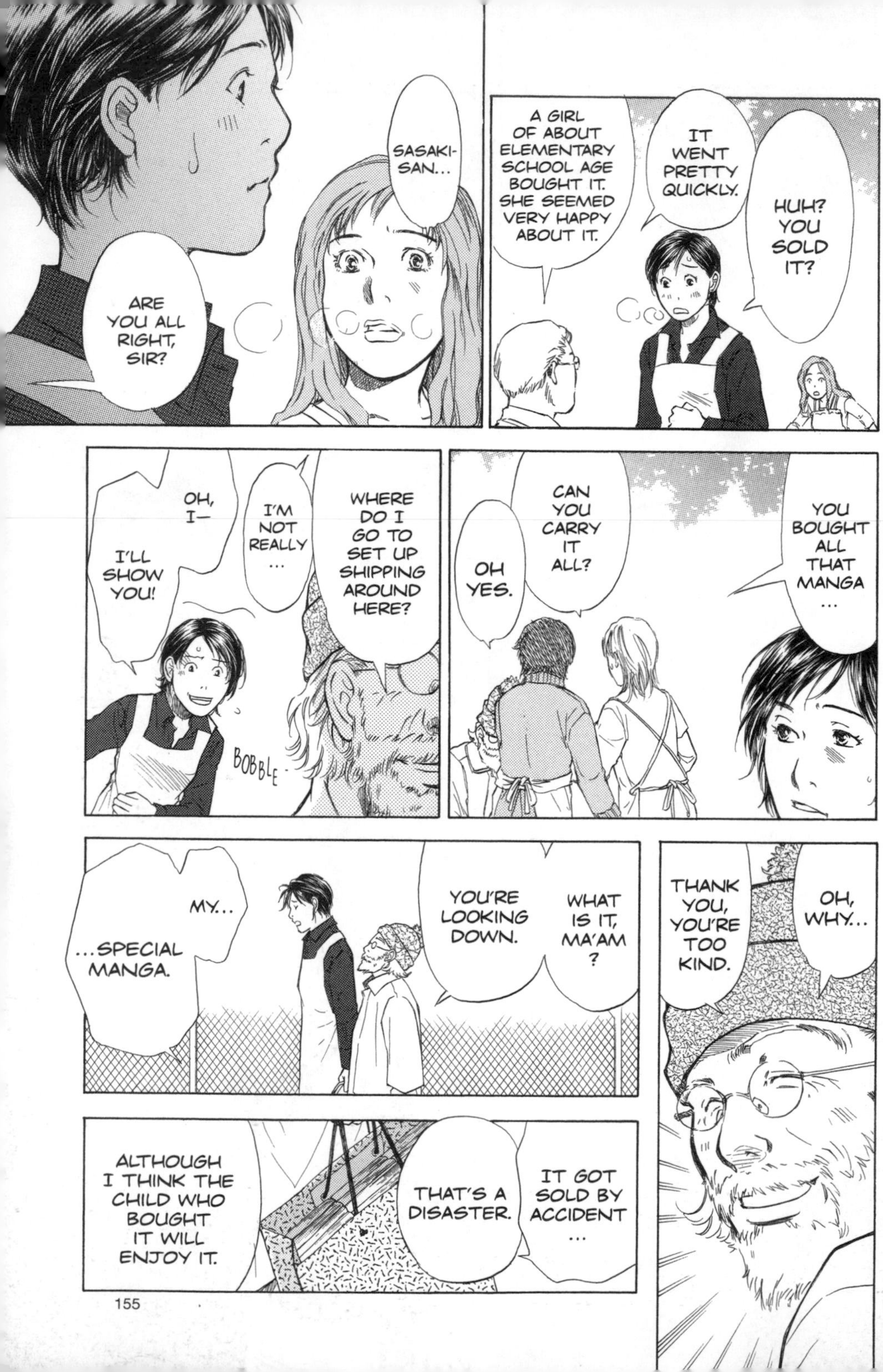
HUH? YOU SOLD IT?
IT WENT PRETTY QUICKLY.
A GIRL OF ABOUT ELEMENTARY SCHOOL AGE BOUGHT IT. SHE SEEMED VERY HAPPY ABOUT IT.
SASAKI-SAN...
ARE YOU ALL RIGHT, SIR?
YOU BOUGHT ALL THAT MANGA ...
CAN YOU CARRY IT ALL?
OH YES.
WHERE DO I GO TO SET UP SHIPPING AROUND HERE?
I'M NOT REALLY ...
OH, I—
I'LL SHOW YOU!
BOBBLE
OH, WHY...
THANK YOU, YOU'RE TOO KIND.
WHAT IS IT, MA'AM ?
YOU'RE LOOKING DOWN.
MY...
...SPECIAL MANGA.
IT GOT SOLD BY ACCIDENT ...
THAT'S A DISASTER.
ALTHOUGH I THINK THE CHILD WHO BOUGHT IT WILL ENJOY IT.

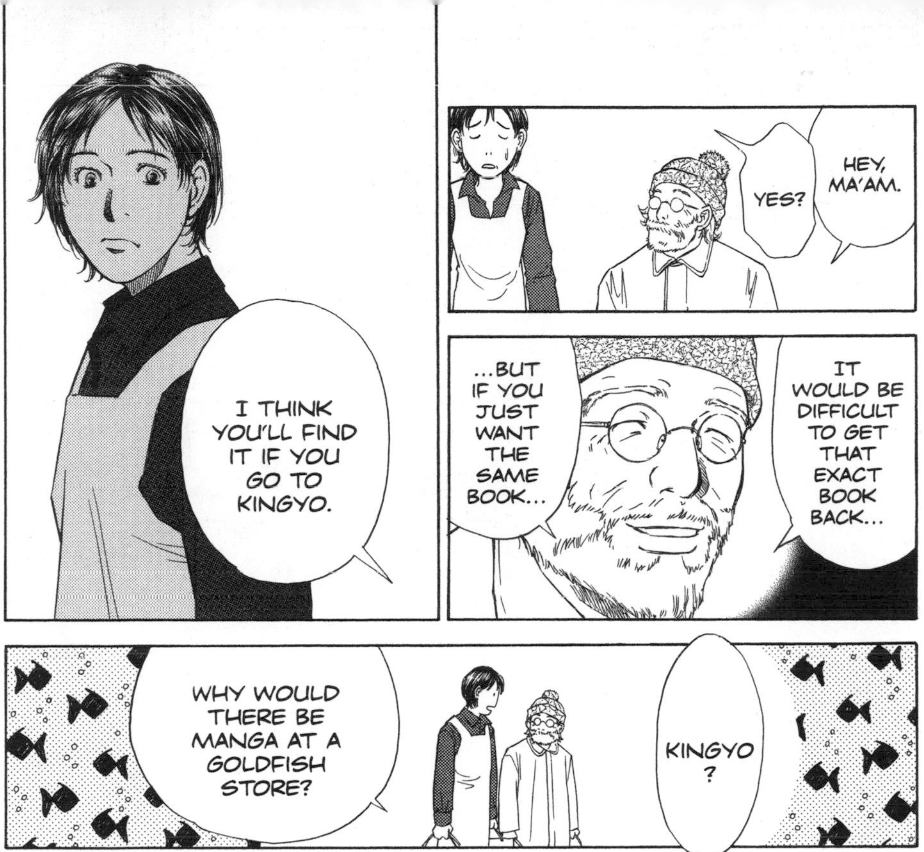
HEY, MA'AM.
YES?
IT WOULD BE DIFFICULT TO GET THAT EXACT BOOK BACK...
...BUT IF YOU JUST WANT THE SAME BOOK...
I THINK YOU'LL FIND IT IF YOU GO TO KINGYO.
KINGYO ?
WHY WOULD THERE BE MANGA AT A GOLDFISH STORE?

REMEMBER: KINGYO MEANS "GOLDFISH" IN JAPANESE–ED.

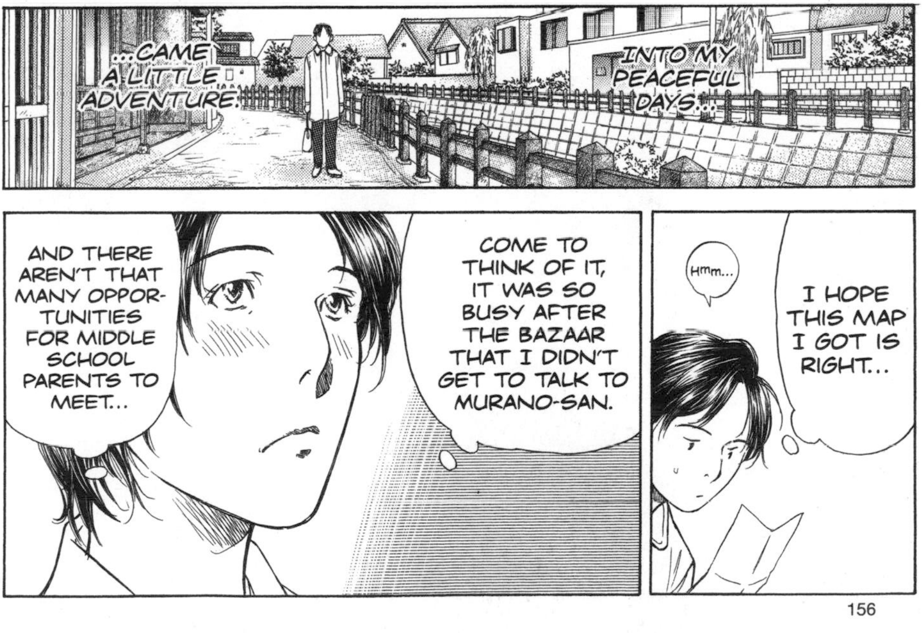
INTO MY PEACEFUL DAYS...
...CAME A LITTLE ADVENTURE.
I HOPE THIS MAP I GOT IS RIGHT...
Hmm...
COME TO THINK OF IT, IT WAS SO BUSY AFTER THE BAZAAR THAT I DIDN'T GET TO TALK TO MURANO-SAN.
AND THERE AREN'T THAT MANY OPPOR-TUNITIES FOR MIDDLE SCHOOL PARENTS TO MEET...

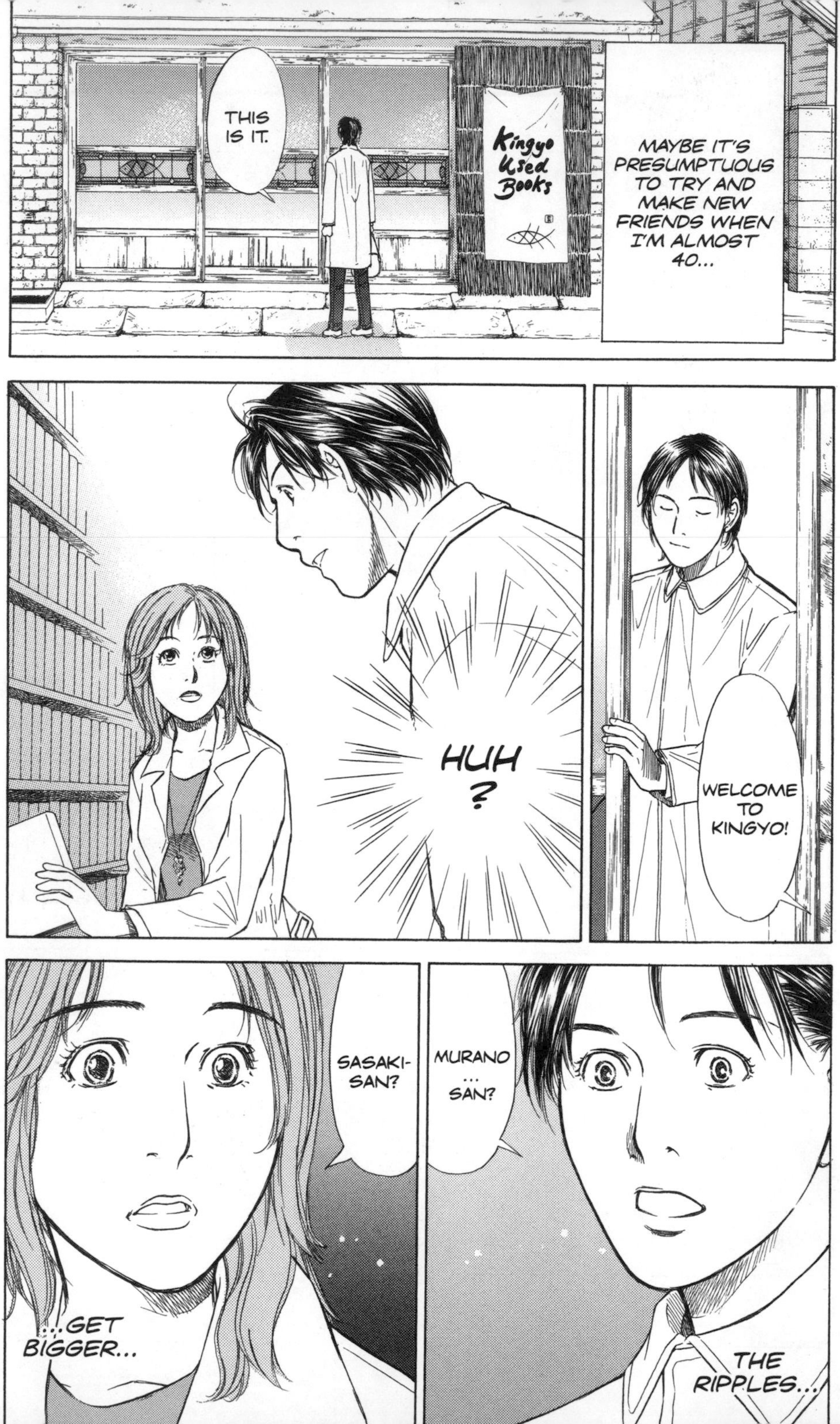
MAYBE IT'S PRESUMPTUOUS TO TRY AND MAKE NEW FRIENDS WHEN I'M ALMOST 40...
Kingyo Used Books
THIS IS IT.
WELCOME TO KINGYO!
HUH ?
MURANO ... SAN?
THE RIPPLES...
SASAKI-SAN?
...GET BIGGER...

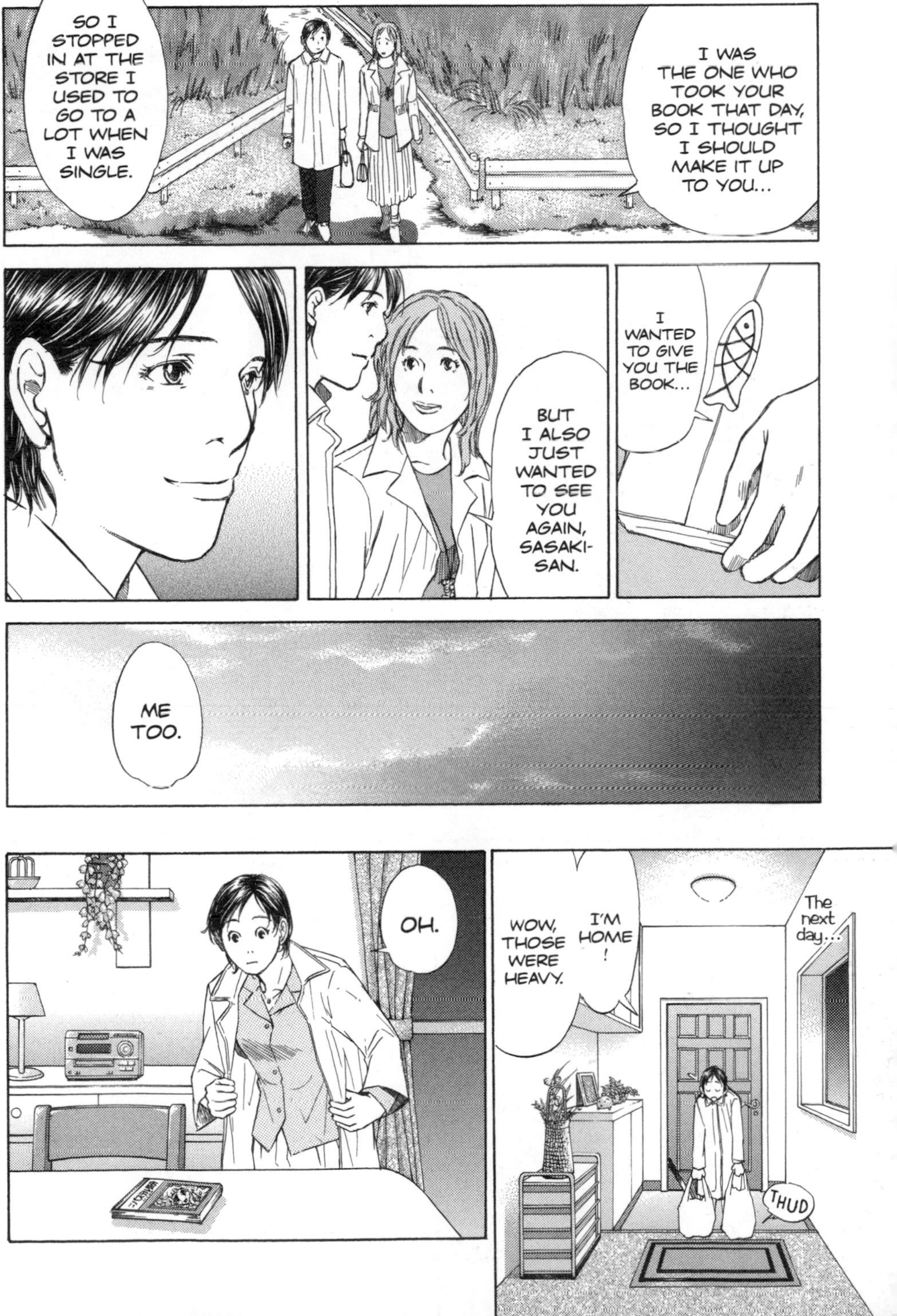
I WAS THE ONE WHO TOOK YOUR BOOK THAT DAY, SO I THOUGHT I SHOULD MAKE IT UP TO YOU...
SO I STOPPED IN AT THE STORE I USED TO GO TO A LOT WHEN I WAS SINGLE.
I WANTED TO GIVE YOU THE BOOK...
BUT I ALSO JUST WANTED TO SEE YOU AGAIN, SASAKI-SAN.
ME TOO.
The next day...
I'M HOME!
WOW, THOSE WERE HEAVY.
THUD
OH.

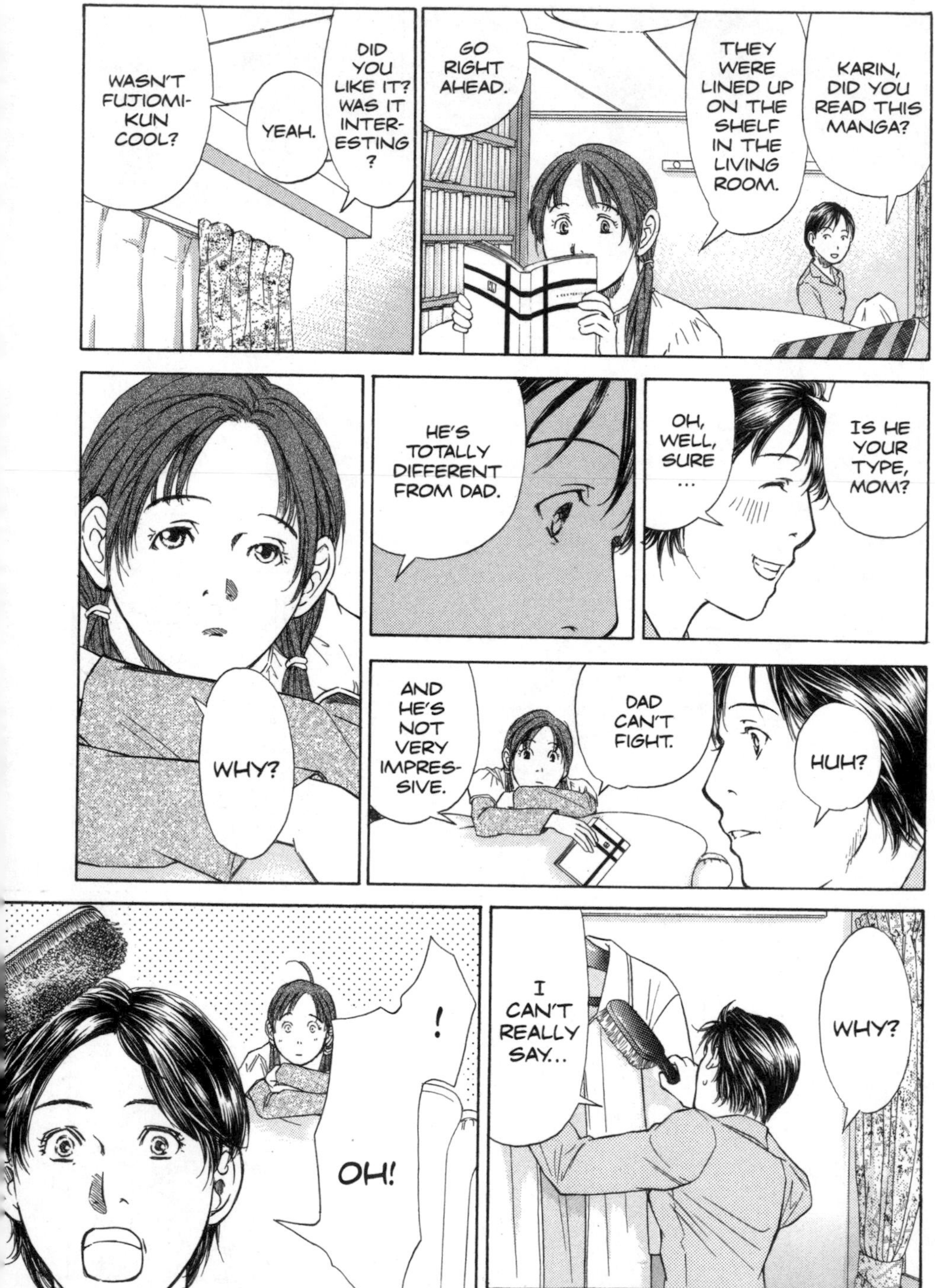

KARIN, DID YOU READ THIS MANGA?
THEY WERE LINED UP ON THE SHELF IN THE LIVING ROOM.
GO RIGHT AHEAD.
DID YOU LIKE IT? WAS IT INTERESTING?
YEAH.
WASN'T FUJIOMI-KUN COOL?
IS HE YOUR TYPE, MOM?
OH, WELL, SURE...
HE'S TOTALLY DIFFERENT FROM DAD.
HUH?
DAD CAN'T FIGHT.
AND HE'S NOT VERY IMPRESSIVE.
WHY?
WHY?
I CAN'T REALLY SAY...
!
OH!

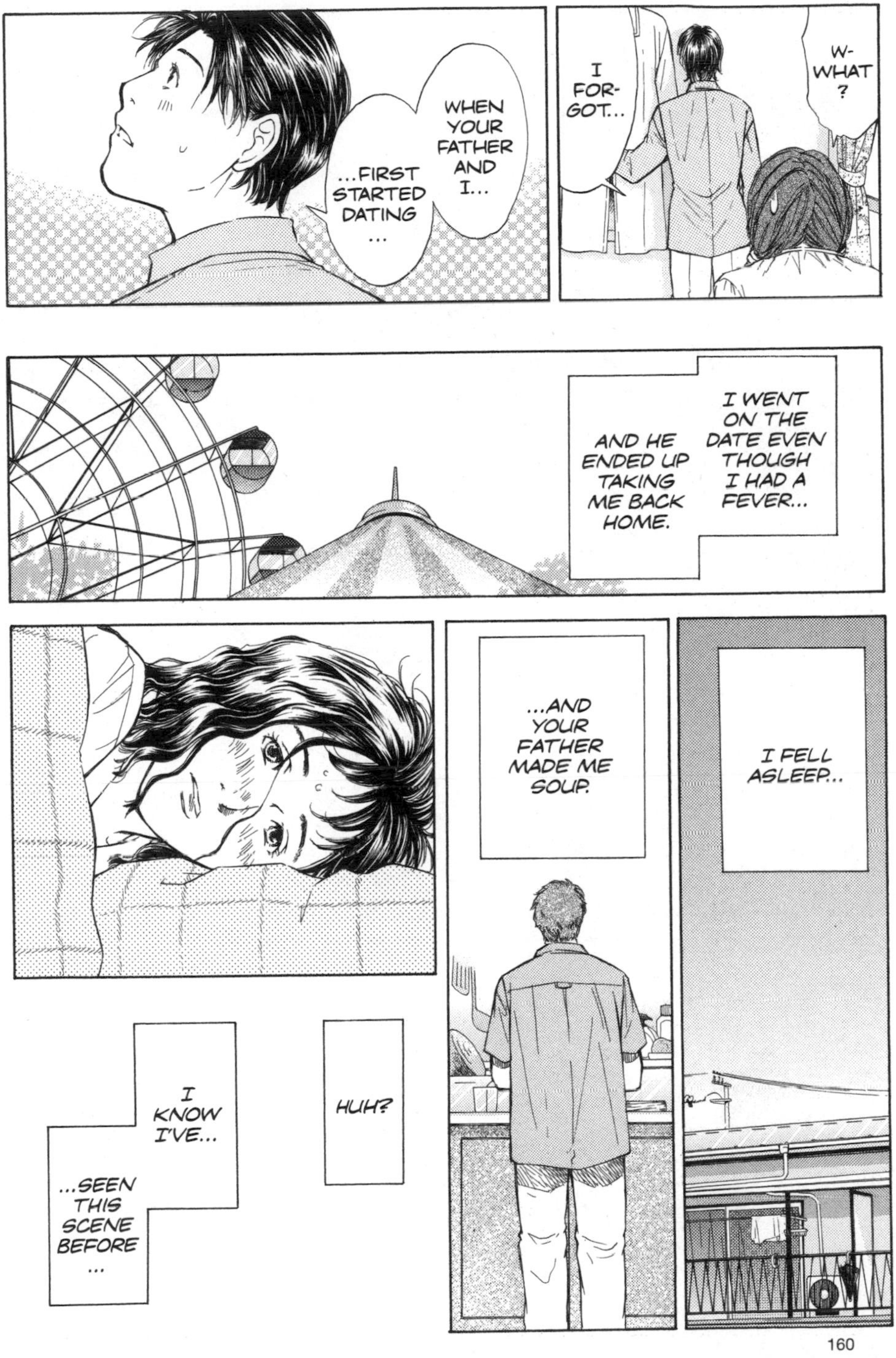
W-WHAT?
I FORGOT...
WHEN YOUR FATHER AND I...
...FIRST STARTED DATING...
I WENT ON THE DATE EVEN THOUGH I HAD A FEVER...
AND HE ENDED UP TAKING ME BACK HOME.
I FELL ASLEEP...
...AND YOUR FATHER MADE ME SOUP.
HUH?
I KNOW I'VE...
...SEEN THIS SCENE BEFORE...

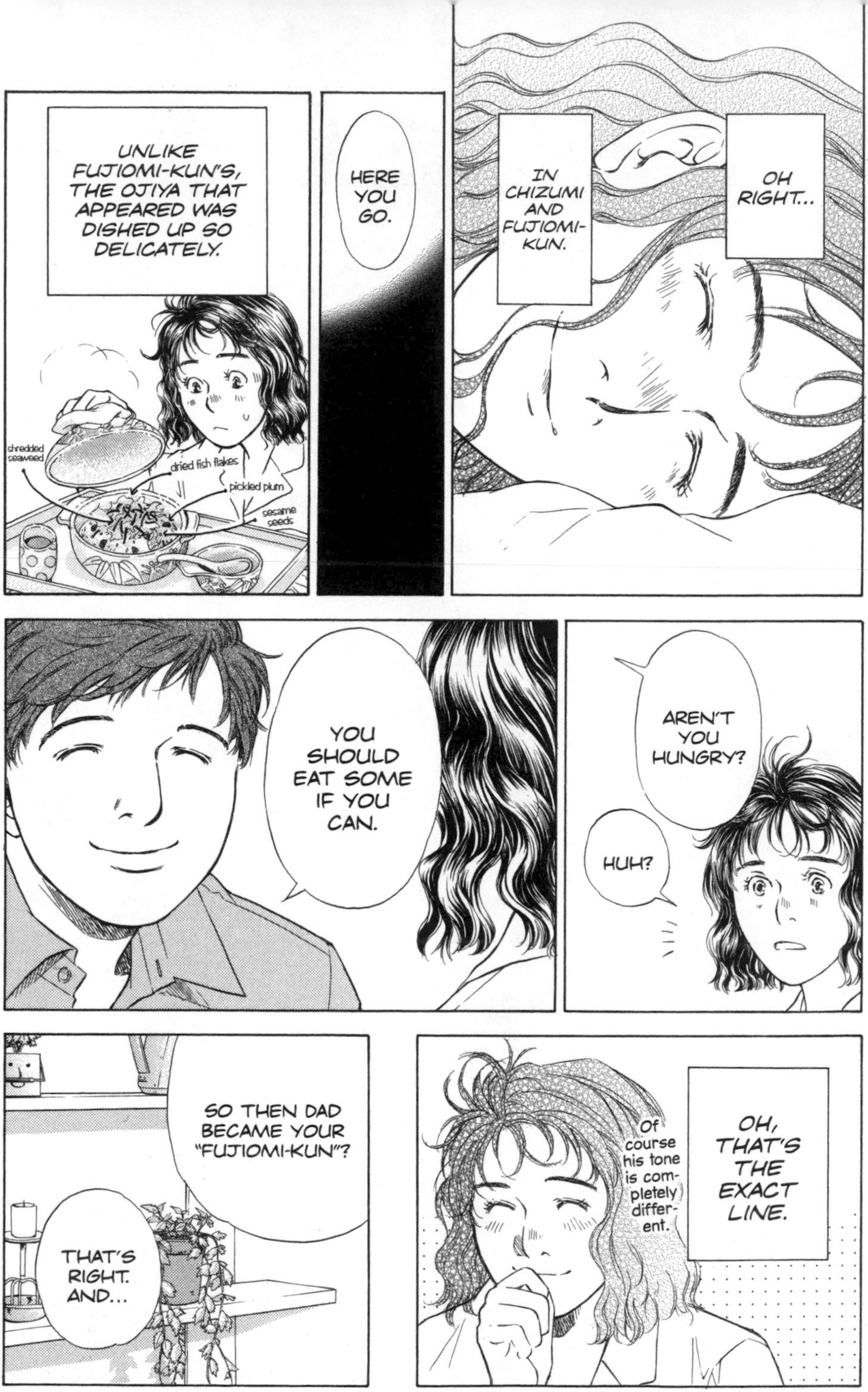
OH RIGHT...
IN CHIZUMI AND FUJIOMI-KUN.
HERE YOU GO.
UNLIKE FUJIOMI-KUN'S, THE OJIYA THAT APPEARED WAS DISHED UP SO DELICATELY.
shredded seaweed
dried fish flakes
pickled plum
sesame seeds
AREN'T YOU HUNGRY?
HUH?
YOU SHOULD EAT SOME IF YOU CAN.
OH, THAT'S THE EXACT LINE.
Of course his tone is completely different.
SO THEN DAD BECAME YOUR "FUJIOMI-KUN"?
THAT'S RIGHT. AND...

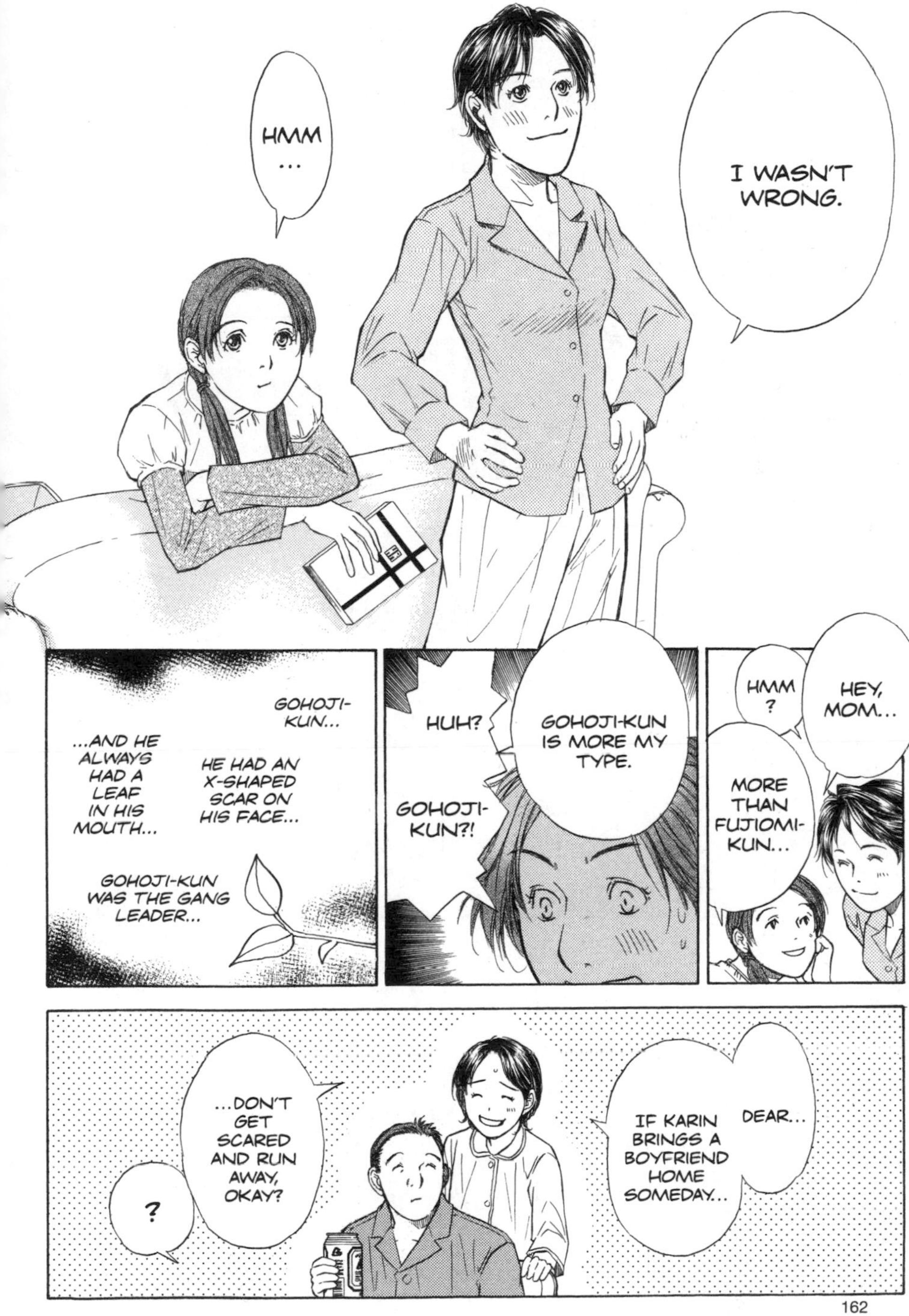
I WASN'T WRONG.
HMM ...
HEY, MOM...
HMM ?
MORE THAN FUJIOMI-KUN...
GOHOJI-KUN IS MORE MY TYPE.
HUH?
GOHOJI-KUN?!
GOHOJI-KUN...
HE HAD AN X-SHAPED SCAR ON HIS FACE...
...AND HE ALWAYS HAD A LEAF IN HIS MOUTH...
GOHOJI-KUN WAS THE GANG LEADER...
DEAR...
IF KARIN BRINGS A BOYFRIEND HOME SOMEDAY...
...DON'T GET SCARED AND RUN AWAY, OKAY?
?

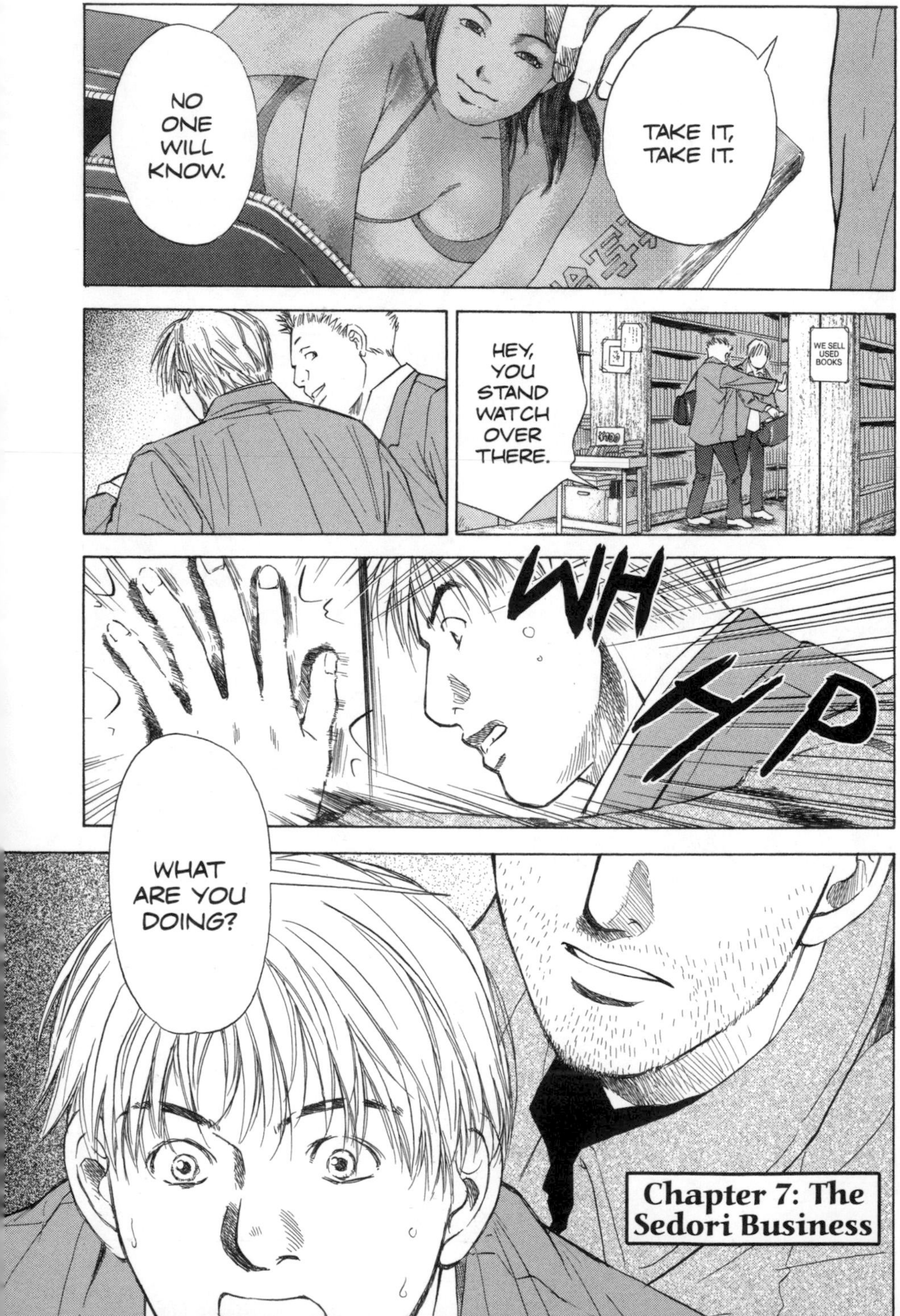
TAKE IT, TAKE IT.
NO ONE WILL KNOW.
HEY, YOU STAND WATCH OVER THERE.
WE SELL USED BOOKS
WHIP
WHAT ARE YOU DOING?
Chapter 7: The Sedori Business

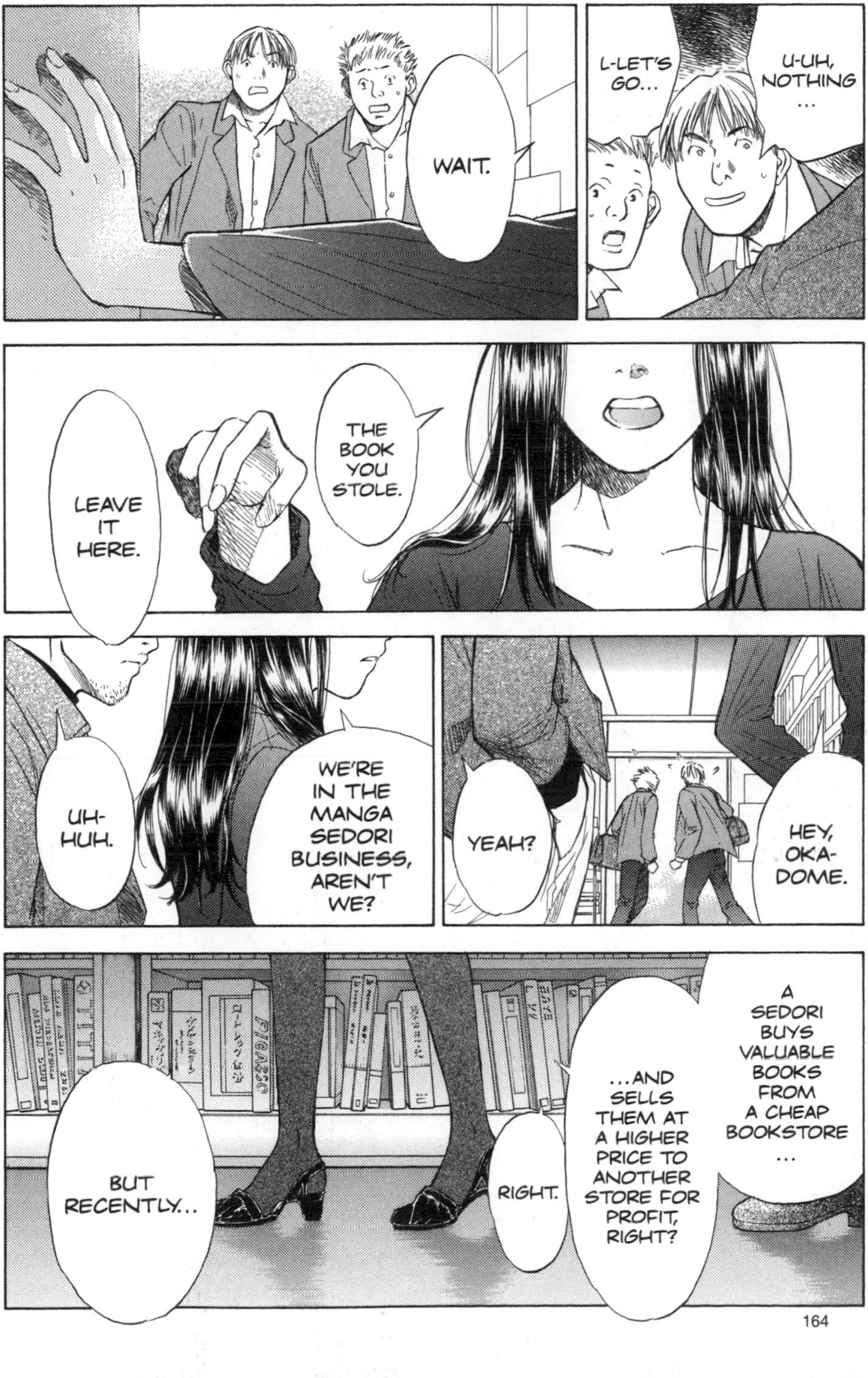
U-UH, NOTHING …
L-LET'S GO…
WAIT.
THE BOOK YOU STOLE.
LEAVE IT HERE.
HEY, OKA-DOME.
YEAH?
WE'RE IN THE MANGA SEDORI BUSINESS, AREN'T WE?
UH-HUH.
A SEDORI BUYS VALUABLE BOOKS FROM A CHEAP BOOKSTORE …
…AND SELLS THEM AT A HIGHER PRICE TO ANOTHER STORE FOR PROFIT, RIGHT?
RIGHT.
BUT RECENTLY…

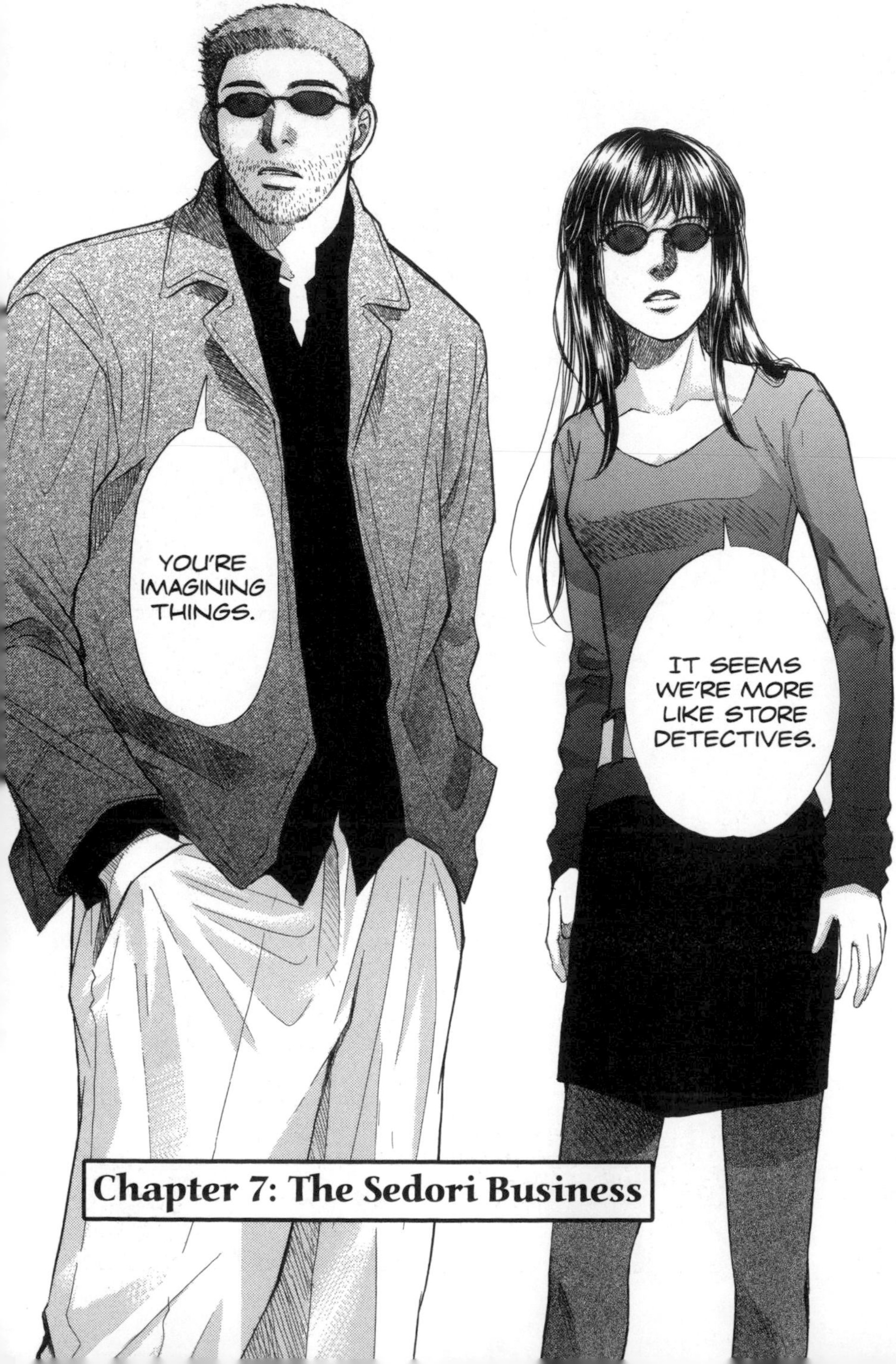
IT SEEMS WE'RE MORE LIKE STORE DETECTIVES.
YOU'RE IMAGINING THINGS.

Chapter 7: The Sedori Business

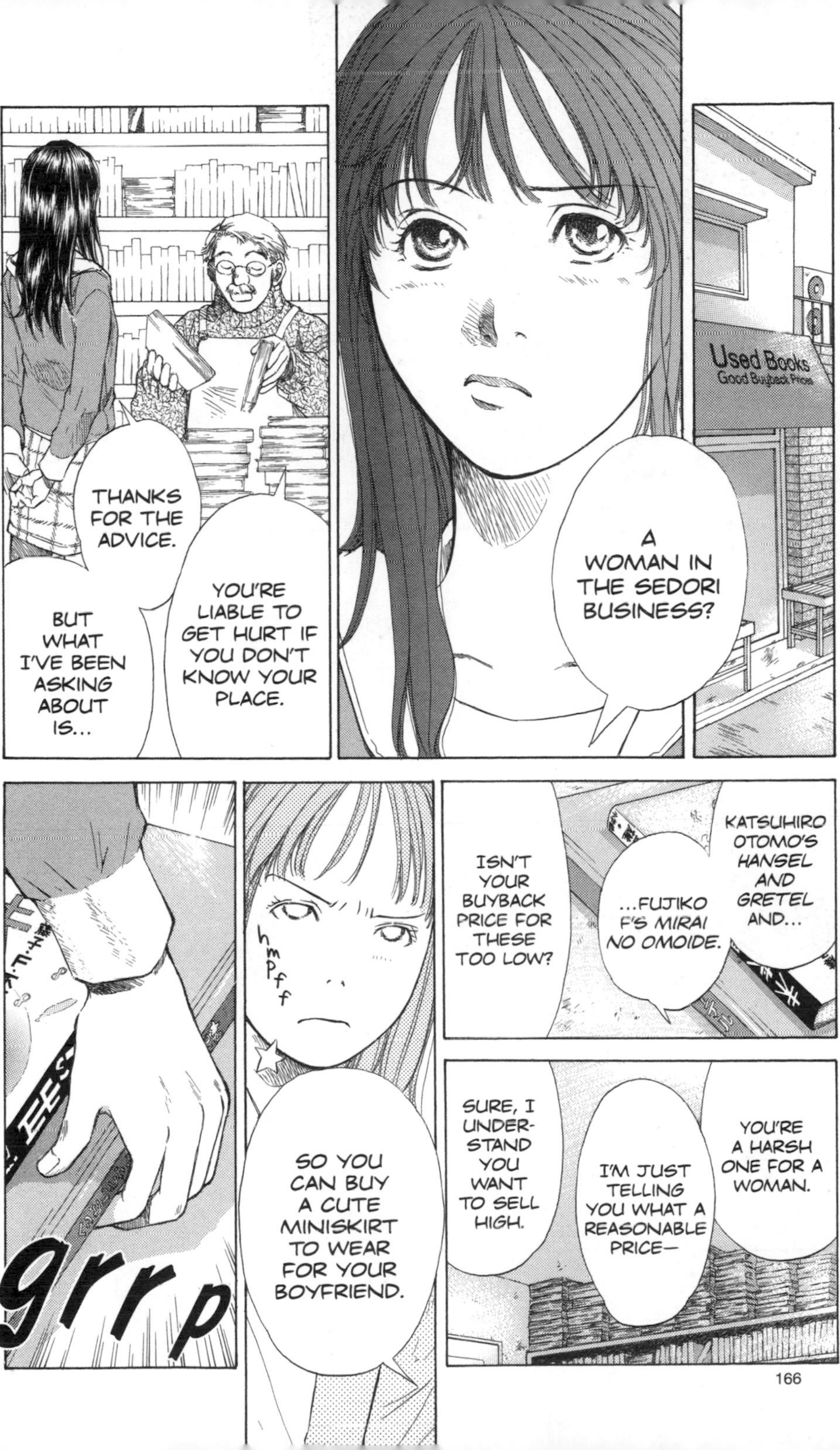

Used Books
Good Buyback Prices
A WOMAN IN THE SEDORI BUSINESS?
YOU'RE LIABLE TO GET HURT IF YOU DON'T KNOW YOUR PLACE.
THANKS FOR THE ADVICE.
BUT WHAT I'VE BEEN ASKING ABOUT IS...
KATSUHIRO OTOMO'S HANSEL AND GRETEL AND...
...FUJIKO F'S MIRAI NO OMOIDE.
ISN'T YOUR BUYBACK PRICE FOR THESE TOO LOW?
YOU'RE A HARSH ONE FOR A WOMAN.
I'M JUST TELLING YOU WHAT A REASONABLE PRICE—
SURE, I UNDERSTAND YOU WANT TO SELL HIGH.
hmpff
SO YOU CAN BUY A CUTE MINISKIRT TO WEAR FOR YOUR BOYFRIEND.
grrp

STUDY!

HANSEL AND GRETEL, A SHORT MANGA COLLECTION BY KATSUHIRO OTOMO PUBLISHED IN 1981. COMPRISED OF REMAKES OF POPULAR CHILDREN'S STORIES INCLUDING THE TITLE STORY, WHICH FIRST APPEARED IN *ZOUKAN YOUNG COMIC* (SPECIAL ISSUE YOUNG COMIC) IN 1978.

STUDY!

MIRAI NO OMOIDE (MEMORIES OF THE FUTURE) BY FUJIKO F. FUJIO, PUBLISHED IN *BIG COMIC* IN 1991. A STORY OF RIHITO NANDO, A MANGAKA WHO RELIVES THE PAST WHILE RETAINING HIS PRESENT MEMORIES. ONE VOLUME. THE AUTHOR'S LAST WORK TO BE SERIALIZED IN A MAGAZINE FOR ADULTS AND WAS ADAPTED INTO A LIVE-ACTION FILM IN 1992.

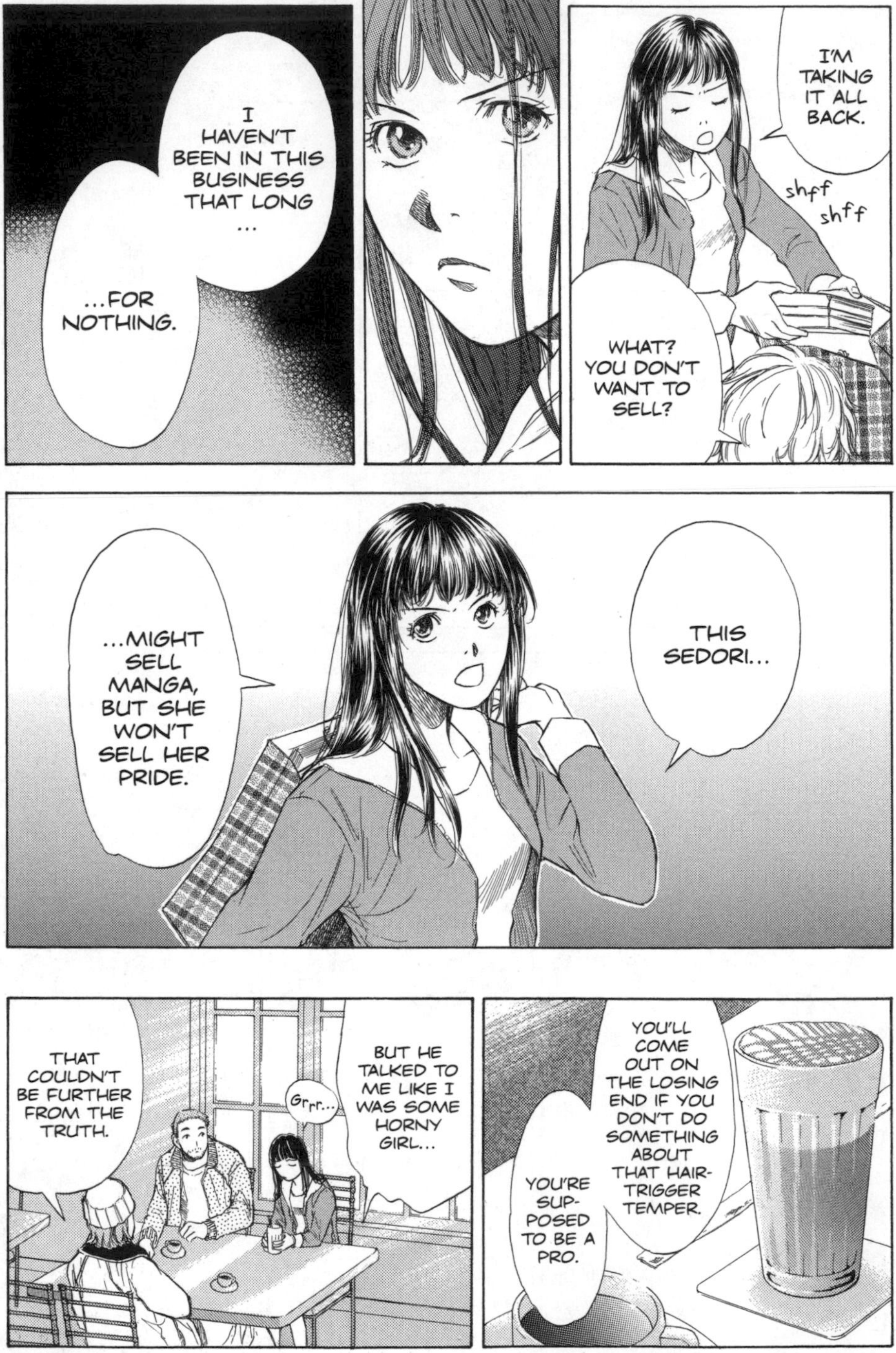
I'M TAKING IT ALL BACK.
shff shff
WHAT? YOU DON'T WANT TO SELL?
I HAVEN'T BEEN IN THIS BUSINESS THAT LONG ...
...FOR NOTHING.
THIS SEDORI...
...MIGHT SELL MANGA, BUT SHE WON'T SELL HER PRIDE.
YOU'LL COME OUT ON THE LOSING END IF YOU DON'T DO SOMETHING ABOUT THAT HAIR-TRIGGER TEMPER.
YOU'RE SUP-POSED TO BE A PRO.
BUT HE TALKED TO ME LIKE I WAS SOME HORNY GIRL...
Grrr...
THAT COULDN'T BE FURTHER FROM THE TRUTH.

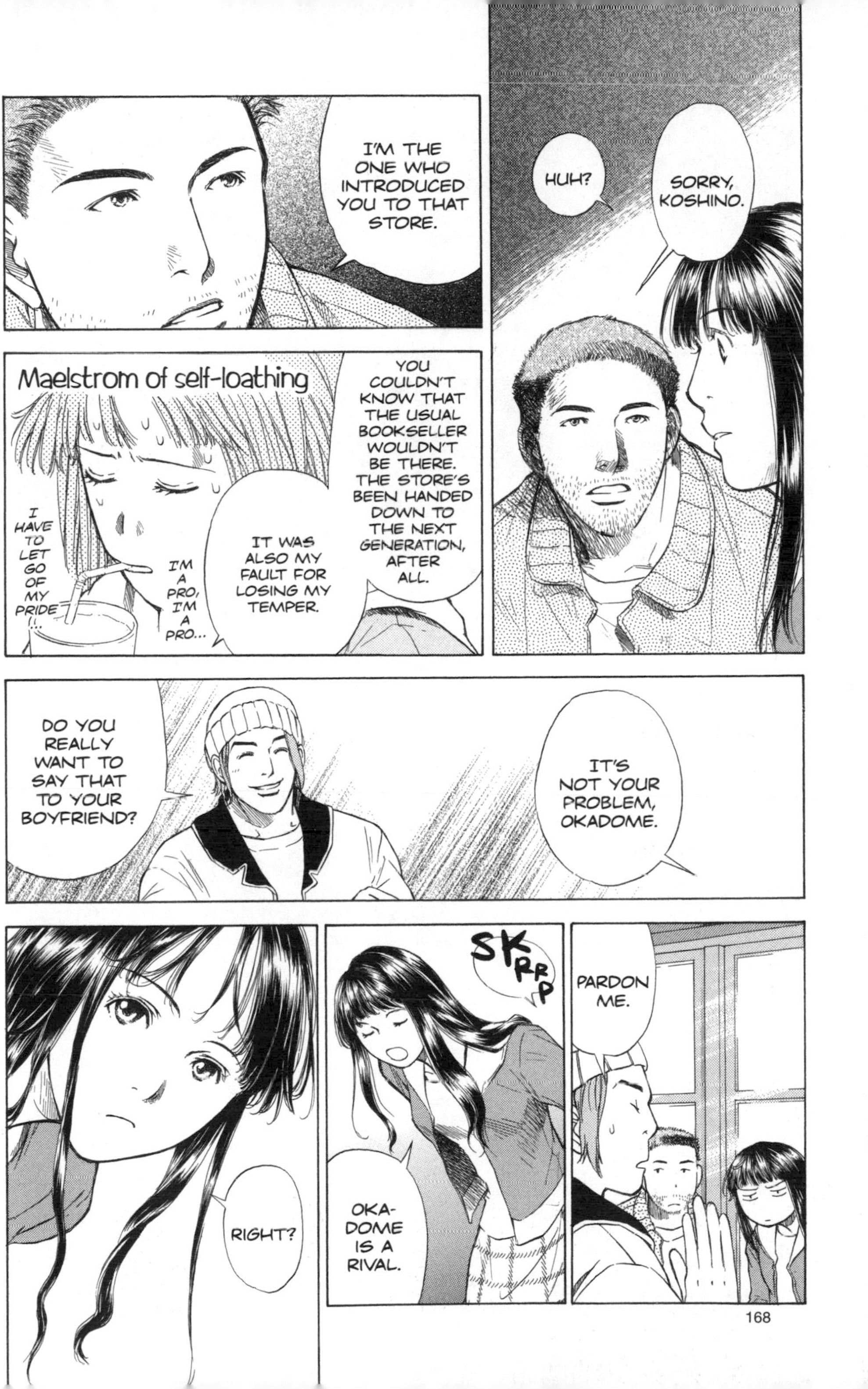
SORRY, KOSHINO.
HUH?
I'M THE ONE WHO INTRODUCED YOU TO THAT STORE.
YOU COULDN'T KNOW THAT THE USUAL BOOKSELLER WOULDN'T BE THERE. THE STORE'S BEEN HANDED DOWN TO THE NEXT GENERATION, AFTER ALL.
IT WAS ALSO MY FAULT FOR LOSING MY TEMPER.
Maelstrom of self-loathing
I'M A PRO, I'M A PRO...
I HAVE TO LET GO OF MY PRIDE!!...
IT'S NOT YOUR PROBLEM, OKADOME.
DO YOU REALLY WANT TO SAY THAT TO YOUR BOYFRIEND?
PARDON ME.
SKRRP
OKA-DOME IS A RIVAL.
RIGHT?

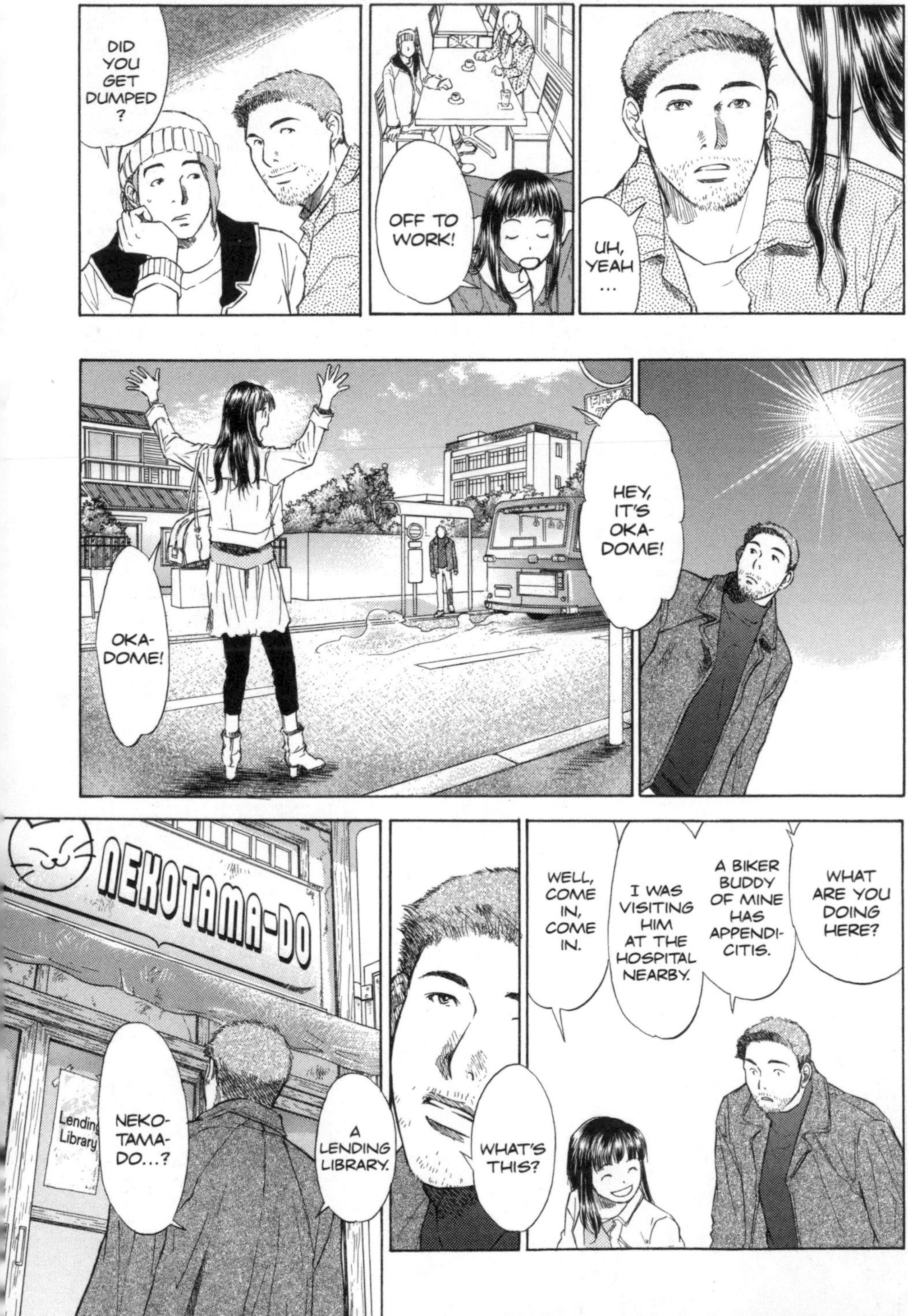
UH, YEAH ...
OFF TO WORK!
DID YOU GET DUMPED?
HEY, IT'S OKA-DOME!
OKA-DOME!
WHAT ARE YOU DOING HERE?
A BIKER BUDDY OF MINE HAS APPENDICITIS.
I WAS VISITING HIM AT THE HOSPITAL NEARBY.
WELL, COME IN, COME IN.
WHAT'S THIS?
A LENDING LIBRARY.
NEKOTAMA-DO
NEKO-TAMA-DO...?
Lending Library

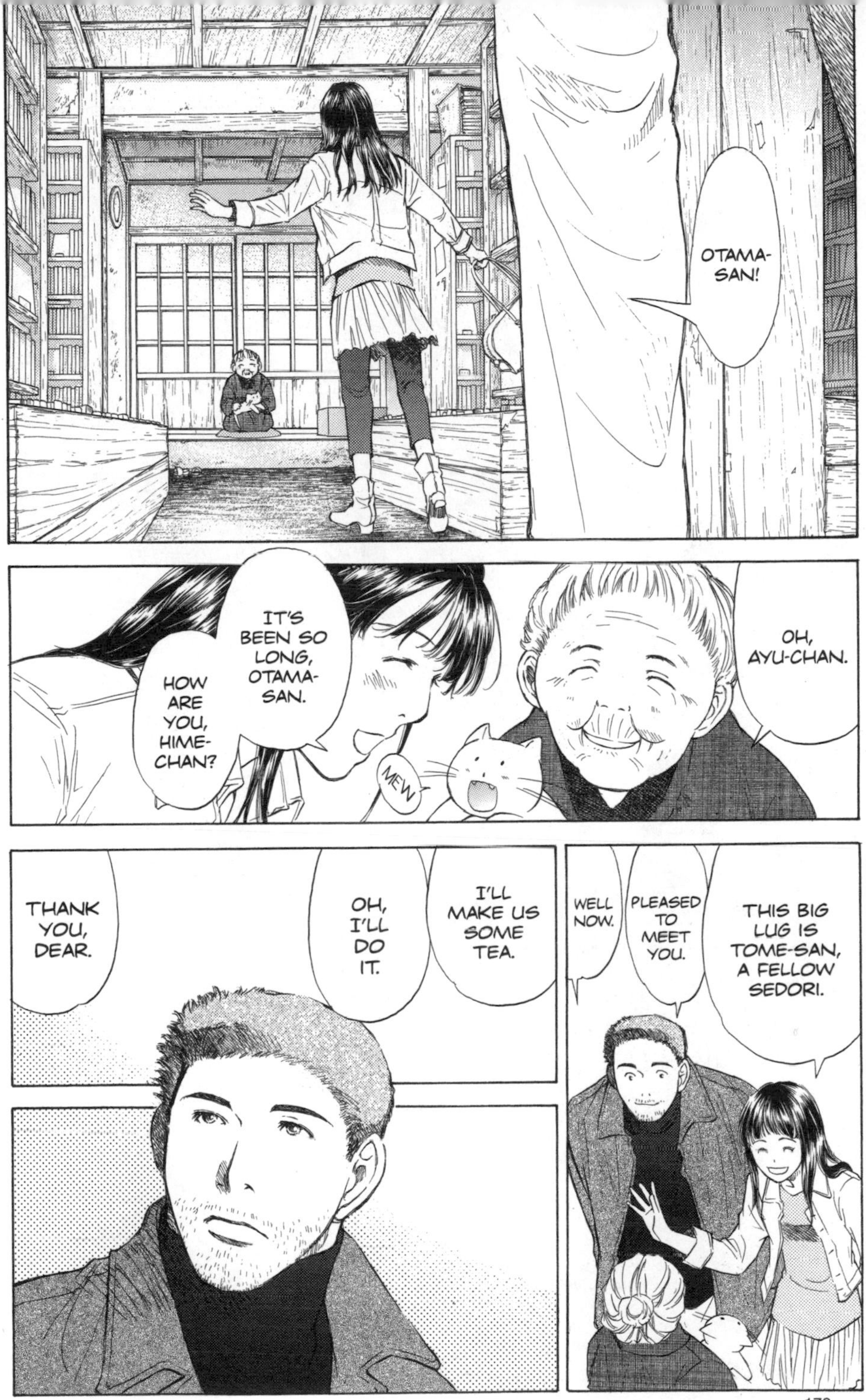
OTAMA-SAN!
OH, AYU-CHAN.
IT'S BEEN SO LONG, OTAMA-SAN.
HOW ARE YOU, HIME-CHAN?
MEW
THIS BIG LUG IS TOME-SAN, A FELLOW SEDORI.
PLEASED TO MEET YOU.
WELL NOW.
I'LL MAKE US SOME TEA.
OH, I'LL DO IT.
THANK YOU, DEAR.

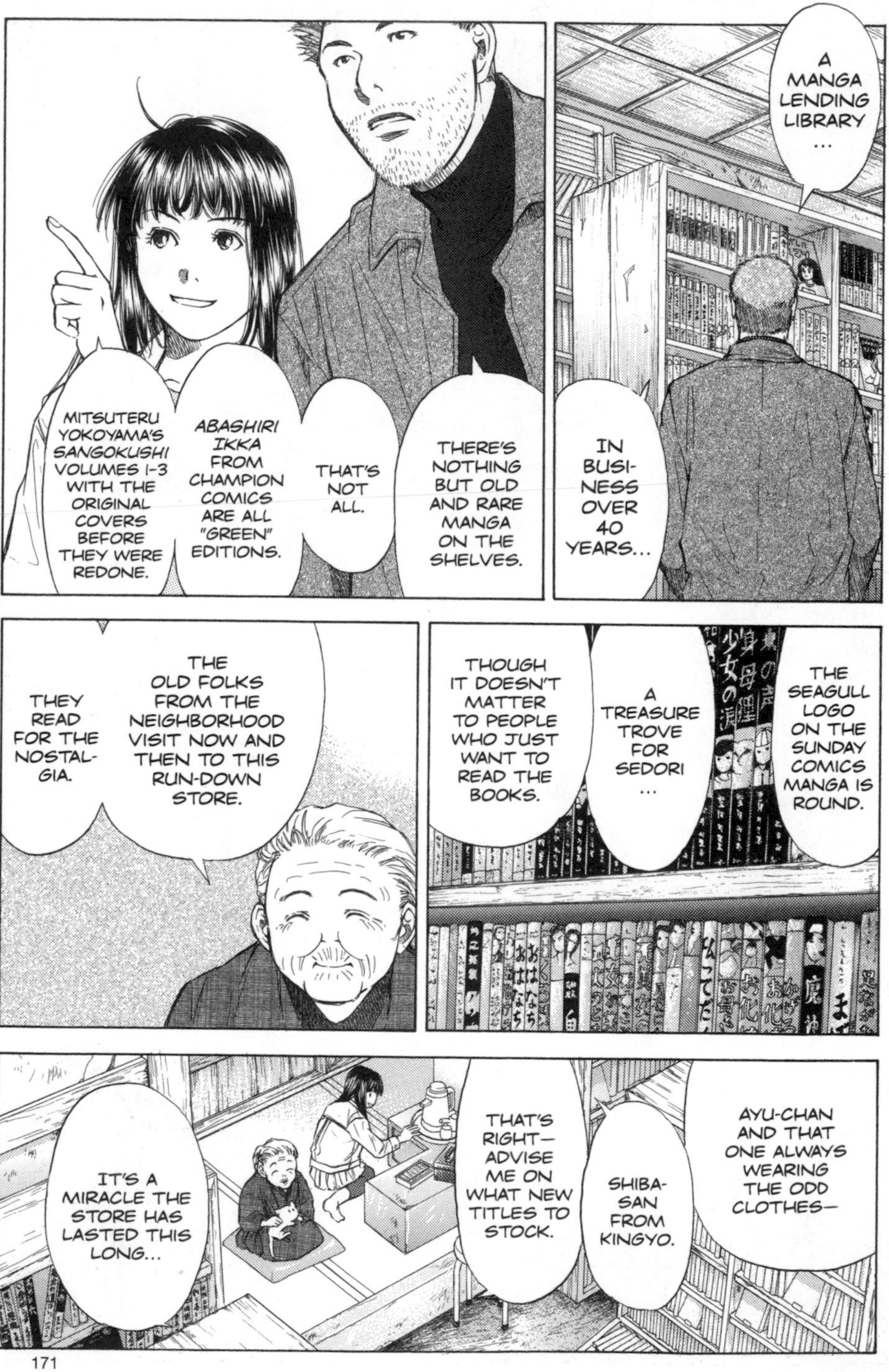
A MANGA LENDING LIBRARY...
IN BUSINESS OVER 40 YEARS...
THERE'S NOTHING BUT OLD AND RARE MANGA ON THE SHELVES.
THAT'S NOT ALL.
ABASHIRI IKKA FROM CHAMPION COMICS ARE ALL "GREEN" EDITIONS.
MITSUTERU YOKOYAMA'S SANGOKUSHI VOLUMES 1-3 WITH THE ORIGINAL COVERS BEFORE THEY WERE REDONE.
THE SEAGULL LOGO ON THE SUNDAY COMICS MANGA IS ROUND.
A TREASURE TROVE FOR SEDORI...
THOUGH IT DOESN'T MATTER TO PEOPLE WHO JUST WANT TO READ THE BOOKS.
THE OLD FOLKS FROM THE NEIGHBORHOOD VISIT NOW AND THEN TO THIS RUN-DOWN STORE.
THEY READ FOR THE NOSTALGIA.
AYU-CHAN AND THAT ONE ALWAYS WEARING THE ODD CLOTHES—
SHIBA-SAN FROM KINGYO.
THAT'S RIGHT—ADVISE ME ON WHAT NEW TITLES TO STOCK.
IT'S A MIRACLE THE STORE HAS LASTED THIS LONG...

STUDY! *ABASHIRI IKKA* (ABASHIRI FAMILY) BY GO NAGAI. BEGAN SERIALIZATION IN 1969 IN *SHONEN CHAMPION*. A RIBALD, FANTASTICAL GAG MANGA FOLLOWING THE EXPLOITS OF THE GANGSTER FAMILY, THE ABASHIRIS. NOW AVAILABLE IN REPRINT EDITION FROM CHAMPION COMICS (15 VOLUMES TOTAL) AND FROM KADOKAWA BUNKO (5 VOLUMES TOTAL).

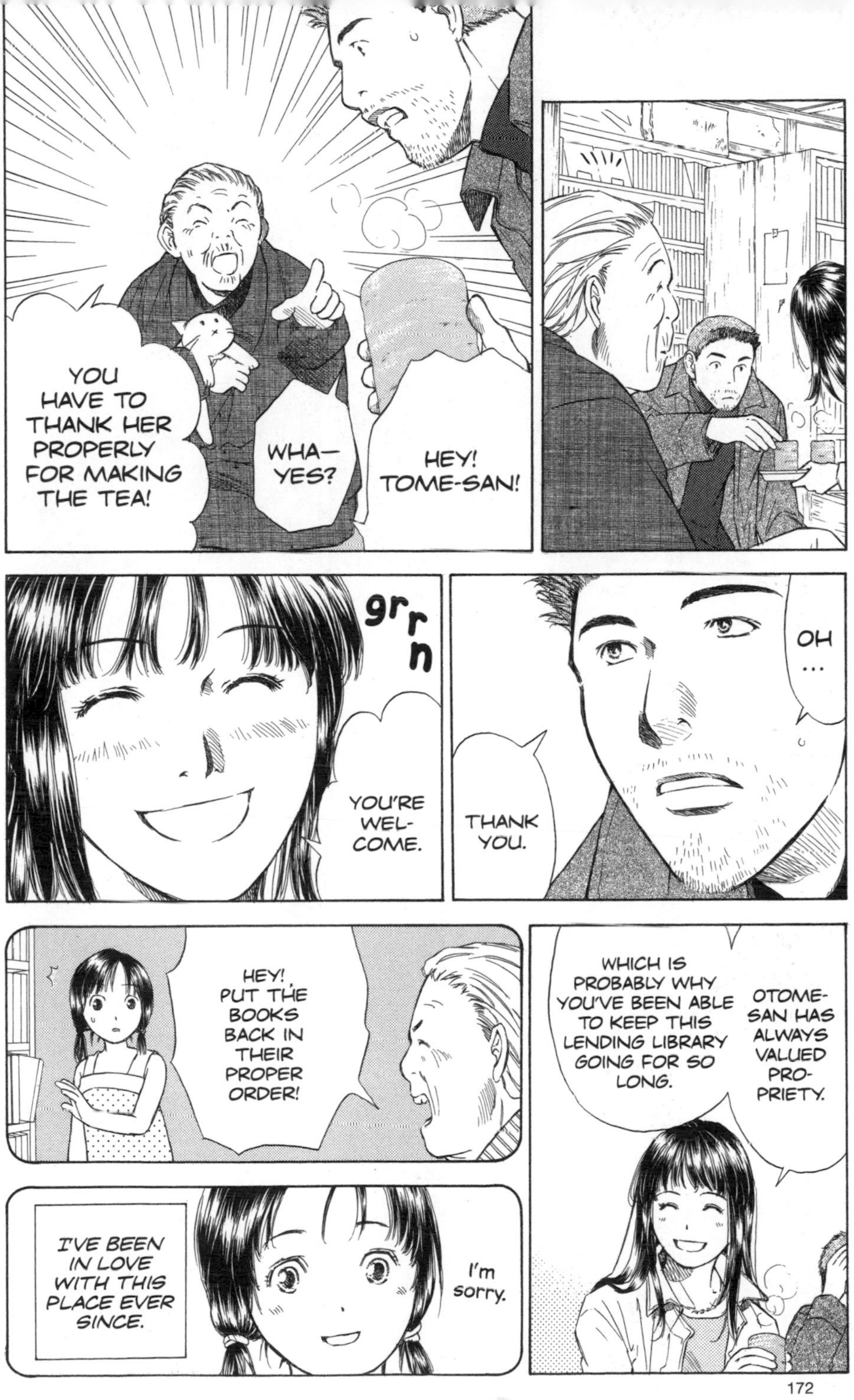

HEY! TOME-SAN!
WHA— YES?
YOU HAVE TO THANK HER PROPERLY FOR MAKING THE TEA!
OH ...
THANK YOU.
grrn
YOU'RE WEL-COME.
OTOME-SAN HAS ALWAYS VALUED PRO-PRIETY.
WHICH IS PROBABLY WHY YOU'VE BEEN ABLE TO KEEP THIS LENDING LIBRARY GOING FOR SO LONG.
HEY! PUT THE BOOKS BACK IN THEIR PROPER ORDER!
I'm sorry.
I'VE BEEN IN LOVE WITH THIS PLACE EVER SINCE.

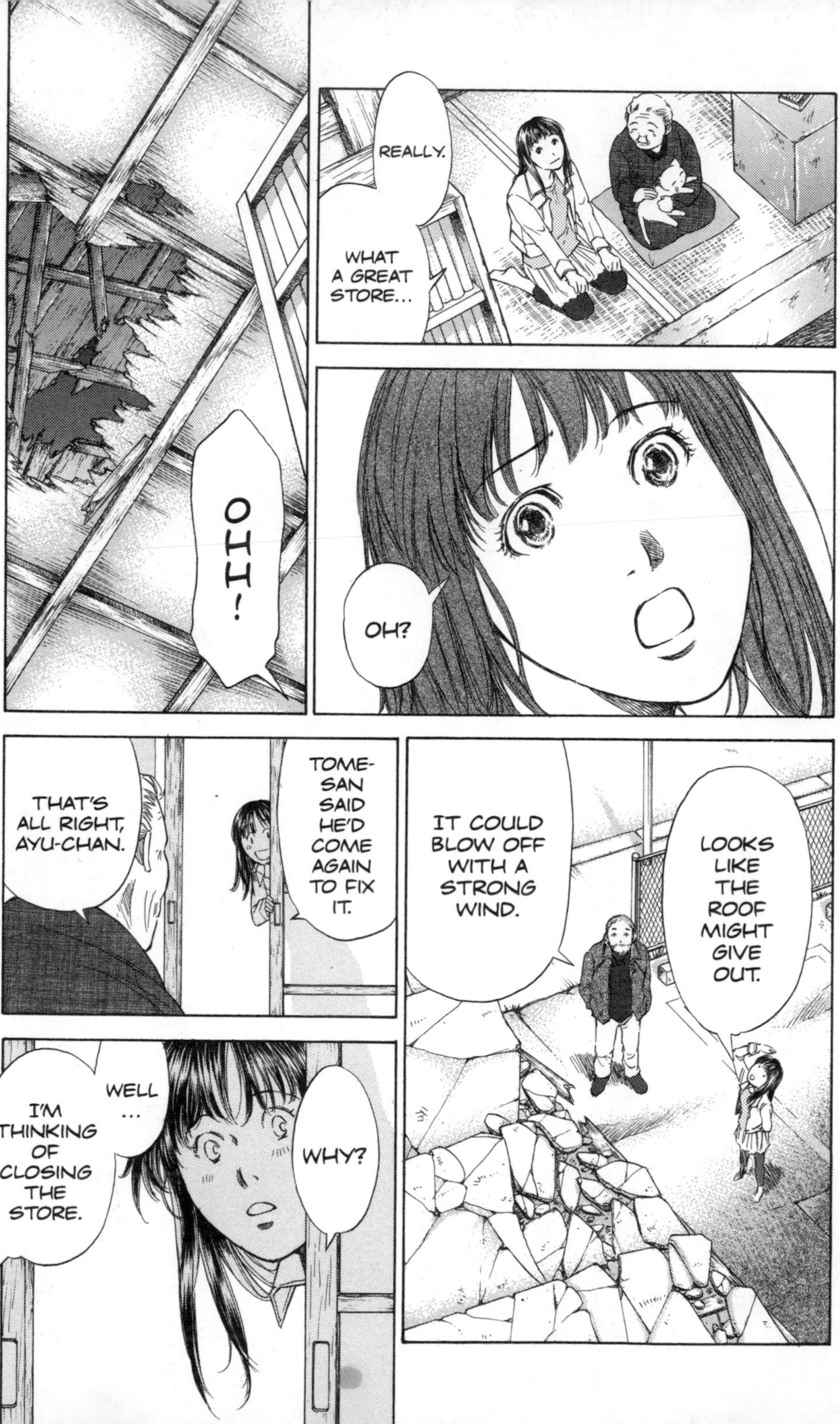
REALLY.
WHAT A GREAT STORE...
OH?
OHH!
LOOKS LIKE THE ROOF MIGHT GIVE OUT.
IT COULD BLOW OFF WITH A STRONG WIND.
TOME-SAN SAID HE'D COME AGAIN TO FIX IT.
THAT'S ALL RIGHT, AYU-CHAN.
WHY?
WELL...
I'M THINKING OF CLOSING THE STORE.

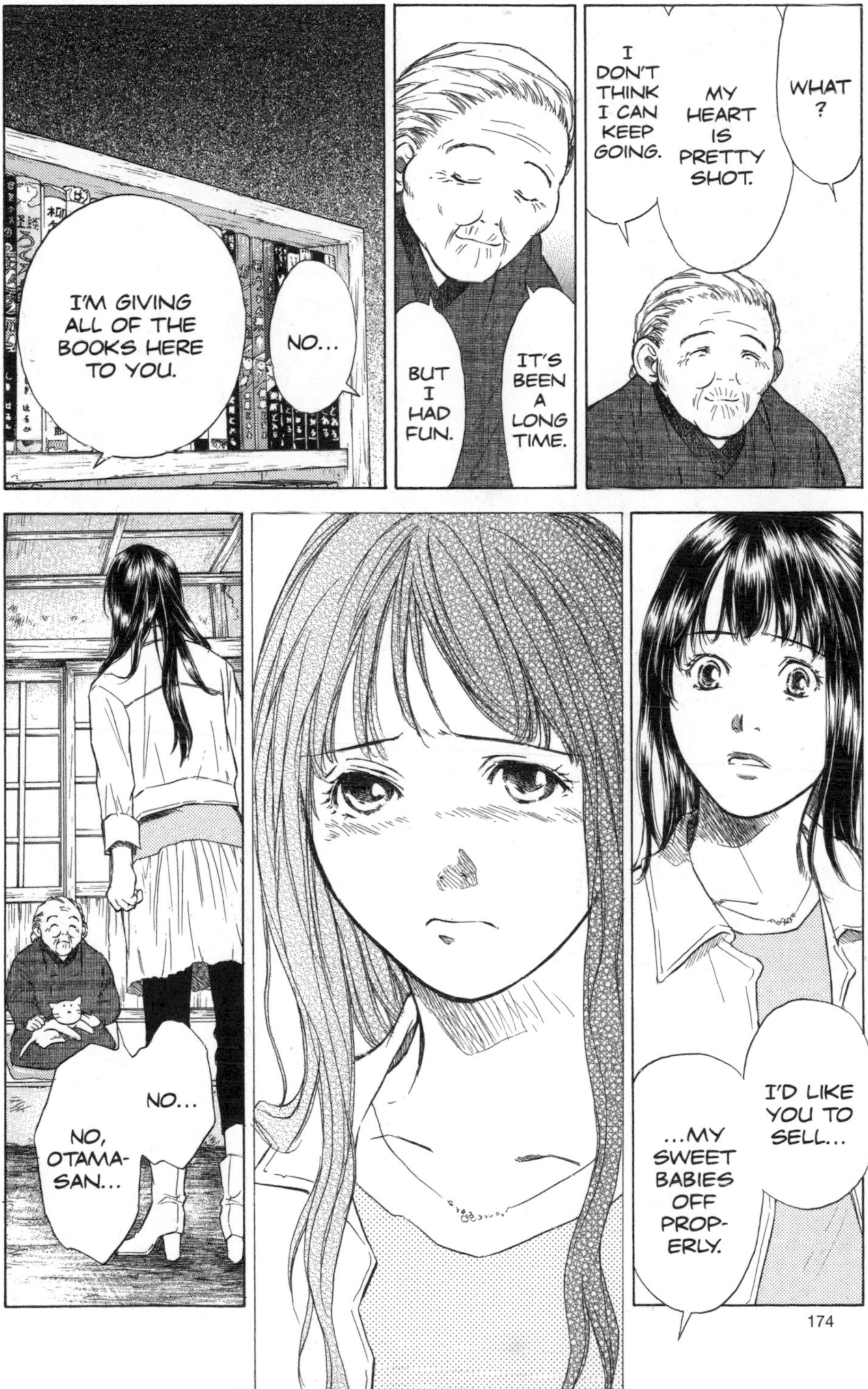
WHAT?
MY HEART IS PRETTY SHOT.
I DON'T THINK I CAN KEEP GOING.
IT'S BEEN A LONG TIME.
BUT I HAD FUN.
NO...
I'M GIVING ALL OF THE BOOKS HERE TO YOU.
I'D LIKE YOU TO SELL...
...MY SWEET BABIES OFF PROPERLY.
NO...
NO, OTAMA-SAN...

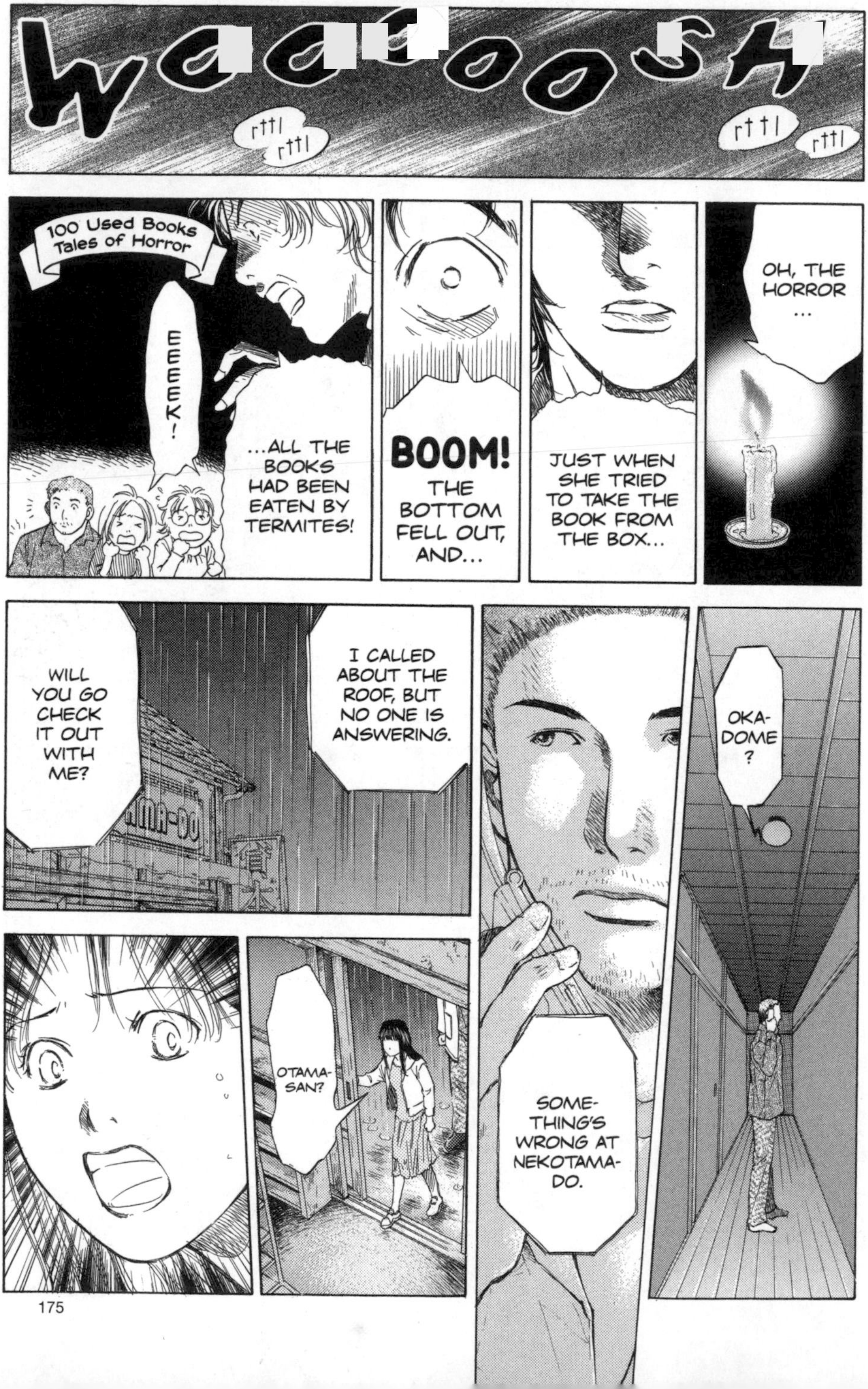
WHOOOOOSH
rttl rttl
rttl rttl
OH, THE HORROR ...
JUST WHEN SHE TRIED TO TAKE THE BOOK FROM THE BOX...
BOOM!
THE BOTTOM FELL OUT, AND...
...ALL THE BOOKS HAD BEEN EATEN BY TERMITES!
100 Used Books Tales of Horror
EEEEK!
OKA-DOME?
SOME-THING'S WRONG AT NEKOTAMA-DO.
I CALLED ABOUT THE ROOF, BUT NO ONE IS ANSWERING.
WILL YOU GO CHECK IT OUT WITH ME?
OTAMA-SAN?

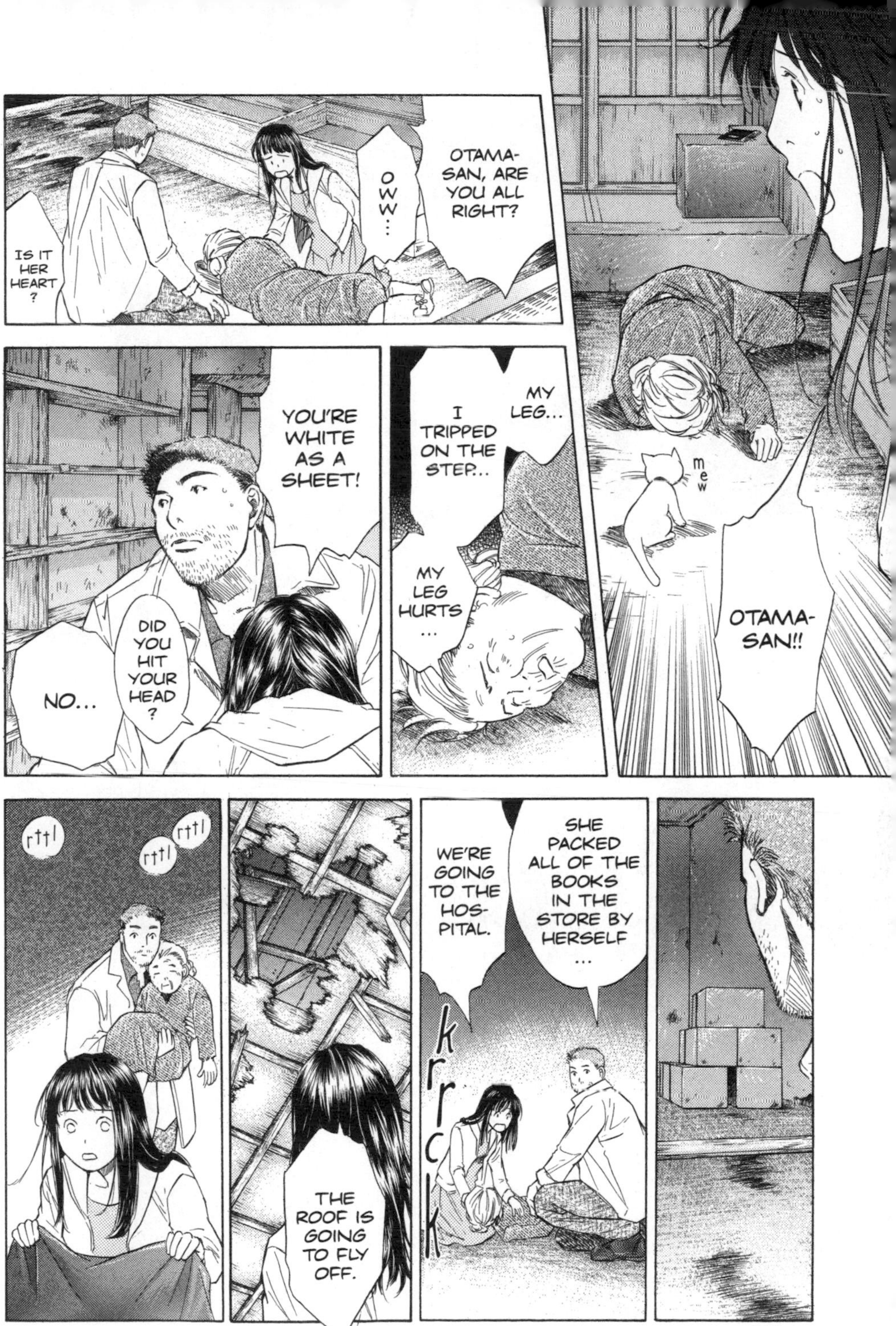
mew
OTAMA-SAN!!
OTAMA-SAN, ARE YOU ALL RIGHT?
OWW...
IS IT HER HEART?
MY LEG...
I TRIPPED ON THE STEP...
MY LEG HURTS...
YOU'RE WHITE AS A SHEET!
DID YOU HIT YOUR HEAD?
NO...
SHE PACKED ALL OF THE BOOKS IN THE STORE BY HERSELF...
WE'RE GOING TO THE HOSPITAL.
krrck
THE ROOF IS GOING TO FLY OFF.
rttl
rttl
rttl

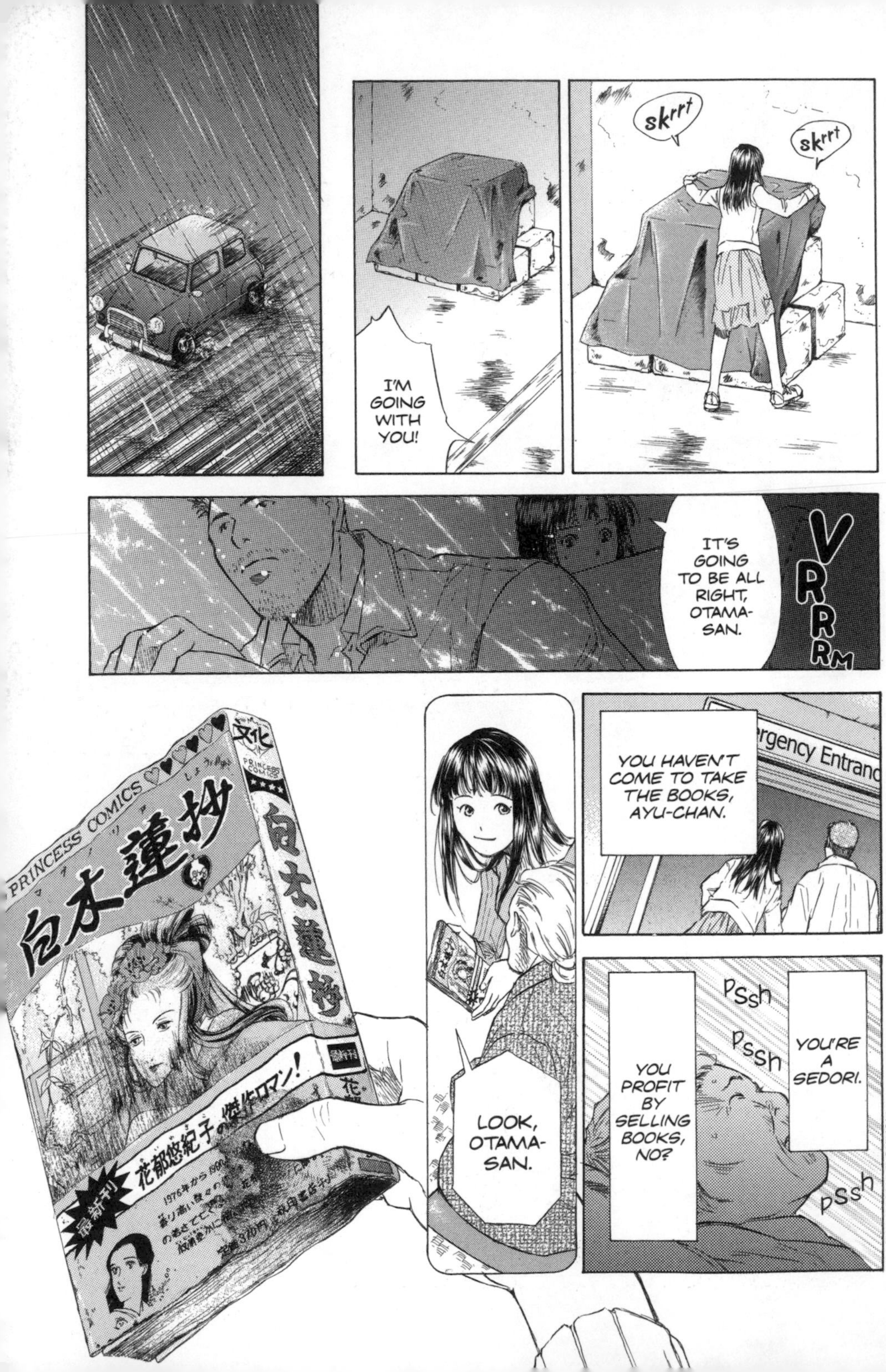
skrrt
skrrt
I'M GOING WITH YOU!
VRRRM
IT'S GOING TO BE ALL RIGHT, OTAMA-SAN.
YOU HAVEN'T COME TO TAKE THE BOOKS, AYU-CHAN.
ergency Entranc
YOU'RE A SEDORI.
pssh
pssh
YOU PROFIT BY SELLING BOOKS, NO?
pssh
LOOK, OTAMA-SAN.
PRINCESS COMICS
文化
白木蓮抄
最新刊
花郁悠紀子の傑作ロマン!

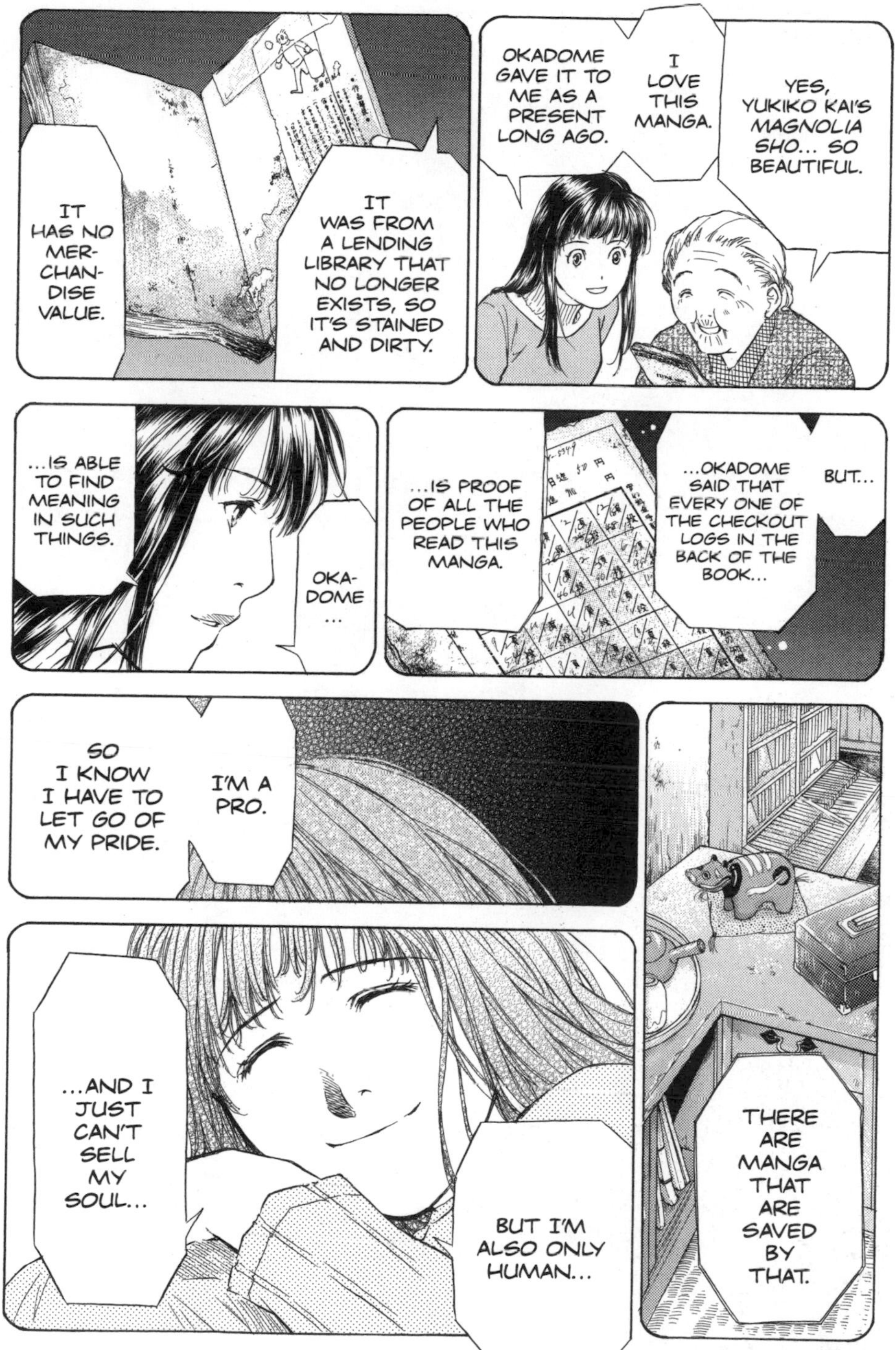
YES, YUKIKO KAI'S MAGNOLIA SHO... SO BEAUTIFUL.
I LOVE THIS MANGA.
OKADOME GAVE IT TO ME AS A PRESENT LONG AGO.
IT WAS FROM A LENDING LIBRARY THAT NO LONGER EXISTS, SO IT'S STAINED AND DIRTY.
IT HAS NO MER-CHAN-DISE VALUE.
BUT...
...OKADOME SAID THAT EVERY ONE OF THE CHECKOUT LOGS IN THE BACK OF THE BOOK...
...IS PROOF OF ALL THE PEOPLE WHO READ THIS MANGA.
OKA-DOME...
...IS ABLE TO FIND MEANING IN SUCH THINGS.
THERE ARE MANGA THAT ARE SAVED BY THAT.
I'M A PRO.
SO I KNOW I HAVE TO LET GO OF MY PRIDE.
BUT I'M ALSO ONLY HUMAN...
...AND I JUST CAN'T SELL MY SOUL...

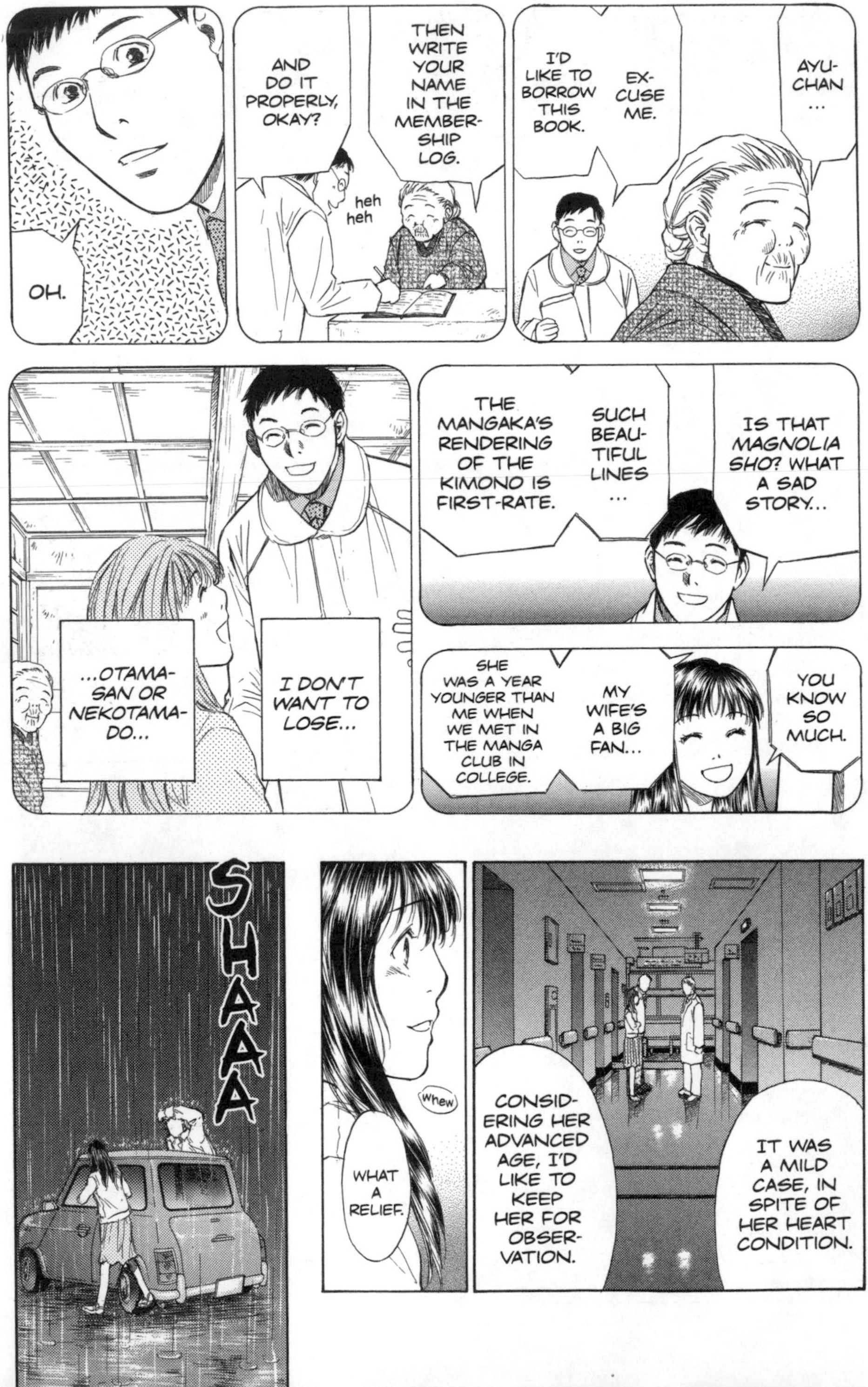
AYU-CHAN ...
EX-CUSE ME.
I'D LIKE TO BORROW THIS BOOK.
THEN WRITE YOUR NAME IN THE MEMBER-SHIP LOG.
AND DO IT PROPERLY, OKAY?
heh heh
OH.
IS THAT MAGNOLIA SHO? WHAT A SAD STORY...
SUCH BEAU-TIFUL LINES ...
THE MANGAKA'S RENDERING OF THE KIMONO IS FIRST-RATE.
YOU KNOW SO MUCH.
MY WIFE'S A BIG FAN...
SHE WAS A YEAR YOUNGER THAN ME WHEN WE MET IN THE MANGA CLUB IN COLLEGE.
I DON'T WANT TO LOSE...
...OTAMA-SAN OR NEKOTAMA-DO...
IT WAS A MILD CASE, IN SPITE OF HER HEART CONDITION.
CONSID-ERING HER ADVANCED AGE, I'D LIKE TO KEEP HER FOR OBSER-VATION.
Whew
WHAT A RELIEF.
SHAAA

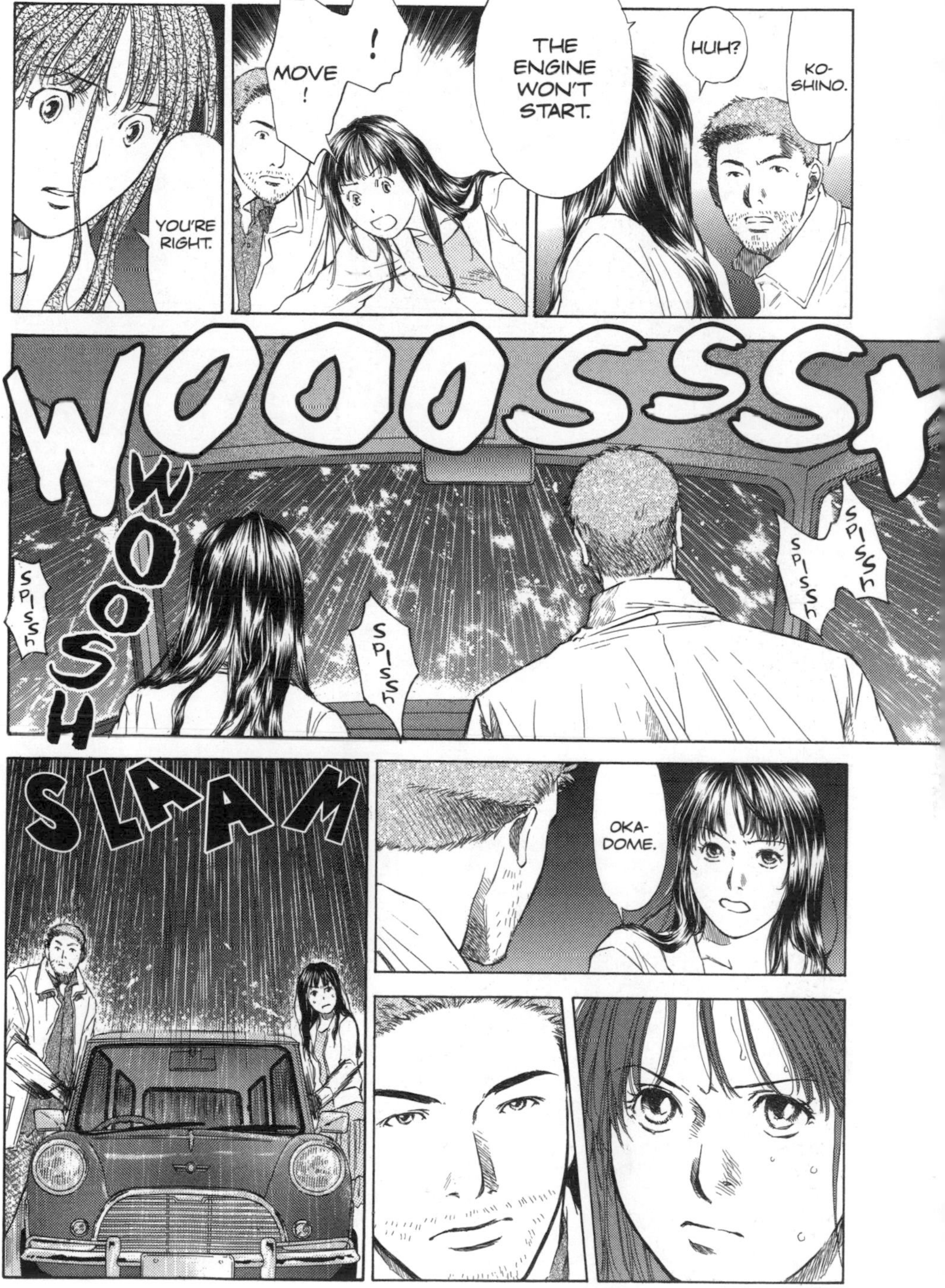
KO-SHINO.
HUH?
THE ENGINE WON'T START.
!
MOVE !
YOU'RE RIGHT.
WOOOSSSH
SPISSH
SPISSH
SPISSH
WOOSH
SPISSH
OKA-DOME.
SLAAM

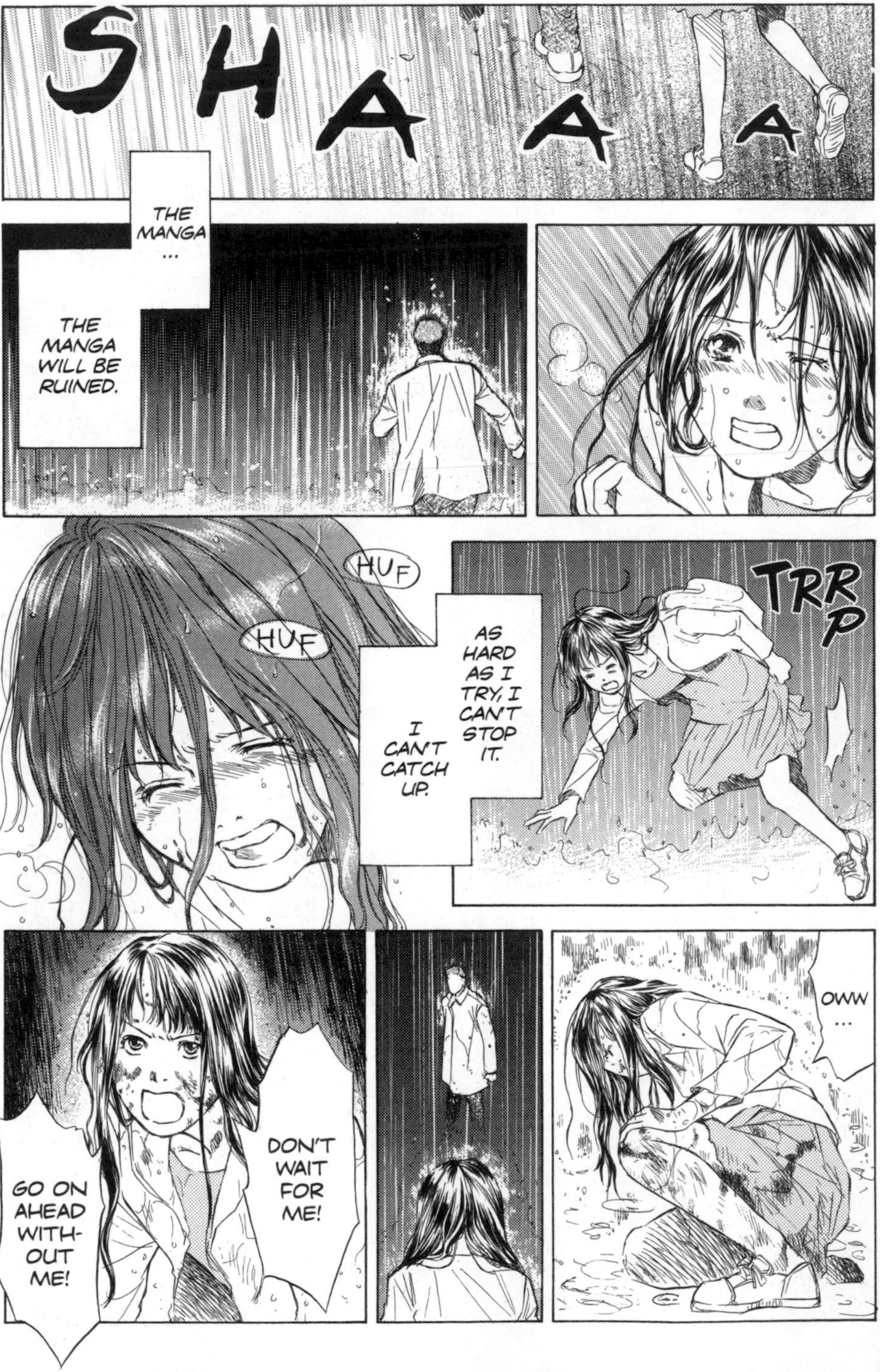
SHAAA
THE MANGA ...
THE MANGA WILL BE RUINED.
TRRP
AS HARD AS I TRY, I CAN'T STOP IT.
I CAN'T CATCH UP.
HUF
HUF
OWW ...
DON'T WAIT FOR ME!
GO ON AHEAD WITH-OUT ME!

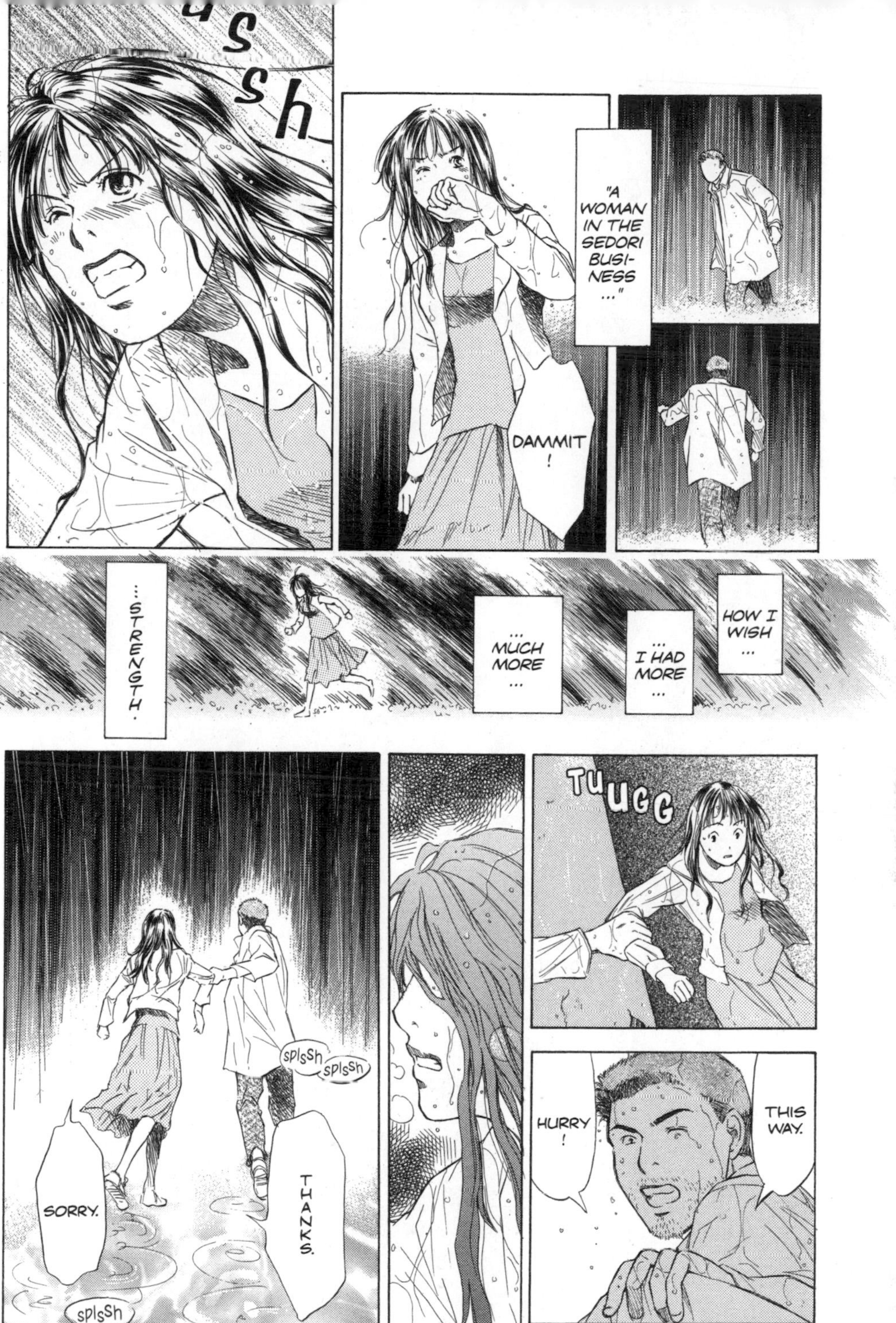

"A WOMAN IN THE SEDORI BUSINESS..."
DAMMIT!
ussh
HOW I WISH...
...I HAD MORE...
...MUCH MORE...
...STRENGTH.
TUUGG
THIS WAY.
HURRY!
THANKS.
SORRY.
splssh
splssh
splssh
splssh

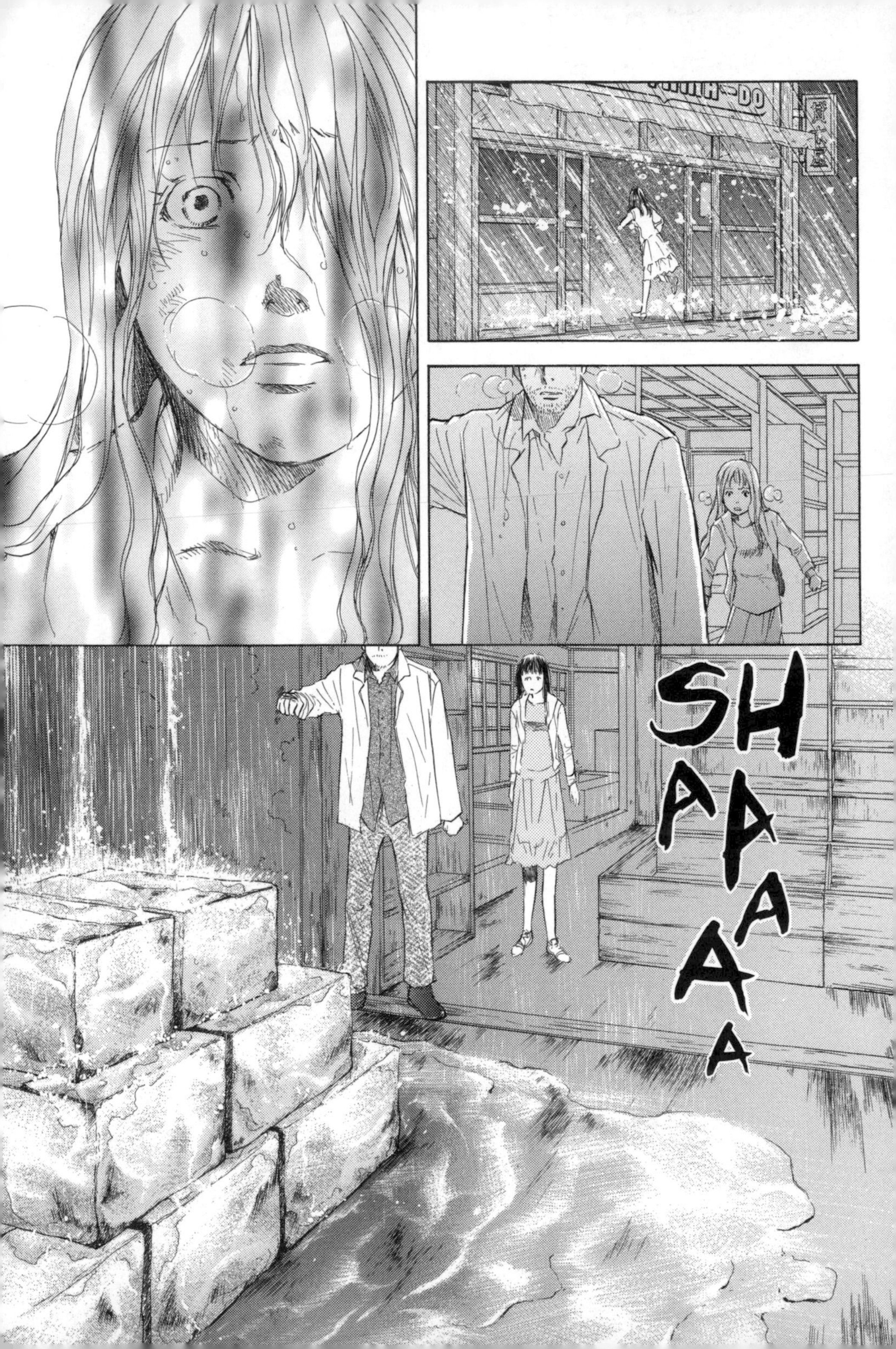
SHAAAAA

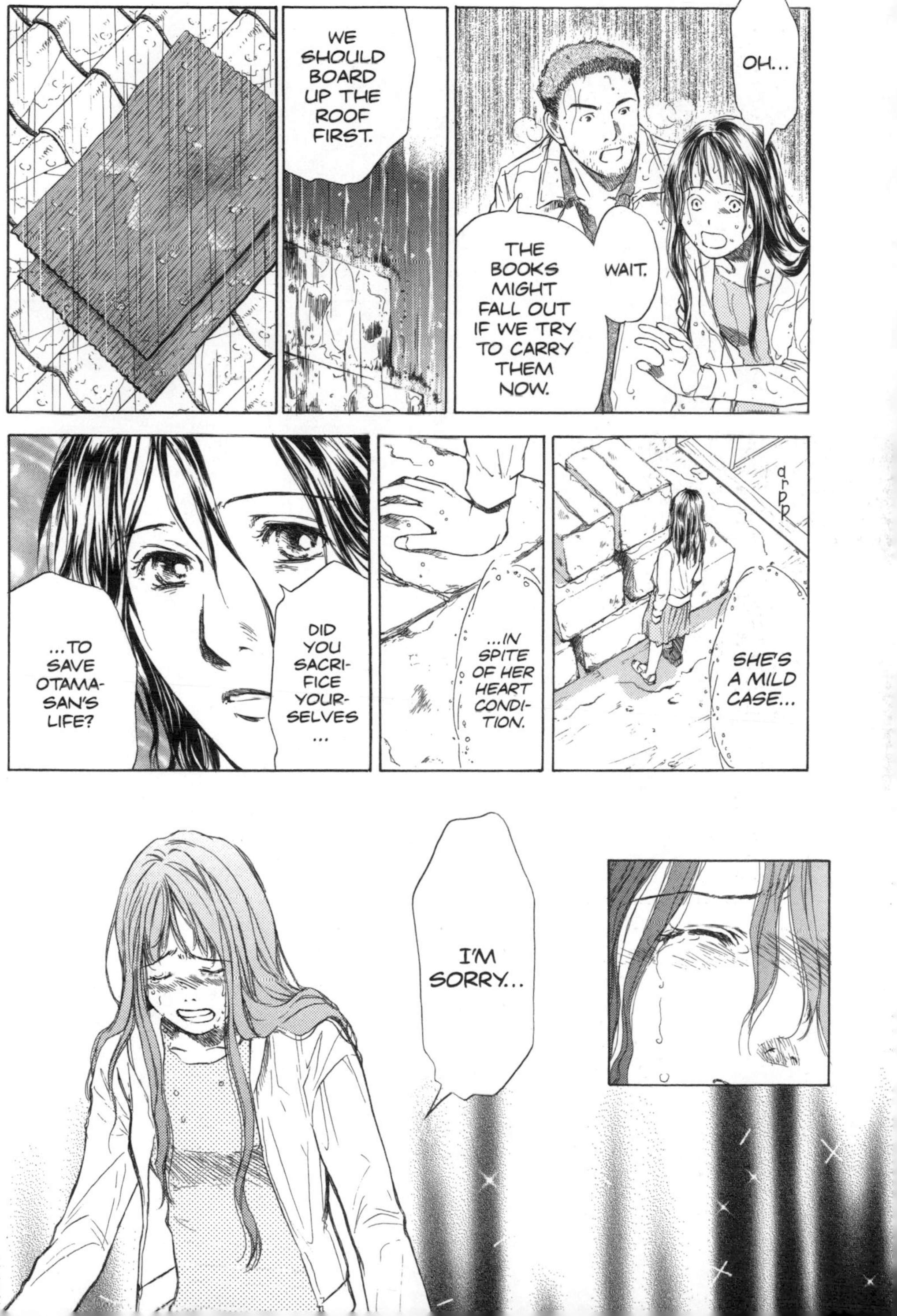
OH...
WAIT.
THE BOOKS MIGHT FALL OUT IF WE TRY TO CARRY THEM NOW.
WE SHOULD BOARD UP THE ROOF FIRST.
drpp
SHE'S A MILD CASE...
...IN SPITE OF HER HEART CONDITION.
DID YOU SACRIFICE YOURSELVES...
...TO SAVE OTAMA-SAN'S LIFE?
I'M SORRY...

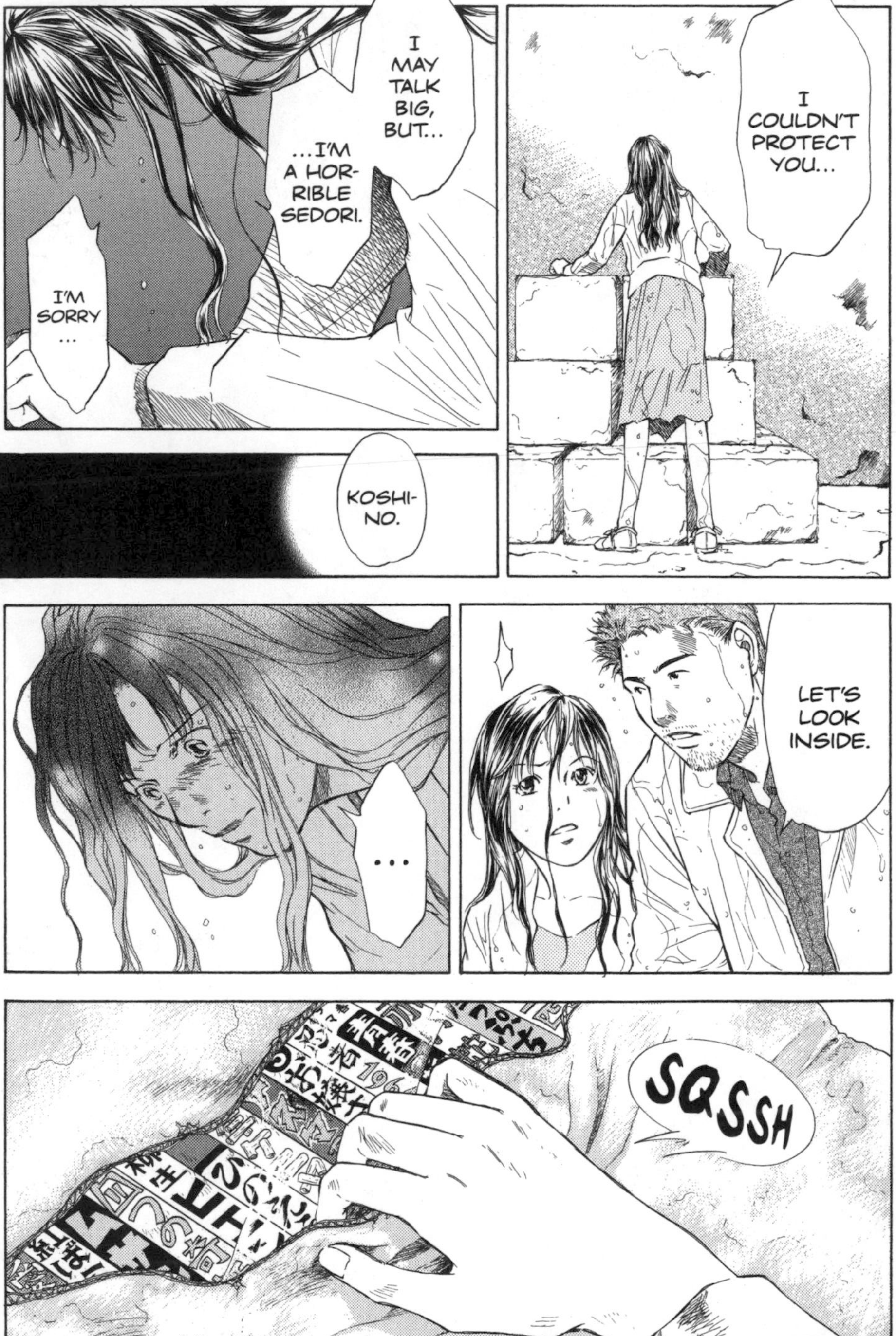
I COULDN'T PROTECT YOU...
I MAY TALK BIG, BUT...
...I'M A HOR-RIBLE SEDORI.
I'M SORRY...
KOSHI-NO.
LET'S LOOK INSIDE.
...
SQSSH

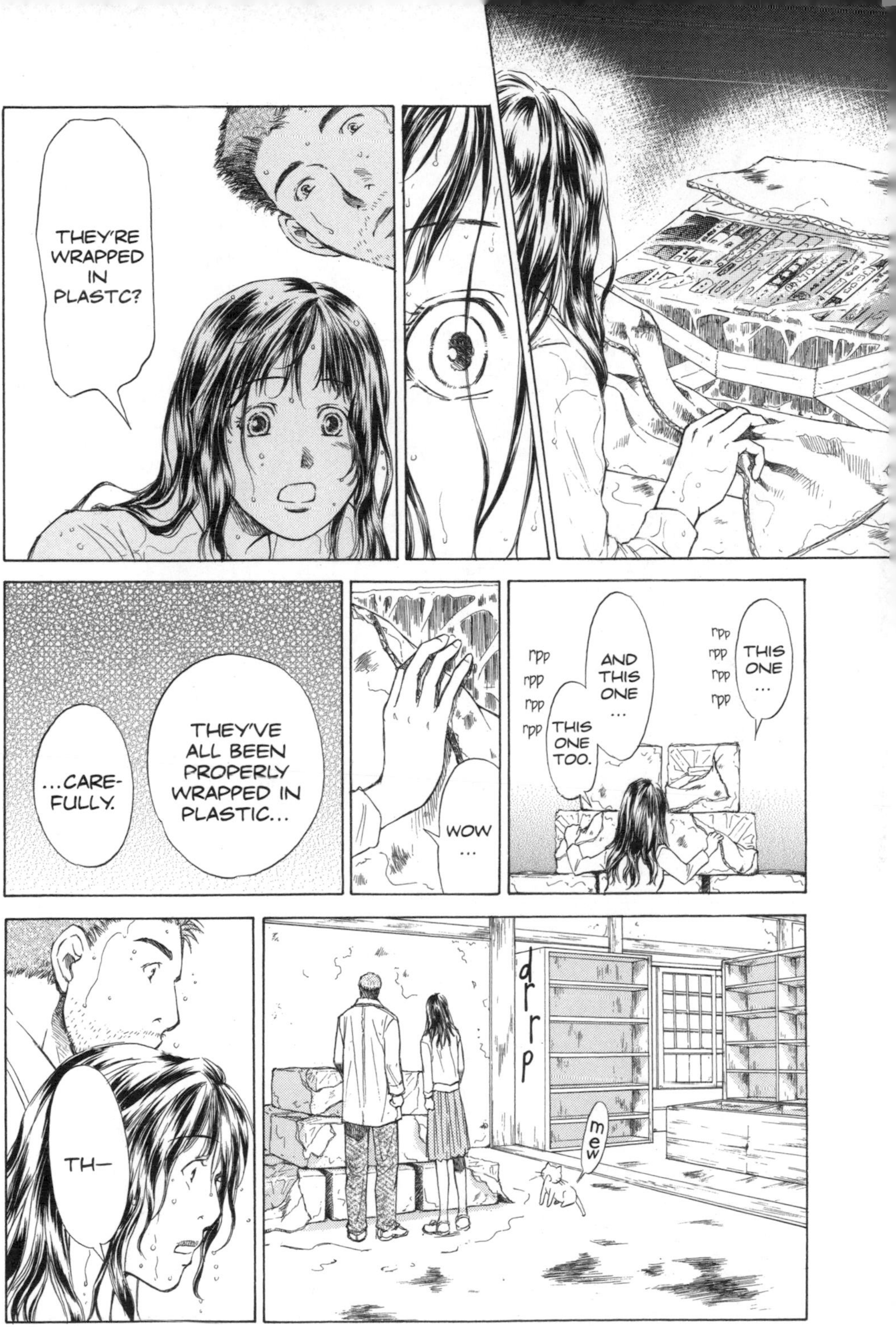
THEY'RE WRAPPED IN PLASTC?
rpp rpp rpp rpp
THIS ONE...
AND THIS ONE...
rpp rpp rpp rpp
THIS ONE TOO.
WOW...
THEY'VE ALL BEEN PROPERLY WRAPPED IN PLASTIC...
...CAREFULLY.
drrp
mew
TH—

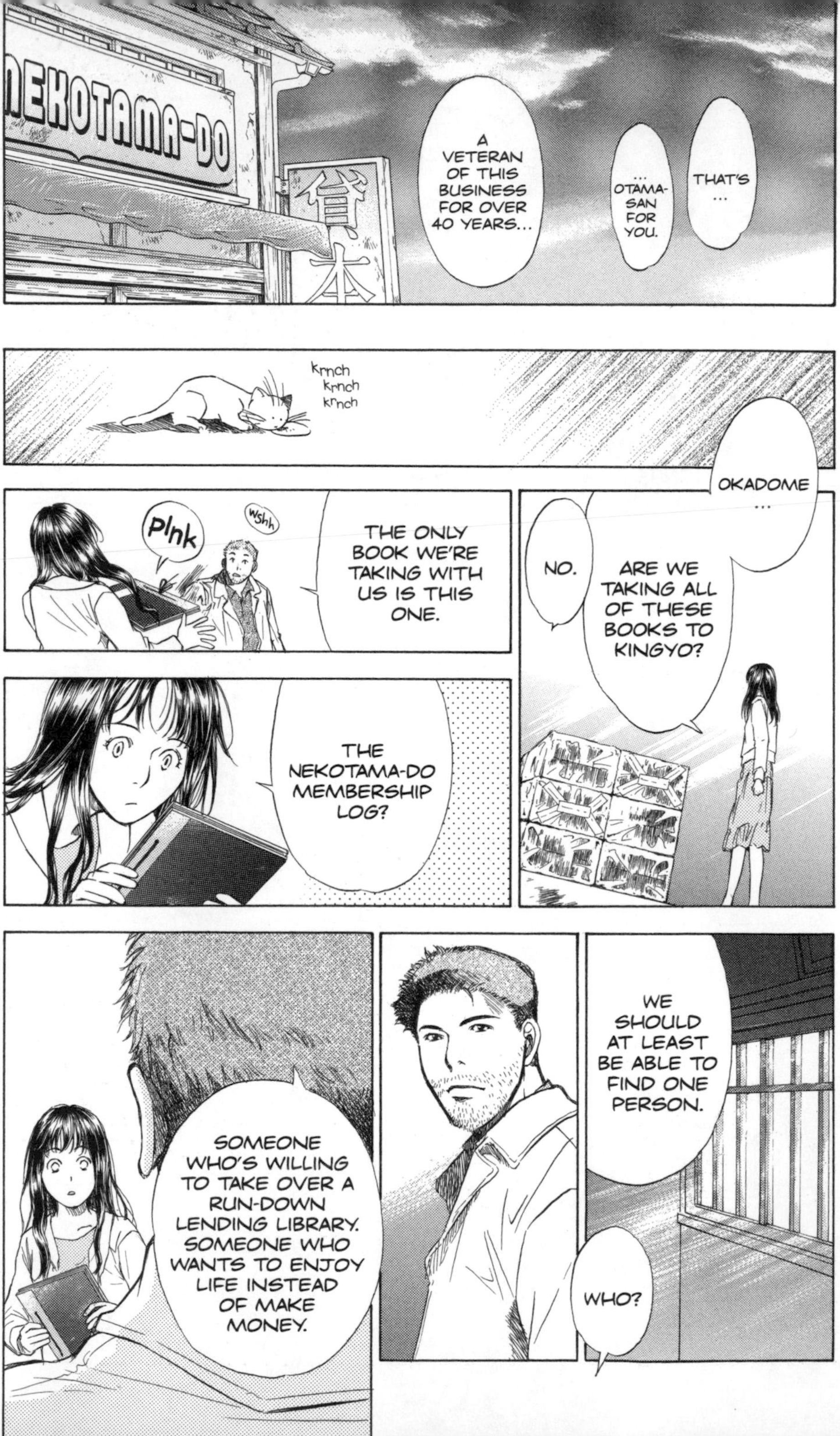
NEKOTAMA-DO
貸本
THAT'S ...
... OTAMA-SAN FOR YOU.
A VETERAN OF THIS BUSINESS FOR OVER 40 YEARS...
krnch krnch krnch
OKADOME ...
ARE WE TAKING ALL OF THESE BOOKS TO KINGYO?
NO.
Plnk
wshh
THE ONLY BOOK WE'RE TAKING WITH US IS THIS ONE.
THE NEKOTAMA-DO MEMBERSHIP LOG?
WE SHOULD AT LEAST BE ABLE TO FIND ONE PERSON.
WHO?
SOMEONE WHO'S WILLING TO TAKE OVER A RUN-DOWN LENDING LIBRARY. SOMEONE WHO WANTS TO ENJOY LIFE INSTEAD OF MAKE MONEY.

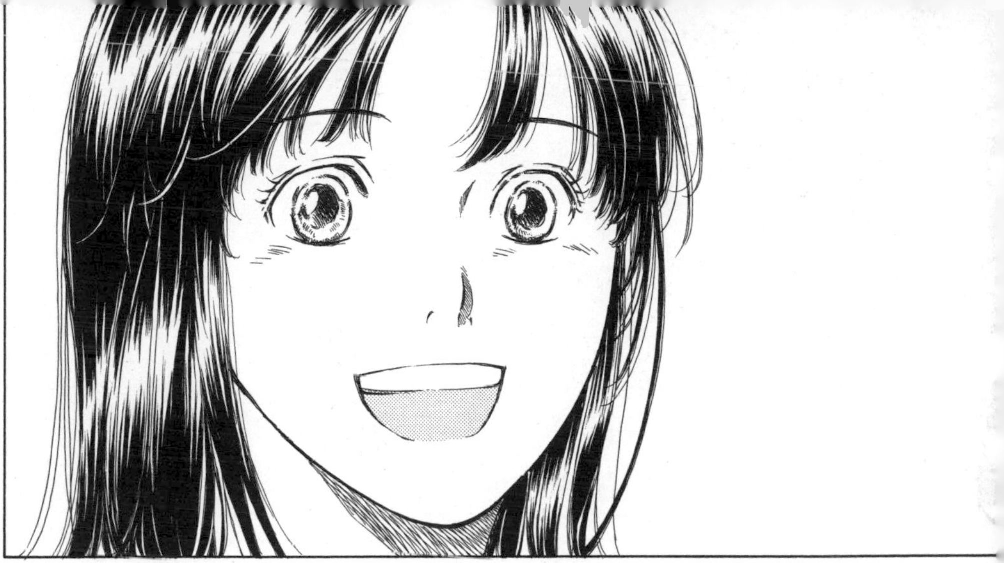

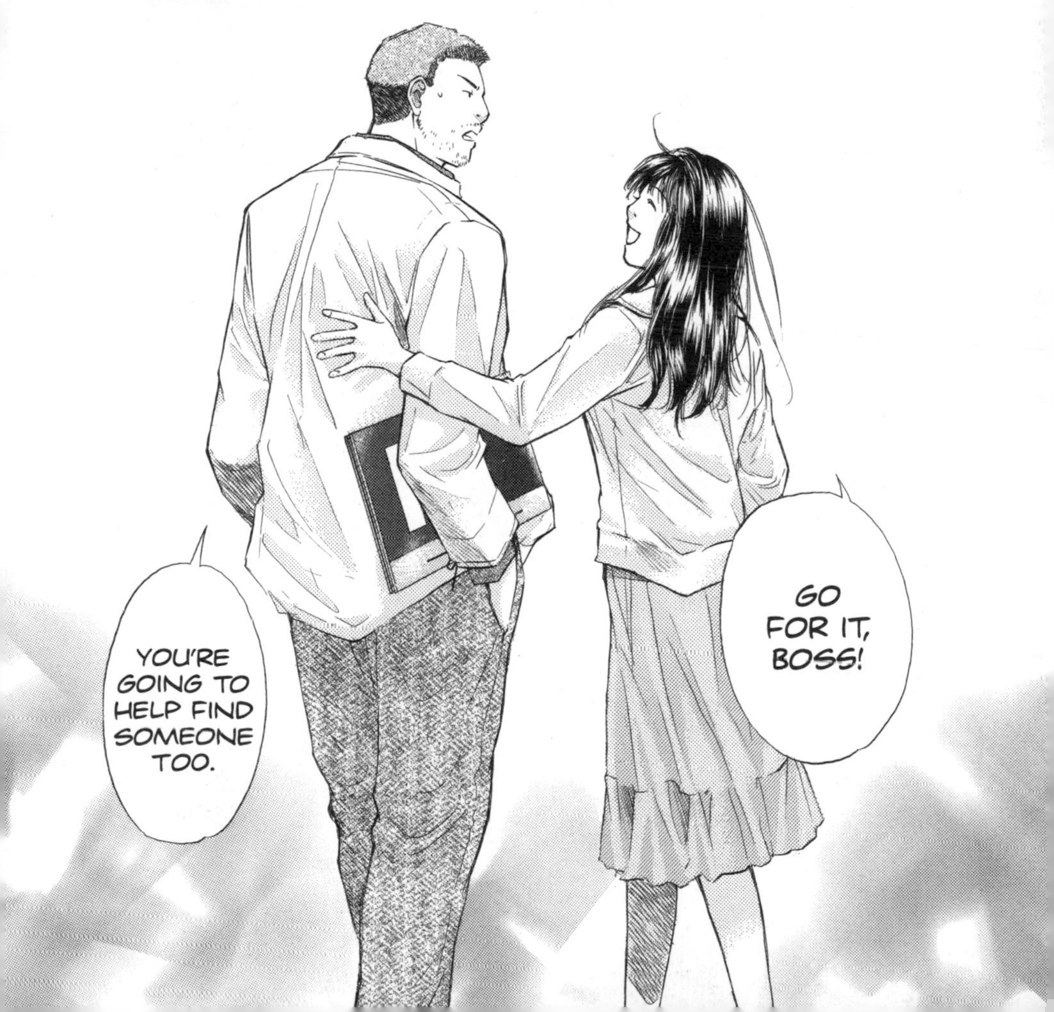
GO FOR IT, BOSS!
YOU'RE GOING TO HELP FIND SOMEONE TOO.

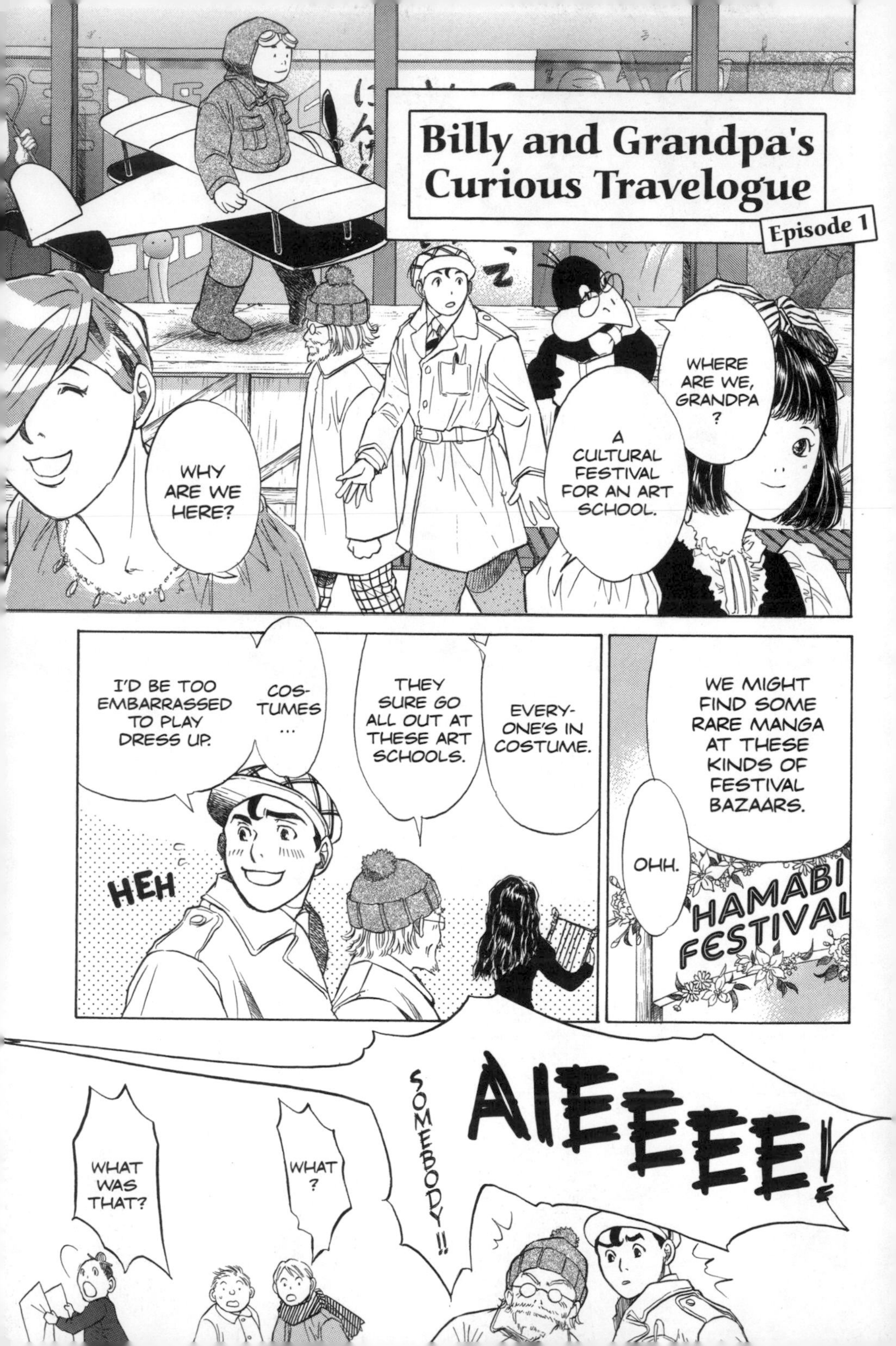

Billy and Grandpa's Curious Travelogue
Episode 1
WHERE ARE WE, GRANDPA?
A CULTURAL FESTIVAL FOR AN ART SCHOOL.
WHY ARE WE HERE?
WE MIGHT FIND SOME RARE MANGA AT THESE KINDS OF FESTIVAL BAZAARS.
OHH.
HAMABI FESTIVAL
EVERY-ONE'S IN COSTUME.
THEY SURE GO ALL OUT AT THESE ART SCHOOLS.
COS-TUMES...
I'D BE TOO EMBARRASSED TO PLAY DRESS UP.
HEH
AIEEEEE!
SOMEBODY!!
WHAT?
WHAT WAS THAT?

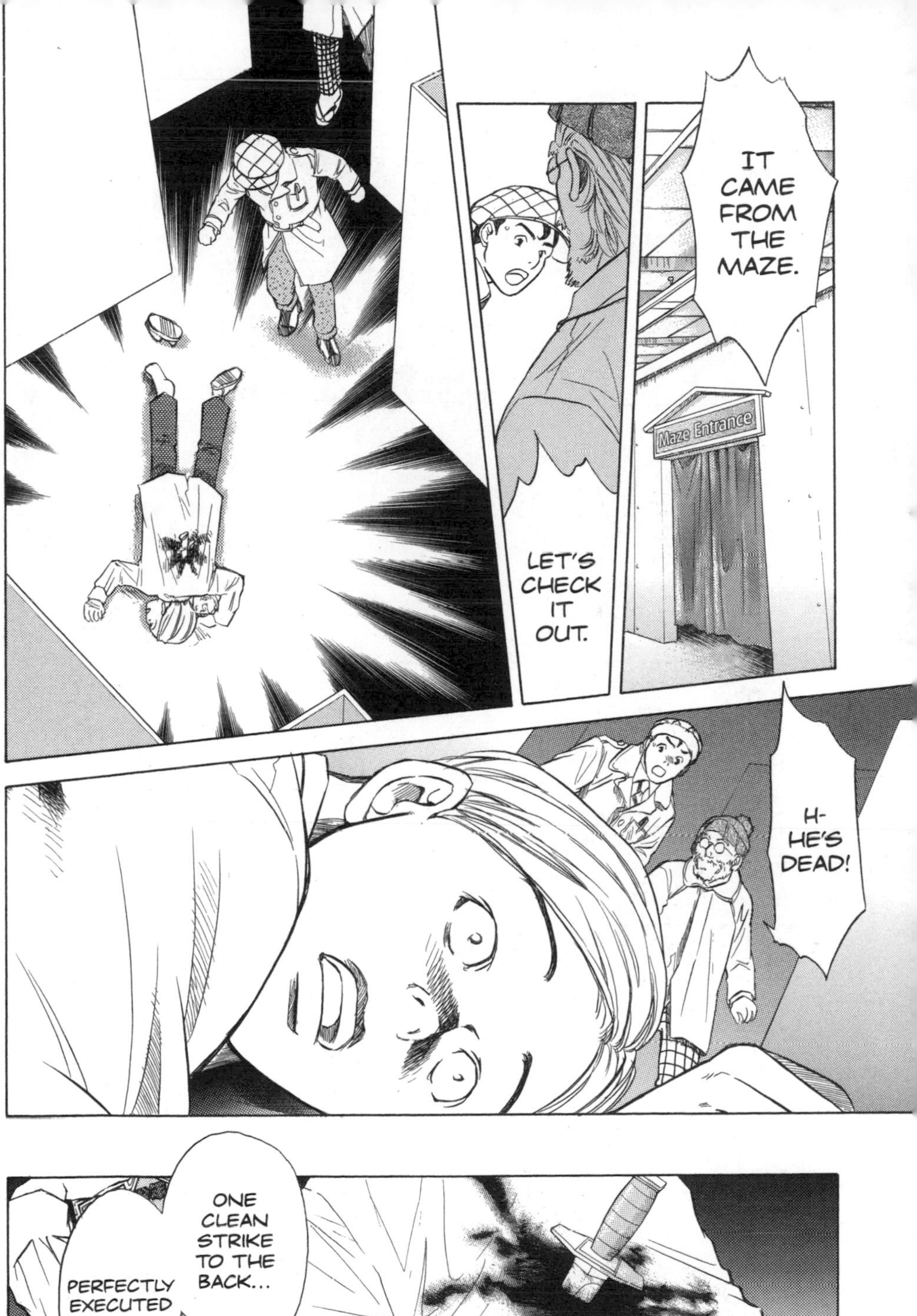
IT CAME FROM THE MAZE.
Maze Entrance
LET'S CHECK IT OUT.
H- HE'S DEAD!
ONE CLEAN STRIKE TO THE BACK...
PERFECTLY EXECUTED ...

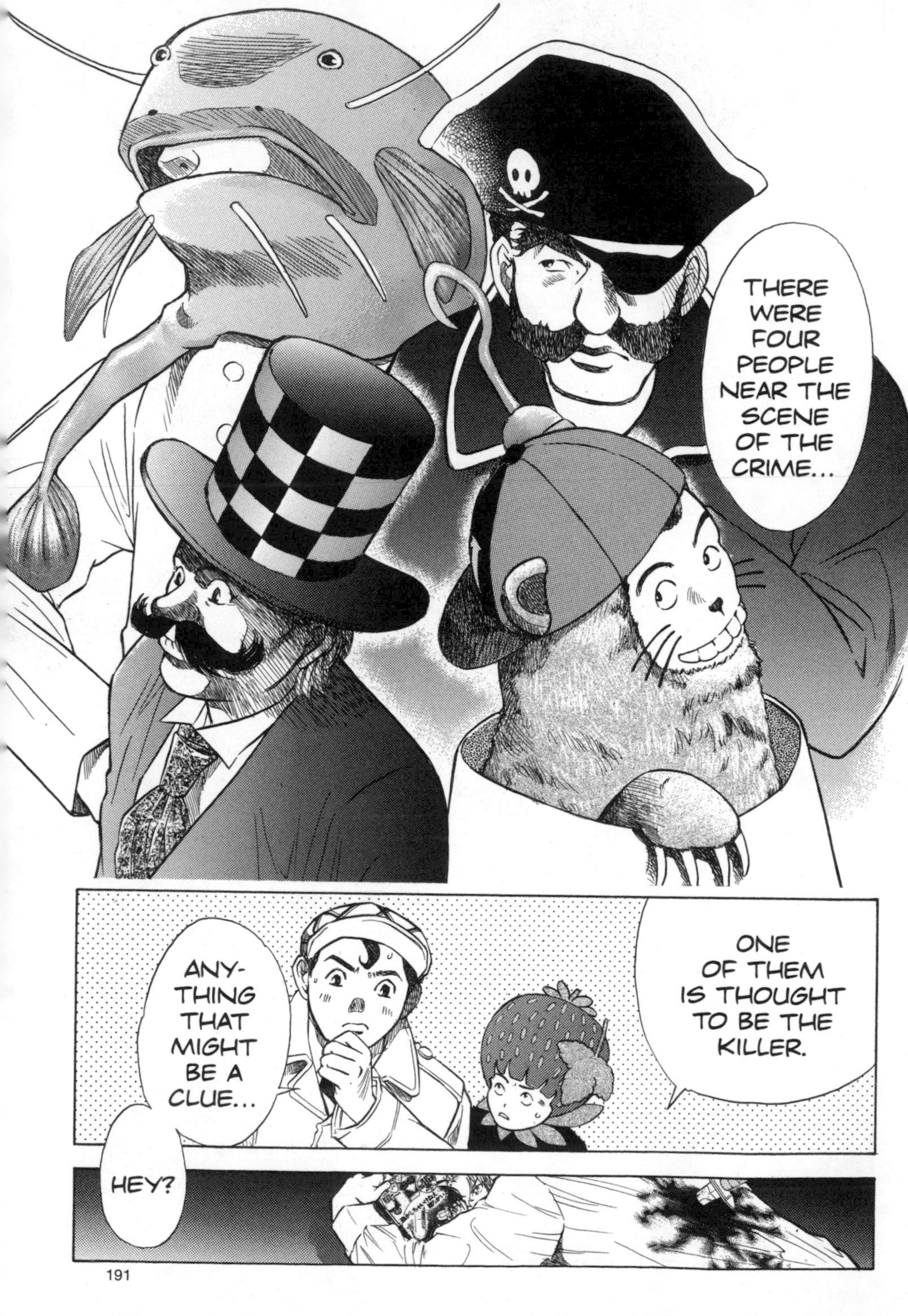
THERE WERE FOUR PEOPLE NEAR THE SCENE OF THE CRIME...
ONE OF THEM IS THOUGHT TO BE THE KILLER.
ANY-THING THAT MIGHT BE A CLUE...
HEY?

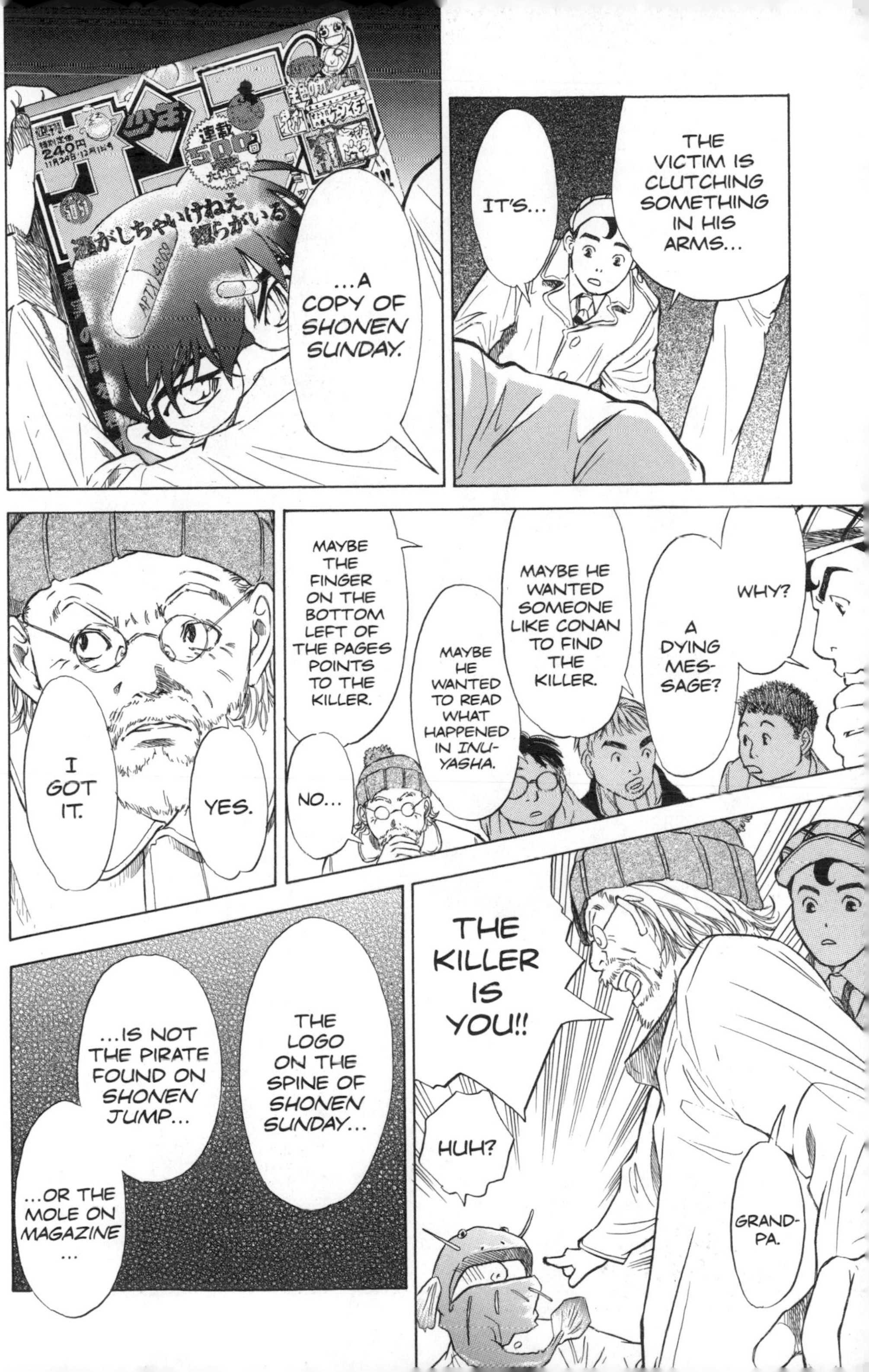
THE VICTIM IS CLUTCHING SOMETHING IN HIS ARMS...
IT'S...
...A COPY OF SHONEN SUNDAY.
WHY?
A DYING MES-SAGE?
MAYBE HE WANTED SOMEONE LIKE CONAN TO FIND THE KILLER.
MAYBE HE WANTED TO READ WHAT HAPPENED IN *INU-YASHA*.
MAYBE THE FINGER ON THE BOTTOM LEFT OF THE PAGES POINTS TO THE KILLER.
NO...
YES.
I GOT IT.
THE KILLER IS YOU!!
GRAND-PA.
HUH?
THE LOGO ON THE SPINE OF SHONEN SUNDAY...
...IS NOT THE PIRATE FOUND ON SHONEN JUMP...
...OR THE MOLE ON MAGAZINE...

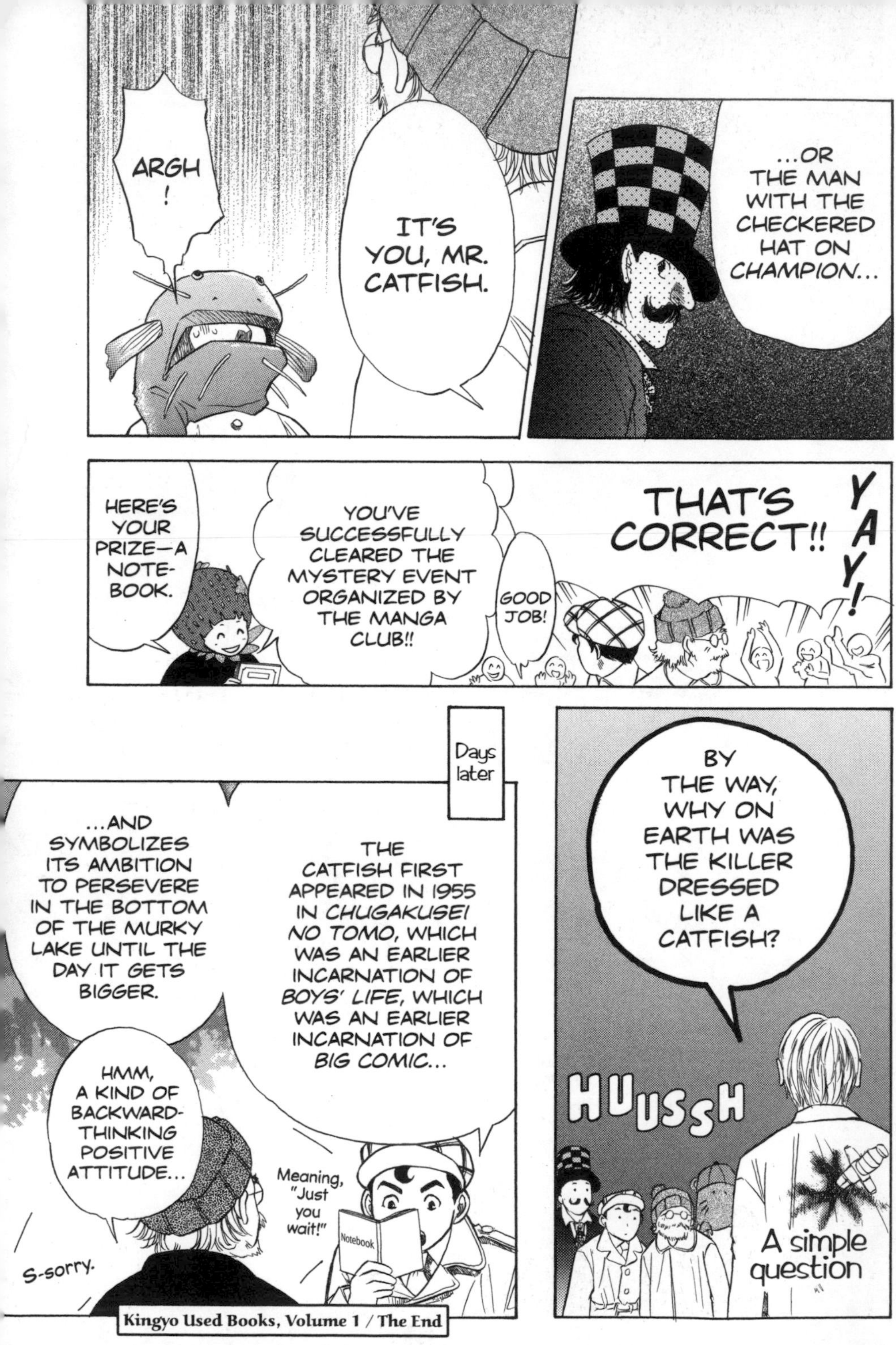

...OR THE MAN WITH THE CHECKERED HAT ON CHAMPION...
IT'S YOU, MR. CATFISH.
ARGH!
THAT'S CORRECT!!
YAY!
GOOD JOB!
YOU'VE SUCCESSFULLY CLEARED THE MYSTERY EVENT ORGANIZED BY THE MANGA CLUB!!
HERE'S YOUR PRIZE—A NOTEBOOK.
BY THE WAY, WHY ON EARTH WAS THE KILLER DRESSED LIKE A CATFISH?
HUUSSH
A simple question
Days later
THE CATFISH FIRST APPEARED IN 1955 IN *CHUGAKUSEI NO TOMO*, WHICH WAS AN EARLIER INCARNATION OF *BOYS' LIFE*, WHICH WAS AN EARLIER INCARNATION OF *BIG COMIC*...
...AND SYMBOLIZES ITS AMBITION TO PERSEVERE IN THE BOTTOM OF THE MURKY LAKE UNTIL THE DAY IT GETS BIGGER.
HMM, A KIND OF BACKWARD-THINKING POSITIVE ATTITUDE...
Meaning, "Just you wait!"
Notebook
S-sorry.

Kingyo Used Books, Volume 1 / The End

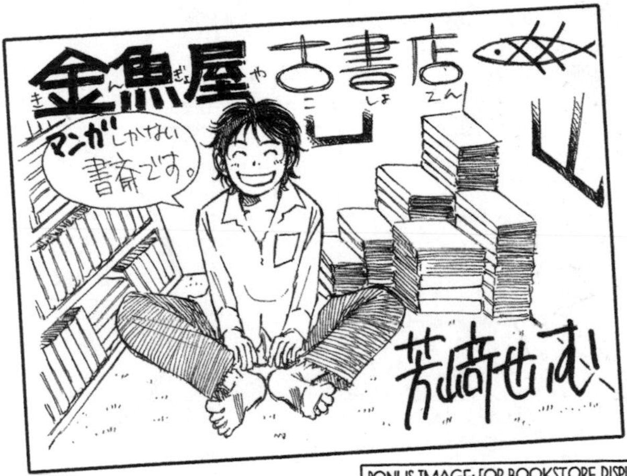
金魚屋古書店
マンガしかない書斎です。
芳崎せいむ

BONUS IMAGE: FOR BOOKSTORE DISPLAY 2

TRANSLATION OF ABOVE IMAGE:
KINGYO USED BOOKS BY SEIMU YOSHIZAKI
SHIBA SAYS, "A MANGA-ONLY SANCTUARY."

KINGYO USED BOOKS NOTEBOOK

More useful information about the manga found on the shelves of **Kingyo Used Books**!

Text by Hiroshi Hashimoto.

Born in 1948 in Kumamoto, Japan. Owner of the used bookstore Kirara Bunko. Aside from running his bookstore, he also teaches at a preparatory school and is active in a nonprofit organization. Fellow alumni of his elementary school include manga commentators Hiroshi Yonezawa and Yukari Fujimoto. His dream is to build a manga library in Aso. Hashimoto was asked to write this column when being interviewed for information for this series.

Kirara Bunko
6-9-9 Kurokami, Kumamoto-shi
860-0860
Tel: 096-345-4991
http://kirarabunko.cool.ne.jp/

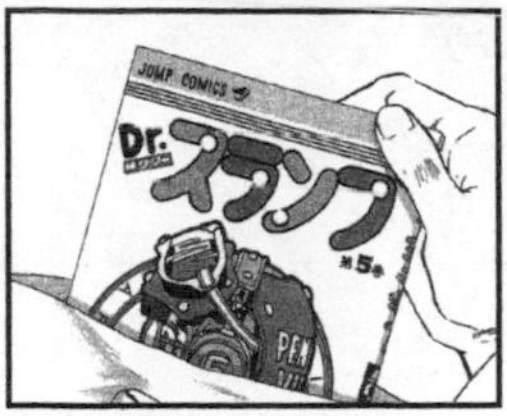
JUMP COMICS
Dr.

This series is featured in Chapter 1: The Components of Memory

Dr. Slump (18 volumes)

By Akira Toriyama

Published by Shueisha beginning in 1980

Akira Toriyama's *Dr. Slump* was serialized in *Weekly Shonen Jump* from 1980 to 1984. Collected into 18 volumes, the series is still readily available in Japan. In a publishing climate where even the most popular manga series eventually goes out of print, the fact that this series is still available twenty years later attests to its popularity. (This fact, however, isn't good news for used bookstores. Since older editions are readily available as reprints, the original editions don't have an especially high collector value.)

Why is the series beloved by so many people? Some say it's the hip West Coast vibe from the U.S. that pervades the story, and others say it's the adorable super-deformed art. I believe its popularity derives from the extreme simplicity and clarity of the story, which appeals to children, adolescents and adults alike.

A lot of mangaka have a tendency to twist their own brains to squeeze out interesting themes, stories, and characters. Often times, however, their best intentions get too complicated and things fall apart. Akira Toriyama never does this.

Much like his heroine Arale, Toriyama has a strong sense of curiosity and tends to operate on instinct. He truly enjoys writing manga. His series has no overreaching storyline or theme or twists. Certainly his artwork is genius, but he draws what he wants to, spouts an endless stream of risqué jokes, and often misses his deadlines after getting too absorbed in his plastic models. *Dr. Slump* seems like it was written by a child. But that's exactly why it works.

Most manga magazines back in 1980 were focused on romantic comedies. But with the publication of *Dr. Slump* and other things geared toward children, *Weekly Shonen Jump* exploded in popularity. The "Golden Era of *Shonen Jump*" had begun. It was around this time that the Shueisha building came to be known as the "Arale-chan Building."

The first printing of the tankobon easily sold over two million copies, astounding numbers for the time. Character merchandise based on the anime also sold like hotcakes. Arale mania hit and became something of a social phenomenon, with "Arale-speak" like "hoyoyo" and "ncha" becoming popular slang. It was a happy time for manga artists, publishers and fans of manga.

Now, over twenty years later, the conditions surrounding manga have changed. The long-term economic downturn makes things tough on mangaka, publishers and bookstores, and no relief seems to be in sight. However, when you read *Dr. Slump* now, the art, storyline and jokes still seem new and fresh. Toriyama's genius has aged well.

We live in an age of cold and stiff interpersonal relationships. Won't you join the customers of Kingyo Used Books and take a trip back to the good old days?

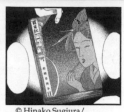

© Hinako Sugiura/
Jitsugyo no Nihon Sha
©杉浦日向子/実業之日本社

Sarusuberi (3 volumes)

By Hinako Sugiura

Published by Jitsugyo no Nihon Sha in 1986

Sarusuberi depicts the lives of Katsushika Hokusai and his daughter Oei, who were fellow *ukiyo* artists during the apex of Edo culture. The series began running in *Manga Sunday* in 1983, was released in three tankobon by Jitsugyo no Nihon Sha in 1986 (currently out of print) and is now available in two volumes from Chikuma Bunko.

During the rainy season, the *sarusuberi* (or crepe myrtle) is laden with crimson blossoms, which fall to the ground only to bloom once again. The author thought of the haiku by Chiyojo which reads, "Sarusuberi, which fades and blooms and fades and blooms," and ended up using it as her title.

Gasso, the author's first tankobon, was published by Seirindo. Along with Yoko Kondo and Murasaki Yamada, she is one of the esteemed "Three Ladies of Garo." ["Garo no Sannin Musume" — Ed.]

During her time at Nihon University College of Art, Sugiura read the manga of Shohei Kusunoki. This made her realize how deeply she could delve into the Edo period using sequential storytelling. Eventually she stopped creating manga and began working as a scholar of Edo-period culture.

Sarusuberi follows Hokusai as he takes on a variety of work, from *shunga* (erotic prints) and *bijinga* (pictures of beautiful women) to *fukeiga* (landscapes). He draws with a single-mindedness that earns him the name "Gakyo Rojin." ["The Old Man Mad with Painting" — Ed.]

Even in his later years when he becomes a great master, Hokusai continues to challenge himself with new genres. In this way, he makes me think of Osamu Tezuka. Tezuka never let his fame hold him back, and he continued to produce a great quantity of manga and was a pioneer until the very end. Hokusai is the *sarusuberi,* but so is Tezuka.

Hokusai's daughter Oei, on the other hand, never loses herself in art to the extent that her father does. She has the talent to rival Hokusai's own, but she has a calmer temperament. Oei is Sugiura herself. She gained some fame but was never a comfortable fit in the world of manga. Tezuka was someone who lived and breathed manga, but Sugiura was a scholar and also an artist. She could never become Hokusai or Tezuka. Perhaps it was her jealousy of the *sarusuberi*'s energy and strength that allowed her to write this manga.

Murao-kun, who appears in chapter 2 of *Kingyo Used Books,* has an amazing talent, but he ends up destroying all his work. When he says, "Something has ended… something inside me. Because I can't get crazy about art," those are Sugiura's own words. On the other hand, Misaki is someone who can't live without drawing. It is really Misaki who is Hokusai, who is Tezuka, who is the *sarusuberi.* She just needs a little more time to bloom and produce fruit. It seems as though it is Kingyo Used Books that will give her that time. My guess is that this chapter is meant to encourage all the young *sarusuberi* who are still trying to blossom.

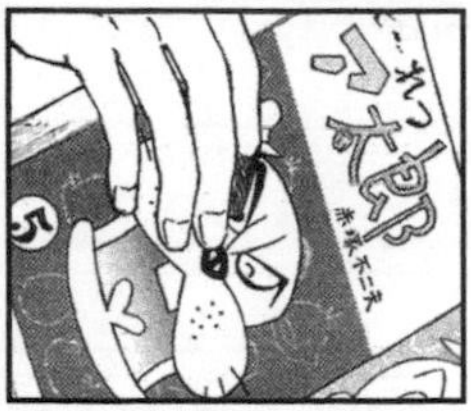

This series is featured in Chapter 3:
Far Away

Moretsu Ataro (12 volumes)

By Fujio Akatsuka

Published by Akebono Shuppan beginning in 1969

The gags in Fujio Akatsuka's manga don't make you think, they just make you laugh. Their impact is so strong that one glance is enough to send the reader into gales of hysterical laughter. And once you've started laughing, you're in trouble. Even after you calm down, if you happen to recall the scene in class or at work, it never ends well.

More than any of his other manga, *Moretsu Ataro* (Note 1), which began running in *Shonen Sunday* in 1967, has more than once brought me to tears. All of a sudden the suit-wearing *tanuki* will do something stupid while saying "Haa Pokkun Pokkun!" and then the cat will come in to be the foil for his joke, yelling "Nyarome! Kishome!" The great pacing and uniqueness of the characters had a huge impact on gag manga to the extent that it was called the Akatsuka Gag Revolution. When I went to take my entrance exam for a certain company, the proctor looked so much like Kokoro no Boss (Note 2) that I started laughing and ended up failing the exam. So it's actually thanks to this manga that I work at a used bookstore now.

While the dynamite gags of Akatsuka's manga instantly send the reader into the world of laughter, the work of Sensha Yoshida, which also appears in this chapter, gives the reader a strange sense of exhaustion. Yoshida's work was called absurdist gag manga because the peculiar phrases he uses and the way he combines things, along with the exquisite line work, create a strange, almost Kafka-like atmosphere.

But what exactly is in that endless stretch of bookshelves below Kingyo Used Books? Who is the Boss? Why does he know so much about manga? The mysteries of Kingyo grow ever deeper.

Note 1: The tankobon were released in 1969 from Akebono Shuppan. Currently the Takeshobo bunkobon (nine volumes) are easily attainable. See Akatsuka's home page for details: www.koredeiinoda.net.

Note 2: One of the characters in *Moretsu Ataro*, the character who appears in the cover on this page. He is the suited *tanuki* boss who often ends sentences with "no kokoro."

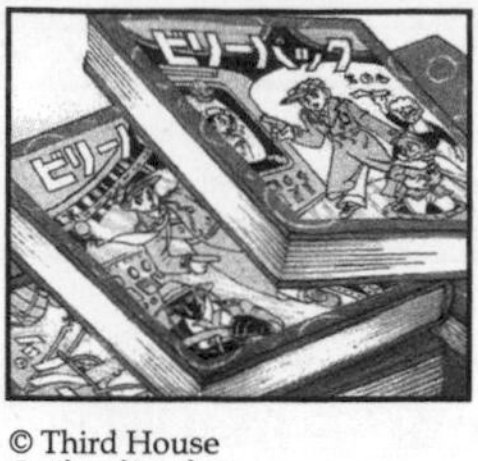
ビリーパック
ビリー

This series is featured in Chapter 4:
The Boy Detective Arrives

Billy Puck (9 volumes)

By Mitsuhiro Kawashima

Published by Shonen Gahosha beginning in 1956

Billy Puck began running in *Shonen Gaho* in 1954, and at the time, it was one of the most popular series, along with Tsunayoshi Takeuchi's *Akado Suzunosuke*, and is the defining work of Mitsuhiro Kawashima, who was one generation before the Tokiwa So Group. [Tokiwa So was an apartment where Osamu Tezuka and several other mangaka lived, which eventually became a kind of studio for cartoonists.—Ed.] The detailed story, the dynamic art, and the Western-style trench coat and hunting cap, combined with Billy's handsome looks, were the keys to the story's popularity.

However, Kawashima fell ill and died in 1961 at the height of his popularity. Kawashima's apprentice Riichi Yajima took over the series, but its popularity fell drastically and the series ended in 1962. Osamu Tezuka mourned Kawashima's death, saying, "With his energetic continuity and broad composition, he had the potential to become the best mangaka in the world. If Kawashima had lived, there's no doubt that he would have become the top artist in the industry."

Shonen Gahosha released the series in tankobon twice, but it is currently out of print. The first edition has a particularly high collector's value due to the extremely low numbers printed, and it is the envy of all serious manga fans. I wish they would bring all the volumes back; it was one of the most notable series in manga history.

The story's setup (a boy who waves around a gun, drives around in a car and fights evildoers along with the police) would be used in later series such as *Maboroshi Tantei* and *Tetsujin 28 Go*. It makes you ask, "What about gun laws? What about traffic laws?" but in the manga and movies of the '50s, a hero was forgiven anything as long as he taught boys a sense of justice. "Everyone, Billy is a brave boy who severely punishes evildoers who torment the weak and commit unjust acts behind the backs of policemen. And he does this so those who are honorable may live in peace. I hope that you all become wonderful boys with just hearts like Billy." (Text taken from the author's preface.)

The words *justice* and *brave* seem almost old-fashioned to today's kids, but no values were more important for boys in the '50s. I was bullied as a child, and I wished in my heart for an ally of justice to save me from the outrageous bullying, and there was always at least one kid in my class who would be that for me. In my eyes, he was Billy Puck. So for me, *Billy Puck* is much more than just manga, it taught me about justice and about admiration.

It seems like Seimu Yoshizaki, the author of *Kingyo Used Books*, shares my fond feelings for *Billy Puck*. *Billy Puck* is the series the Boss's granddaughter is assessing in the first chapter, and then it makes a reappearance in this chapter. With the hold this series has on the hearts of manga lovers, it could be called a classic among classics.

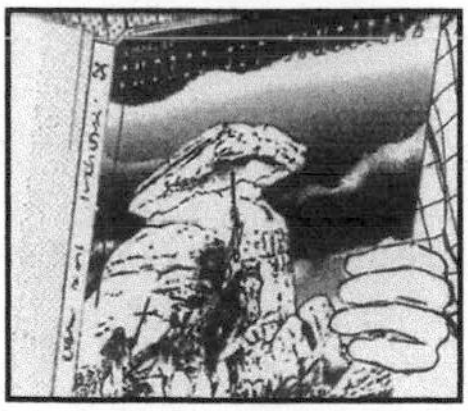

BLUEBERRY • Ombres sur Tombstone

This series is featured in Chapter 5:
A Country Without Manga

Blueberry

By Charlier & Giraud

Published by Dargaud beginning in 1965

The series that appears in chapter 5 is Jean Giraud's *Blueberry*. The author Jean Giraud is well-known in Japan under his pen name Moebius. He has worked on many films as a designer and is arguably one of the most famous comic book artists in the world. In France, comics are called BD (bande dessinée), and while in Japan people look to manga for entertainment, French comics are highly praised for their art.

Perhaps that's the reason that not many French comics have been brought to Japan. Translations of *Blueberry* are available in many countries, but it has never been published in Japan. As a manga fan, that only makes me want to read it more. A live-action movie has recently been released in France, so I hope they'll use this chance to release the comic along with it.

Giraud is still working on the series, which he began in his teens. The series could be classified as a French-style Western, and the bold plot, fierce originality of the hero and polished artwork have garnered it much attention. It's also well-known for the influence it had on the "New Wave," typified by the work of Katsuhiro Otomo, which hit Japan's manga world in the 1980s.

However, there was only one Japanese mangaka who was not only influenced by the series but was able to make the world of the comic his own. Thirty years ago, a single page in a magazine lent to him by a friend had a huge influence on one mangaka. It was Jiro Taniguchi, who was drawing a series for a third-class comic magazine but still had yet to find his own unique style. With that single page, he realized instantly what he wanted to express through manga. Destiny had brought those two mangaka together. After that, he collected all of Jean Giraud's works, as though possessed, and began to express something Giraud-like in his own manga. It was a turning point for his work.

Thirty years later, Jiro and Giraud released their first collaboration called *Ikaru*. *A Distant Neighborhood,* Taniguchi's most recent work, won all three of Europe's biggest manga awards. France has finally accepted Japan's manga, which it had previously ridiculed for "only drawing violence and sex." A French comic boom may not be far behind.

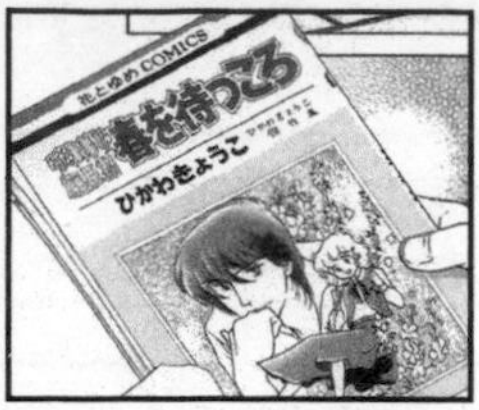
春を待つころ
ひかわきょうこ

This series is featured in Chapter 6: Fujiomi-kun

The Chizumi and Fujiomi-kun Series (3 volumes)

By Kyoko Hikawa

Published by Hakusensha beginning in 1980

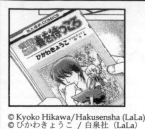

The series featured in chapter six is Kyoko Hikawa's debut work, *Chizumi and Fujiomi-kun*. The series first appeared with *Akikaze Yurete* in the *LaLa Deluxe* Winter Issue in February of 1979. It continued until 1985's *Giniro Ehon* and was collected into three volumes, which are now out of print. Recently it was re-released in bunko format (see note below).

Many of the manga titles adored by girls in the '80s are once again in demand. For example, Yoko Shoji's masterpiece *Seito Shokun!* was re-released by popular demand. *Chizumi and Fujiomi-kun* must be another of those that women want to see again.

The women who were in their teens when the series ran in the magazine are now in their mid-thirties. Their days are very busy. Maybe they have started to remember the shojo manga that once set their hearts aflutter.

Fujiomi-kun is an athlete, a man of few words but full of compassion. He would never cheat; instead he gives everything he has to protect one woman. Chizumi is unreliable and clumsy, but she has a great inner strength. The two characters may seem overly stereotypical today, but they had a huge impact on girls back then.

Chizumi is always trying to do her best. Fujiomi-kun is deeply in love with her, but he remains resolute. Chizumi is both grateful for and respectful of him. Maybe it's those things that we've forgotten—resolution, gratitude and respect—that make this manga shine.

We read the romance manga of the '80s to cheer up our tired hearts. At Kingyo Used Books, those cheerful books are sitting on the shelves, waiting to be rediscovered.

Note: The Hakusensha bunko editions of *Haru wo Matsu Koro* and *Giniro Ehon* are currently the most widely available.

[Kyoko Hikawa's 14-volume fantasy series *From Far Away* (*Kanatakara*) was published in English by VIZ Media—Ed.]

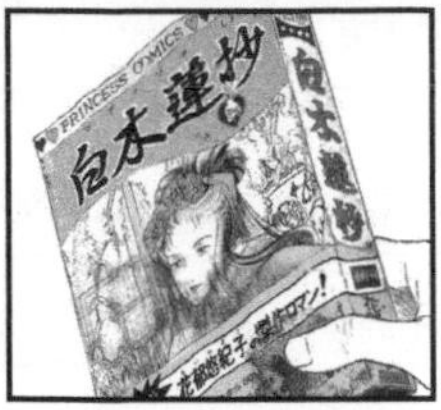
白木蓮抄

This title is featured in Chapter 7:
The Sedori Business

Magnolia Sho (1 volume)

By Yukiko Kai

Published by Akita Shoten in 1981

The manga featured in chapter seven is Yukiko Kai's *Magnolia Sho*. It was published in *Princess* in 1979 and released as a tankobon (Princess Comics) in 1981 and also in bunko format in 1999 (see note below).

Yukiko Kai worked as an assistant to Moto Hagio and debuted in 1976 with *Anastasia no Sutekina Otonari*. She gained popularity with a body of work featuring delicate, aesthetic fantasies. She passed away from stomach cancer at age 26.

According to the wishes of her readers, five volumes of her collected works were published after her death with a eulogy by Moto Hagio and Shio Sato in the appendix. In 1982 a special Yukiko Kai tribute issue of *Ryu* magazine was released. It was an unprecedented response to the death of a mangaka.

Her death was a major event for fans who were reading her work at the time. How must they have felt when their connection between reader and author was cut so short?

Shio Sato's eulogy described their feelings:

"A whole world of possibilities was cut short; the end has come without being able to see what had been and what would be possible. What a pity that is, for her and for the people around her."

After this, Kai's work passed into legend. Her readers chose to honor her memory by continuing to read and talk about her work. One woman said, "Characters so cold and beautiful they give you shivers, the elaborately planned plots, the beauty of destruction that reminds you of Mishima [Yukio] or Dazai [Osamu]. Kai-san's work deserves to have a place in the future."

Oh, the indomitable Yukiko Kai! If you want to read all of her work, your only choice is to go to Kingyo Used Books. I'm sure the sedori have provided them with the super-rare first editions still with their original obi book bands.

Note: The Akita Shoten Bunko edition is the most widely available.

The information in this volume is current up to December 2004. This includes all manga footnotes and all the columns comprising the Kingyo Used Books Notebook.

Thanks to every creator, publisher and property owner of manga titles mentioned in this volume for your understanding and cooperation.

Information provided by Gendai Manga Toshokan/Kirara Bunko.

KINGYO USED BOOKS
Volume 1
VIZ Signature Edition

Story and Art by **SEIMU YOSHIZAKI**

© 2005 Seimu YOSHIZAKI/Shogakukan
All rights reserved.
Original Japanese edition "KINGYOYA KOSHOTEN"
published by SHOGAKUKAN Inc.

BLUEBERRY albums have been first published in French by DARGAUD.
www.dargaud.com - Charlier & Giraud
All rights reserved

Original Japanese cover design by Kei Kasai

Translation: Adrienne Weber, HC Language Solutions, Inc.
(Chapters 1–6); Mini Eda (Chapter 7)
Touch-up Art & Lettering: Ben Costa
Design: Sean Lee
Editor: Eric Searleman

VP, Production: Alvin Lu
VP, Sales & Product Marketing: Gonzalo Ferreyra
VP, Creative: Linda Espinosa
Publisher: Hyoe Narita

Printed in the U.S.A.

Published by VIZ Media, LLC
P.O. Box 77010
San Francisco, CA 94107

10 9 8 7 6 5 4 3 2 1
First printing, April 2010

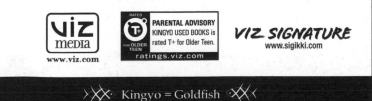

PARENTAL ADVISORY
KINGYO USED BOOKS is
rated T+ for Older Teen.
ratings.viz.com

VIZ SIGNATURE
www.sigikki.com

www.viz.com

⟩✕✕⟨ Kingyo = Goldfish ✕✕⟨

All My Darling Daughters

Story & Art by **Fumi Yoshinaga**

Eisner-nominated author and creator of *Antique Bakery* and *Ōoku*

As an adult woman still living at home, Yukiko is starting to feel a little bit… stuck. When her mother gets engaged to an ex-host and aspiring actor who's younger than Yukiko, will it be the motivation she needs to move on and out?

Follow the lives of Yukiko and her friends in five short stories that explore their lives, relationships, and loves.

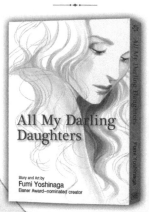

US **$12.99** | CAN **$16.99**
ISBN: 978-1-4215-3240-0

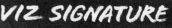
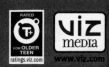

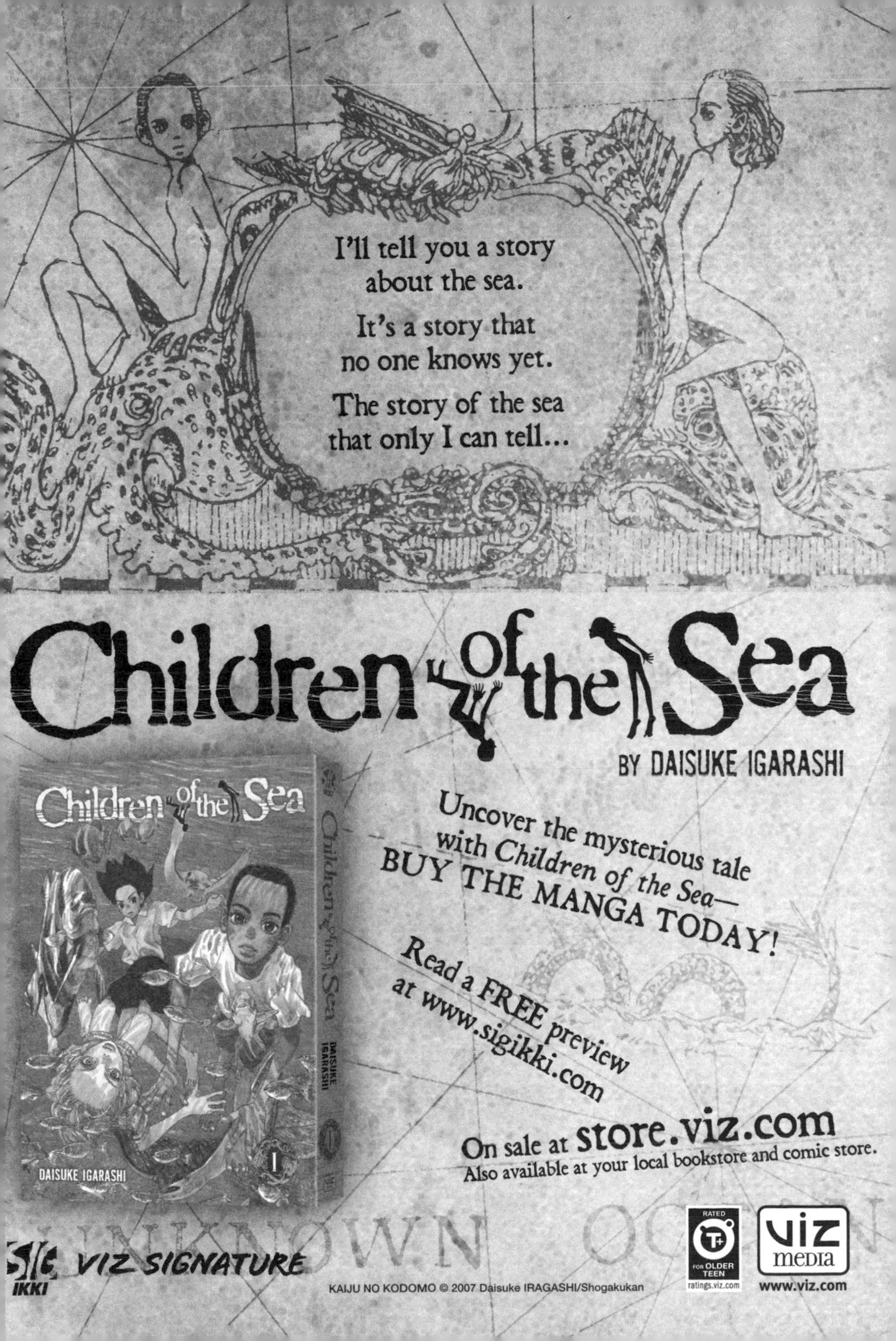
I'll tell you a story
about the sea.
It's a story that
no one knows yet.
The story of the sea
that only I can tell...
Children of the Sea
BY DAISUKE IGARASHI
Children of the Sea
DAISUKE IGARASHI
1
Uncover the mysterious tale
with *Children of the Sea*—
BUY THE MANGA TODAY!
Read a FREE preview
at www.sigikki.com
On sale at store.viz.com
Also available at your local bookstore and comic store.
UNKNOWN OCEAN
SIG IKKI
VIZ SIGNATURE
KAIJU NO KODOMO © 2007 Daisuke IRAGASHI/Shogakukan
RATED T+ FOR OLDER TEEN
ratings.viz.com
viz media
www.viz.com

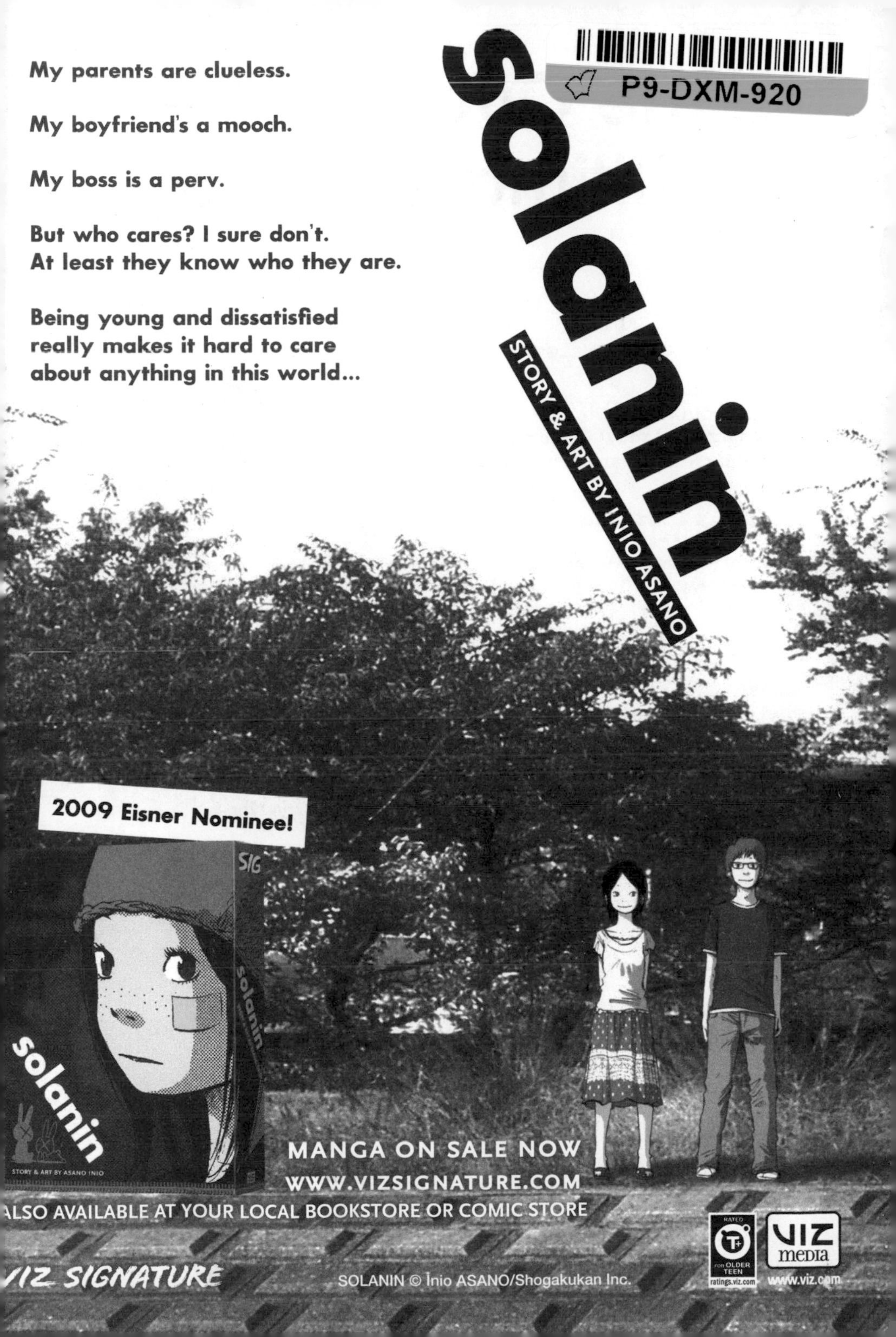
P9-DXM-920
My parents are clueless.
My boyfriend's a mooch.
My boss is a perv.
But who cares? I sure don't.
At least they know who they are.
Being young and dissatisfied
really makes it hard to care
about anything in this world...
solanin
STORY & ART BY INIO ASANO
2009 Eisner Nominee!
SIG
solanin
solanin
solanin
STORY & ART BY ASANO INIO
MANGA ON SALE NOW
WWW.VIZSIGNATURE.COM
ALSO AVAILABLE AT YOUR LOCAL BOOKSTORE OR COMIC STORE
VIZ SIGNATURE
SOLANIN © Inio ASANO/Shogakukan Inc.
RATED
T+
FOR OLDER TEEN
ratings.viz.com
VIZ media
www.viz.com